Entertaining Lisbon

Currents in Latin American & Iberian Music

WALTER CLARK, SERIES EDITOR

Nor-tec Rifa!
Electronic Dance Music from Tijuana to the World
Alejandro L. Madrid

From Serra to Sancho:
Music and Pageantry in the California Missions
Craig H. Russell

Colonial Counterpoint:
Music in Early Modern Manila
D. R. M. Irving

Embodying Mexico:
Tourism, Nationalism, & Performance
Ruth Hellier-Tinoco

Silent Music:
Medieval Song and the Construction of History in Eighteenth-Century Spain
Susan Boynton

Whose Spain?
Negotiating "Spanish Music" in Paris, 1908–1929
Samuel Llano

Federico Moreno Torroba:
A Musical Life in Three Acts
Walter Aaron Clark and William Craig Krause

Representing the Good Neighbor:
Music, Difference, and the Pan American Dream
Carol A. Hess

Danzón:
Circum-Caribbean Dialogues in Music and Dance
Alejandro L. Madrid and Robin D. Moore

Agustín Lara:
A Cultural Biography
Andrew G. Wood

In Search of Julián Carrillo and Sonido 13
Alejandro L. Madrid

Tracing Tangueros:
Argentine Tango Instrumental Music
Kacey Link and Kristen Wendland

Playing in the Cathedral
Music, Race, and Status in New Spain
Jesús A. Ramos-Kittrell

Entertaining Lisbon
Music, Theater, and Modern Life in the Late 19th Century
João Silva

Entertaining Lisbon

*Music, Theater, and Modern Life
in the Late 19th Century*

JOÃO SILVA

OXFORD
UNIVERSITY PRESS

Oxford University Press is a department of the University of Oxford. It furthers
the University's objective of excellence in research, scholarship, and education
by publishing worldwide. Oxford is a registered trade mark of Oxford University
Press in the UK and certain other countries.

Published in the United States of America by Oxford University Press
198 Madison Avenue, New York, NY 10016, United States of America.

© Oxford University Press 2016

All rights reserved. No part of this publication may be reproduced, stored in
a retrieval system, or transmitted, in any form or by any means, without the
prior permission in writing of Oxford University Press, or as expressly permitted
by law, by license, or under terms agreed with the appropriate reproduction
rights organization. Inquiries concerning reproduction outside the scope of the
above should be sent to the Rights Department, Oxford University Press, at the
address above.

You must not circulate this work in any other form
and you must impose this same condition on any acquirer.

Library of Congress Cataloging-in-Publication Data
Names: Silva, João, 1980– author.
Title: Entertaining Lisbon : music, theater, and modern life in the late 19th century / João Silva.
Description: New York, NY : Oxford University Press, [2016] | ?2016 |
Includes bibliographical references and index.
Identifiers: LCCN 2016004796| ISBN 9780190215705 (cloth : alk. paper) |
ISBN 9780190628680 (epub)
Subjects: LCSH: Musical theater—Social aspects—Portugal—Lisbon—History—19th century. |
Music—Portugal—Lisbon—19th century—History and criticism. | Lisbon (Portugal)—Social life and
customs—19th century. | Nationalism in music. | Fados—Portugal—History and criticism. |
Music trade—Social aspects—Portugal—Lisbon—History—19th century. |
Sound recordings—Social aspects—Portugal—Lisbon—History—19th century.
Classification: LCC ML3917.P6 S55 2016 | DDC 780.9469/09034—dc23
LC record available at http://lccn.loc.gov/2016004796

1 3 5 7 9 8 6 4 2
Printed by Sheridan Books, Inc., United States of America

To my parents, Amílcar and Fátima

But history was real life at the time when it could not yet be called history.
José Saramago, History of the Siege of Lisbon

CONTENTS

Acknowledgments ix

Introduction 1

1. The Long 19th Century in Portugal and the Transformation of Lisbon 26

2. Opera, Operetta, and *Revista*: Music and Entertainment in Lisbon 75

3. Song Collection in Portugal: Between Domestic Entertainment and Scientific Objectivity 151

4. Programs, Postcards, *Coplas*, and Sheet Music 186

5. The Mechanization of Everyday Life: Mechanical Instruments, Phonography, and Modernity 234

Conclusion 283

Glossary 294
References 295
Index 319

ACKNOWLEDGMENTS

This book started as a doctoral thesis about Portuguese popular music theater. Its initial research began in Portugal in 2007, and the book was written between two cities: Newcastle-upon-Tyne and Lisbon. During this period, I have encountered many people who helped me and to whom I am greatly indebted. The book is also yours.

The research for this book was made possible by a scholarship of the Fundação para a Ciência e Tecnologia, for which I am very grateful. It allowed me to concentrate exclusively on my research and to study at the International Centre for Music Studies in Newcastle University. I am also deeply indebted to my supervisors, Dr. Ian Biddle and Dr. Nanette de Jong for their constant support and friendship throughout this process. Their insightful comments and our discussions were key in the development of this project since I first arrived at Newcastle. I would also like to thank my friends and colleagues of Newcastle University for creating a welcoming environment and for the valuable conversations we had there. This book would have been completely different without you.

To my colleagues and friends from INET-MD (Universidade Nova de Lisboa), especially Professor Salwa Castelo-Branco, for allowing me to consult the information produced by the project titled the Recording Industry in 20th Century Portugal. I am also deeply grateful to Leonor Losa, Susana Belchior, and Isaac Raimundo for our ongoing conversations concerning mechanical music in Portugal. The conversations I had with Gonçalo Antunes de Oliveira on Portuguese theater and with Luísa Cymbron on 19th-century music were instrumental in shaping my thought. Their support and friendship was instrumental in this project.

Furthermore, I would like to thank the Museu Nacional do Teatro, especially Sofia Patrão. Her knowledge of Portuguese theater and of the collections of the museum were extremely valuable for a student who was abroad. The National

Library of Portugal was another place where I found important information. Thus, I want to thank Maria Clara Assunção for her ongoing support. Many images of this book were generously supplied by the Hemeroteca Municipal de Lisboa, and this work would look very different without them. I am also grateful to Miguel Ângelo Ribeiro for supplying me with valuable data associated with the library of Lisbon's Conservatoire, and to João Pedro Mendes dos Santos for allowing me to look at his collection on Portuguese music.

Thanks to Suzanne Ryan and Walter Clark, whose support, patience, and generosity cannot be overstated. They believed in this project from the start and helped me through the good times and the bad times. I would also like to thank the other people at Oxford University Press who helped this book to see the light: Jessen O' Brien, Adam Cohen, Daniel Gibney, and Eden Piacitelli. My gratitude goes to Jonathan Fox, who proofread the book, and to Tom Astley, who provided the index. Their generosity and friendship made the process much easier.

Finally, I would like to thank my parents Amílcar and Fátima for their continuous support from the beginning of this project, helping me to get through this slow and difficult process. This book could not have been written without them.

Entertaining Lisbon

Introduction

"There is no impression of how Lisbon looked in the days that followed the glorious date of the proclamation [of the Portuguese Republic]. The streets had so much traffic, and the thousands of republican flags gave it such a festive appearance, that people gladly forgot the bloody hours of combat."[1] Such testimony illustrates the confidence some people had in the Portuguese Republic, established on 5 October 1910 after a military uprising. This book studies the connections between construction of the modern Portuguese nation-state and popular entertainment between 1867 and 1910, focusing on theatrical music. The cultural fabric of Lisbon is examined by integrating historical and cultural studies, concentrating on a historical interpretation of experience. This polyphonic narrative binds music, space, class, gender, ethnicity, and technology together through the use of a variety of primary sources. Using voices of the past to write history is a complicated task. Who are we listening to? Why do we choose to listen to specific voices? Who do we ignore? Are these voices representative of their time? Is it possible to reconstruct experience? What is the role played by images? Can we develop a coherent narrative from an overwhelmingly fragmentary set of sources? Whose history is being told? These questions were raised over and over again during the writing of this book, and the answers were always temporary. On each visit, the archives reframed these issues, and the results of this enterprise are fleeting and precarious, just like Lisbon's theatrical world.

An important reason for dedicating this study to nationalism is my ongoing suspicion of these narratives. However, when trying to understand how nationalism was lived by ordinary people I encountered the opacity of a multivocal social life. This confirmed my suspicion that the "ordinary people" is a myth. Different people had distinct experiences, expectations, and tastes. Therefore, there is a multiplicity of actions and processes happening simultaneously

---

[1] Hermano Neves, *Como triumphou a Republica* (Lisbon: Empreza Liberdade, 1910), 133.

within a complex social life. This interweaving posed obstacles to my early intent of writing a popular history or a history from below. Nevertheless, some passages of this book resonate with the work of historians like E. P. Thompson, Raphael Samuel, Richard Cobb, Carolyn Steedman, or William Fishman. The influence of both cultural studies and sociology, especially the work of Stuart Hall and Pierre Bourdieu, gave theoretical substance to the study of the asymmetries of both class and gender. Nevertheless, the historical use of these perspectives is both partial and complex. The idea that culture is ordinary was put forward by Raymond Williams who, despite not being a professional historian, developed a line of thinking that was historically informed. Moreover, his focus on lived experience played an important part in reconstructing obfuscated passages of Portuguese history.[2] These include the squalor of Lisbon's poorest districts and the marginal settings where fado (an urban popular music genre) was performed. The extensive use of primary sources allows the historical other to speak. This does not mean the book is a positivist work. It relies on sources that are socially constructed and manipulated. By taking a fragmentary approach to a historical narrative, it engages with different modes of experiencing everyday life.

This work focuses on Lisbon's theatrical activity between 1867 and 1910 and traces the complex relation between a cultural nation-state and popular entertainment. Moreover, it examines the development of a local nationalism independent from monarchist symbols. Geographically, I chose Lisbon as a case study for this work because, as the country's capital, it was where theatrical activity thrived. Despite the financial constraints associated with the theatrical business, subsidized and unsubsidized companies coexisted and performed a large number of shows. Moreover, the city underwent a significant process of urban development during this period. New forms of urbanism point out the complex interaction between public and private spaces as well as the foregrounding of the representational value of various products. This was only possible because space began to be used in a modern way. This was part of a process that superimposed traits of a modern capital on Lisbon's urban fabric. A planned modern urban layer intertwined with other layers that were already in place, complicating an already complex interaction between space, culture, and everyday life. Moreover, the old city continued to emerge through the cracks of the new one, and its traces, sounds, and smells were ubiquitous. However, selecting one city to illustrate the rise of nationalism poses significant problems of scale, including the risk of taking Lisbon to represent

---

[2] Raymond Williams, "Culture Is Ordinary," in Williams, *Resources of Hope* (London: Verso, 1989), 3–18.

the entire kingdom. Consequently, it becomes impossible to take Lisbon's cultural fabric as representative of a heterogeneous Portugal, a predominantly rural country. Nevertheless, the capital concentrated several institutions that represented Portugal, like the royal family and both chambers of parliament. Moreover, the entertainment venues of this city provide a fertile ground in which to address the role that popular musical theater played in the symbolic construction of the Portuguese nation.

The chronological limits for this book were selected to include a set of events that had a significant impact on Portuguese society. The Teatro da Trindade opened in 1867 and soon became an important venue for the performance of operetta, evidencing the expansion of Lisbon's theatrical activity. The new forms of entertainment both reflected and were accompanied by a different attitude toward leisure. However, not everything was fun and frolic. The end of the 19th century proved to be disastrous for Europe, including Portugal. The partition of Africa among the European colonial powers resulted in the British Ultimatum of 1890, a memorandum sent to the Portuguese Government on 11 January 1890, which demanded the retreat of Portuguese military forces from areas of British interest in Africa, such as parts of the Shire River valley. Lord Salisbury's memorandum was the apex of an ongoing issue between Portugal and Britain concerning the borders of the African colonies of both countries. This was soon followed by a failed republican military coup in Porto, Portugal, and, in the following year, Portugal declared a sovereign default on external debt.[3] This was associated with the Baring crisis of 1890, triggered by the near insolvency of the Barings Bank in London, and aggravated the country's precarious condition. The epicenter of the crisis was in Latin America but European countries that had strong commercial interests there, such as Portugal and Spain, were deeply affected. Both the Ultimatum and the default were read as signs of national decadence and were effectively employed by the republican movement to criticize the monarchist regime and to increase its own influence. For the republican journalist João Chagas, Portuguese politics was entering a new stage: "The circumstances are exceptional. The institutions have always been criticized but this did not cause them to cease to exist.... Now, however, the institutions are not discussed in the abstract: the King is concretely criticized, and not only by the republican members of parliament."[4]

Moreover, the 1908 regicide precipitated the fall of the Portuguese monarchy. It was shocking news for the European monarchies because many of

---

[3] Pedro Lains, "The Power of Peripheral Governments: Coping with the 1891 Financial Crisis in Portugal," *Historical Research*, 81/213 (2008), 485–506.

[4] João Chagas, *1908: Subsidios criticos para a historia da dictadura* (Lisbon: João Chagas, 1908), 48.

them shared family ties with the ruling dynasty. The magazine *O Ocidente* stated: "The King D. Carlos of Bragança [Portugal], assassinated in broad daylight in one of the squares of the capital of his kingdom, and the teacher Buíça, his assassin, both sought to rescue, in this anguished historical moment, the Portuguese character from the discredit it had fallen into."[5] These words resonate with a shared feeling of national decay. Nevertheless, this condition was not exclusive to Portugal. For Teixeira Bastos,

> the crisis that afflicts the Portuguese nation, and that reveals itself under multiple forms—economic crisis, financial crisis, agricultural crisis, industrial crisis, monetary crisis, labor crisis, political crisis— it is, partly, a succession of internal causes, such as the accumulated mistakes of successive governments, and of an international conflict, like the English question [the Ultimatum], but also derives from a set of circumstances that characterize the situation of contemporary societies, Portugal is one of the members of the great modern civilization.[6]

There is a striking parallel between the Portuguese response to the British Ultimatum and the Spanish reaction to Spain's defeat in the Spanish-American War. These events determined the aspirations of the Iberian empires and had a strong impact on the public opinion of both countries. However, concern about the decadence of the Iberian nations was circulating prior to these events. In 1871, a group of intellectuals led by the poet and philosopher Antero de Quental promoted a series of conferences in the Casino Lisbonense, in Lisbon. These conferences aimed to discuss current political and social matters, to disseminate modern theories in Portugal, such as the ideas of Pierre-Joseph Proudhon, and to reform the country. Antero de Quental, a leading intellectual of the time, gave a presentation on the causes of the decadence of the Portuguese and Spanish peoples. He pointed out that Tridentine Catholicism (especially the Inquisition) and the absolute monarchies played a major role in this.[7] This blend fostered "an invincible horror of labor and a deep contempt for the industry," and the political inertia of the population allowed both centralism and militarism to spread.[8] Therefore, a break with the

---

[5] Alfredo Mesquita, "Chronica occidental," in *O Occidente*, 10 February 1908, 26.

[6] Teixeira Bastos, *A crise: estudo sobre a situação política, financeira, económica e moral da nação* (Porto: Livraria Internacional de Ernesto Chardron, 1894), VII–VIII.

[7] Antero de Quental, *Conferencias democraticas: Causas da decadencia dos povos peninsulares nos ultimos tres seculos* (Porto: Typographia Commercial, 1871).

[8] Quental, *Conferencias democraticas*, 46.

past was needed. "We are a decayed race for having rejected the modern spirit, we will regenerate ourselves by frankly embracing this spirit."[9] However, in 1907–1908 Manuel Laranjeira criticized the relationship between Portuguese pessimism and the country's decadence, stating that the current state of affairs did not represent the "twilight of a people."[10] Across the border, Ganivet argued that the Spanish decadence started in the 16th century, with the failure of the imperial project of Philip II.[11] He argued that modern Spain was living an unprecedented political problem, and advised against a break with the past. This break would be a "violation of natural laws, a coward relinquishing of our duties, a sacrifice of the real for the imaginary."[12] In 1898, the Spanish-American War confirmed his fears. Thus, ideas of decadence were circulating in both Spain and Portugal, but their interpretations and answers varied.

Nevertheless, at the time of Quental's conference, Portuguese society was changing. An important sector of civil servants was being created, and a heterogeneous set of manual and industrial laborers occupied delimited spaces in the cities. Some of these developed cooperative organizations, which created their own schools, libraries, wind bands, and newspapers. Moreover, they were crucial in the intellectual development of Lisbon's popular segments. Their adherence to socialist, anarchist, republican, and trade unionist ideas kept the authorities alert and fueled the fear of a revolution in the city. Thus, Quental's ideal of an industry "of the people, for the people, and to the people," and unmediated by the state, lingered after his suicide in 1891.[13]

The centennial of the Portuguese Republic was celebrated with an increase of publications concerning that period. However, these tend to neglect the entertainment market. Given the traumatic events mentioned above, it is not surprising that the history of popular culture was overlooked. Nevertheless, this struck me as odd, bearing in mind the prominence of entertainment in naturalizing an idea of Portugal that was independent from monarchist values. The popular music theater did not limit itself to prefiguring the perspectives on Portugal that would be adopted by the newborn republic. It also reflects a larger tendency for modernization in which patriotism was embedded. Moreover, music theater was part of a wide cultural complex in which the shared, contradictory, and competing aspects of the modern nation-state were displayed and negotiated on stage. This openness fostered an engagement of the audience. Therefore, it was a space for the active production of modern

---

[9] Quental, *Conferencias democraticas*, 48.
[10] Manuel Laranjeira, *O pessimismo nacional* (Lisbon: Padrões Culturais Editora, 2008), 27.
[11] Angél Ganivet, *Idearium español* (Granada: n.p., 1897), 116–117.
[12] Ganivet, *Idearium español*, 138–139.
[13] Quental, *Conferencias democraticas*, 48.

everyday life, allowing personal experiences to surface. Moreover, the theater generated products and ideas that circulated in Lisbon, penetrating both public and private spaces.

I aim to address a gap in the knowledge of these subjects by focusing on Lisbon's theatrical scene and the relationship between musical presentations and a changing theatrical panorama that transformed the city's leisure rituals. New forms of music theater (the operetta and the *revista*) created a space for the display and representation of modernity, in which the notion of the cultural nation-state was embedded. The *revista* is "a topical, satirical show consisting of a series of scenes and episodes, usually having a central theme but not a dramatic plot, with spoken verse and prose, sketches, songs, dances, ballet and speciality acts."[14] Thus, the nation was commodified and disseminated through entertainment, relying on the pervasiveness of popular theater. The idea of a modern Portugal had to be appealing to facilitate its acceptance by the people. Furthermore, music is part of a wide context and forges relationships with larger forces, such as a free market economy, patronage culture, secularization, or a nationalist agenda. Thus, it relates symbolic forms of expression to modes of history.[15]

Most works concerning the revue theater (*teatro de revista*) in Portugal were published in the late 1970s and in the early 1980s, and approached the musical aspects of the genre superficially.[16] Therefore, a musicological study of the *revista* is yet to be conducted, especially during the period when the genre became dominant. What strikes me most in the extant scholarship on the popular music theater is that the significance of these genres in the local theatrical scene is not reflected in the available bibliography. This can be explained by the role that musicology has played in the polar relation between art, embodied by opera (even in periods when it was conceived as popular entertainment) and the public concert, and entertainment, predominantly associated with popular spectacles like the *revista*. Until recently, historical approaches to 19th-century Portuguese music have concentrated on opera and on concert music, neglecting the popular entertainment market. However, tracing the boundary between art and entertainment in Portugal between 1867 and 1910 is highly problematic, given the blurred distinction between these areas. This is further complicated

---

[14] Andrew Lamb, et al., "Revue," *Grove Music Online*, ed. L. Macy, <www.oxfordmusiconline.com>, accessed 5 December 2009. For an overview of the genre in Portugal during this period see Vítor Pavão dos Santos, *A revista à portuguesa* (Lisbon: O Jornal, 1978), 11–27.

[15] Michael Pickering, *History, Experience and Cultural Studies* (London: Macmillan, 1997), 10.

[16] See Vítor Pavão dos Santos, *A revista à portuguesa* (Lisbon: O Jornal, 1978) and Luiz Francisco Rebello, *História do teatro de revista em Portugal*, 2 vols (Lisbon: Publicações D. Quixote, 1984).

with the flow of a large number of people in Lisbon's theatrical scene. For example, orchestra musicians of the Real Teatro de S. Carlos (Lisbon's opera house) composed operettas and *revistas* for the popular stage, demonstrating the working porosity between art and entertainment. Conversely, including the vernacular in the opera plots points to an aesthetic that draws from naturalistic paradigms. This is reinforced by the role the "popular" began to play in the cultural imaginary of more "artistic" entertainment genres.

A phonographic market was slowly established in Portugal at the end of the 19th century, and the *revista* and the operetta became the dominant repertoires in this process. This evidences the importance and the ubiquity of the popular music theater in urban everyday life. Despite the rising interest by musicologists in studying the recording industry, a broader perspective on the early phonographic period is needed. Thus, I present a chronologically concentrated study of the early days of sound reproduction, a process that relied on both local entrepreneurs and international companies.[17] This study addresses and engages with a body of music that has been overlooked both by musicologists who concentrate on the study of 19th-century opera and concert music and by popular music scholars who tend to focus their research on the Anglo-American context of a later period. Moreover, it draws extensively from primary sources and archival materials that are unavailable for English-speaking audiences, contributing to a broader understanding of the popular entertainment market in Lisbon and its relationships with other cities, such as Rio de Janeiro, Madrid, and Paris.

Negotiating Modernity in Lisbon

The profound transformation of Lisbon's everyday life under the sway of modernity is key to understanding this period. Moreover, the ways people reacted to novelty was both heterogeneous and fascinating. However, my use of the term "modernity" is not in the sense of a *longue durée* that falls sometime between the Renaissance and the Second World War. For Osborne,

> modernity plays a peculiar dual role as a category of historical periodization: it designates the contemporaneity of an epoch to the time

---

[17] Leonor Losa, "Indústria fonográfica," in Salwa Castelo-Branco (ed.), *Enciclopédia da música em Portugal no século XX*, vol. 2 (Lisbon: Círculo de Leitores, 2010), 633–634; Leonor Losa and Susana Belchior, "The Introduction of Phonogram Market in Portugal: Lindström Labels and Local Traders (1879–1925)," in Pekka Gronow and Christiane Hofer (eds.), *The Lindström Project: Contributions to the History of the Record Industry: Beiträge zur Geschichte der Schallplattenindustrie*, vol. 2 (Vienna: Gesellschaft für Historische Tonträger, 2010), 7–11.

of its classification, but it registers this contemporaneity in terms of a qualitatively new, self-transcending temporality, which has the simultaneous effect of distancing the present from even that most recent past with which it is thus identified.[18]

In this sense, I pose modernity as a novel mode of experience of space and time and not as a chronological period. This can be related to the pervasiveness of the term "modern." The ideas of modern music, modern housing, modern fashion were tropes that were also emic categories. Moreover, they were used efficiently in the marketing strategies of a wide range of businesses in Portugal. For example, large department stores like the Grandes Armazéns do Chiado published their seasonal fashion catalogues emphasizing the idea of novelty, which reflects the transient nature of consumer culture in the 1900s.[19] Of course, this means that "modern" was a positive category in Portugal, a tendency that was widely circulating at the time. Raymond Williams points to the favorable English view of the "modern" in the 19th century and, especially, the 20th century, when it was presented as a synonym for "improved."[20] Moreover, the terms *Neuzeit* and *modernité* were frequently used in the second half of the 19th century, which illustrates modernity's self-reflexive tendency, a defining characteristic of the period, according to Habermas. The social forms of experience in the late 19th century valued fleeting categories like novelty, fashion, and aesthetic modernism.[21] In this context, "the urgent need for Portugal to open its eyes and resurge to modern life in fast leaps" is reflected in many cultural practices, from the household kitchen, which served new products (such as Nestlé's Milk Flour), to the walls of the buildings, with their *Art Nouveau* touches.[22] Despite the spread of "modernity," a perspective that marks the opposition between "modern" and "ancient" or "traditional" has to be historically framed, given the role these categories played in Lisbon's urban life and in the shaping of the "rural" as the city's constitutive outside. "The constitutive outside is a relational process by which the outside—or 'other'—of any category is actively at work on both sides of the constructed boundary, and is thus always leaving its trace within

---

[18] Peter Osborne, "Modernity Is a Qualitative, Not a Chronological, Category," *New Left Review*, 1/192 (1992), 73.

[19] Grandes Armazéns do Chiado, *Catálogo de Novidades: Inverno de 1910* (Lisbon: A Editora, 1910).

[20] Raymond Williams, *Keywords* (London: Fontana Press, 1988), 208.

[21] Osborne, "Modernity Is a Qualitative," 71.

[22] Fialho d'Almeida, *Saibam quantos* . . . (Lisbon: Livraria Clássica Editora, 1912), 167.

the category."[23] However, these views place modernity as a radical break with the past, a perspective that placed the present at the forefront of history.[24] David Harvey criticizes this by retrieving the positions of both Saint-Simon and Marx in which "no social order can achieve changes that are not already latent within its existing condition."[25] Therefore, a perspective that perceives the world "as a tabula rasa, upon which the new can be inscribed without reference to the past" is put into question.[26]

"Modernity is the transient, the fleeting, the contingent, one half of the art, the other being the eternal, the immutable."[27] This statement has been frequently quoted and encapsulates the aesthetic thought of a material witness to modernity as it unfolded as a category of human experience. During Baudelaire's life, the pace of Parisian modern life was transformed by people like Georges-Eugène Haussmann (1809–1891). New developments indicate the growing rationalization of space that aimed to trace a clear boundary between the public and the private, and to promote the movement of both capital and labor. Therefore, the rise of a consumer culture, associated with strategies that enhance the representational value of commodities, is associated with the development of leisure activities for people who could not have afforded them before.[28] In this sense, commodified leisure is an important part of modernity.

"The deepest problems of modern life derive from the claim of the individual to preserve the autonomy and individuality of his existence in the face of overwhelming social forces, of historical heritage, of external culture, and of the technique of life."[29] Thus, the concentration of capital and labor intensifies the internal and external stimuli to which the modern metropolitan spectator is subjected. The link between modernity and urbanization is clear in the work of Leo Charney and Vanessa Schwartz, to whom modernity's stage is predominantly urban.[30] In this environment, the movement of people and

---

[23] Wolfgang Nater and John Paul Jones III, "Identity, Space, and Other Uncertainties," in Georges Benko and Ulf Strohmayer (eds.), *Space and Social Theory: Interpreting Modernity and Post-Modernity* (London: Blackwell, 1997), 146.

[24] Henri Lefebvre, *Introduction to Modernity: Twelve Preludes* (London: Verso, 1995), 168.

[25] David Harvey, *Paris, Capital of Modernity* (London: Routledge, 2005), 1.

[26] Harvey, *Paris*, 1.

[27] Charles Baudelaire, "Le Peintre de la vie moderne," in *Œuvres complètes de Charles Baudelaire*, vol. 3 (Paris: Calmann Lévy, 1885), 69.

[28] Vanessa Schwartz, *Spectacular Realities: Early Mass Culture in Fin-de-Siècle Paris* (Berkeley: University of California Press, 1998).

[29] Georg Simmel, "The Metropolis and Mental Life," in Gary Bridge and Sophie Watson (eds.), *The Blackwell City Reader* (Cambridge: Blackwell, 2002), 11.

[30] Leo Charney and Vanessa Schwartz, "Introduction," in Charney and Schwartz (eds.), *Cinema and the Invention of Modern Life* (Berkeley: University of California Press, 1995), 3.

commodities (whose roles sometimes overlap, as with the prostitute) define not only modernity but the city itself in the second half of the 19th century.[31] This was a period when industrial capitalism and consumerism were expanding on an unprecedented scale, traversing spaces and cultures.

Building on the Freudian idea that our sense organs develop strategies to protect the system against an unbearable level of stimuli, Benjamin puts forward a neurological perspective of modernity as a process embedded in the development of capitalism that reconfigured human experience.[32] Good examples of these excesses are the sensationalist strategies employed by Portuguese media in the period when photographs became widely available. For example, the magazine *Ilustração Portuguesa* published a story on the 1908 regicide that included photographs taken in the morgue of the corpses of the perpetrators and of one bystander shot by the police.[33] This strengthening of stimuli under both chaotic and rationalizing tendencies of metropolitan life is also a part of Marshall Berman's take on modernity, a mode of experiencing space and time that "pours us all into a maelstrom of perpetual disintegration and renewal, of struggle and contradiction, of ambiguity and anguish."[34]

However, modernity and modern life were not homogeneous categories in a complex and differentiated world. A myth about modernity is the clustering of its tendencies in specific spaces and times that embody and radiate them.[35] This was certainly the case of Paris in the Second Empire, exporting urban planning, entertainment, and fashion. However, even if peripheral countries like Portugal imported these ideas and goods from Paris, the negotiation between the local and the foreign was constant. For Straw, "the manner in which musical practices within a scene tie themselves to processes of historical change occurring within a larger international musical culture will also be a significant basis of the way in which such forms are positioned within that scene at the local level."[36] Therefore, performing Parisian operettas in Lisbon relied on their translation and adaptation to suit the demands of the local audience. This was essential to the profitability of the theatrical venture. In this sense, Lisbon's entertainment market was both local and global in a particular way. On the one hand, it presented cosmopolitan genres like Italian opera

---

[31] Charney and Schwartz, *Cinema and the Invention of Modern Life*, 3.

[32] Ben Singer, "Modernity, Hyperstimulus, and the Rise of Popular Sensationalism," in Charney and Schwartz (eds.), *Cinema and the Invention of Modern Life*, 72.

[33] "O attentado de 1 de Fevereiro," *Illustração Portugueza*, 10 February 1908, 169.

[34] Marshall Berman, *All That Is Solid Melts into Air: The Experience of Modernity* (London: Verso, 1983), 15.

[35] David Harvey, *Paris, Capital of Modernity*, 1.

[36] Will Straw, "Systems of Articulation, Logics of Change: Communities and Scenes in Popular Music," *Cultural Studies*, 5/3 (1991), 373.

performed by Italian singers. On the other hand, it incorporated local vernacular styles that were captured by multinational recording companies and then disseminated to other countries, like Brazil. Thus, modernity in Portugal followed its own path in which both homogenizing and differentiating trends were operating simultaneously, a key aspect in the embedding of the cultural nation-state in its narrative. Furthermore, the notion of a modern Portuguese nation-state was deeply associated with its empire. Therefore, the assimilation of colonial or post-colonial elements in the consumer culture of the late 19th century evidences the complex relationship between Europe and its colonial others. This happened when industrial capitalism expanded to large parts of the globe, and posits the notions of both center and periphery as contingent.

The Portuguese Nation: A Mosaic of Theories

Nation-building is a contended field in the social sciences that encompasses competing theories. Most classic theories of nationalism address macro-processes, such as modernization, as key factors for creating the nation-state. This is very useful for understanding the transformation of European society during the long 19th century, but it fails to explain the individual attachment that nationalism has to promote to be efficient. Furthermore, it overlooks the mechanisms through which this attachment is developed by concentrating its study on the role of the privileged, like the state or the intellectuals. I aim to trace a link between the macroscopic view of the "nation" and individual action that explains the importance of the idiosyncratic agency of some Portuguese musicians in promoting patriotism through the theatrical stage. They did it in both conspicuous and subtle forms. However, for this to be effective, audiences had to develop an individual engagement with the plays that were presented. Moreover, they actively constructed their attachment to the sometimes contradictory symbols of the nation-state.

Ernest Gellner associates the nation-state with a Weberian theory of modernization and centralization. Thus, nationalism is posed as a consequence of industrialization and of bureaucracy. Nation was a product of both modernity and differentiation. According to him, "industrialization engenders a mobile and culturally homogeneous society, which consequently has egalitarian expectations and aspirations, such as had been generally lacking in the previous stable, stratified, dogmatic, and absolutist agrarian societies."[37] This is very problematic because it creates an unhelpful polar relation between dynamic industrial

---

[37] Ernest Gellner, *Nations and Nationalisms* (Oxford: Blackwell, 2006), 71.

societies and stable agrarian societies, disregarding their internal characteristics. For example, Portugal was a predominantly agrarian country with a small number of industrialized areas. This evidences the coexistence of different types of social organization within the same territory, a characteristic that is shared by many countries. Moreover, the teleological reliance on industrialization as the most important homogenizing factor is debatable, given that pre-industrialized or incipiently industrialized countries developed cultural nation-states during the 19th century. This is certainly the case of Portugal, a peripheral European country that maintained large colonial possessions and whose industrial activity was small and concentrated in particular places and activities. However, if we bring the development of a bureaucratic culture to this picture, it becomes more plausible to associate modernization with the Portuguese nation-state in the 19th century. The establishment of a constitutional monarchy and the bureaucratization of public organisms point to the role played by urbanization and modernization in local nation-building. This was visible in Lisbon, especially the growth of the public sector. "The public offices, almost without exception, have too many employees, and this superabundance of workers does not prevent that the indispensable work of the public services is slow and poorly conducted."[38] This sector included heterogeneous people who had both a stable job and income. Moreover, a private sector that catered for their needs, including their leisure activities, was developed. This was crucial for the growth of Lisbon's entertainment circuit, whose variety reflects important tendencies in Portuguese society.

Anthony D. Smith proposes an ethnosymbolic paradigm for the study of nationalism that argues that actual nations are not result of a break during modernity, but a reformulation of a much older construct. One convincing aspect of his approach is the reliance on shared national symbols that were encoded in an earlier period. This partly resonates with Hobsbawm's perspective in which the attempt to ground nation-states in a remote past and the use of their alleged antiquity is part of a validation strategy.[39] This presented a contingent formation as an old and inevitable presence. A nation that relies on a continuous narrative from time immemorial was part of the working of Portuguese ethnologists. If identifying a nation with a culture and a state has been a modern phenomenon, this does not exclude the selection of pre-modern symbols as their cultural markers. For example, the writer and historian Alexandre Herculano places the creation of the Portuguese nation in the 12th century, contrasting with a view that identifies the Portuguese with the Lusitanian.[40]

[38] Bastos, *A crise*, 273–274.
[39] Eric J. Hobsbawm, "Introduction," in Eric J. Hobsbawm and Terence Ranger (eds.), *The Invention of Tradition* (Cambridge: Cambridge University Press, 1992), 14.
[40] Alexandre Herculano, *História de Portugal*, vol. 1 (Lisbon: Casa da Viúva Bertrand e Filhos, 1853 [1846]), 47.

The second view presents a continuous national narrative since pre-Roman times and was frequently used since the Renaissance to attest the antiquity of the Portuguese people. Thus, as a validation strategy, the Lusitanian hypothesis was brought back into focus by people like Adolfo Coelho, Teófilo Braga, or Leite de Vasconcelos in the end of the 19th century. Is it understandable that nationalism plays a key role in naturalizing "the recency and contingency of the nation-state through providing its myths of origin."[41] If nationalism poses the models for identification, it also blocks other possible articulations of the system, privileging some aspects to the detriment of others.

Furthermore, European nation-states that emerged in the second half of the 19th century were multi-ethnical and culturally heterogeneous. This complicates a straightforward theory of nation-building based on ethnicity. To make the argument more flexible, Anthony D. Smith proposes the concept of "dominant ethnie" as a sort of hegemonic set of biological and cultural traits that exert dominance within a given territory.[42] This stress on ethnicity raises important questions in the late 19th century in both metropolitan and colonial Portugal, where people like Basílio Teles, Alberto Sampaio, and Alberto Pimentel questioned the unity of the country. They promoted a North/South divide based on ethnic grounds, segmenting the country into a Celtic North and a Semitic South. Therefore, this perspective poses interesting questions concerning both biology and culture, revealing an internal division that has surfaced frequently, predominantly associated with regionalist policies. In this divide Lisbon was part of a purportedly Semitic South, given its Moorish influences. Moreover, the comparison between a commercial and bourgeois Porto and a capital that concentrates many civil servants is frequently made. Ethnicity is always a murky territory, above all because of the binding of biology and culture that it entails. Furthermore, this racial discussion is further complicated when one studies the Portuguese colonies. The metropolitan cities articulated colonial life and Lisbon had a large black community. Thus, the ghostly presence of the colonial world in metropolitan daily life was deeply felt, showing that the homeland became cross-culturalized. Moreover, the colonial ideology of effective occupation promoted several expeditions to both Africa and India, and the explorers were seen as national heroes. These honors were extended to the military officers who led successful African "pacification" campaigns, like Mouzinho de Albuquerque, Aires de Ornelas, or Alves Roçadas. Moreover, the end of the 19th century was marked by the reinforcing

---

[41] Anthony Giddens, *A Contemporary Critique of Historical Materialism: The Nation State and Violence* (Cambridge: Polity Press, 1985), 221.

[42] Anthony D. Smith, *The Ethnic Origins of Nations* (Oxford: Blackwell, 1987).

of the colonial order in the metropolis through propaganda, leading to the spread of national symbols throughout the empire.

By stating that traditions rely on invented rituals, Hobsbawm stresses a constructivist view of the nation. His theory focuses on the manufacturing of symbols by intellectuals and institutions and their imposition on the "people." This unilateral and oversimplified way of seeing the dynamics of nationalism is questioned in a later work, where he points to the inadequacy of taking the nationalist ideas from a literate minority to represent a people that included a vast majority of illiterates.[43] This was clearly the Portuguese case. Moreover, a model that privileges the building of national symbols can even undermine its own workings. According to Tilly,

> Top-down nationalism generated bottom-up nationalism as its antithesis and mirror image. Political brokers who had strong investments in alternative definitions of language, history, and community rallied supporters in the name of oppressed and threatened nations, demanding protection from top-down nationalizers. Having insisted on the correspondence between state and nation, top-down nationalizers were caught in a trap of their own devising: to the extent that interlocutors for regional populations could establish that they constituted distinct, ancient nations, they made credible cases for political autonomy.[44]

This resonates with Hall's perspective, in which the historicized nation is the result of "concrete interactions between people in projects and networks," emphasizing the role some agents play in this process.[45] In this sense, nation-building can fuel contradictory expectations and attachments in the people. In an insightful Foucauldian reading of nationalism, Askew argues that "rather than an abstract ideology produced by some to be consumed by others, nationalism ought to be conceptualized as a series of continually negotiated relationships between people who share occupancy in a defined geographical, political or ideological space."[46] This perspective emphasizes the ongoing process of nation-building, to which the circulation of both power and resistance

---

[43] Eric Hobsbawm, *Nations and Nationalism since 1780: Programme, Myth, Reality* (Cambridge: Canto, 1992), 48.

[44] Charles Tilly, "The State of Nationalism," *Critical Review: A Journal of Politics and Society*, 10/2 (1996), 304.

[45] Patrik Hall, "Nationalism and Historicity," *Nations and Nationalism*, 3/1 (1997), 17.

[46] Kelly Askew, *Performing the Nation: Swahili Music and Cultural Politics in Tanzania* (Chicago: University of Chicago Press, 2002), 12.

is fluid and inextricably embedded.⁴⁷ Moreover, a top-down theory of nationalism emanates from a top-down model of history. Thus, listening to often overlooked voices is part of a strategy of adding new layers to an already contested space, a view that stresses the discontinuity and heterogeneity of historical processes. Placing the people as the basis for nationality and as a political agent is at the core of this problem. So, by situating the people as representing the "cutting edge between the totalizing powers of the 'social' as homogeneous, consensual community, and the forces that signify the more specific address to contentious, unequal interests and identities within the population," Bhabha complicates an essentialist view that perceives the nation as an emanation of its people.⁴⁸

A Herderian perspective of nationalism was present during Portuguese Romanticism, and the first ethnologists relied mainly on texts. This was transformed with the spread of positivist ideas from the 1870s onward. Moreover, this approach presented popular culture as a residual trace of the past, a past that was framed in a multi-ethnical perspective. This view was part of the scientific validation of Portugal, and it was mainly grounded in capturing what was perceived as the "authentic tradition," what was peculiar, picturesque, or unusual.⁴⁹ However, Portuguese anthropology underwent a significant change in the 1890s, favoring a more inclusive concept of popular culture that comprised art, architecture, technologies, and forms of economic and social life.⁵⁰ The rising interest in material culture was fundamental for the archaeology and ethnology of this period, a tendency that was reflected in a renewed interest in museums.⁵¹ Moreover, museums can be an important part of nation-building, in this case, presenting Portuguese culture in a way that appealed to the public. By the end of the 19th century, Portuguese anthropology had become legitimated by its involvement with the two foremost scientific organizations of the time: the university and the museum.⁵² In the beginning of the 20th century,

---

⁴⁷ Michel Foucault, *Histoire de la sexualité: La volonté de savoir*, vol.1 (Paris: Gallimard, 1976).

⁴⁸ Homi K. Bhabha, "Dissemination: Time, Narrative and the Margins of the Modern Nation," in Bhabha, *The Location of Culture* (London: Routledge, 1994), 146.

⁴⁹ João Leal, *Antropologia em Portugal: mestres, percursos e transições* (Lisbon: Livros Horizonte, 2006), 178.

⁵⁰ João Leal, *Etnografias portuguesas (1870–1970): cultura popular e identidade nacional* (Lisbon: Publicações D. Quixote, 2000), 43.

⁵¹ Orvar Löfgren, "Scenes from a Troubled Marriage: Swedish Ethnology and Material Culture Studies," *Journal of Material Culture*, 2 (1997), 111.

⁵² George W. Stocking Jr. (ed.), *Objects and Others: Essays on Museums and Material Culture* (Madison: University of Wisconsin Press, 1985); Nélia Dias, "The Visibility of Difference: Nineteenth-Century French Anthropological Collections," in Sharon Macdonald (ed.), *The Politics of Display: Museums, Science, Culture* (London: Routledge, 1998), 36–52.

Manuel Laranjeira wrote that "the life of a nation is not a political fiction, it is not a conventional lie to divide peoples, it exists."[53] Thus, the concreteness of the Portuguese nation was taught in the university and disseminated in the museums.

Benedict Anderson focuses on "imagined communities" as the basis of the modern nation. In his view, communities are bound by symbols that emphasize their uniqueness and distinction. This affinity is created through media and relies on the capitalist development of the printing industry. For Anderson, print capitalism promoted the possibility of "rapidly growing numbers of people to think about themselves, and to relate themselves to others, in profoundly new ways."[54] Moreover, "the convergence of capitalism and print technology on the fatal diversity of human language created the possibility of a new form of imagined community, which in its basic morphology set the stage for the modern nation."[55] Accordingly, the publishing business created a national public sphere by introducing a new kind of relationship between the members of a linguistic community. However, the prominence given by Anderson to print media does not reflect the role media like music play in building national identities.[56] Furthermore, taking print capitalism as a major creator of national bonds is problematic in Portugal, given its enormous illiteracy rate. This relies on a top-down model of nationalism that concentrates on literate elites and does not take account of the uneven spread of literacy in a country, as the literacy rate varies with age, gender, class, and geography. According to the 1890 census, there was a much greater prevalence of illiteracy in rural areas than in cities.[57] In both Lisbon and Porto, Portugal's second largest city, the illiteracy rate was significantly smaller for both men and women than it was in the country's rural areas. This clearly reinforces the idea that Lisbon's cultural market cannot be extrapolated to represent the entire country. Moreover, the data do not relate literacy to income or activity, which complicates the study of Lisbon's literate audiences. Nevertheless, there was a noteworthy growth of the press, when periodicals enlarged their scope and audience. To make a more nuanced reading, taking literacy as a barrier that excludes the participation of a large part of the people from the contact with periodicals can be misleading. For Chartier and González,

---

[53] Laranjeira, *O pessimismo nacional*, 36.

[54] Benedict Anderson, *Imagined Communities: Reflections on the Origin and Spread of Nationalism* (London: Verso, 1991), 36.

[55] Anderson, *Imagined Communities*, 46.

[56] Askew, *Performing the Nation*, 271.

[57] Portugal, Direcção Geral de Estatística, *Relatorio sobre o censo da populaçao* (Lisbon: Imprensa Nacional, 1896), graphic VII.

Reading is not only an abstract operation of the intellect: it puts the body into play and is inscribed within a particular space, in a relation to the self or to others. This is why attention should particularly be paid to ways of reading that have been obliterated in our contemporary world: for example reading out loud in its double function-communicating that which is written to those who do not know how to decipher it, and binding together the interconnected forms of sociability which are all figures of the private sphere (the intimacy of the family, the conviviality of social life, the cooperation of scholars).[58]

For example, reading aloud has been a prevalent mode of providing access to written texts since early modernity, and Abel Botelho's novel *Amanhã!* includes a scene in which a character reads aloud from the republican newspaper *O século* to his fellow-thinkers.[59]

Imagined communities are interconnected to imagined geographies and create a dynamic that binds culture, memory, and place. Selecting national symbols has to be twofold: they must be efficient for the "people" to attach to them, and they must be open enough to contain ambiguity and to be continuously re-encoded to achieve that efficiency. Furthermore, Stavrakakis and Chrysoloras state the importance of personal investment in the identification and the construction of collective identities.[60] They also argue against the reduction of identity to a discursive form because of its insufficiency to account for aspects that escape both the attachment to a set of symbols and the historical kernel of identity. Therefore, the non-representative character of music, whose ambiguity is cultivated for various purposes, establishes a complex dialectic between existing and projected identities that include the past, the present, and the future. In this sense,

> music can variably both construct new identities and reflect existing ones. Sociocultural identities are not simply constructed in music; there are "prior" identities that come to be embodied dynamically in musical cultures, which then also form the reproduction of those identities—no passive process of reflection.[61]

---

[58] Roger Chartier and J. A. González, "Laborers and Voyagers: From the Text to the Reader," *Diacritics*, 22/2 (1992), 53.

[59] Abel Botelho, *Amanhã!* (Porto: Livraria Chardron, 1902), 398–399.

[60] Yannis Stavrakakis and Nikos Chrysoloras "(I Can't Get No) Enjoyment: Lacanian Theory and the Analysis of Nationalism," *Psychoanalysis, Culture & Society*, 11/2 (2006), 144–163.

[61] Georgina Born and David Hesmondhalgh, "Introduction," in Georgina Born and David Hesmondhalgh (eds.), *Western Music and Its Others: Difference, Representation, and Appropriation in Music* (Berkeley: University of California Press, 2000), 31–32.

This dialectic is essential for understanding the dynamic in which popular theater worked in Portugal. Given the constant demand for political and economic reform, plays and songs were used to comment on the state of affairs from varied perspectives. Moreover, the constraints imposed on the theater promoted the allegorical staging of symbols, which fostered a curious ambiguity. For example, republican playwrights refrained from promoting the direct overthrow of the regime but kept on criticizing it within the legal boundaries, a move that places them side by side with playwrights of other political persuasions. Thus, the burlesque subversion of social conventions on which the revue theater relied became the common ground which a heterogeneous amalgam of people understood. This is evidenced in the association between the playwright and member of parliament Eduardo Schwalbach and the professional musician with collectivist inclinations Tomás Del Negro. Together they penned some of the most successful *revistas* that were performed in the end of the 19th century.

My focus on popular theater is a way to address the role leisure played in facilitating the spread of ideas that include the modern nation-state. Given its wide audience, popular theater was pivotal in naturalizing the idea of modern Portugal, through the integration of its many contradictory features in a pleasurable entertainment. Music occupied an important space in these shows. Moreover, the various types of extra-musical connotations that derive from the non-representational quality of musical sound are naturalized and projected so they appear to derive from sound itself.[62] This is central to understanding the affective and political implications of sound in Portuguese nation-building and the association made between local genres like fado and nationalism. Moreover, the revue theater acted as a commentator of everyday life and presented symbols that could be decoded by both literate and illiterate spectators. "The art of the theater is the only art that doesn't demand previous studies from the spectator for its reception," argues José Simões Coelho, a writer for the libertarian magazine *Amanhã*.[63] However, the article stresses the need of a "theater by the people and for the people" that presents "scientific truth."[64] Staging theatrical shows that aimed to elevate the people and were devoid of artifice resonates with both positivist and realist ideals. Moreover, Coelho asserts that a theater that does not rely on capitalist profit should be created. For him, most theaters limited their offerings to a form of "prostituted art" in order to obtain financial

---

[62] Georgina Born, "Music and the Materialization of Identities," *Journal of Material Culture*, 16/4 (2011), 377.

[63] José Simões Coelho, "O povo e o teatro," *Ámanhã*, 1 August 1909, 4.

[64] Coelho, "O povo e o teatro," 3–4.

gain.⁶⁵ Despite this critique, the article demonstrates the importance of the theater in the entertainment routines of some workers.

This expands and elaborates on established theories of nationalism, tracing a circuit that accounts for the asymmetry of the social world. In this context, differentiated forms of modernity and nation-building were working in Lisbon. Technological innovations, aesthetic, political, and economic changes provide a fertile ground in which to analyze the reshaping of local culture. Moreover, these materials were interwoven in the fabric of everyday life, creating an efficient narrative in which the modern nation-state operates. Hence, a discourse of nation-building that relies on commonality became a key aspect for the grounding of a Portuguese nation that was independent from the Bragança Dynasty. This created the space for the replacement of the Constitutional Monarchy by a regime inspired by the French Third Republic. Furthermore, the construction of Portugal was a complex process in which heterogeneous and sometimes incompatible perspectives were articulated in a set of symbols that strove to attract the investment and promote the attachment of the Portuguese people. However, nationalism as a mutual rapport between individuals always carries the possibility of dissension, due to the active role people play in this relationship.⁶⁶ A good example is the spread of internationalist tendencies among workers, illustrated in a passage from *Amanhã!*: "Patriotism is one of the many crafty forms of oppression that the rich and powerful have invented to crush us and remain unpunished."⁶⁷ To complicate this, both internationalist and protectionist tendencies were circulating. Therefore, the everyday life of workers was ambivalently linked with both trends, reflecting the internal tensions of a country in which migration is a key factor for understanding the local economy.

Research Methods

Studying the complex relations between the Portuguese nation and a changing entertainment market where popular music theater dominated requires a variety of methods. Moreover, an interdisciplinary approach to nationalism implies employing several types of sources and methods. The main sources for this study include periodicals, books, posters, postcards, sheet music, and sound recordings. Also, a period of intense transformation provides fertile

---

⁶⁵ Coelho, "O povo e o teatro," 3–4.
⁶⁶ Askew, *Performing the Nation*, 12.
⁶⁷ Botelho, *Amanhã!*, 65.

ground in which to analyze the reshaping of culture. This created a symbiotically articulated system that produced a heterogeneous set of products (such as theatrical presentations, printed material, and sound reproductions), which were rapidly incorporated in the everyday routines of Lisbon's population.

> A heterogeneity of human involvement is therefore equivalent to a heterogeneity of results as well as of interpretative skills and techniques. There is no center, no inertly given and accepted authority, no fixed barriers ordering human history, even though authority, order, and distinction exist.[68]

To make an efficient reading of these heterogeneous materials I draw on distinct methods and bodies of theory. Therefore, the book embodies the interdisciplinary approach that grounds it as well as the fragmentary nature of establishing the modern cultural nation-state in Portugal effectively. Moreover, this polyphonic character associated with my own suspicions toward master narratives raised important methodological questions. For example, relying on modes of inquiry associated with microhistory poses a problem of scale, especially when studying large processes such as nationalism. These methods have proven to be efficient for reconstructing passages of the past and are part of the work of people like Carlo Ginzburg or Robert Darnton. Telling a coherent story from scattered, disordered, varied, and contradictory traces is part of my strategy. Moreover, these methods place the reader as a willing participant in the unfolding of the argument by making extensive use of primary sources. This process is like the collective effort of assembling a large puzzle, and the reader will be swamped with details, people, and sounds. Sounds of voices, of music, and of everyday life are woven in a way that embraces difference. To complement the pitfalls of microhistory, especially the application of this approach to large social processes, I draw from the work of historians like Roger Chartier or Peter Burke. Therefore, a microscopic view of history is articulated with the study of long periods in cultural history. Moreover, reading Hobsbawm's *The Age of Empire* has made a strong impression in me. As an undergraduate student of musicology, connecting with a history that is both engaged and engaging transformed the way I understood writing. Thus, I intend to create a space where both microhistory and macro-processes coexist. This space is both unstable and contested, and it is where the tensions between the local and the global are played out. Moreover, I do not intend to create a third

---

[68] Edward Said, "Opponents, Audiences, Constituencies, and Community," *Critical Inquiry*, 9/1 (September 1982), 12.

dimension by blurring the tensions between these levels. By tearing the fabric of history and by emphasizing discontinuity I aim to open windows to the past. Nevertheless, these windows are anything but clear.

Finding a balance between my own voice and the voices of others without losing sight of the larger picture has also been a difficult part of writing. A key concern has been building a shifting and sometimes irregular polyphony of written, visual, and auditory traces. I also intend to develop ways in which both history and cultural studies mutually inform each other. However, the relationship between these areas has not always been peaceful, and tensions are bound to arise. These contested grounds sometimes overlap but this has not been always true. Thus, perspectives that were mainly developed to study contemporary societies are used to understand lives from the past. Conversely, a multilayered set of sources that both contrast and resonate with current matters emerges. Therefore, placing this research in another contested intersection was a personal choice. Macro and micro levels, history and cultural studies, private and public spaces, lived and projected experiences, popular and learned cultures, art and entertainment are part of the story being told. Furthermore, a narrative that is placed on these contested grounds will inevitably have loose ends. These are not always dead ends, and some can even be productive moments for launching future research. Sometimes, they are there just to remind us that incoherence and incompleteness is an important part of human experience.

The periodicals were the starting point for the research. A large survey of the press allowed me to have a general understanding of the variety of sources that could be used to study everyday life. These were often incompatible and contradictory but they gave me a special insight into the role played by the iconography in creating a faithful depiction of reality as well as a satirical exaggeration of the agents involved. The collection of periodicals of the National Library of Portugal and of the Hemeroteca Municipal de Lisboa raised my awareness of the variety of publications that were circulating. The variety of political orientations, of aesthetic values, and of intended audiences was evidenced in this survey. Of course, lived experience is not contained in periodicals. Nevertheless, the newspapers can help to show how reality was socially constructed. Quantitative data were mainly drawn from the population censuses of 1878, 1890, 1900, and 1911. Coeval bibliography, such as history books, historical accounts, novels, and diaries were key to establishing the context in which the popular theater developed. These sources were important in tracing the polyphonic matrix of Lisbon's population. Of course, I am aware that using fiction as a source for historical inquiry can lead to questionable results. Nevertheless, these novels and poems give important clues to how experiences were lived, especially aspects of everyday life that were not meant to become public. Moreover, some works portray illiterate social groups who were not able to voice themselves for posterity. Despite their realistic intents, the aesthetic construction of the poorer segments of society tended to include aspects of living that were perceived as unusual. Thus, the work of writers who focus on urban contexts resonates with the work carried out by the contemporary ethnologists concerning popular culture. In this process, authors like Fialho d'Almeida projected their own anxieties on them, sometimes with a deeply moralistic tone, and these sources are important traces of a past that is still taught in Portuguese language courses.

Operetta and *revista* epitomize a methodological concern that emerges from studying ephemeral repertoires: the nature of the sources. In these genres, a significant part of the surviving traces is printed material associated with the shows, especially the *coplas* (booklets that contained the sung texts of the revue theater) and the sheet music of some sketches. On the one hand, it is impossible to reconstruct the entire plays with these materials. Conversely, these goods were sold because of their popularity. Therefore, they reflect the success of specific parts of the play, obfuscating not only other parts of the show but also a large number of unsuccessful plays. Despite the scarcity of sources, some manuscripts containing both text and music are part of the collections of the National Library of Portugal and of the National Music Theater. Given the economic difficulties of the companies that performed unsubsidized theater, the large quantity of materials that were drawn from these plays is surprising. Nevertheless, the fragmented sources reveal the difficulties of studying ephemeral genres of the entertainment market. A study of these plays requires a particular methodological approach. Therefore, I privilege the reconstruction of the universe in which these repertoires operated in detriment of using the re-creation of an entire play as a case study. Nevertheless, sources are scarce concerning the staging of both *revista* and operetta. There is a large quantity of iconographic evidence that is helpful in reconstructing the visual aspects of the plays. However, there is also a major lack of information when it comes to stage movements, lighting, and choreography. Many musical sources containing music notation have been consulted. My work uses musical analysis tangentially and focuses on other forms of analysis. Nevertheless, it would be impossible to understand how sound circulated without knowing which music was played and heard. To map this circuit, I have surveyed Portuguese music collections, especially those in the National Library of Portugal and the National Theater Museum. The majority of manuscripts consulted are part of the first collection, and most of the sheet music is held in the museum. The manuscripts of operettas and *revistas* by Filipe Duarte are especially relevant for this study. Moreover, the National Library holds a copy of the most comprehensive collection of Portuguese traditional music, the *Cancioneiro de músicas populares*.[69] Most player piano rolls and some recordings I have consulted are part of the collection of the Music Museum (Lisbon). To study phonography in Portugal I have consulted a wide variety of sources, from public institutions, like the EMI Archives, parts of which are accessible in the British Library, to private collectors who hold unique information. Moreover, the complex dialectic between the local and the global played a prominent role in the Portuguese phonographic market, where both local entrepreneurs and multinational companies developed their business. Thus, the polyphony of sources is reflected in a multivocal narrative.

To produce a comprehensive study requires a broad approach to distinct types of sources and methodologies. Moreover, these sources are multiple traces of a fragmentary past that need to be interpreted and contextualized, avoiding a predominantly historicist reading that aims to reconstruct a period in a continuous and coherent fashion. With this move, I aim to critique a modern and evolutionist perspective on history as "a narrative of the victor who legitimizes his victory by presenting the previous development as the linear continuum leading to his own final triumph."[70] Consequently, it includes competing and heterogeneous modes of living, including the popular segments of Lisbon's society. By examining popular repertoires, my book stresses cultural practices that were integrated in the everyday life of people, many of them living in social spaces whose history remains yet to be written.

Outline of the Book

The first chapter introduces the historical background of the book, beginning with the 1820 Liberal Revolution. It traces the transformations of Portuguese society until 1910, giving special attention to the changes introduced in Lisbon. "And here she is [Lisbon] overflowing the lugubrious piles of the old districts, Alfama, Mouraria, Estrela; breaking the belt of walls in a charivari of filthy chic buildings, transforming the environs into centers; climbing the hills or spreading like a nomad camp by the river."[71]

Chapter 2 concentrates on Lisbon's theatrical life from 1867 to 1910, a period when urban expansion was closely associated with paradigms of modernity as it was perceived at the time. This produced new spaces in the urban fabric, some of them directly connected with the development of a market for

---

[69] César das Neves and Gualdino de Campos, *Cancioneiro de músicas populares*, 3 vols. (Porto: Tip. Ocidental—Empresa editora César, Campos & Cª, 1893, 1895, 1898).

[70] Slavoj Žižek, *Enjoy Your Symptom!* (London: Routledge, 2008), 92–93.

[71] Fialho d'Almeida, *Lisboa Galante* (Porto: Livraria Civilisação, 1890), 16.

cultural goods. "The audience goes to the theater to spend an evening. Here [in Lisbon] the theater is not a curiosity of the spirit, it is a Sunday leisure."[72] This remark by the writer Eça de Queirós reflects the important role theater played in Lisbon's population. The chapter concentrates on the staging of unsubsidized theatrical spectacles in Lisbon, such as operetta, *zarzuela* (the Spanish equivalent to operetta), and *revista*. Furthermore, the processes through which the vernacular is aestheticized and commodified are central to understanding how popular culture operates. Staging the vernacular became an important tendency of realist aesthetics but it was also reflected in allegorical genres like the *revista*. The *revista* included, absorbed, and metabolized everyday life, translating it into an imaginary in which a set of conventions was recurrently revisited by the playwrights. This imagery contributed to the creation and naturalization of a "composite image" of Portuguese (mostly) urban society that embodies the modern nation. In this sense, popular entertainment became an important area for the dissemination of nationalist ideas.

The third chapter discusses the study, collection, and publication of music from predominantly rural contexts as part of Portuguese ethnology. It studies the emergence of a historiographical narrative that concentrated on fado. This move emphasized its specificity as a genre when the term "fado" was used almost indiscriminately to name popular songs. Studying traditional music was not the main concern in the work of ethnographers and historians. Nevertheless, several collections of transcriptions of Portuguese traditional music were published. These publications later became key sources for the study of those repertoires and are still part of the Portuguese folklore revival. When examining these works, I focus on the inherent politics of repertoire selection, transcription, and commercialization.

The fourth and fifth chapters study the circulation of musical products and the role played by the commodity form in Lisbon. To understand this commodification, a process in which technology, class, and gender were embedded, I examine a heterogeneous set of goods that circulated in Lisbon's entertainment market. Chapter 4 studies domesticity and activities like collecting and playing the piano. The parlor piano occupies a prominent place in bourgeois sociability, and condensed attributes like gender and class. Moreover, the trade in goods such as *coplas* or sheet music promoted the consumption of theatrical repertoires in domestic spaces. Consequently, the circulation of repertoires that relied on differentiated goods promoted the ubiquitous presence of theatrical music in everyday life.

---

[72] Ramalho Ortigão and Eça de Queirós, *As farpas: crónica mensal da política, das letras e dos costumes* (Lisbon: Typographia Universal, 1872), 53.

Chapter 5 studies the development of technologies for sound and music recording and reproduction, such as the phonograph, the gramophone, and the player piano. These innovations transformed Lisbon's entertainment market and pose interesting theoretical questions concerning the storage media and their materiality. The positioning of these media in a market that relied on local sheet music retailers and importers transformed the local offer of cultural goods. These innovations were essential to the production, reproduction, and dissemination of theatrical repertoires. Furthermore, the chapter addresses the introduction of mechanical music in the Portuguese market in its two main forms: mechanical instruments and phonography. It discusses their cultural implications, when the possibility of music reproduction introduced by mechanization was portrayed as an embodiment of modernity. This helped to reconfigure domestic space and time around new technologies, allowing for a redistribution of cultural capital in the social networks. Therefore, modernity and nationalism were ubiquitous ideas in Portugal, where cosmopolitanism and localism were constantly interacting. Thus, the stage of the popular theater, the contingent space between shadows and light, becomes a passageway for the study of a reality that is simultaneously familiar and distant.

1

The Long 19th Century in Portugal and the Transformation of Lisbon

Historical Background

"The Portuguese society resembles a group of slaves that, indifferent, inert, and half-naked, watch the bartering of the price for which they should be sold, caring little whether they are the property of this or of that lord, just waiting humbly for their meagre sustenance."[1] This is how the politician Augusto Fuschini describes Portuguese society at the end of the nineteenth 19th century. However, Portugal had changed significantly in the previous decades. This chapter begins with the 1820 Liberal Revolution and addresses the transformations carried out in Portugal in the subsequent ninety years. The first half of the nineteenth 19th century was an unstable period for the country, when the balance between a society of the ancien régime, embodied by aristocratic landowners, was transformed with the rising of a bourgeois order. However, this was not simple or straightforward. A tendency to raise to nobility those citizens whose political and economic action was profitable for the government was intensified, and the Portuguese political institutions reflected the heterogeneous constitution of the upper stratum of Portuguese society, comprising old aristocrats and the wealthy bourgeois.

The Peninsular War, a conflict which pitted the Napoleonic Empire against Britain, Spain and Portugal, marked the beginning of the Portuguese turmoil in the first half of the 19th century. The royal family and the court had to move to Brazil, and Rio de Janeiro became the capital of the Portuguese Empire. Rio was greatly transformed with the presence of the court, and the seeds of independence would soon be harvested in Brazilian lands, paving the way for the colony's independence a few years later, under the rule of D. Pedro I of Brazil.

---

[1] Augusto Fuschini, *O presente e o futuro de Portugal* (Lisbon: Companhia Typographica, 1899), 334.

D. Pedro was the son of the Portuguese king D. João VI and also ruled briefly in Portugal as D. Pedro IV. To repel the French offensive, Portugal relied on the Anglo-Portuguese alliance, a relationship that became central to understanding Portuguese foreign policy and strategies of economic development in the 19th and early 20th centuries. Dependence on the British Empire amplified the trauma of the 1890 Ultimatum in Portugal, fostering strong anti-British feelings that were efficiently manipulated by the local republicans. In 1820, a constitutional monarchy was established after a liberal uprising in Porto, Portugal. This system lasted until the establishment of the Portuguese Republic in 1910, with a short interruption during the absolutist rule of D. Miguel, brother of D. Pedro IV. The historian Oliveira Martins argues that the revolution was, in itself, just another episode of slow decomposition: it could not become anything else. The heap of misfortunes of the preceding years had caused it; those misfortunes and the famine would take history to the final convulsions of absolutism, presenting a social epilepsy to the world, predecessor of the end. . . . The spontaneous anarchy wore a bland character until the beginning of the century. Now, after the [French] invasion, after 20, after the independence of Brazil, the lost, ragged, naked, starving society, rudderless or without governance falls into a fierce anarchy.[2]

Creating a new system in a predominantly rural country with high illiteracy rates relied on a topdown model: "The political history of the Portuguese nation, from the beginning of the liberal struggles [1826] until now [1911], can be said to be limited to the parties, or, at most, to the common effort of the ruling classes."[3] Therefore, the coincidence of interests between the liberal aristocracies and bourgeoisies was reflected in the leisure activities enjoyed by the upper social stratum. Attending balls, musical and literary soirées, and the opera were part of the sociability routines of Lisbon's elegant society, and these activities reinforced social ties. The court, the wealthy financiers and businessmen, the diplomats, and the men of letters gathered in Lisbon's opera theater, the Real Teatro de São Carlos.[4] This hall became part of Portuguese public life and attendance there was a mark of prestige, where a web of relationships between people from similar backgrounds was woven and reinforced. Gossip and intrigue took place in its boxes and halls, where current matters were discussed. The divas attracted great attention from their admirers, and courtship and romance spiced the everyday life of the theatergoers.

---

[2] Oliveira Martins, *História de Portugal*, vol. 2 (Lisbon: Bertrand, 1887), 256–257.

[3] Veiga Simão, *A nova geração; estudo sobre as tendencias actuaes de litteratura portuguesa* (Coimbra: F. França Amado, 1911), 12.

[4] Maria de Lourdes Lima dos Santos, *Intelectuais portugueses na primeira metade de Oitocentos* (Lisbon: Editorial Presença, 1988), 201.

The musical and literary soirées replaced the old ancién régime salon. These gatherings were promoted by the affluent bourgeoisie and were pivotal to the affirmation of a Romantic culture in Portugal.[5] Poets and writers recited their works and musicians performed varied compositions. The heterogeneous soirées accommodated both amateur and professional performances that ranged from songs, instrumental pieces, and opera selections to full performances of theatrical plays. The Count of Farrobo (1801–1869), a wealthy businessman who had risen to the aristocracy, was a master in this form of ostentation. With the help of professional musicians he staged full operas in his private theater, in which he and his family participated. Farrobo was also an important patron of the arts and became the impresario of several theaters until he went bankrupt. However, people like Oliveira Martins criticized the changes brought to Portugal by these new ideas: We have traded the Gospel for Liberty; the sermon for the speeches in S. Bento [the Portuguese Parliament]; the processions for the dances in the tivolis; the solemn Te Deum with long copes worked with gold and glittering of gemstones ... for the opera performances that Farrobo directs, for the *soirées* of his small theater in Laranjeiras, an Eden of a rich grocer.[6] He points to the substitution of religious solemnity for secular bourgeois entertainment. This sets the tone for the main ideas of this book, whereby urban entertainment becomes crucial for the way both modernity and patriotism are staged and played out in Lisbon.

In the meantime, Portuguese history was agitated. A liberal constitution was approved in 1822. The document was inspired by the first French constitutions and by the Constitution of Cadiz, and represented the progressive wing of the liberal movement. In the same year, Brazil became independent. This carried strong implications in Portugal's positioning in both the colonial and the metropolitan worlds. Nevertheless, both countries maintained an intense exchange of people, goods, and ideas, fostering a transatlantic entertainment market for theatrical genres like the operetta and the *revista*. In 1826 the constitution was replaced by a constitutional charter granted by D. Pedro IV, then emperor of Brazil. The charter aimed to balance various sectors of Portuguese public life by adding a new power apart from the legislative, the judiciary, and the executive. It was the "moderating power" and rested with the monarch, placing him or her in the center of the political arena. Under the 1820 constitution the parliament had one elected chamber, whereas under the charter it was bicameral. To the elected chamber of parliament was added a chamber of peers, who were hereditary and chosen by the monarch. In this system,

---

[5] Santos, *Intelectuais portugueses*, 279–298.

[6] Oliveira Martins, *Portugal contemporâneo*, vol. 2 (Lisbon: António Maria Pereira, 1895), 16–17.

the government's stability depended on the appointed peers. The charter was revised several times, and some reforms concerned the peerage system. This document was suspended between 1828 and 1834, when D. Miguel I ruled as an absolute sovereign. However, the final part of his reign was marked by a bloody civil war that lasted until 1834. With the threat of foreign intervention, the war was stopped, and D. Pedro's daughter, D. Maria II, restored the constitutional order.

> In the cataclysm of 34, when the assets belonging to the religious orders and to the Crown were confiscated, there was a large grain field to share; and in different ways, that property mass passed (as always) from the hands of the loser to the hands of the victor. This, however, could not influence the nation's economy, and the old poverty continued as before. The Treasury, a beggar, groaned under the weight of the traditional obligations, now aggravated by the army of new people that was necessary to feed.[7]

This apparent stability did not last long, and a revolution fueled by the ideals of 1820 broke in 1836. Its promoters (the *setembristas*) approved a new constitution two years later, aiming to balance the charter with the 1822 constitution. This short period lasted until 1842, when a military coup restored the constitutional charter under the authority of António Bernardo da Costa Cabral. "The old aristocracy had resigned, it is true; but liberty and competition had created a new and real power, a plutocracy: the class of the rich bourgeois that could not leave their power, their interests, at the mercy of the chance of elections. . . . The money, therefore, created for itself a new doctrine, that had a defender in Costa-Cabral."[8] This statement displays the role political leaders had in the development of the Portuguese economy, supporting either protectionism or free trade according to their convenience. Cabral's authoritarian reformism was rapidly contested and a popular revolt, the Maria da Fonte, broke in 1846. It began in the North but it worked as a fuse for the civil war of the Patuleia that lasted until 1847. In this conflict the *cabralistas* (the supporters of Costa Cabral) were opposed by a broad coalition of forces that ranged from the *setembristas* to the absolutists. Nevertheless, the chartists associated with Cabral remained in power until 1851, when another military coup started the Regeneração (Regeneration). According to Oliveira Martins, this period sped up the country's downfall because "the revolution and the war, crumbling the card castle

---

[7] Oliveira Martins, *Historia de Portugal*, vol. 2 (Lisbon: Livraria Bertrand, 1887), 295.

[8] Oliveira Martins, *Portugal contemporâneo*, vol. 2, 140.

of Cabral's usury, had ruined, in its fall, the Portuguese fiduciary circulation. It was another step in the path of an economic decadence, declared since the beginning of the century, and that, up to now, liberalism was not able to correct."[9] The unrest in Portuguese society of the first half of the 19th century had strong implications for the musical life of the country. The theaters were closed for long periods, and musical practice was confined to private spaces. Musical soirées, domestic concerts, amateur opera performances, or dances were already part of the aristocratic and bourgeois lifestyle. With the theaters closed and a generalized feeling of unrest, these people had to find entertainment in their homes. Relative peace and prosperity was enjoyed under the Regeneração. The political system was based on two large parties, the Partido Regenerador and the Partido Histórico (Partido Progressista after 1876). The main political leaders of the time were Fontes Pereira de Melo (1819–1887) for the Partido Regenerador and Nuno de Moura Barreto, Duke of Loulé, (1804–1875), for the Partido Histórico. Both parties shared their power under the auspices of an updated constitutional charter and the monarch's supervision. Moreover, they depended on the charismatic authority of their leaders and on the network of influences their notables held in the provinces. This was amplified by a strong investment in public works and an increase of public service jobs, creating new opportunities for their followers and sponsors.[10] "Since 1851 the material transformation of the country has been carried, rendered in the construction of roads, of telegraph lines, of bridges, ports, and railways, whose building expenses had to be paid through resources obtained from credit in foreign countries."[11] Thus, rapid modernization became the mantra of many politicians. It aimed to reduce Portugal's endemic backwardness and raise the country to a status more comparable to that of other European nations. This stability was reflected in various aspects of Portuguese life, including the development of the theatrical scene as well as of public works concerning the modernization of Lisbon, an issue addressed below. The *revista* was a shrewd witness to and commentator on these events that transformed Lisbon's everyday life. The "material improvements" (*melhoramentos materiais*) carried out in Portugal in the second half of the 19th century were mocked in the *revista* titled *Os melhoramentos materiais*, premièred in the Teatro do Ginásio in 1860.[12] However, in

---

[9] Oliveira Martins, *Portugal contemporâneo*, vol. 2, 261.

[10] Teixeira Bastos, *A crise: estudo sobre a situação política, financeira, económica e moral da nação* (Porto: Livraria Internacional de Ernesto Chardron, 1894), 3.

[11] Teixeira de Sousa, *Para a história da Revolução*, vol. 1 (Coimbra: Moura Marques & Paraísos, 1912), 38.

[12] Andrade Ferreira, *Os melhoramentos materiais: revista de 1859. Comédia satírica e fantasmagórica em 3 actos e 4 quadros por um curioso observador* (Lisbon, Typ. de Joaquim Germano de Sousa Neves, 1860).

a weak economy this major venture had to be financed by borrowed capital. The practice of widespread borrowing became unsustainable toward the end of the century, and a time of hardship reached the National Treasury in 1890.[13] "The Regeneração was a historical moment that, if it could not lift Portugal up to the level of the great nations in Europe, and give it the preponderance of past eras, mainly in the early days of the conquests, would have placed it in an advantageous and dignified situation."[14] This apparent prosperity was important for capturing foreign investment. However, in a "poor and ignorant country" it became "an untamed field for all castes of foreign adventurers, and a profitable market for the banks, commissioned by us to raise funds we did not have for the works we were projecting."[15] The growing foreign debt had to be reduced with increased taxes, a strategy that was not popular. Moreover, "the parties fell on personal rivalries without any historical reach, fighting the power for the power's sake.... Cunning became the main quality to dominate, and systematic corruption became its main process."[16]

The apparent security fostered by the Regeneração was threatened toward the end of the century. The deaths of Fontes Pereira de Melo and of Anselmo José Braamcamp (1817–1885), then leader of the Partido Progressista, triggered a political crisis. This was intensified because the political system relied on the charisma of its leaders, therefore complicating their succession. The first republican members of parliament were elected in 1878. However, the rise of republicanism in Portugal was not a continuous and simple process of increasing social influence but a complex issue that intertwined foreign and local policies as well as demographic shifts in the urban population, the most important space for the dissemination of its doctrine.[17] Paralleling republicanism, anarchist and socialist tendencies began to circulate among the urban population of the 1870s. Clubs were created and rapidly became spaces that facilitated networking and the dissemination of political agendas. They tended to reflect social segmentation, as the republican clubs were dominated by shopkeepers and civil servants while socialist clubs were primarily frequented by "respectable workers."[18] With the growing public perception of national decadence, the opposition from outside the parliamentary system

---

[13] Teixeira de Sousa, *Para a história da Revolução*, vol. 1, 38.

[14] Bulhão Pato, *Memórias: homens politicos*, vol. 2 (Lisbon: Typographia da Academia Real das Sciencias, 1894), 77–78.

[15] Oliveira Martins, *Historia de Portugal*, vol. 2, 295.

[16] Teixeira Bastos, *A crise*, 1.

[17] Fernando Catroga, *O republicanismo em Portugal* (Lisbon: Editorial Notícias, 2000), 65.

[18] Maria Filomena Mónica, "Os fiéis inimigos: Eça de Queirós e Pinheiro Chagas," *Análise social*, 36/160 (2001), 720; Daniel Ribeiro Alves, "A República atrás do balcão: os lojistas de Lisboa na fase final da Monarquia (1870–1910)," Ph.D. thesis (Universidade Nova de Lisboa, 2010).

became more acute, especially after the British Ultimatum of 1890, the apex of a question between Portugal and Britain involving the borders of the African colonies of both countries. The republican, trade unionist, and socialist press thrived in the final years of the monarchy. *A voz do operário* ("The Worker's Voice" or "The Voice of the Worker") was established in 1879 as the weekly periodical of the Associação de Socorros Mútuos União Fraternal dos Operários do Tabaco (a society of tobacco workers).[19] Its main writer, Custódio Brás Pacheco (1828–1883) soon established himself as a remarkable working-class journalist, a voice of a largely illiterate and heterogeneous community to which the newspaper appealed. *A voz do operário* was independent from political parties, but some of its contributors developed close ties with the Portuguese Socialist Party, a small organization.[20] To survive and maintain efficiency *A voz do operário* created a cooperative society in February 1883, the Sociedade Cooperativa A Voz do Operário, and was represented in the Possibilist International Workers Congress held in Paris in 1889. This society became an important space for workers and a supporter of education for the working class. Toward the end of the 19th century its newspaper reflected the rise of anarcho-syndicalism in Portugal and the institution grew during the Portuguese First Republic (1910–1926). Its schools and library are still working today. The anarchists disseminated their ideas in the poorer districts of Lisbon. This is documented in Abel Botelho's *Amanhã!*, where the protagonist Mateus spent his finest hours in Alcântara, in the *grémios* [associations], on the streets, on the *ilhas* [sets of small houses for workers], through the taverns, in the vehement analysis, in the painful auscultation of the intimate living of the many thousands of proletarians that slowly agonize in this insalubrious and sad district.[21]

The growth of working-class societies brought important transformations for music. Some institutions had a wind band (a *banda*). They became a place of gathering for the community and an important source of music education for people who otherwise could not afford to study. Wind bands became a popular sight in European cities, towns, and villages in the second half of the 19th century and were perceived as a way of democratizing the people's access to music. Therefore, both performers and audiences could enjoy music that was not otherwise within easy reach. For example, workers would not go to the opera in the Real Teatro de São Carlos but they played operatic selections with their wind band. The same was true for the audience, who could

---

[19] Fernando Piteira Santos, "A fundação de "A voz do operário"—do "abstencionismo político" à participação no "congresso possibilista" de 1889,' *Análise social*, 17/67–69 (1981), 681–693.

[20] Piteira Santos, "A fundação de "A voz do operário," 691.

[21] Abel Botelho, *Amanhã!* (Porto: Livraria Chardron, 1902), 217.

now listen to live band music in Lisbon's public spaces. Bandstands were built in the city's gardens and people would gather around them on Sundays to listen to their music. However, the large variety of musical societies established in the end of the 19th century complicates a straightforward reading in which wind bands are a product of working-class life. Many of these ensembles were based in the districts known for having a large working-class population. Nevertheless, they also became part of the music education of the lower middle class. Apart from the public gardens, the *bandas* provided music for the society's dances, played in religious processions, and were frequently summoned to perform in a new public form of civic and political participation, the rally. Figure 1.1 depicts a republican rally held in the Avenida D. Amélia in 1907, where the new perspectives of urban planning were being implemented. It is interesting to see how the city conquered its rural surroundings, the space where the border between country and city was being blurred.

Despite the frequent criticisms concerning their boisterous style and lack of musicality, the *bandas* have played an important role in Portuguese music since the 19th century. Their repertoire was varied and is discussed in Chapter 4.

Figure 1.1 Joshua Benoliel, Comício Republicano, Lisbon, 1907, Arquivo Fotográfico de Lisboa, Colecção Joshua Benoliel, PT/AMLSB/JBN/003595. Joshua Benoliel, Republican Rally, Lisbon, 1907.

The acceptance of the British Ultimatum by Portuguese authorities was used to create a backlash against the cabinet and the monarchy. Republican newspapers mounted a vigorous campaign to shape unfavorable public opinion toward the government.[22] King Carlos I, who had recently ascended to the throne, faced an important diplomatic crisis that was aggravated by the country's disappointing economic prospects. Despite the resignation of the cabinet, the republicans kept up their effective propaganda. Attributing the Ultimatum's responsibility to the government was a way of safeguarding national interest.[23] Nevertheless, the republicans soon moved the emphasis of this crisis from government toward the regime.[24] By exploring the anti-British hatred generated by colonial policy, they took advantage of their recently acquired prestige to openly criticize the monarchy.[25] The outcome of this process was perceived as an attack on the inefficiency of monarchic institutions. Therefore, a rift between king and Motherland was created. This division was paramount to criticisms of the regime and to the dissemination of republicanism in Portugal.[26] Nevertheless, this was only a small part of a long and complicated process. In the aftermath of the Ultimatum, republican power rose in Lisbon. However, support for republicans declined throughout the rest of the 19th century, a tendency that was only overturned in the 1906 elections.[27] Lisbon's streets were often the site of republican demonstrations. The Portuguese Republican Party conducted an effective strategy by promoting rallies and parades that often ended in violent confrontations with the forces of authority.[28] These situations were intentionally caused by the party to confirm the repressive character of the monarchy and were amplified by the republican press to enlist supporters for their cause.[29] The discredit of the political institutions and the spread of republicanism caused important figures from the monarchist parties to join the movement, raising the suspicions of staunch republicans like Machado Santos, who played a crucial role in the successful uprising of 1910: "I was surprised with the ease with which the Republican Party admitted in its

---

[22] José Tengarrinha, *Imprensa e opinião pública em Portugal* (Coimbra; Edições Minerva, 2006), 167–171.

[23] Nuno Severiano Teixeira, "Politica externa e politica interna no Portugal de 1890," *Análise social*, 23/4 (1987), 698.

[24] Teixeira, "Politica externa e politica interna no Portugal de 1890," 703.

[25] Catroga, *O republicanismo em Portugal*, 77.

[26] Tengarrinha, *Imprensa e opinião pública em Portugal*, 168–170, and Rui Ramos, *A segunda fundação*, vol. 6 in José Mattoso (ed.), *História de Portugal* (Lisbon: Círculo de Leitores, 1994).

[27] Catroga, *O republicanismo em Portugal*, 63–67.

[28] Vasco Pulido Valente, *O poder e o povo: A Revolução de 1910* (Lisbon: Alhetheia, 2010), 80.

[29] Valente, *O poder e o povo*, 80.

ranks the defectors of the monarchy, and with the trust deposited in them right from the beginning."[30]

The military provided a fertile ground for republican propaganda, and an unsuccessful coup, a "barracks revolt," broke in Porto on 31 January 1891.[31] "The revolution in Porto, a madness as useless as splendid, should remind the monarchy how rigorous is the prognostic that we have made more than once here, and will make the republicans see the inconvenience of proceeding in detached groups."[32] The threat of an organized revolution haunted the local monarchy, and the punishment of the people involved was vigorous. Nevertheless, the revolutionary spirit lingered in the minds of the republicans, of the anarchists, and of the socialists. As stated above, a generalized atmosphere of protest was generated by the Ultimatum and heightened by the republican press. In this context, some people defended the creation of an Iberian federation to counteract national decline and to regain the prestige of both Portugal and Spain.[33] Despite surfacing in several moments of crisis, the federalist solution was never adopted. The overall feeling of decay was intensified by a sovereign default on external debt declared in 1892.[34] "After 40 years, under the influence of the free-trade theoretical doctrines that were badly understood and poorly applied, Portuguese statesmen let our industry wither and lag behind and let the gold that entered every year in the treasury leave rapidly in waves, in the form of onerous foreign loans."[35] Thus, the default was a consequence of the foreign loans that were used to finance the country's modernization and had strong repercussions on the national budget deficits, reaching a breaking point with the international economic depression of the 1890s.[36] For the socialist Teixeira Bastos, the crisis extended to all civilized countries and, despite local variables, was caused by excessive consumption.[37] For him, the worldwide crisis was a result of the new forms of capitalism that relied on mechanization, on the exploitation of the proletariat, and on the increasing division of labor.[38] This worldwide crisis appeared as a local political and financial crisis that was caused by the Portuguese rulers

---

[30] Machado Santos, *A Revolução Portuguesa: relatorio de Machado Santos* (Lisbon: Papelaria e Typographia Liberty, 1911), 10.

[31] Machado Santos, *A Revolução Portuguesa*, 16, and Basílio Teles, *Do ultimatum ao 31 de Janeiro: esboço de Historia politica* (Porto: B. Telles, 1905).

[32] "Gloria aos vencidos!," *Pontos nos ii*, 5 February 1891, 42.

[33] Magalhães Lima, *La Fédération Ibérique* (Paris: Imprimerie Gautherin, 1892).

[34] Pedro Lains, "The Power of Peripheral Governments: Coping with the 1891 Financial Crisis in Portugal," *Historical Research*, 81/213 (2008), 485–506.

[35] Augusto Fuschini, *O presente e o futuro de Portugal* (Lisbon: Companhia Typographica, 1899), 160.

[36] Teixeira de Sousa, *Para a história da Revolução*, 38.

[37] Teixeira de Sousa, *Para a história da Revolução*, XVIII.

[38] Teixeira de Sousa, *Para a história da Revolução*, 110.

and parties, whose ambition and individualism had damaged the country's finances.[39] Therefore, the international crisis was intensified by local particularities, especially the public debt accumulated through foreign credit. Despite the ubiquity of the idea that decadence had led to the economic downfall in the end of the 19th century, the leisure industry was reaching a larger number of people. Managing popular theater companies was a tricky business and could easily end in bankruptcy. However, the financial crisis provided fertile ground for this ephemeral activity. Satire formed the core of the *revista*, and the genre thrived in this period. Laughter seemed the best medicine for the people in times of uncertainty. Moreover, the rise of Lisbon's population fueled the growth of the entertainment market and the access to leisure widened significantly. From the opera theater to the fairground attractions, a large number of spectacles were available. However, different people followed distinct paths, as the hierarchies of taste tended to reflect the social order.

The long national crisis and the frequent scandals penalized the two main parties, and their dominance was criticized. A need for a profound reform had emerged and this transformation had to rely on the authority of King D. Carlos. The last stage of Portuguese liberalism was dominated by João Franco (1855–1929) and José Maria de Alpoim (1858–1916). Franco had ties with the Partido Regenerador (Regenerator Party) and, after a break with the party leader Hintze Ribeiro (1849–1907), established the Centro Regenerador Liberal (Liberal Regenerator Center) in 1901. He later became prime minister and promoted significant reforms. His cabinet was partly supported by the Partido Progressista, and promoted significant reforms. However, the Partido Progressista (Progressive Party) withdrew their support and Franco had to rule as a dictator. To do this, he had to be supported by D. Carlos. The king was interviewed by the French newspaper *Le temps* and showed his agreement with Franco's policies, assuring the full cooperation between Crown and cabinet.[40] Ruling in dictatorship was not unusual in Portuguese liberalism. This meant that the cabinet ruled by decree and without parliamentary opposition until the following elections.[41] For example, Passos Manuel and Costa Cabral had ruled in dictatorship in the earlier part of the century. Franco's dictatorship was highly criticized by several political forces and ended with the 1908 regicide. João Chagas, writing under the pseudonym João Rimanso, shared his thoughts on João Franco in *A paródia*:

---

[39] Teixeira de Sousa, *Para a história da Revolução*, 110.

[40] Joseph Galtier, "Visite au Portugal: Déclarations de S. M. D. Carlos Ier," in *Le temps*, 14 November 1907, 1.

[41] Rui Ramos, *João Franco e o fracasso do reformismo liberal (1884–1908)* (Lisbon: Imprensa das Ciências Sociais, 2001).

> Your Excellency puts the political question on these terms: either the institutions support Your Excellency, or the cataclysm. You have banned the conservative parties. You have replaced them with yourself. In reality, you replaced everyone with yourself. . . . You will drag in your wake all the hopes that you proudly wanted to be the sole depositary, will undo the tale of the conservative messianism, of which the *revistas d'anno* already took over to make a definitively skeptic audience laugh and, when abandoning the institutions, leave them without the moral strength to rule.[42]

The same Chagas wrote in 1908 that João Franco "does not understand that Portuguese democracy has made so much progress that it became impossible to come to an understanding with the monarchy."[43] On the other side of the political divide, José Maria de Alpoim was a member of the Partido Progressista and worked in several cabinets. He was perceived as a desirable leader for the party until he left to create the Dissidência Progressista (Progressive Dissidence) in 1905, a force that maintained close negotiations with the republicans. With a failed coup of 28 January 1908 that was supported by the republicans and by Alpoim's party, he fled to Salamanca. Alpoim returned to Portugal after the republic, and supported the new regime. Thus, the political reform that D. Carlos actively promoted was interrupted with his assassination, paving the way for the end of the Portuguese monarchy.[44]

To add to this situation, general pessimism was circulating in Europe. This trend reached Portugal and was reflected in the work of some fin-de-siècle ethnologists. However, Manuel Laranjeira published a set of essays that criticized the association between pessimism and Portuguese decadence. For him, "one of the most typical aspects of Portuguese life and one of its more ill-fated conditions is its prodigious messianic fertility."[45] Messianism has occupied an important place in Portuguese history since, at least, the Battle of Ksar El Kebir in 1578, when King Sebastião was probably killed. After the financial crisis of the 1890s the country went through "a new period in our political history; the series of extra-party cabinets started, or the experience of the predestined saviors that proclaimed their elixirs [their ideas concerning Portugal] to be marvelous or who were acclaimed by a band of admirers and friends."[46] The

---

[42] João Rimanso, "Epistola ao sr. conselheiro João Franco—salvo o devido respeito," in *A paródia*, 4 May 1907, 2.

[43] João Chagas, *1908: subsidios criticos para a historia da dictadura* (Lisbon: João Chagas, 1908), 26.

[44] Rui Ramos, *D. Carlos* (Lisbon: Círculo de Leitores, 2006).

[45] Manuel Laranjeira, *O pessimismo nacional* (Lisbon: Padrões Culturais Editora, 2008), 39.

[46] Teixeira Bastos, *A crise*, 160.

Republic, "the true political form of the triumphant middle classes" embodied this messianism, and people believed that a regime change would be "a solution to all social problems, a remedy to all particular grievances."[47] The *revista* often mocked this messianism, especially during João Franco's rule, presenting him frequently as the chosen Messiah.

However, the crisis was not limited to politics and economics, and Teixeira Bastos argued that the most important crisis is manifested

> in the dissolution of the characters, in the corruption of the consciences, in the lack of energy and of deliberation, in the hatred of the principles and the ideals, in the complete absence of convictions, in the self-seeking selfish utilitarianism that directs all actions, and in a thousand small things, alas, that every day we can observe in the bosom of our decadent and demoralized society.[48]

Nevertheless, both Laranjeira and Teixeira Bastos believed in the country's recovery, pointing out that "from the current ruins a new society will come," and that there were still stored energies to remake "a whole new Portugal."[49]

This spirit imbued in messianism was associated by the republicans with the overthrow of the monarchy. Figure 1.2 is a postcard showing the winning side of the military uprising that broke in Lisbon in 3 October 1910. After hours of fighting and the participation of the civilian revolutionary organizations, especially the Portuguese Carbonari, the Portuguese Republic was established two days later.[50] The photograph shows a heterogeneous mix of people, many of them civilians, who fought in the Rotunda. Amélia Santos, a woman who took part in the fighting is the center of the postcard.

The republic was deemed inevitable, given the discredit the monarchist institutions had fallen into. The revolt also relied on the effective republican and anarchist propaganda, especially in some military units and in urban populations. Machado Santos, a republican who played an important part in the revolt, argued that "to take part in a revolution one has to have faith, and that faith was extinct in the ruling classes of the Country."[51] Thus, Machado Santos echoes the idea of national decadence that was circulating. Celestino Steffanina, another republican involved in the revolutionary

---

[47] Neno Vasco, *Da Porta da Europa: factos e ideias, 1911–1912* (Lisbon: Biblioteca Libertas, 1913), 21, 233.

[48] Teixeira Bastos, *A crise*, 449.

[49] Teixeira Bastos, *A crise*, 473, and Laranjeira, *O pessimismo nacional*, 51.

[50] Jorge de Abreu, "Da Monarchia á República (Narrativas da revolução de 4 e 5 de Outubro de 1910)," in *A capital: diário republicano da noite*, 21 November 1910, 4.

[51] Machado Santos, *A Revolução Portuguesa*, 17.

Figure 1.2 N.A., Na Rotunda da Avenida, a heroína Amélia Santos [postcard], [Lisbon]: Typ. A Editora,1910, Biblioteca Nacional de Portugal, PI—3157——P. The Hero Amélia Santos in the barricades of the Rotunda da Avenida, October 1910.

operations, returned from Brazil "with the fixed idea of doing something to bring down the knavery in which the Country was sinking."[52] Despite the enthusiasm with the new regime, and given the expectations nurtured by the working poor, the euphoria soon turned into disappointment. There was no rise in the standard of living of the people who had deposited their confidence in the new order. These were "the proletarians, the hungry, the rabble, the ones who guarded the banks and houses of their enemies as they would guard their homes and their belongings, if only they owned any of these."[53] This atmosphere was captured by the libertarian socialist Neno Vasco, who summarized the Portuguese Republic in these terms:

> The Republic, a bourgeois regime, will always defend its class, with cunning or with energy, in Portugal as well as in all the countries where it is instated. And on the day that the class struggle becomes more intense and irreversible here, it will not hesitate, if needed, to use all processes of forthright dictatorship against the dominated

---

[52] Celestino Steffanina, *Subsidios para a historia da Revolução de 5 de Outubro de 1910* (Lisbon: Typographia do Commercio, 1913), 5.
[53] Machado Santos, *A Revolução Portuguesa*, 174.

and exploited class. But, being aware of this, we and the all the people our propaganda reaches will not stop preferring unquestionably the Republic, the full regime of the middle classes.[54]

The Nation as a Scientific Fact

The development of the social sciences contributed to understanding Portugal as a nation-state. A broad field of studies whose object was the Portuguese nation encompassed geography, geology, archaeology, ethnology, philology, and folklore studies, and played a key role in local nation-building. This interaction between local agents and transnational knowledge was crucial to the shift from a Romantic notion of the nation toward a perspective that gave prominence to ethnicity or geography. The return of a theory that places the roots of the Portuguese nation in the tribe of the Lusitanians (portrayed either as Celtic or pre-Celtic Indo-Europeans) is a consequence of this transformation and contradicts the idea presented by Alexandre Herculano in the first half of the 19th century. For him, Portugal was a product of the "political action of the medieval aristocracy."[55] Thus, the Portuguese nation dated from the 12th century and was created by local nobility who promoted independence from León and Castile. Competing nation-building theories provide valuable insight into the construction of the historical past as a coherent narrative. This story is "assembled and arranged into sets of evidence and data which are mediated by the organization of their presentation as texts, images or artefacts."[56] This more scientific approach was demonstrated by the recognition of anthropology as an academic discipline in Portugal and the establishment of archaeological and ethnological museums. However, there was still a complex relation between an ethnology predominantly concentrated on the rural areas of Portugal and the imperial background of the nation. In this process, the construction and naturalization of the colonial other as well as its incorporation in the coeval public discourse worked as a form of promotion of the Portuguese Empire.

Folklorization is "the process of construction and institutionalization of performative practices, perceived as traditional, and constituted by fragments

---

[54] Neno Vasco, *Da Porta da Europa*, 237.

[55] José Manuel Sobral, "Race and Space in the Interpretation of Portugal: The North-South Division and Representations of Portuguese National Identity in the Nineteenth and Twentieth Centuries," in Sharon R. Roseman and Shawn S. Parkhurst (eds.), *Recasting Culture and Space in Iberian Contexts* (New York: SUNY Press, 2008), 209; João Leal, *Etnografias portuguesas (1870–1970): cultura popular e identidade nacional* (Lisbon: Publicações D. Quixote, 2000), 63–82.

[56] Michael Pickering, *History, Experience and Cultural Studies* (London: Macmillan), 6.

drawn from popular culture, mainly from rural areas."⁵⁷ The disjointed nature of this process points to the prominent role ethnographers played in the construction of the popular through a partial selection of elements. This "nationalization of the people" was part of a civic task associated with the new forms of bourgeois thought that emerged in the last third of the 19th century.⁵⁸ Moreover, an essentialist dichotomy between the rural and the urban is played within folklorization. In this process a particular perspective on the nation and its popular culture takes form. The first generation of Portuguese researchers embodied what Dias designated as its philological-positivist period.⁵⁹ They were conscious of their dilettantism, and drew from different approaches and methodologies that were circulating in Europe to systematize their study of popular culture.⁶⁰ At the time, positivism interacted with the historicist Romantic ideals of nationalism established in the earlier part of the 19th century.⁶¹ As stated above, the presentation of the nation as a "scientific fact" established competing narratives about the origins of Portugal, a process that paralleled the developments in other countries.⁶² Therefore, the idea of belonging to one shared background was presented by positivist thinkers to the populations of modern states, contributing to naturalize the nation-state as a form of social bond.⁶³ Moreover, the folklorists cultivated a civic culture and patriotism in the Portuguese liberal state.

The foremost researchers were Teófilo Braga (1843–1924), Adolfo Coelho (1847–1919), Consiglieri Pedroso (1851–1910), and Leite de Vasconcelos (1858–1941). Braga worked predominantly on literature and history. He had a strong interest in Portuguese literature and theater, and developed a political career as a republican, rising briefly to the Portuguese presidency. Despite his affiliation with a Romantic perspective in an earlier stage of his academic career, he became an important promoter of positivism in Portugal. With the doctor and psychiatrist Júlio de Matos (1856–1922) Braga published the periodical *O positivismo: revista de filosofia* between 1878 and 1884. Adolfo

---

⁵⁷ Jorge Freitas Branco and Salwa Castelo-Branco (eds.), *Vozes do povo: a folclorização em Portugal* (Oeiras: Celta Editora, 2003), 1.

⁵⁸ Jorge Freitas Branco, "A fluidez dos limites: Discurso etnográfico e movimento folclórico em Portugal," *Etnográfica*, 3/1 (1999), 27.

⁵⁹ Jorge Dias, "Bosquejo histórico da etnografia portuguesa," *Revista Portuguesa de Filologia*, 2 (1952), 1.

⁶⁰ Branco, "A fluidez dos limites," 26; João Leal, *Antropologia em Portugal: mestres, percursos e transições* (Lisbon: Livros Horizonte, 2006), 11; João de Pina Cabral, "A antropologia em Portugal hoje," in Pina Cabral, *Os contextos da antropologia*, (Lisbon: Difel, 1991), 23–26.

⁶¹ Rui Ramos, "A ciência do povo e as origens do estado cultural," in Branco and Castelo-Branco (eds.), *Vozes do povo*, 26–27.

⁶² Ramos, "A ciência do povo," 26–27.

⁶³ Ramos, "A ciência do povo," 28.

Coelho delivered one lecture of the Democratic Conferences held in the Casino Lisbonense as part of the reformist group known as Geração de 70, and worked in pedagogy, linguistics, and ethnology. Pedroso researched oral literature and popular mythology, and pursued a career as a republican politician. Vasconcelos, despite his training in natural sciences and in medicine, worked in philology, ethnology, and archaeology. These individuals drew on distinct frameworks to study vernacular culture. Apart from a positivist background and a shared reference to comparative mythology, some authors like Teófilo Braga or Adolfo Coelho were influenced by pre-evolutionist trends, like the theories of Theodor Benfey (1809–1881) or François Lenormant (1837–1883), while Pedroso and Coelho drew from evolutionism.[64]

The heterogeneity of their work is reflected in the outcomes of Portuguese ethnology. For instance, Teófilo Braga relied on bibliographic studies and on secondary sources, whereas Leite de Vasconcelos collected his data directly from the rural populations.[65] The scarcity of direct contact between most scholars and the performers of popular culture allowed for "the people" to be presented as an empty signifier.[66] Nevertheless, this was precisely what held ethnology in place, occupying an important space in the ideological apparatuses of the time. In Figueiredo's dictionary, the "people" are "the inhabitants of a country who are subjected to the same laws," "the inferior and more numerous class of a country," or "the inferior class of society."[67] This places "the people" as the entirety of Portugal's population as well as its lower class, reflecting the political and ethnographical strategies that were in place, especially the "nationalization of the people."

The dominant ethnological perspective on Portugal during the 1870s and 1880s considered popular culture to be uniform and homogeneous, seeing Portugal as a unified nation.[68] A textual approach to popular culture pervaded and was reflected in the interest in popular literature (popular poetry, balladry, lyrics, and folk tales) and on popular traditions (beliefs, cyclical festivities, or rites of passage).[69] This is similar to the philological work that was being undertaken in other countries and is permeated by a comparative approach to mythology. The collection and publishing of Portuguese folk tales from the late 1870s onward illustrate this tendency. Coelho, Pedroso, Braga, and Leite

[64] João Leal, *Etnografias portuguesas*, 42–43.
[65] Ramos, "A ciência do povo," 28, and Leal, *Antropologia em Portugal*, 103.
[66] Leal, *Antropologia em Portugal*, 102.
[67] Cândido de Figueiredo, *Novo diccionario da língua portuguesa*, vol. 2 (Lisbon: Livraria Tavares Cardoso & Irmão, 1899), 352.
[68] Leal, *Etnografias Portuguesas*, 55, and Leal, *Antropologia em Portugal*, 114.
[69] Leal, *Etnografias Portuguesas*, 41; Teófilo Braga, *Cancioneiro e romanceiro geral portuguez* (Porto: Typographia Lusitana, 1867).

de Vasconcelos collected a large number of folk tales. The Folk-Lore Society published the tales collected by Pedroso in English, revealing a transnational interest on this subject matter.[70]

However, by the end of the 19th century and with the rise of ethnographic methodologies, the prevailing perspective changed to one that favored internal diversity, and shifted its emphasis from the national to the regional and local levels.[71] Along with folk tales, song lyrics occupied an important place in Portuguese ethnology, and Leite de Vasconcelos published an article in his *Revista Lusitana* on popular songs, attributing their forms and vocabulary to a purported "spontaneity" and "simplicity."[72] This take on popular songs points to the positive view of popular culture that circulated among the first generation of Portuguese ethnologists.[73] Despite an initial interest in texts (a symptom of a Romantic and Herderian concept of nationalism), several researchers embraced the tendency to expand the subject matter of ethnology that developed toward the end of the century. A less textual approach to popular culture developed in the 1890s, expanding its scope beyond popular literature to include art, architecture, technologies, and forms of economic and social life.[74] Therefore, topics such as kinship or material culture became part of their work and interacted with their earlier experiences. In this approach, popular culture was perceived as a trace of the past and promoted an ethnogenealogical perspective. It was predominantly grounded in the desire to capture the "authentic tradition," what was peculiar, picturesque, or unusual.[75] This broadened view indicates a more complex consideration of popular culture in the 1890s that had risen with the British Ultimatum and the country's default, in which certain traits of popular culture were perceived as symptoms of Portuguese decay.[76]

Despite Portuguese ethnology's focus on nation-building, there was an understated comment on the country's imperial condition.[77] The cartographic expeditions to Africa and India that took place in the last decades of the 19th

---

[70] Consiglieri Pedroso, *Portuguese Folk-Tales* (London: Folk-Lore Society, 1882), and Leal, *Antropologia em Portugal*, 15.

[71] Leal, *Antropologia em Portugal*, 15.

[72] Leite de Vasconcelos, "Observações sobre as cantigas populares," *Revista Lusitana*, 1 (1889), 143–157.

[73] Vasconcelos, "Observações sobre as cantigas populares," 143.

[74] Leal, *Etnografias Portuguesas*, 43.

[75] Leal, *Antropologia em Portugal*, 178.

[76] Leal, *Etnografias Portuguesas*, 56.

[77] João Leal, "The Hidden Empire: Peasants, Nation Building, and the Empire in Portuguese Anthropology," in Roseman and Parkhurst (eds.), *Recasting Culture and Space in Iberian Contexts*, 41.

century collected important ethnographical data of people from the colonies, and the awareness of the empire raised by the Ultimatum provided a fertile ground for this work. Naval officers Hermenegildo Capelo and Roberto Ivens conducted an expedition from Benguela (in coastal Angola) to the interior of the African continent between 1877 and 1880. This expedition was widely covered by the press, revealing an interest in the exotic and the colonial other. Moreover, the coverage naturalized imperial ideology among the papers' intended readership. Capelo and Ivens followed the courses of several rivers and gathered information on the region's geographical and hydrographical profiles. They also studied the fauna and flora, and the people. Their account was published as a serial in *O Ocidente* and as a book that was soon translated into English.[78] Several years later, Capelo and Ivens embarked on another cartographic expedition that lasted from 1884 to 1886. This time they traveled from Angola to coastal Mozambique and published their findings in the book *De Angola à contra-costa*.[79] The role that nationalist ideologies played in the study of the Portuguese colonies is reflected in the dedication of both books: *From Benguella to the Territory of Yacca* is dedicated to the Portuguese nation. The dedication of *De Angola à Contra-costa*'s includes King D. Luís, Manuel Pinheiro Chagas, and the Portuguese people. Pinheiro Chagas (1842–1895) was the Navy and Overseas Minister at the time of the expedition. The officer Serpa Pinto (1846–1900) was part of Capelo and Ivens' first expedition, but separated from them and followed a route to Pretoria and Durban. A London printer published his account in Portuguese in 1881.[80] In his expedition, Pinto collected the same kind of information as his colleagues Capelo and Ivens. Moreover, he included many illustrations. Maps, village schematics, genealogical trees, utensils, and people were depicted in his book. Some people were portrayed in the context of their everyday activities, revealing an ethnological interest by Serpa Pinto. Thus, in Portuguese anthropology "the construction of an Other in the colonial world was part of the process of constructing the Same in the homeland."[81]

---

[78] Hermenegildo Capelo and Roberto Ivens, *De Benguella ás terras de Iácca; descripção de uma viagem na Africa central e occidental*, 2 vols. (Lisbon: Imp. Nacional, 1881); Hermenegildo Capelo and Roberto Ivens, *From Benguella to the Territory of Yacca: Description of a Journey into Central and West Africa*, 2 vols. (London: Sampson Low, Marston, Searle, & Rivington, 1882).

[79] Capelo and Ivens, *De Angola á contra-costa*, 2 vols. (Lisbon: Imprensa Nacional, 1886).

[80] Serpa Pinto, *Como eu atravessei Africa: Do Atlantico ao mar Indico*, 2 vols. (London: Sampson Low, Marston, Searle, and Rivington, 1881).

[81] Miguel Vale de Almeida, "Anthropology and Ethnography of the Portuguese-Speaking Empire," in Prem Poddar, Rajeev S. Patke, and Lars Jensen, *A Historical Companion to Postcolonial Literature: Continental Europe and Its Empires* (Edinburgh: Edinburgh University Press, 2008), 436.

Accompanying a growing interest in the synchronic study of the Portuguese colonies was a new diachronic perspective on these territories. This was predominantly based on historical approaches and was developed by people like Pinheiro Chagas and Oliveira Martins. As noted earlier, Chagas supported expeditions to the African colonies, and during his time as Navy and Overseas Minister (that lasted from 1883 to 1886) he made important strategic decisions for these territories. Among these were the installation of the telegraph from Angola to Portugal and construction of a railroad system in Angola and Mozambique.[82] In 1890, after the British Ultimatum, Chagas published an account of Portuguese colonialism during the 19th century, presenting the latest developments as an elegy to Portuguese expansion and colonization. A "veil of mourning" covered the country's recent history.[83] *As cólonias portuguezas no seculo XIX* offers a factual narrative of Portuguese colonialism from 1811 to 1890 and his personal account as a member of cabinet. This helps us to understand how the African continent was partitioned among European countries toward the end of the century.[84]

Oliveira Martins embodies a paradigmatic shift in Portuguese historiography that developed in the late 19th century. He drew from Herculano's perspective in which the origins of Portugal were based on a rational and contractual relation among subjects . However, toward the end of his career Martins adopted an approach that valued the racial aspect of Iberian civilization, emphasizing its specificity within the European context.[85] This move is visible in *O Brasil e as colónias portuguesas* (published in 1880) and in *As raças humanas e a civilização primitiva* (published in 1881).[86] A racist perspective created a hierarchical and evolutionary relation of races, promoting Aryan superiority. This view circulated widely in Europe in the second half of the 19th century and is epitomized by the work of Arthur de Gobineau (1816–1882), author of the *Essai sur l'inégalité des races humaines*. The ethnological interest in the Portuguese colonies complicates a straightforward binary in the history of anthropology that opposes nation-building to empire-building anthropological traditions. The popular culture of the metropolis dominated Portuguese ethnography. Nevertheless, the study of the colonial environment should not be overlooked.

---

[82] Mónica, "Os fiéis inimigos," 713–714.

[83] Pinheiro Chagas, *As colonias portuguezas no seculo XIX* (Lisbon: António Maria Pereira, 1890), 221.

[84] Pinheiro Chagas, *As colonias portuguezas no seculo XIX*, 194–221.

[85] Valentim Alexandre, "Questão nacional e questão colonial em Oliveira Martins," *Análise Social*, 31/135 (1996), 194.

[86] Oliveira Martins, *O Brazil e as colonias portuguezas* (Lisbon: Livraria de António Maria Pereira, 1888); Oliveira Martins, *As raças humanas e a civilização primitiva*, 2 vols. (Lisbon: Bertrand, 1881).

Therefore, the history of Portuguese anthropology carried elements of both traditions, privileging a narrative that focused on nation-building.

Archaeology and physical anthropology introduced and legitimated anthropology in the Portuguese university. In this process the works of the Geological Commission of Portugal cannot be overlooked. Formed in 1857, the commission was led by Pereira da Costa (1809–1888) and Carlos Ribeiro (1813–1882), with the assistance of Nery Delgado (1835–1908). Despite its changing status and a small interruption of its activities, the commission contributed to the study of the country, publishing Portugal's first geological map.[87] The map resulted from a survey undertaken by Ribeiro and Delgado, military engineers whose work was grounded in extensive fieldwork. Moreover, their method proved its value in later archaeological efforts. The archaeological works of the commission strived to fill the gap left in Portuguese history by the Romantic historians, and it used a positivist paradigm to study the "natural history" of the Portuguese people.[88] As stated above, the link between the Lusitanians and the modern Portuguese people was reemerging, which points to the presence of ethnogenealogical theories on the origins of the nation. For this to become a fact, it had to rely on scientific methods, and the archaeological work developed by Martins Sarmento and Leite de Vasconcelos was essential in validating this assumption. Their work established a grounded myth of common descent and ethnic origin.[89] The search for a common ethnic ancestor of the Portuguese people occupied an important place in the work of Martins Sarmento, the archaeologist responsible for reexamining the link between the Lusitanians and the modern Portuguese, a paradigm followed by his colleague Leite de Vasconcelos.[90] This resonates with Hobsbawm's theory of the modern nation. For a recent construction to be legitimized it needs to be tied to the past.[91] Archaeological evidence was used to attest to the antiquity of the Portuguese nation.[92] Thus, "nationalism was an attempt to promote cultural homogeneity as a means for resolving class and cultural contradictions

---

[87] Nery Delgado and Carlos Ribeiro, *Carta geológica de Portugal* (Lisbon: Direcção Geral dos Trabalhos Geodésicos, 1876), Shelfmark PTBN: C. Par. 70, National Library of Portugal.

[88] Gonçalo Duro dos Santos, *A escola de antropologia de Coimbra, 1885–1950* (Lisbon: Imprensa das Ciências Sociais, 2005), 75.

[89] Anthony D. Smith, *The Ethnic Origins of Nations* (Oxford: Blackwell, 1987), 24–25.

[90] Leal, *Antropologia em Portugal*, 63–82; Martins Sarmento, *Os Lusitanos: questões de etnologia* (Porto: Typ. de Antonio José da Silva Teixeira, 1880); Martins Sarmento, "Para o pantheon lusitano," *Revista Lusitana*, 1 (1888/1889), 227–290.

[91] Eric J. Hobsbawm, "Introduction," in Eric J. Hobsbawm1 and Terence Ranger (eds.), *The Invention of Tradition* (Cambridge: Cambridge University Press, 1992), 14.

[92] Philip L. Kohl, "Nationalism and Archaeology: On the Constructions of Nations and the Reconstructions of the Remote Past," *Annual Review of Anthropology*, 27 (1998), 223–246.

Figure 1.3 J. Gonçalves, Bernardino Machado giving his anthropology lesson in the University of Coimbra, in *Illustração portugueza*, 2 January 1911, 23, Hemeroteca Municipal de Lisboa. Bernardino Machado giving his anthropology lesson in the University of Coimbra.

within states, and a notion of race as something settled and based in fate could contribute ideologically to nationalization."[93]

The University of Coimbra integrated anthropology as part of the curriculum of the Natural Philosophy Faculty in 1885.[94] This discipline reflected a prevalent association with physical anthropology, indebted to the naturalist inclination of some authors.[95] Figure 1.3 depicts a lesson in anthropology given by Bernardino Machado (1851–1944). He developed a political career and occupied high places during the Constitutional Monarchy and the First Republic.[96] During the monarchy Machado was a member of parliament, and rose to hold the post of Public Works, Commerce, and Industry Minister. Later, he joined the Republican Party and became president of the Portuguese Republic twice. The lesson depicted craniometry, the

---

[93] Sobral, "Race and Space in the Interpretation of Portugal," in Roseman and Parkhurst (eds.), *Recasting Culture and Space in Iberian Contexts*, 212.
[94] Santos, *A escola de antropologia de Coimbra*, 77.
[95] Santos, *A escola de antropologia de Coimbra*, 87.
[96] Santos, *A escola de antropologia de Coimbra*, 98–122.

measurement of human skulls, to compare the differences between people. This method became very important in the colonial discourse of the time, and the University of Coimbra still holds a large collection of skulls and skeletons from different places.

In late 1893, when Machado was a member of the cabinet, he created the Museu Etnológico Português (Portuguese Ethnological Museum). This reflects the recognition of archaeology and ethnology, now legitimated by association with the two foremost scientific institutions of the time, the university and the museum. The rise of the mass consumption of goods reveals a growing interest in material culture during the 19th century,[97] and the museum, a space not exclusively dedicated to the display of modern scientific developments, was also a mechanism through which modernity itself is constituted, performed, and presented to the public.[98] The museum was established by Leite de Vasconcelos, who directed it until 1929.[99] The collection was divided into several periods of the "Portuguese civilization" (prehistoric, proto-historic, Roman, "barbarian," Arabic, Portuguese-medieval, Renaissance, and modern). Its aim was to "educate the public, making him know and love the motherland," and fostered a national consciousness based on scientific knowledge about Portugal.[100] The main concern of the "modern Portuguese epoch" was to display objects that were both "characteristic and ancient," and related to everyday life (such as buildings, furniture and household objects, clothing, means of transportation, tools, or religious artifacts, for example).[101] Moreover, the museum published a journal concerned with the Portuguese archaeological heritage, *O arqueólogo português*.[102] The main sources of the museum inventory were the private collections of Estácio da Veiga (1828–1891) and of Leite de Vasconcelos.[103] Veiga was a prominent Portuguese archaeologist who did most of his fieldwork in southern Portugal, founded the Museu Arqueológico do Algarve in 1880, and wrote a four-volume work on the paleoethnology of the region of

---

[97] Orvar Lofgren, "Scenes from a Troubled Marriage: Swedish Ethnology and Material Culture Studies," *Journal of Material Culture*, 2 (1997), 111.

[98] Sharon Macdonald, "Preface," in Sharon Macdonald (ed.), *The Politics of Display: Museums, Science, Culture* (London: Routledge, 1998), ix.

[99] Leal, *Etnografias Portuguesas*, 70.

[100] Leite de Vasconcelos, "Museu ethnographico português," *Revista Lusitana*, 3 (1895), 194, 197.

[101] Leite de Vasconcelos, "Museu ethnographico português," 217.

[102] *O archeólogo português*, 1 (1895).

[103] Leite de Vasconcelos, *História do Museu Etnológico Português* (Lisbon: Imprensa Nacional, 1915).

Algarve.[104] Apart from his ethnological production, Leite de Vasconcelos's archaeological work is reflected in the collection and by his rising interest in the study of the Lusitanians as the interpretative framework for Portugal's pre- and proto-historical past.[105]

Changing the City, Reshaping the Social

Lisbon's urban fabric was radically transformed between 1867 and 1910. New planning strategies created modern facilities and aimed to develop Lisbon as a modern capital. This introduced profound changes in the city, intensified by internal migration. A large number of people went to Lisbon to find work and had to be accommodated. The resulting transformation was similar to what was occurring in many cities of the time that were responding to industrialization. Despite Lisbon's incipient industrialization, the need for housing grew and the supply was limited. The city's landscape was transformed to cater to the workers. Existing structures were remodeled and new spaces were built. Most works took place in the vicinities of industrial sites, changing the landscape in the districts of Alcântara, Graça, Xabregas, and Poço do Bispo. Old palaces became quarters for a large number of poor families, jeopardizing their own health and well-being. In the early stage of industrialization, workers rented rooms in existing spaces, like converted palaces or convents, and in makeshift accommodations.[106] The environment of these places, where entire families lived in overcrowded spaces, was obviously insalubrious, and diseases thrived. Living conditions were appalling but affordable housing was rare. Building *pátios* (courtyards) and *vilas* (multifamily housing constructions for those on low incomes) became an important strategy for accommodating workers.[107] The Pátio da Castelhana (Figure 1.4) was situated in Mouraria, and its poor conditions are evident in the photograph. However, this courtyard predates the new manifestations of urbanism. On the floor there are animal skins, which indicate the presence of a tanner. This shows the incipient industrialization of the country, where a significant part of the manufactured goods was still produced in domestic workshops. Moreover, it shows that, in

---

[104] Estácio da Veiga, *Antiguidades monumentaes do Algarve: tempos prehistoricos*, 4 vols. (Lisbon: Imprensa Nacional, 1886, 1887, 1889, 1891).

[105] Leite de Vasconcelos, *Religiões da Lusitania: na parte que principalmente se refere a Portugal*, 3 vols. (Lisbon: Imprensa Nacional, 1897, 1905, 1913).

[106] Nuno Teotónio Pereira, "Pátios e vilas de Lisboa, 1870–1930: a promoção privada do alojamento operário," *Análise social*, 29/127 (1994), 509–524.

[107] Teotónio Pereira, "Pátios e vilas de Lisboa," 511.

Figure 1.4 N.A., Pátio da Castelhana, Lisbon, [1898–1908], Arquivo Fotográfico de Lisboa, PT/AMLSB/FAN/002510. Pátio da Castelhana, a Lisbon courtyard.

these crowded places, space had to have multiple uses. The same floor where the tanner spread the skins was used as a place for children to play or where the family clothesline was hung. Thus, forced socialization fostered a porosity between work and leisure that reflects the shortage of space.

Later, a mix of private entrepreneurs, industrials, or cooperatives started to buy land to build housing for workers, and the first *vilas* were born.[108] Thus, physical and cultural spaces merge in a narrative of class, sociability and living area. These residential areas became important sites for the contact between the regional cultures of the people who migrated there and a vernacular culture thrived. With the rise of realism the vernacular was commodified and became an important part of everyday culture. The rise of positivism in the visual arts and in literature translated the vernacular in an appealing way and the theaters staged popular dramas. The porosity of boundaries and the forced sociability of the city's poor were clearly illustrated in the arts. However, Lisbon's growth was not confined to the developing working class. The demands of a rising housing market for a growing sector of shopkeepers, civil servants, or teachers expanded the city limits. This required a planned urbanization of new

---

[108] Teotónio Pereira, "Pátios e vilas de Lisboa," 511.

spaces and resulted in residential areas like Estefânia or Campo de Ourique.[109] Thus, the 19th-century city simultaneously established and transgressed new boundaries between high and low, creating modern forms of social division and exclusion.[110]

The Making of a Modern Capital

The opening of the Avenida da Liberdade transformed Lisbon in a profound way. It was a wide avenue that expanded the city center to the newly urbanized areas farther north. This destroyed the Passeio Público, a public park built in the 18th century, and other entertainment venues like theaters and circuses. Despite constant efforts to make the Passeio Público more appealing, it was only during the second third of the 19th century that the garden became fashionable and attractive to aristocratic and bourgeois families. This is shown in Figure 1.5, displaying the entrance gate of the Passeio Público, where couples and families, including the royal family, would stroll in their leisure time.

Its fence demarcated it as public, yet restricted, space, literally evidencing the gatekeeping strategies of the local society. Furthermore, clothing restrictions were imposed until 1852. Men had to wear jacket and tie and women wearing cloaks were not admitted. The theatrical revue *Revista of 1858* commented on the then recent transformation of the Passeio, where the "most candid maidens" would entertain boys in the presence of the authorities.[111] The importance of the Passeio in Lisbon's circuits of sociability is evident in *O primo Basílio*, a 1878 novel by Eça de Queirós. The protagonists Jorge and Luísa met in the Passeio Público on a summer evening and were married afterward.[112] When Jorge was away from Lisbon, Luísa committed adultery with her cousin Basílio. This was discovered by the housemaid Juliana, who began to blackmail Luísa. Juliana became a frequenter of the Passeio Público to show off the clothing and shoes she bought with the profits of her extortion. This happened mostly on Sundays, when the people would parade in the garden. Thus, the people who frequented the Passeio had changed toward its final stage. The mimicking of bourgeois behavior by a servant reveals a general tendency to copy the lifestyle of the higher social stratum. Nevertheless, the

---

[109] Teotónio Pereira, "Pátios e vilas de Lisboa," 510.

[110] Peter Stallybrass and Allon White, *The Poetics and Politics of Transgression* (Ithaca, NY: Cornell University Press, 1986), 126.

[111] Joaquim Augusto de Oliveira, *Revista de 1858: em dois actos e dez quadros* (Lisboa: Escriptorio do Teatro Moderno, 1859), 47.

[112] Eça de Queirós, *O primo Basílio, episódio doméstico* (Porto/Braga: Livraria Chardron, 1878), 9.

Figure 1.5 F. A. Serrano, Passeio Publico do Rocio, Lisbon, Lith. da Rua Nova dos Mártires [1850–?1869], Biblioteca Nacional de Portugal, E—1689—P. Passeio Público (Public Promenade) of Rossio.

Passeio Público remained a cultural marker of urbanity as well as an important gathering point for Lisbon's society.

The idea of "Passeio" (promenade or stroll) was important in the everyday routines of the bourgeois and aristocratic milieu during Portuguese Romanticism.[113] This comprised all aspects of public life, like theaters, cafés, the circus, the bullring, and the houses of parliament. Thus, the Passeio Público represents bourgeois lifestyle in Lisbon during the second third of the 19th century. For a journalist writing in 1853, Lisbon's life spanned from the Teatro do Ginásio (in Trindade) to the Teatro de D. Maria II (in Rossio), a small area when compared to the actual size of the city.[114] He stressed the importance of the theaters for the circulation of the "elegant" society, and narrowed the city to the areas where public bourgeois life took place. However, he did not mention the Passeio Público, which may indicate that the space was not yet incorporated in the routines of people despite its recent refurbishment. As stated above, the opera house was an important part of public life, and *A Revolução de Setembro* stated that the season opening of the Real Teatro de S. Carlos was of

---

[113] José-Augusto França, *O Romantismo em Portugal: estudo de factos socioculturais* (Lisbon: Livros Horizonte, 1974), 364.

[114] *A Revolução de Setembro*, 24 January 1853, 1.

central importance for the writers of *feuilletons* (a newspaper column devoted to culture and entertainment).¹¹⁵ Displaying one's social status was one of the main focuses of the "Italian theater," another name for the Teatro de S. Carlos. For Júlio César Machado, this was more important than the operatic performances in the Real Teatro de S. Carlos.¹¹⁶ Regulars predominated in the audience, indicating the role that theater played in the everyday life of Lisbon's well-to-do society.¹¹⁷ People maintained lively conversations throughout the performances, ignoring the new auditory culture associated with the rise of "absolute music" (and, therefore, of a bourgeois Enlightenment aesthetic).¹¹⁸ Furthermore, Machado stresses the dull programming of the theater: the audience knew both the operas and the people who attended them by heart.¹¹⁹

Lisbon grew with the construction of the Avenida da Liberdade on the same site as the Passeio Público. This process began in 1879 and lasted for several decades, transforming a Romantic pleasure garden into a modern boulevard. Just as the Passeio Público stood for the everydayness of bourgeois life, so the Avenida da Liberdade is emblematic of its time. The discontinuity between the Passeio Público and the Avenida da Liberdade is presented in the novel *Os Maias*, by Eça de Queirós. The protagonist Carlos da Maia returns to Lisbon after a long absence brought by the tragic outcome of his incestuous relationship, and goes for a walk in the city. He finds the Passeio Público transformed into the Avenida, a set of geometrically organized heavy buildings that was frequented by the new generation of Lisbon's men.¹²⁰ Figure 1.6 clearly illustrates the contrast between the fenced pleasure garden that was associated with a Romantic idea of leisure and the broad and bright Avenida, a modern thoroughfare surrounded by new buildings.

The construction of the Avenida had been long in planning. The city council had intended to build it since at least 1859.¹²¹ However, the new strategy of urban planning was set in motion by the engineer Frederico Ressano Garcia (1847–1911). Having studied in Portugal and in France, Garcia was appointed to head the technical department of the city's council in 1874.¹²²

---

[115] *A Revolução de Setembro*, 7 December 1850, 1.

[116] Júlio César Machado, *Os theatros de Lisboa* (Lisbon: Mattos Moreia, 1875).

[117] Machado, *Os theatros de Lisboa*, 8.

[118] James Johnson, *Listening in Paris: A Cultural History* (Berkeley: University of California Press, 1996).

[119] Machado, *Os theatros de Lisboa*, 10–11.

[120] Eça de Queirós, *Os Maias: episódios da vida romântica*, vol. 2 (Porto: Livraria Chardron/Casa Editora Lugan & Genelioux Successores, 1888), 511–512.

[121] Isabel Maria Rodrigues, "As avenidas de Ressano Garcia," *Boletim Lisboa Urbanismo*, 13 (Sept./Oct. 2000), 20–23; 14 (Nov./Dec. 2000): 30–34.

[122] Raquel Henriques da Silva (ed.), *Lisboa de Frederico Ressano Garcia, 1874–1909* (Lisbon: Câmara Municipal de Lisboa/Fundação Calouste Gulbenkian, 1989).

Figure 1.6 N.A., Lisboa (Portugal) Centro da Avenida da Liberdade [postcard], Lisbon, F. A. Martins, editor, c. 1908, private collection. Central view of the Avenida da Liberdade.

While in Paris he became aware of the new views on urbanism that were being realized under the initiative of Louis-Napoléon Bonaparte (1808–1873) and Georges-Eugène Haussmann (1809–1891). The so-called Haussmanization of Paris had a tremendous impact on urban planning, as it began to be emulated in Lisbon. Moreover, other capitals experienced similar changes in this period. For example, Rio de Janeiro, a city that maintained an important transatlantic relationship with Lisbon, and the capital of the recently established Republic of Brazil, was subjected to the reforms promoted by its mayor Pereira Passos that resonated with both Paris and with Lisbon.[123] Another striking example of this type of urban reform is Madrid's Gran Via, started in 1910, which concentrated companies, major shopping outlets, and entertainment venues. Lisbon was deeply transformed when Garcia became the leading planner of the new cityscapes, and its landscape reflected this process. Modern districts were built and linked to new and broad avenues, like the Avenida da Liberdade and the Avenida das Picoas. In this context, the Avenida da Liberdade can be compared to the wide Parisian boulevards built according to Haussmann's vision.

---

[123] Jaime Benchimol, *Pereira Passos: um Haussmann tropical* (Rio de Janeiro: Secretaria Municipal de Cultura, Turismo e Esportes, 1992).

Figure 1.7 N.A., Ascensor de St.ª Justa—Lisboa [postcard], Lisbon: Tabacaria Costa, early 20th century, private collection. The Santa Justa Lift, Lisbon.

A network of omnibuses and streetcars was created to facilitate the circulation of people inside Lisbon.[124] These transports were first drawn by horses but soon relied on electrical power. The transport system was further developed with the construction of funiculars and elevators, such as the Ascensor Ouro-Carmo (nowadays known as the Elevador de Santa Justa, Figure 1.7), the

---

[124] Manuela Mendonça (ed.), *História da Companhia Carris de Ferro de Lisboa em Portugal*, 2 vols. (Lisbon: Companhia Carris de Ferro de Lisboa, S.A./Academia Portuguesa de História, 2006); António Lopes Vieira, *Os transportes públicos de Lisboa entre 1830 e 1910* (Lisbon: Imprensa Nacional-Casa da Moeda, 1982).

Ascensor da Bica, the Elevador do Município, the Ascensor do Lavra, and the Ascensor da Glória.[125] These last two led to the new Avenida da Liberdade and facilitated circulation through the steep hills of the city. The railway system that led to Lisbon facilitated the circulation of both people and goods.

The Sud-Express linked Lisbon to Paris, shrinking the gap between Portugal and the capital of modern life; consequently, Parisian culture took less time than earlier to travel to Lisbon. Regional railways (like the West and the Sintra railways) transported hundreds of thousands of people to and from Lisbon every year. To accommodate these travelers, a new railway station was built at the southern end of the Avenida da Liberdade. The Estação da Avenida (Avenida Station, nowadays called the Rossio Railway Station) recreated the *manuelino*, a late Gothic style of Portuguese Renaissance which mixed medieval architecture with complex ornamentation, and was inaugurated in 1890. Thus, passengers left their train and entered Lisbon where the old and the new parts of the city met. With the modernization of the city under the influence of Art Nouveau, iron became a visible material. The rattles, hisses, creaks, thumps, and squeaks of the new materials transformed Lisbon's soundscape. This was intensified in the last decade of the 19th century, when the automobile was introduced.[126]

A strong concern of urban planning in Lisbon was public health, as a significant number of people lived in precarious situations and in places where contagious diseases prevailed.[127] The renewal of the sewer network and the creation of indoor markets improved the city's sanitary conditions. Markets such as Mercado da Ribeira Nova and the Mercado de Alcântara (inaugurated in 1882 and 1905, respectively), reflect this tendency. Figure 1.8 depicts the daily routines of the fish sellers in the Alcântara Market. The *varinas*, female migrants from the coastal region of Aveiro, are shown unloading fresh fish to sell in the market's stalls. They bought fish from the local fishermen and sold them door-to-door or in the markets. Their cries and costumes became part of Lisbon's everyday life until the late 20th century. Nowadays, they live on in souvenirs for tourists and in the names of a few commercial establishments. As a child, I remember seeing them carrying the *canastra* (something between a basket and tray where they carried the fish) on their heads while proclaiming the freshness of the fish. Despite its modernization, Lisbon's urban fabric was anything but homogenous and the old practices coexisted with modern trends. In this respect, Lisbon's heterogeneous mixture of buildings of several epochs and styles embodies the multilayered complexity of urban spaces.

---

[125] "Por encostas e ladeiras," *Illustração portugueza*, 8 February 1909, 165–168.

[126] Alfredo Mesquita, "Do omnibus ao automóvel," *Illustração portugueza*, 24 September 1908, 233–238.

[127] Lisboa, *Os engenheiros em Lisboa*, 151–177.

Figure 1.8 Joshua Benoliel, A faina matinal no mercado do peixe, in *Illustração portugueza*, 27 September 1909, 400, Hemeroteca Municipal de Lisboa.
The morning labor in Lisbon's fish market.

"In this scaly and phosphorescent monster's body that is Lisbon by night, made of plates, bumps, legs, and ankyloses, there is an arterial system drawn with gas lights through which large vessels cart motion and life."[128] The electrification of transports and of public lighting changed the way people circulated in the city. The shift of public lighting from gas or oil to electricity started in 1889 and was an uneven process throughout the city. Initially, electrification benefited both the newly developed areas and the areas traditionally associated with trade and entertainment. Electrical lighting was first installed in Chiado, Rua do Ouro, Praça D. Pedro IV (Rossio), Praça do Município, Praça dos Restauradores, and Avenida da Liberdade.[129] A delimited corridor for a new kind of public life was created in Lisbon, highlighting sites such as shops, theaters, public buildings, and cafés. This intensified the idea of the promenade that served both people and goods, integrating the representational value of commodities in the everyday nature of the modern city. Therefore, "consumption becomes an aesthetic experience; space and consumption are merged

---

[128] Fialho d'Almeida, *Lisboa galante* (Porto: Livraria Civilisação, 1890), 211.
[129] Abílio Fernandes, *Lisboa e a electricidade* (Lisbon: EDP, 1992), 15–63.

in the spatial practice producing spaces of consumption."[130] These "spaces of consumption" affected both public and private spaces. Therefore, the representational value of goods was enhanced with the new forms of display. In this sense, "consumption is always spatial: it is based on the spatial-aesthetic arrangement, associations, and display of commodities in social space."[131]

Lisbon's shopping experience was transformed at the end of the 19th century with the opening of the first multistory department stores inspired by the Parisian *magasins*. The Companhia dos Grandes Armazéns do Chiado was established in 1894 by two French immigrants; it lasted three years and traded in clothes, jewelry, and perfumery. The store was then occupied by other businesses until the opening of the Grandes Armazéns do Chiado, a department store owned by the company Santos, Cruz & Oliveira, Lda in 1904.[132] The beginning of the summer season in the Grandes Armazéns do Chiado is captured in Figure 1.9. The store advertised its "factory prices" over a bustling street where a curious mix of people from all walks of life circulated.

The Armazéns Grandella belonged to the entrepreneur Francisco Grandella (1853–1934). To supply his store, Grandella kept factories in Benfica (a civil parish that was incorporated in Lisbon in 1885) and in Alhandra (a village in the eastern periphery of Lisbon).[133] To provide accommodation for his workers, Grandella built a district in Benfica that included a school (the Bairro Grandella, 1903), a way of "reproducing the labor hierarchy in the place of habitation," evidencing a paternalistic view of the employer toward the workers.[134] Grandella was a prominent republican who became part of Lisbon's city council in the 1908 elections.

Walter Benjamin studied the modern cityscape as "a site of disambiguation and rationalisation of social space through either privatisation and atomisation . . . or collectivisation . . . of built space.[135] These tendencies were reflected in the lives of the people who circulated in these spaces."[136] A tendency for a stricter separation of public and private spaces in Paris started in the reign of

---

[130] Alexander Styhre and Tobias Engberg, "Spaces of Consumption: From Margin to Centre," *Ephemera*, 3/2 (2003), 116–117.

[131] Styhre and Engberg, "Spaces of Consumption" 121.

[132] Hélder Ferreira and António Azevedo, *Armazéns do Chiado: 100 anos* (Mafra: Elo, 2001).

[133] Joaquim Palminha Silva, "Armazéns Grandella: como nasceram e o que foram," *História*, 112 (1988), 4–27; João Mário Mascarenhas (ed.), *Grandella, o grande homem* (Lisbon: Câmara Municipal de Lisboa, 1994).

[134] Teotónio Pereira, "Pátios e vilas de Lisboa," 518; Andrea Tone, *The Business of Benevolence: Industrial Paternalism in Progressive America* (Ithaca, NY: Cornell University Press, 1997).

[135] Peter Schmiedgen, "Interiority, Exteriority and Spatial Politics in Benjamin's Cityscapes" in Andrew Benjamin and Charles Rice (eds.), *Walter Benjamin and the Architecture of Modernity* (Prahran: re.press, 2009), 147.

[136] Schmiedgen, "Interiority, Exteriority and Spatial Politics," 147.

Figure 1.9 Advertisement of Grandes Armazéns do Chiado, in *Illustração portugueza*, 16 April 1906, Hemeroteca Municipal de Lisboa. Advertisement of Grandes Armazéns do Chiado.

Louis-Philippe I (1830–1848).[137] This was intensified in the Second Empire, when Paris was transformed to suit the needs of an imperial capital of an industrial state, largely through the efforts of Napoleon III and of Haussmann.[138] Thus, the reworking of space was inherent to the development of modern cities. For Benjamin, the pervading tendency of the Second Empire was "to ennoble technical exigencies with artistic aims," where "the institutions of the worldly and spiritual rule of the bourgeoisie, set in the frame of the boulevards, were to find their apotheosis."[139] He also expands on the Marxian element of

---

[137] Walter Benjamin, "Paris—Capital of the Nineteenth Century," *New Left Review*, 1/48 (1968), 83.

[138] Bill Risebero, *Modern Architecture and Design: An Alternative History* (Cambridge, MA: MIT Press, 1982), 79–84.

[139] Benjamin, "Paris," 86.

phantasmagoria, an image a "commodity-producing society ... produces of itself ... and that it customarily labels as its culture."[140] Therefore, modern forms of urban life stressed the representational value of goods. Large and decorated shop windows proliferated in the boulevards, aiming to draw the customers in. Fialho d'Almeida describes the sensuousness of a shop window in Lisbon, emphasizing the new paradigm:

> There, under the gas that gushes from above, a wide shop window shows winter cushions with austere embroideries on pale backgrounds, pleated electrics, nuanced in mordant hues, and appears to be instructing the light little heads on an entire code of shameless living.[141]

Porosity and Boundaries in Lisbon

Extending the analogy of the recently built areas of Lisbon with Benjamin's Paris, I suggest a relationship between the old districts of Lisbon, like Alfama, Madragoa, or Bairro Alto, with Benjamin and Lacis's Naples.[142] Their essay on Naples values the porosity of the architecture of a southern European city, in which "building and action interpenetrate in the courtyards, arcades, and stairways."[143] This relates with the way people lived in the Páteo da Castelhana mentioned above. For them, poverty imposed a form of socialization that was reflected in a "passion for improvisation, which demands that space and opportunity be at any price preserved."[144] For them, a prominent aspect in Naples was the interpenetration of the public and the private, a distinction they stress when comparing that city with its northern European peers. However, different notions of privacy circulated in Lisbon. The affluent bourgeoisie cultivated forms of private and public life that contrasted with the lived experience of the poorer people. To implement the Victorian ideas of privacy efficiently one needed to have enough living space. This excluded a significant part of the people who lived in the poorer districts of Lisbon, where "buildings are used as a popular stage," and they were all "divided into innumerable, simultaneously animated theaters."[145] In places like the Páteo da Castelhana "each

---

[140] Walter Benjamin, *The Arcades Project* (Cambridge, MA: Harvard University Press, 1999), 669; Susan Buck-Morss, *The Dialectics of Seeing: Walter Benjamin and the Arcades Project* (Cambridge, MA: MIT Press, 1991), 81–82.

[141] Fialho d'Almeida, *Lisboa galante*, 43.

[142] Walter Benjamin and Asja Lacis, "Naples," in Walter Benjamin, *Reflections: Essays, Aphorisms, Autobiographical Writings* (New York: Schocken Books, 2007), 163–173.

[143] Benjamin and Lacis, "Naples," 165.

[144] Benjamin and Lacis, "Naples," 166–167.

[145] Benjamin and Lacis, "Naples," 167.

private attitude or act is permeated by streams of communal life."[146] This becomes evident when looking at Lisbon's older districts, like Alfama, Mouraria, or Madragoa where the boundaries between individual and collective living are very difficult to trace, as shown in Figure 1.10. Here, we can see how "the house is far less the refuge into which people retreat than the inexhaustible reservoir from which they flood out."[147] "Balcony, courtyard, window, gateway, staircase, roof are at the same time stage and boxes" in a life that had to be communal.[148]

Moreover, a vernacular culture in Lisbon developed in these sites. The theatricality of everyday life in the old districts included a curious mix of urban and rural music that became part of the leisure rituals of the people. Playwrights used popular characters and vernacular music to reinforce the realism of their works, and there was not a strict division between the entertainment industry and vernacular culture. Poorer audiences, the protagonists of vernacular culture in the end of the 19th century, took part in this entertainment, and many performers associated with the popular theater came from underprivileged backgrounds. Conversely, the idea of a vernacular culture that relies on unstructured forms of sociability is problematic. Are we to think that people who make music every night in a café or in a tavern as part of a professional routine are taking part in an unstructured event?. How can we accurately differentiate the structured from the unstructured in a porous environment? Thus, an opposition between a purportedly authentic and spontaneous vernacular culture and manufactured entertainment is misleading. The rationalization of boundaries between public and private that is in place in the modern industrial cities contrasts with a chaotic and almost archaic city like Lisbon, where traces of a pre-capitalist organization are always visible.[149] This is evident in Abel Botelho's description of Ilha do Grilo, a quarter for workers in the industrial area of Beato:

> A double rank of hovels, of simple wood and thin walls, poorly assembled, filthy, almost without eaves, without caulking, without window-glass, all drawn with the same pattern, resembling gallows ... where the light came in, the wind, the rain, the cold, the heat, and all sources of inclemency would also enter. The walls were a nutshell, the foundations an abstraction, the safety a myth, and the hygiene an impossible. Open, each of these raffish slums was a square; closed it was a grave.[150]

---

[146] Benjamin and Lacis, "Naples," 171.
[147] Benjamin and Lacis, "Naples," 171.
[148] Benjamin and Lacis, "Naples,"167.
[149] Jennifer Robinson, *Ordinary Cities: Between Modernity and Development* (London: Routledge, 2006), 33.
[150] Abel Botelho, *Amanhã!* (Porto: Livraria Chardron, 1902), 28.

Figure 1.10 N.A., Lisboa antiga, Rua de S. Pedro de Alfama [postcard], Lisbon: Tabacaria Costa, c.1903, private collection. Old Lisbon, Rua de S. Pedro, a street in Alfama.

To complicate a straightforward reading of notions of porosity in the 19th century, David Harvey relates the creation of commercial spaces and entertainment venues with an increased flexibility of the boundary between public and private spaces, a limit that became porous.[151] This seems to make Harvey's perspectives on Haussmann's Paris incompatible with the work of Benjamin. However, they are addressing distinct types of porosity. On the one hand, Harvey emphasizes a porosity that facilitates the circulation of capital, people, and goods. On the other, Benjamin's porosity was based on the forced socialization of the people who lived in the poor districts of southern European cities. Therefore, porosity is used differently by Benjamin and Harvey to study distinct aspects of urban life. This reveals multilayered and shifting ideas of public life and domesticity that cannot be consistently translated into a polarity between the public and the private. Moreover, porosity is a quality common to all cities, consisting in a spatial metaphor for a "variety of temporal dimensions embedded in physical space" that reflects multiple "layers of time and history, social problems, as well as ingenious techniques of urban survival."[152] Thus, porosity allows for aspects of the old Lisbon to be always visible and audible between the cracks of the modern layer of the cityscape. Traces of the medieval Moorish city are within walking distance from 18th-century buildings and from the new boulevard.

The poem *O sentimento de um ocidental* ("The feeling of a Westerner") is a good place to study the porosity in Lisbon. It was written by Cesário Verde (1855–1886) and published in the newspaper *Jornal de viagens* in 1880. It was later included in a posthumous compilation of Cesário Verde's poetry.[153] The narrator strolls in Lisbon, witnessing its transformation between dusk and late at night. The poem is divided into four sections, representing different times (the *"Avé Marias"*—Hail Marys, the *"Noite Fechada"*—Dark Night, *"Ao gás"*—When the gas lighting is turned on, and *"Horas Mortas"*—Late Hours). The subject in the poem experiences the city by walking, echoing Michel de Certeau's work on everyday life.[154] Moreover, the poem represents an experience in which "the moving about that the city multiplies and concentrates makes the city itself an immense social experience of lacking a place."[155] It is the narrative of a *flâneur*, a strolling spectator of urban life who "could no

---

[151] David Harvey, *Paris, Capital of Modernity* (London: Routledge), 207.

[152] Svetlana Boym, *The Future of Nostalgia* (New York: Basic Books, 2001), 77.

[153] Cesário Verde, *O livro de Cesário Verde* (Lisbon: Typographia Elzeveriana, 1887).

[154] Michel de Certeau, *The Practice of Everyday Life*, vol. 1 (Berkeley: University of California Press, 1988), 93.

[155] de Certeau, *The Practice of Everyday Life*, vol. 1, 103.

longer fully identify his sense of modernity with the actual empirical city of Paris [or Lisbon], nor could he celebrate it in the social types and everyday life he observed in the urban landscape."[156]

The *flâneur* has been mostly associated with Paris and with the writings of Charles Baudelaire and Walter Benjamin on the Second Empire. However, Harvey argues that the same character is part of Balzac's earlier works.[157] "Balzac's flaneur or flaneuse maps the city's terrain and evokes its living qualities. The city is thereby rendered legible for us in a very distinctive way."[158] As a Parisian "type" the *flâneur* has been taken to exemplify the masculine and bourgeois privilege of modern public life in Paris. The *flâneur* delighted in the sight of the city and its tumultuous crowd, while allegedly remaining aloof and detached from it.[159]

Nevertheless, the problematic association of the *flâneur* with the masculine has been brought into question in the past decades.[160] Furthermore, the "*flâneur*'s representations of everyday life could not, in the final analysis, transcend the fragmentations of the modern city and the compromises of the cultural market."[161] In modern life, "*flânerie* became a cultural activity for a generalized Parisian public."[162] Moreover, the "*flâneur* is not so much a person as *flânerie* is a positionality of power—one through which the spectator assumes the position of being able to be part of the spectacle and yet command it at the same time."[163] Therefore, *flânerie* is not necessarily passive and alienating, and "the consumption of life as spectacle" could have "liberating and even democratizing effects" for people who lived in modern cities.[164] Democratizing the access to leisure transformed the way people spent their time and interacted with each other in the heterogeneous environment of the metropolis, where public spaces were shared by a larger number of individuals. Therefore, the *flâneur* witnesses urban life as he circulates among the crowds.

---

[156] Mary Gluck, *Popular Bohemia: Modernism and Urban Culture in Nineteenth-Century Paris* (Cambridge, MA: Harvard University Press, 2005), 100.

[157] Harvey, *Paris*, 23–57.

[158] Harvey, *Paris*, 55.

[159] Vanessa Schwartz, *Spectacular Realities: Early Mass Culture in Fin-de-Siècle Paris* (Berkeley: University of California Press, 1998), 9.

[160] Janet Wolff, "The Invisible Flâneuse: Women and the Literature of Modernity," *Theory, Culture & Society*, 2/3 (1985), 37–46, and Deborah L. Parsons, *Streetwalking the Metropolis: Women, the City, and Modernity* (Oxford: Oxford University Press, 2000).

[161] Gluck, *Popular Bohemia*, 95.

[162] Schwartz, *Spectacular Realities*, 9.

[163] Schwartz, *Spectacular Realities*, 16.

[164] Schwartz, *Spectacular Realities*, 131.

The narrator of *O sentimento de um ocidental* is a *flâneur* who shares his experience while walking in Lisbon. His individuality is never absorbed into the urban crowd he contemplates and the poem starts with the shipwrights hopping around the scaffoldings and the caulkers returning home from their shift in the shipyards near the river Tejo. The barefooted *varinas* return to their homes in the districts where diseases thrived and infections were triggered.[165] The social landscape changes in the following section of the poem ("*Noite Fechada*"), when the narrator arrives in Chiado, Lisbon's elegant district. He hears the noises of the nearby jail, watches the turning on of the lights in the flats, observes the cafés, the tobacconists, the *tascas* (eating houses), the *tendas* (small groceries), and the horsed patrols that cross his path. The florists and the seamstresses were leaving work, yet some of them were going to perform as extras or chorus girls in the theaters.[166] "*Ao gás*" marks an abrupt change of the city, where the bourgeois women are seen returning from their religious services. The *flâneur* then witnesses a young mischief-maker examining the shop windows, and sees the fashion and fabric shops, where the suffocating smells of face powder linger through "clouds of satin."[167]

A boundary between day and night is traced with the reference to gas lighting. This resonates with the writings of Benjamin on Baudelaire, where "the appearance of the street as an *intérieur* in which the phantasmagoria of the *flâneur* is concentrated is hard to separate from gas lighting."[168] The dim gas lighting reinforced the phantasmagoric appearance of the commodity-in-display in the city's shopping districts, and the nauseating smell of the leaking gas intensified the oppressive atmosphere that permeated *O sentimento de um ocidental*. Despite the prominence given to a bourgeois social space, "Ao gás" finishes with the narrator hearing a hoarse lottery seller and meeting an old beggar, his former Latin teacher.[169] The last section of the poem moves to the gates of the private houses of the wealthy, where the *flâneur* pictures the "chaste wives" nestling "in mansions of transparent glass."[170] Then, the subject walks past the taverns where drunken men sing, sees the guards searching the stairways and the "immorals" smoking on the balcony in their

---

[165] Cesário Verde, "O sentimento de um ocidental," in Cesário Verde, *O livro de Cesário Verde*, 61–62.

[166] Verde, "O sentimento de um ocidental," 62–64.

[167] Verde, "O sentimento de um ocidental," 64–66.

[168] Walter Benjamin, *The Writer of Modern life: Essays on Charles Baudelaire* (Cambridge, MA: Harvard University Press, 2006), 81.

[169] Verde, "O sentimento de um ocidental," 66.

[170] Verde, "O sentimento de um ocidental," 66.

dressing gowns.[171] The poem finishes with the stanza: "And, huge, in this irregular mass/of sepulchral buildings sized like hills/the human Pain searches the broad horizons,/and has tides, of gall, like a sinister sea!"[172] A narrative poem, *O sentimento de um ocidental* illustrates the multiplicity of the urban spaces in Lisbon and how they were lived. It describes the transformations of the social and physical landscape, and hints at the porosity in the city's districts. In this sense, the dialectic between the old and the new that was lived in Lisbon embodied traits of both Paris and Naples, as they were presented by Walter Benjamin.

As a topical show, the revue theater (*teatro de revista*) commented on the ongoing transformations that were reshaping the capital. Moreover, its sketches relied frequently on elements that stand in polar opposition, commenting on everyday life. For example, *O anno em hora e meia* includes a sketch that opposes three elegant areas, the Chiado, the Avenida da Liberdade, and the Rua Áurea, to three poor streets, the Rua dos Canos, the Rua do Capelão, and the Rua dos Vinagres.[173] The play was written by Baptista Diniz and Esteves Graça, and premièred in the Teatro Chalet in 1905. The Chiado, the Avenida, and the Rua Áurea are "dandies with monocles and gaiters" who seduced Lisbon's population.[174] Chiado describes itself as old, but still elegant, while the Avenida is both cocotte and honorable, with many people walking up and down in the afternoons.[175] The writer Bulhão Pato reinforces this in his memoirs, when he states that the city was growing and the elegant society strolled daily up and down the Avenida.[176] The Rua Áurea is the banking center of the city, between the Armazéns Grandella and the arcades of the Praça do Comércio, where badmouthing takes place and the unions fabricate rumors.[177] The other three are "the poor districts, the badly frequented streets, which do not harbor nobles."[178] In the Rua dos Canos the *tascas* served cod with potatoes with "brawl sauce and three stabs" and the Rua dos Vinagres, with its dark inns and *fadistas* (fado singers, associated with Lisbon's outcasts), made the city's prisons its branches.[179] The Rua do Capelão, where A Severa used to live, smelled

---

[171] Verde, "O sentimento de um ocidental," 67.

[172] Verde, "O sentimento de um ocidental," 68.

[173] Baptista Diniz and Esteves Graça, *Coplas de O anno em hora e meia* (Lisbon: Imprensa Lucas, 1905), 10–12.

[174] Diniz and Graça, *Coplas*, 10.

[175] Diniz and Graça, *Coplas*, 10.

[176] Bulhão Pato, *Memorias: homens politicos*, vol. 2 (Lisbon: Typographia da Academia Real das Sciencias, 1894), 81.

[177] Diniz and Graça, *Coplas*, 10.

[178] Diniz and Graça, *Coplas*, 11.

[179] Diniz and Graça, *Coplas*, 11.

like wine and looked like a worm in Lisbon's intestines.[180] This sketch illustrates and caricatures the differences between the respectable and bourgeois Lisbon and the shady parts of the city, presenting the newly developed areas as the "arteries of the new city."[181]

Theaters and the New Entertainment Circuits

The entertainment business was not immune to the transformation of the urban landscape. For d'Almeida, "this so-to-speak restoration of the architectonic type, this revolution in residence, coincided with another no less absolute [transformation] of the customs, of the character, and of the pleasures."[182] From the Liberal Revolution of 1820 until 1846, most theatrical activity in Lisbon was concentrated on three 18th-century theaters: the Real Teatro de S. Carlos—established in 1793 to perform mostly opera in Italian, run by an impresario and subsidized by the state; the Teatro da Rua dos Condes—established in 1765 and mostly dedicated to drama and, occasionally, comic opera; and the Teatro do Salitre—established in 1783, presenting the same genres as the Teatro da Rua dos Condes.[183] The prominent role played by the romantic historical drama in the theatrical market of this period contributed to the shaping of a dialectic relationship between the local and the cosmopolitan. The new political and aesthetic orientation toward historicism fostered the promotion of Portuguese history. Nevertheless, most of this historicism followed models imported from Paris, a city where a significant number of Portuguese liberals were exiled during the absolutist reign of D. Miguel.

The interaction between French historical drama and Portuguese history surfaces clearly in the French theatrical company that performed in the Teatro da Rua dos Condes from 1835 to 1837. It included the actor and stage director Émile Doux, who played a key role in the Portuguese scene by importing French Romantic theater (especially the plays of Victor Hugo and Alexandre Dumas) and performing them with the historicist staging required at the time. Furthermore, Doux trained performers and directed theaters in Lisbon until his departure for Brazil. Given the importance the liberal *setembristas* (the Portuguese left-wing who were in office from 1836 to 1842) gave to theatergoing

---

[180] Diniz and Graça, *Coplas*, 11.
[181] Diniz and Graça, *Coplas*, 11.
[182] Fialho d'Almeida, *Lisboa galante*, 25.
[183] Luísa Cymbron, "A ópera em Portugal 1834–1854: o sistema produtivo e o repertório nos teatros de S. Carlos e de S. João," Ph.D. thesis (Universidade Nova de Lisboa, 1998).

as a way of civilizing the people, Minister of the Kingdom (interior minister) Manuel da Silva Passos (1801–1862) called on the writer, poet, and playwright Almeida Garrett (1799–1854) to organize a Portuguese state theater. Between 1836 and 1841, Garrett was appointed Inspector-General of the Theaters and Spectacles. He created the Conservatório Geral de Arte Dramática—Escola de Música e Escola de Teatro e Declamação (General Conservatoire of Drama—School of Music and School of Theater and Declamation) in 1836. Directed by Garrett, it was a state school of theater and dance, and incorporated the Music Conservatoire (established in 1835 and directed by the composer João Domingos Bomtempo, 1775–1842). In 1840, the Conservatório changed its designation to Real Conservatório de Lisboa (Royal Conservatoire of Lisbon).[184]

This large venture included building a new theater according to the emerging needs since most theaters were shoddily built. The Teatro Nacional D. Maria II opened in Rossio in 1846 and transformed Lisbon's theatrical scene.[185] Its programming by Garrett reshaped the city's cultural market.[186] The Teatro do Ginásio opened in the same year, and was mostly devoted to drama. According to Sousa Bastos, Doux introduced vaudeville in Portugal when he was directing the company of the Teatro do Ginásio.[187] In addition to drama, this theater also staged comic operas, mostly composed by António Luís Miró (1815–1853).[188] Comic operas were regularly performed in Portuguese in Lisbon since 1841. The Count of Farrobo (the Médicis-Farrobo, in the words of Oliveira Martins) was the impresario of the Teatro da Rua dos Condes, where translations of both French and Italian comic operas were performed.[189] Farrobo also commissioned comic operas from local composers and staged them with the help of Émile Doux and of the composer João Guilherme Daddi (1813–1887).[190] Performing opera broke the monopoly of the São Carlos, and Lisbon's less-reputed venues also performed repertoires

---

[184] Joaquim Carmelo Rosa, "'Essa pobre filha bastarda das artes': a Escola de Música do Conservatório Real de Lisboa nos anos de 1842–1862," master's thesis (Universidade Nova de Lisboa, 1999).

[185] Júlio César Machado, Os theatros de Lisboa, 65–190.

[186] Luiz Francisco Rebello, O teatro romântico (1838–1869) (Lisbon: Instituto de Cultura e Língua Portuguesa, 1980), 31–48; Maria de Lourdes Lima dos Santos, "Para a análise das ideologias da burguesia," Análise social, 14/53 (1978), 39–80.

[187] António de Sousa Bastos, Diccionario do theatro portuguez (Lisbon: Imp. Libânio da Silva, 1908), 343.

[188] Sousa Bastos, Diccionario, 343.

[189] Isabel Gonçalves, "A introdução e a recepção da ópera cómica nos teatros públicos de Lisboa entre 1841 e 1851," Revista portuguesa de musicologia, 13 (2003), 93–111.

[190] Gonçalves, "A introdução e a recepção da ópera cómica nos teatros públicos de Lisboa entre 1841 e 1851," 93–111.

that were part of the cosmopolitan market for cultural goods.[191] According with the actor Isidoro, there was a decrease of theatrical activity after the Maria da Fonte rebellion, due to the political instability that caused audiences to stop frequenting the theaters, led some performers to relocate to Brazil, and caused other performers to abandon their profession.[192] However, after 1847 the situation began to change and theatrical activity increased in the 1850s. The success of the Teatro do Ginásio was associated with the performance of comic operas and with the signing of Francisco Taborda (1824–1909), who became an extremely popular actor.[193] Moreover, the theater staged the first *revistas*, a genre that would become dominant in the decades to follow. The Teatro de D. Fernando opened between 1849 and 1859 and presented drama in Portuguese and in French along with *opéra comique* and *zarzuela*. Frequent financial losses caused the theater to close; it was transformed into a tobacco factory.[194] This shows the volatility of the theatrical business in Lisbon in the middle of the 19th century.

Many theaters opened and closed in Lisbon during this period, reflecting the transience of these ventures. The Teatro do Salitre changed its name to Teatro das Variedades in 1858. It was demolished in 1879, one of the buildings destroyed to make way for the Avenida da Liberdade.[195] The Circo Price also disappeared with the avenue. Its story reveals the circulation of entertainment in Iberian culture. In the late 1850s Thomas Price established a space in Madrid where he presented circus (acrobats, gymnasts, and trained horses) and, occasionally, operetta and *zarzuela*. In the following year the Circo Price opened in Lisbon and presented the same shows.[196] Such spectacles circulated between both capitals, sometimes promoted and performed by the same people. During the second half of the 19th century the number and types of theaters increased in Lisbon, Madrid, and Rio de Janeiro; these theaters often shared a name, like Variedades or Apolo (the name given to the Teatro do Príncipe Real in the Portuguese Republic). The Teatro da Rua dos Condes opened in 1765 and closed down in 1882. During the last years of the Teatro da Rua dos Condes, the most important source of income was

---

[191] Luísa Cymbron, "O teatro de Scribe em Lisboa após a vitória liberal (1834–1853), in Luísa Cymbron, *Olhares sobre a música em Portugal no século XIX* (Lisbon: Edições Colibri/CESEM, 2012), 206.

[192] Isidoro Sabino Ferreira, *Memorias do Actor Izidoro* (Lisbon: Imprensa de J.G. de Sousa Neves, 1876), 164.

[193] Isidoro Sabino Ferreira, *Memorias do Actor Izidoro*, 165.

[194] Sousa Bastos, *Diccionario*, 331.

[195] *O Occidente*, 15 September 1879, 138–140.

[196] *O Occidente*, 11 April 1883, 83, 85.

Figure 1.11 Casellas, O novo Theatro da Rua dos Condes—Inaugurado em 23 de Dezembro de 1888, in *O Occidente*, 1 Fev. 1889, 29, Hemeroteca Municipal de Lisboa. The new theater of the Rua dos Condes—Inaugurated 23 December 1888.

the *revistas*, and the same repertoire was also dominant in its successor, a provisional theater that was built on the same grounds and lasted only three seasons, the Teatro Chalet da Rua dos Condes.[197] After the Teatro Chalet was demolished, the new Teatro Condes was built. It opened in 1888 and performed operettas and *revistas*. The hall also had a café-concert, where "saucy songs" were performed with a "French grace."[198] The Teatro Condes, depicted in Figure 1.11, belonged to Francisco Grandella and was initially run by the impresarios Salvador Marques (1844–1907) and Casimiro d'Almeida.[199] Unlike its predecessors, the theater's facade is oriented toward the Avenida da Liberdade and not toward the Rua dos Condes. This exemplifies the transformations that occurred in the area surrounding the Avenida. A new, comfortable theater, it catered to the needs of a growing audience looking for songs and laughter. The opening of three theaters on the same plot shows that this space was part of Lisbon's entertainment circuit over a long period of time. A spatial *habitus* was in place, and that place became part of the leisure routines

---

[197] Sousa Bastos, *Diccionario*, 325, 359–361; Luiz Francisco Rebello, *História do teatro de revista em Portugal*, vol. 1 (Lisbon: Publicações D. Quixote, 1984), 84.

[198] *O micróbio*, 16 December 1894, 182.

[199] Sousa Bastos, *Diccionario*, 359.

of several generations of individuals. A cinema, the Cinema Condes, replaced the theater in 1950 and the building is now a theme restaurant of an international chain.

In retrospect, of the theaters working in the first forty years of the 19th century, only the Real Teatro de S. Carlos, the Teatro de D. Maria II, and the Teatro do Ginásio survived and maintained regular activity throughout the century. With increasing theatrical activity, an important number of theaters were built in Portuguese cities, towns, and villages in the last third of the 19th century. Despite the precarious nature of the business, some venues presented the new genres of musical theater that were becoming dominant in Lisbon: the operetta and the *revista*. Situated in the district of Mouraria, the Teatro do Príncipe Real opened its doors in 1865, and presented drama and operetta.[200] The Teatro da Trindade opened in 1867 and had two halls. The main hall accommodated theater, especially operetta and *revista*, and the Salão housed concerts and balls.[201] The theater was built by a society, and its director, Francisco Palha (1826–1890), had managed the Teatro da Rua dos Condes in the previous season.[202] The Teatro Taborda, situated in the Costa do Castelo and concentrating especially on drama, was inaugurated in 1870.[203] The Real Coliseu de Lisboa opened in 1887 and was mostly dedicated to circus. It also presented opera, comic opera, operetta, and *zarzuela*. Starting in 1896, film became part of its programming. This new type of entertainment was soon presented in other places, like the Teatro D. Amélia, and in rooms built especially for that purpose, like the Animatógrafo do Rossio (established in 1907). The Teatro da Avenida began its activity in 1888, performing comedies and *revistas*.[204] It was one of the first buildings of the Avenida da Liberdade. Close to this theater was the short-lived Teatro da Alegria. Opened in 1890 on the grounds of the Rua Nova da Alegria where a provisional theater once stood, it was dedicated to spoken drama.[205] The biggest venue in Lisbon, the Coliseu dos Recreios opened in the same year. It still stands as an octagonal hall with a glass and iron dome, reflecting the new architectural tendencies. Despite a première with a comic opera by an Italian company, its programming consisted predominantly of circus shows. Nevertheless, it also accommodated musical theater (especially operetta, *zarzuela*, and Italian opera), concerts, film (with

---

[200] Sousa Bastos, *Diccionario*, 355.
[201] Tomaz Ribas, *O Teatro da Trindade: 125 anos de vida* (Porto: Lello & Irmão, 1993), 13; Luiz Francisco Rebello, *O teatro naturalista e neo-romântico (1870–1910)* (Lisbon: Instituto de Cultura Portuguesa, 1978), 53–54.
[202] Sousa Bastos, *Diccionario*, 372–373.
[203] Sousa Bastos, *Diccionario*, 371.
[204] Sousa Bastos, *Diccionario*, 312, 318.
[205] Sousa Bastos, *Diccionario*, 316; *O Occidente*, 1 June 1890, 123.

Edison's Projectoscope), and wrestling.[206] An operetta inaugurated the Teatro D. Amélia in 1894. It is located in Chiado and its current name is São Luiz Teatro Municipal. The D. Amélia presented spoken drama and comedy, and cinema.[207]

By interlocking theaters and other public places, it is possible to see that many of the recently built spaces were in the areas that were traditionally associated with leisure. However, the growth of the city with the Avenida da Liberdade enlarged the theatrical circuit. Most of these venues were situated in the nearby streets of the Avenida and not in the boulevard itself, favoring the development of these areas well into the 20th century.[208] Another popular entertainment in Lisbon was the bullfight, frequently held in Lisbon since the last years of the 18th century (first in Salitre, in the plot the Circo Price would occupy, later in the Campo de Santana). Because of the modernization of the city, a new space specifically designed for the bullfight opened in 1892, the Praça de Touros do Campo Pequeno. However, Lisbon's entertainment offer was not confined to its theaters, cinemas, and bullrings. Some entertainment took place during seasonal events, like the annual Alcântara fair. In these events theaters coexisted with other popular amusements, such as shooting galleries, clowns, carnival oddities, food stalls, taverns, cafés with live music, and other attractions. For example, the 1905 fair included two large theaters (Chalet and Água d'Ouro), a circus, and puppet show booths.[209] A significant number of distinguished operetta and revue performers began their careers in these itinerant troupes and were then hired to perform in the city's theaters, displaying the strategies of the popular theater impresarios of the time (Table 1.1).[210]

Ticket pricing did not play a major role in audience segmentation. Apart from the Real Teatro de São Carlos, the theaters had identical admission prices, a fact that complicates a straightforward use of pricing as a gate-keeping strategy.[211] For example, the most expensive boxes in the Real Teatro de S. Carlos cost 22.000 *réis* (the currency of the Portuguese monarchy) in 1910, whereas the equivalent seats in the Teatro da Trindade cost 4.000 *réis* in the same year.[212] However, there is no significant difference between the ticket prices

---

[206] Mário Moreau, *Coliseu dos Recreios: um século de história* (Lisbon: Quetzal Editores, 1994), 17–20, 25, 38, 205–206.

[207] Sousa Bastos, *Diccionario*, 332–333.

[208] Manuel Villaverde, "Rua das Portas de Santo Antão e a singular modernidade lisboeta (1890–1925): arquitectura e práticas urbanas," *Revista de História da Arte*, 2 (2006), 142–176.

[209] *Illustração Portugueza*, 8 May 1905, 428–429.

[210] *Ilustração Portugueza*, 8 May 1905, 428–429.

[211] Rui Leitão, "A ambiência musical e sonora da cidade de Lisboa no ano de 1890," master's thesis (Universidade Nova de Lisboa, 2006), 163–164, 307–308.

[212] *Almanach de A Lucta* (Lisbon: Empreza de Propaganda Democratica, 1909), 65–66.

Table 1.1 **Lisbon's Main Venues and Repertoires**

Venue	Show
Real Teatro de S. Carlos	Opera
Teatro D. Maria II	Drama, high comedy
Teatro da Rua dos Condes	Drama, comic opera, later *revista*
Teatro do Ginásio	Drama
Teatro do Salitre, later Variedades	Drama
Circo Price	Circus
Teatro Condes	Operetta, *revista*
Teatro do Príncipe Real	Drama, operetta
Teatro da Trindade	Operetta, *revista*, drama
Real Coliseu de Lisboa	Circus, opera, comic opera, operetta and *zarzuela*
Coliseu dos Recreios	Circus, operetta, *zarzuela*, Italian opera, concerts, film, and wrestling
Teatro de D. Amélia	Drama, high comedy, film

of Teatro da Trindade, Teatro Avenida, and Teatro Gymnasio.[213] The Real Teatro de São Carlos charged the most expensive prices in almost all sections, reinforcing the notion of this theater as a selective space. This illustrates that operagoing was part of a strategy of social distinction promoted by the upper stratum of Lisbon's society.[214] According to Bourdieu, "It is true that one can observe almost everywhere a tendency toward spatial segregation, people who are close together in social space tending to find themselves, by choice or by necessity, close to one another in geographic space."[215] Toward the end of the century, the Coliseu dos Recreios began to stage Italian opera in the summer, complicating the association of the genre with a social and spatial demarcation of Lisbon's audiences.[216] Nevertheless, the Real Teatro de São Carlos retained its symbolic capital and kept its role in the sociability circuits of the upper stratum of the city. "S. Carlos is not just a theater, it is a meeting point: it is a sociability element in this classic land of the ombre, of the whist, of the ten o'clock tea, and of the invariable turning of the light at eleven in the evening."[217] In

---

[213] *Almanach de A Lucta*, 65–66.
[214] Pierre Bourdieu, *La distinction. Critique social du jugement* (Paris: Éditions de Minuit, 1979).
[215] Pierre Bourdieu, "Social Space and Symbolic Power," *Sociological Theory*, 7/1 (1989), 16.
[216] Moreau, *Coliseu dos Recreios*, 20.
[217] *A Revolução de Setembro*, 1 December 1848, 1.

his analysis of Lisbon's audiences, Rebello states that the Real Teatro de São Carlos, the Teatro Nacional de D. Maria II, and the Teatro D. Amélia attracted the haute and middle bourgeoisie, and the other theaters had a predominantly popular audience.[218] Thus, the audience segmentation was related to theatrical genres. The operas that were performed in the Real Teatro de São Carlos and the drama and the high comedy presented in the Teatro Nacional de D. Maria II and in the Teatro D. Amélia attracted the bourgeoisie and the aristocracy.[219] Operetta, *revista*, and circus attracted the popular segments of Lisbon's theatergoers.[220] Therefore, the ability to attract specific audiences was indebted to the type of entertainment that was offered. Moreover, famous performers were used to attract the people, a strategy that is evident in the advertising of the theaters.

This chapter sets the scene for the book, mapping the most important transformations that took place in Portugal and in its capital. Lisbon was coming to grips with modernity while holding on to its past. I have tried to show how culture and space are inextricably bound. Thus, one thinks of space as both corporeal and discursive and as a category that "is never ontologically given."[221] Moreover, space is not as an "a priori or ontological entity," and my work emphasizes the historical processes and strategies through which space is produced.[222] This unfolds a complex dialectic between culture and space that "emphasizes the symbolic meaning and significance of particular spaces, in effect how spaces are culturalized, but also how culture is spatialized, how practices are lived in space."[223]

---

[218] Rebello, *O teatro naturalista*, 53–54.

[219] Rebello, *O teatro naturalista*, 53–54.

[220] Rebello, *O teatro naturalista*, 53–54.

[221] James Clifford, *Routes: Travel and Translation in the Late Twentieth Century* (Cambridge, MA: Harvard University Press, 1997), 54.

[222] Kanishka Goonewardena, et al., "On the production of Henri Lefebvre," in Kanishka Goonewardena, et al. (eds.), *Space, Difference, Everyday Life: Reading Henri Lefebvre* (London: Routledge, 2008), 9.

[223] Deborah Pellow, "The Architecture of Female Seclusion in West Africa," in Denise Lawrence-Zúñiga and Setha M. Low (eds.), *The Anthropology of Space and Place: Locating Culture* (Cambridge: Blackwell, 2003), 161.

2

Opera, Operetta, and *Revista*

Music and Entertainment in Lisbon

Introduction

Lisbon's urban expansion was closely associated with paradigms of modernity. The newly built Avenida da Liberdade created new spaces in the urban fabric, which transformed the local entertainment market. Therefore, theatrical life reflected the new trends, as new leisure activities became available. The growing audience in search of a good time encouraged development of a volatile yet significant theatrical business that relied on new forms of show, namely, the operetta and the *revista*. These genres were imported from Paris and represented modern cosmopolitanism. However, they had to please local audiences. Therefore, local layers were added to a transnational form of entertainment in a way that transformed the genres themselves. In this process, popular entertainment packaged the modern nation in an appealing way for the audiences.[1] Given the prevailing atmosphere of decadence toward the end of the 19th century, laughter was a form of engaging with reality. To provide a theoretical ground for this study I draw from anthropology and from psychoanalysis to understand the mechanisms that displayed and naturalized the Portuguese nation through leisure. Leisure was central to the creation of liaisons, albeit temporary, between individuals in different parts of the social spectrum.[2] The audience of the Real Teatro de São Carlos was fairly homogeneous when compared with the people who frequented the operetta and the *revista*. Thus, the boxes and stalls of the popular theaters harbored a mixed crowd that paid their admission to be entertained with the satirization

---

[1] José de Oliveira Barata, *História do teatro português* (Lisbon: Universidade Aberta, 1991), 255–302.

[2] Dave Russell, *Popular Music in England, 1840–1914: A Social History* (Manchester: Manchester University Press, 1987), 11.

of current events. Moreover, the multivocality of the symbols and the openended form of the *revista* favored the rapid integration of everyday life in the genre's plots, where shifting, competing, and even contradictory readings of both modernity and nation could surface. In these plays, laughter made the audience lower their guard, making it easier for people to incorporate political and social ideas. Therefore, pleasure derived from the entertainment market facilitated the circulation of ideas concerning the nation-state. To counter a pervasive stance that sees nation-building as a top-down process, I will show that personal attachment and motivation were crucial for the efficient spread of nationalism. According to Young's work on Spanish *zarzuela*, popular nationalist music demonstrates that nationalism was not a completely topdown, static, state-driven process. For theatrical composers, librettists, and audiences, nationalism might mean a critique of the state; it might also mean suggestions of how the masses themselves could unite to solve what they viewed as problematic with the state.[3]

This is especially noticeable in Lisbon's stages between 1867 and 1910, when political turmoil exacerbated patriotic feelings. Moreover, the multivocality of symbols of the *revista* allowed for competing and sometimes contradictory perspectives of the nation to circulate. Despite the ubiquity of the "nation" on the Portuguese stage, several spaces developed different strategies for presenting it. The Real Teatro de S. Carlos relied on imported material, dominated by Italian opera. Thus, nationalism was played out in a different way than in the popular theaters, where local genres in Portuguese flourished. This illustrates a segmented market, in which some theatrical genres were associated with the display of social status. However, this division is misleading and often oblivious to the dynamic nature of social interaction. If music merely reflected social distinctions it would have been far less effective in the spread of nationalism than it was. Moreover, people and repertoires circulated in an entertainment market that catered to socially heterogeneous audiences.

The Real Teatro de São Carlos and Opera

The Real Teatro de São Carlos was the most important place in the social life of the higher social stratum, for which the display of prestige was crucial.[4] This theater was a place to be seen and a gathering point that encouraged the "investment in social relations with expected returns" for Lisbon's aristocracy

---

[3] Clinton David Young, "Zarzuela: or Lyric Theater as Consumer Nationalism in Spain, 1874–1930," Ph.D. thesis (University of California San Diego, 2006), 380.

[4] Mário Vieira de Carvalho, *Eça de Queirós e Offenbach* (Lisbon: Edições Colibri, 1999), 29–37.

and bourgeoisie.[5] The opera house provided a suitable setting for socializing in a period when face-to-face interaction was central. It was frequented by the Portuguese crème de la crème who "did not understand anything of the art of singing" and went there to parade themselves and to maintain their prestige.[6] Like most European opera houses, the Real Teatro de São Carlos focused on Italian opera, performed in Portuguese, and was run by an impresario. It employed an Italian company for a large part of its activity. Italian singers were ubiquitous on the European stages:

> It can be argued that in Italy the art industry introduces extremely important values in the country. In singing, mainly, Italians have a natural monopoly and its products, forgive my expression, are the many singers of all orders and qualities, who collect the artistic tax that humankind duly pays to the Italian genius in every part of the globe.[7]

Augusto Fuschini uses Italian opera an example of an international monopoly. Fuschini knew what he was writing about. Son of Eduardo Maria Fuschini, a musician of Italian ancestry, he was a Portuguese politician who became a member of the cabinet during the financial crisis of 1891. Despite being a private enterprise, the Real Teatro de S. Carlos relied on government subsidies.[8] Given its association with the high society who cherished cosmopolitan forms of entertainment, its shows reflected the European operatic scene, featuring works of composers such as Rossini, Donizetti, Bellini, and Verdi.[9] For example, of the seventeen operas performed in the 1864–1865 season, thirteen were by these composers.[10] During a significant part of the 19th century, and despite the frequent performance of operas like Rossini's *Il barbiere di Siviglia*, theatrical programming relied on novelty and on staging recent works. However, by the middle of the century, a more or less fixed canon had reshaped the structure of the opera seasons, and frequent performance of the same operas reduced the

---

[5] Nan Lin, "Building a Network Theory of Social Capital," *Connections*, 22/1 (1999), 30.

[6] António de Sousa Bastos, *Diccionario do theatro portuguez* (Lisbon: Imp. Libânio da Silva, 1908), 118.

[7] Augusto Fuschini, *O presente e o futuro de Portugal* (Lisbon: Companhia Typographica, 1899), 30.

[8] Francisco da Fonseca Benevides, *O Real Theatro de S. Carlos de Lisboa: memorias 1883–1902* (Lisbon: Typographia & Lithographia de Ricardo de Sousa Salles, 1902), 375–376; Rui Vieira Nery and Paulo Ferreira de Castro, *História da música* (Lisbon: Imprensa Nacional-Casa da Moeda, 1991), 152.

[9] Luísa Cymbron (ed.), *Verdi em Portugal 1843–2001* (Lisbon: Biblioteca Nacional de Portugal, 2001) [exhibition catalogue].

[10] Francisco da Fonseca Benevides, *O Real Theatro de S. Carlos de Lisboa desde a sua fundação em 1793 até à actualidade: estudo histórico* (Lisbon: Typ. Castro Irmão, 1883), 312–313.

role played by new operas. Most premières in the Real Teatro de São Carlos, however, were of recent operas by prominent living composers.

On the one hand, this change indicates a narrowing of the repertoire and a homogenization of operatic performances. Conversely, the shift is crucial for understanding the changes of the musical canon in a peripheral city like Lisbon. The frequent performance of the same operas created an informal archive of operas and of related artifacts in the São Carlos. This collection is an important source for the study of music in Lisbon; however, it is not without difficulties. Portuguese theaters did not have an actual archive but maintained a collection of manuscripts or printed materials for their own use.[11] Theatrical activity in Portugal was volatile, and attitudes toward their collections were utilitarian. Because of the informal and unsystematic nature of the archive, changes in the management of the theater, and the ephemerality of the repertoire, materials were lost or misplaced and never found their way into the collection.[12] The materials bought by the impresario became part of the theater's inventory, and the buyer was refunded in the end of the contract.[13] Later, they were owned by the firms who ran the theater. Because no attempt was made to create an actual archive of materials, it is difficult for the historian to reconstruct the actual theatrical scene of the time.

Apart from complete operas and ballets, the Real Teatro de São Carlos staged benefit shows for people associated with the theater and with the musical life of Lisbon. In these events, the net profit was delivered to a person or institution. The show usually focused on a musician or an institution, but some benefit shows were organized for the technical personnel of the theater. Because benefits were not included in the season tickets, their profit depended on the ticket office revenue. They were almost like a season within the opera season. For them to be profitable, they had to appeal to a wide audience. Thus, the choice of repertoire was crucial for their success. These varied programs were similar to the heterogeneous repertoire performed in the public concerts. They could include a complete act of an opera or a selection of its most important arias and, if the beneficiary was an instrumentalist, they included solo pieces performed by him or her. The season of the Real Teatro de São Carlos was shorter than most venues in Lisbon. It usually lasted from October to March or April, whereas most theaters worked six to eight months a year.[14] The writer Júlio César Machado (1835–1890) compared the São Carlos to a cloak,

---

[11] Bastos, *Diccionario*, 16.
[12] Benevides, *O Real Theatro de S. Carlos*, 307–309.
[13] Benevides, *O Real Theatro de S. Carlos*, 307–309.
[14] Bastos, *Diccionario*, 58; Benevides, *O Real Theatro de S. Carlos*, 385.

because it was only worn during the winter.[15] Nevertheless, its short season allowed other companies to use the building during the long summer break and let its orchestra musicians work in other theaters. This allowed the circulation of people between spaces, and some musicians of the orchestra doubled as composers for the popular theater. The actor Augusto Rosa wrote in 1916:It is during the winter that the new plays are staged; it is in the winter we see the top artists, who are touring or resting during the summer; it is in the winter that all the life of the big capital is boiling up, it scalds.[16]

In the other parts of the year, empty rooms were let for other uses. National and foreign drama companies performed in the Real Teatro de S. Carlos, and many political meetings were held in the city's theaters, where the rooms accommodated a large number of people.[17] During Carnival season, many masked balls took place in Lisbon's theaters, societies, and private salons. In the 1878 season the impresarios of the Real Teatro de S. Carlos gave four balls and three operatic performances (the fourth being included in the regular season). As part of an entrepreneurial strategy these events created a separate season ticket.

Allowing other groups to use the S. Carlos during the theater's break diversified its program. In May 1866 the *zarzuela* company that performed in Circo Price staged works by Francisco Barbieri (1823–1894), Joaquín Gaztambide (1822–1870), Manuel Caballero (1835–1906), and José Rogel (1829–1901) in S. Carlos.[18] In May and June 1870, the company performed their usual *zarzuelas* by Barbieri, Gaztambide, and Emilio Arrieta (1821–1894). However, they also staged a Spanish version of *La vie parisienne* and of *Barbe-Bleu* by Jacques Offenbach.[19] This demonstrates the pervasiveness of French operetta in Portugal in the late 1860s and 1870s. However, these performances were usually in Portuguese. Because the genre relied on a satirical look at everyday life and was aimed at a popular audience, the language was one the locals understood. However, a Spanish *zarzuela* company performing in Portugal used their native language. This shows the complexity of naming theatrical genres at this time, especially in the popular entertainment market. Does a French operetta become a *zarzuela* when a Spanish company performs it in Spanish? Was the music adapted to suit the tastes of the traditional audience of the *zarzuela*? Given the available sources, these questions cannot be answered. However, Sousa Bastos contrasts *zarzuela* with French operetta and emphasizes the national character of the latter. Unlike Parisian operetta, *zarzuela*

---

[15] Júlio César Machado, *Os theatros de Lisboa* (Lisbon: Mattos Moreia, 1875), 7.
[16] Augusto Rosa, *Memórias e estudos* (Lisbon: Livraria Ferreira, 1917), 75.
[17] Benevides, *O Real Theatro de S. Carlos*, 320, 347, 372, 336.
[18] Benevides, *O Real Theatro de S. Carlos*, 316–317.
[19] Benevides, *O Real Theatro de S. Carlos*, 330.

included "popular songs," patriotic marches, and dances such as *seguidillas* or *malagueñas*.[20] This echoes the role *zarzuela* played in Spanish nation-building, especially its *genero chico*, a shorter show which contained vernacular characters and local music.[21]

The most important feature of the Real Teatro de S. Carlos in the second half of the 19th century was the constitution of an operatic canon. Nevertheless, this canon was dynamic and subject to change. New operas by active composers became regular presences in on the European stages and the rise of new aesthetic movements was reflected in the repertoires. Notwithstanding the dominance of the Italian music, the S. Carlos began to stage French opera in the late 1830s. Nevertheless, these performances were rare. Starting in the 1860s the theater staged regularly operas by Gounod, Auber, Thomas, Massenet, Délibes, and Bizet. *Lohengrin* premièred in S. Carlos in 1883 but Wagner's music dramas were only staged on a regular basis in the 1890s. Furthermore, the frequent performance of *verismo* operas marked the seasons of the 1890s in the S. Carlos and in other theaters that were not devoted to opera.[22] Despite being written in French and in German, the vast majority of these operas were performed in Italian given the presence of an Italian company. However, this changed at the beginning of the 20th century. The satire of the *revista* was based on current events, which the genre mocked. Thus, performing operas in several languages was commented on in the *revista A nove*, premièred in the Teatro da Avenida on 28 February 1909. Its author Sousa Bastos includes a sketch about Lisbon's theaters stating that people were performing in so many languages in the S. Carlos that they would end up singing "in ox tongue."[23] This statement exaggerates the transformation that took place in the opera theater and places the *revista* as a keen observer of theatrical activity, a show that does not merely display current matters but also reflects on them.

The growth of the operatic repertoire was a transnational process that transformed the markets for cultural goods in the last third of the 19th century. With this background, the Real Teatro de S. Carlos is a good case for studying how French and German opera were received within the tradition of Italian theater. This goes back to the 1840s. When two operas by Saverio Mercadante were staged in 1842, the newspaper *A Revolução de Setembro* portrayed him

[20] Bastos, *Diccionario*, 157.

[21] Young, "Zarzuela," 380; Carmen del Moral Ruiz, *El género chico: Ocio y teatro en Madrid (1880–1910)* (Madrid: Alianza Editorial, 2005).

[22] Bastos, *Diccionario*, 261–262; Mário Moreau, *O Teatro de S. Carlos: dois séculos de história*, vol. 1 (Lisbon: Hugin Editores, 1999), 88–157.

[23] Sousa Bastos, *A nove: revista em 3 actos e 15 quadros* (Lisbon: Impr. Lucas, 1909), 16.

(who had already worked in the Real Teatro de S. Carlos) as someone who mixed the melodies of the Italian tradition with the techniques of Viennese late Classicism.[24] Mercadante's *Il bravo* and *La vestale* led to a comparison with Meyerbeer. Meyerbeer stood as the model of German opera for southern European audiences, despite his cosmopolitanism and his association with French *grand opéra*.[25] However, his reception changed toward the end of the century. Writing about the late 1860s, Jaime Batalha Reis (1847–1935) argued that the supreme art form in Lisbon was Italian opera and that Meyerbeer's productions, albeit in the Italian model, were representative of the German tradition.[26] This is because his operas were performed in Italian and adapted to the Italian company of the Real Teatro de S. Carlos.[27] Thus, the specter of an Austro-German musical culture surfaces periodically in Portugal throughout the 19th century, sometimes through a reference to France.

The rise of Wagner as the German model for the musical theater is illustrated by Portuguese writers toward the end of the century.[28] Ramalho Ortigão and Jaime Batalha Reis, who belong to the so-called 1870 generation (Geração de 70), saw in Wagner a quasi-messianic character before the performance of his musical dramas in Portugal. In 1876 Ramalho Ortigão had argued that Offenbach's operettas were the worthy substitute for the Wagnerian art form for Lisbon's audience.[29] This was written before Wagner's operas were staged in the S. Carlos and reinforces a 19th century trope that placed Italian opera as superficial entertainment and Austro-German music as art. In this hierarchy, French music stands somewhere between these poles. Batalha Reis wrote a series of articles on Wagner under the initials V. de D. in *O Ocidente*.[30] These were published less than a month after the composer's death and coincided with Lisbon's première of *Lohengrin* on 13 March 1883. Batalha

---

[24] *A Revolução de Setembro*, 2 August 1842, 1.

[25] Michael Wittmann, "Meyerbeer and Mercadante? The Reception of Meyerbeer in Italy," *Cambridge Opera Journal*, 5/2 (1993), 115–132; Fabrizio della Seta, "L'imagine di Meyerbeer nella critica italiana dell'Ottocento e l'idea di 'dramma musicale,'" in Maria Teresa Muraro, *L'opera tra Venezia e Parigi* (Florence: Olschki, 1988), 147–176.

[26] Jaime Batalha Reis, "Introdução," in Eça de Queirós, *Prosas bárbaras* (Porto: Lello & Irmão, 1912), 17.

[27] Carvalho, *Eça de Queirós e Offenbach*, 96.

[28] Maria João Rodrigues de Araújo, "The Reception of Wagner in Portugal (1880–1930)," Ph.D. thesis (University of Oxford, 2004).

[29] Ramalho Ortigão and Eça de Queirós, *As farpas: crónica mensal da política, das letras e dos costumes*, vol. 7 (Lisbon: Typographia Universal, 1876), 71–72; Carvalho, *Eça de Queirós e Offenbach*, 76, 121–125.

[30] *O Occidente*, 1 March 1883, 50–51; 11 March 1883, 59; 21 March 1883, 67; 1 April 1883, 78; 21 April 1883, 94, and 1 May 1883, 100–102; Adriano da Guerra Andrade, *Dicionário de pseudónimos e iniciais de escritores portugueses* (Lisbon: Biblioteca Nacional de Portugal, 1999), 269.

Reis studied in a German school in Lisbon, the Roeder, and he wrote a biography of the composer that was consistent with the myths that Wagner himself promoted.[31] These were in wide circulation in Europe, and the articles focus on the Bayreuth Festspielhaus and on the texts of Wagner's dramas. Batalha Reis described the illusionist apparatus of the Bayreuth Theater as a way of satisfying the full aesthetic experience for those attending a performance of a Wagnerian musical drama.[32] Thus, he reinforced the dichotomy between the German art and Italian entertainment.

After the première of *Lohengrin*, it took almost a decade for Wagnerian music dramas to return to Lisbon's stages. *Lohengrin* was performed again in the 1892–1893 season, during which *Der fliegende Holländer* and *Tannhaüser* were given their premières.[33] The performance of Wagner's work in the S. Carlos reflected the shift in the repertoire performed on the Italian stages after the 1870s. Freitas Brito, the impresario of S. Carlos in that season, played a key role in this process.[34] The première of *Tristan und Isolde* was scheduled for 1 February 1908. The royal family returned to Lisbon from Vila Viçosa to attend. However, the journey proved to be fatal as on that afternoon, King Carlos I and the Prince D. Luís were killed in Lisbon. After being postponed, *Tristan und Isolde* premièred on 10 February 1908.[35] Wagner's *Der Ring des Nibelungen* was staged in the following season for the first time. It was sung in German, a fact that illustrates the transformation of the repertoire and the end of the monopoly of Italian companies in the Real Teatro de S. Carlos.[36] Also, the Portuguese audience saw *Salome*, by Richard Strauss, for the first time in that season.

The performances of *Der Ring des Nibelungen* were widely covered in the press. *Ilustração portuguesa* published a series of articles on the operas. The articles began by imagining how these operas would be received in S. Carlos. They indicate the role played by this theater in the social life of the city and criticize the superficiality and snobbery of its audience.[37] "More than a strong and sincere artistic interest, the curiosity and the exhibitionism will certainly fill the room and, if not all are impressed with the brilliant greatness of the

---

[31] Maria José Marinho, "Jaime Batalha Reis e Celeste Cinatti: diálogo sobre um retrato incompleto," *Análise social*, 42/182 (2007), 281–284; Richard Wagner, *My Life* (London: Constable & Robinson, 1996).

[32] *O Occidente*, 1 April 1883, 78.

[33] Moreau, *O Teatro de S. Carlos: dois séculos de história*, vol. 1, 128. For a review of the première of *Der fliegende Holländer* and of the première of *Tannhaüser* see *A semana de Lisboa*, 5 March 1893, 78, and 26 March 1893, 103, respectively.

[34] Nery and Castro, *História da música*, 152.

[35] Moreau, *O Teatro de S. Carlos*, vol. 1, 157.

[36] Nery and Castro, *História da música*, 152–153.

[37] *Illustração portugueza*, 1 March 1909, 278.

Wagnerian work, by the lack of aesthetic capacities and of musical education, they will, at least, be impressed by the novelty and the magnitude of the *mise-en-scène*."[38] This illustrated the purpose of the articles—to prepare an audience that was accustomed to Italian models to watch a new type of opera. The writing also recommended that the public cough less, be more punctual, and read about Wagner beforehand.[39] Paulo Osório published four illustrated articles, one discussing each opera of *Der Ring*.[40] They summarized the plots of each opera and related the musical motifs with the overall narrative. This mirrors the analysis of Wagner's dramas that was circulating at the time, an approach initially developed by his associate Hans von Wolzogen.[41]

Much later, the magazine *Contemporânea* published an article telling how a small number of musicians from Porto connected with Wagner's music dramas.[42] The writer, Manuel Ramos (1862–1931), described the performances of the piano reductions of *Tannhäuser* and *Lohengrin* by the pianist and composer Miguel Ângelo Pereira (1843–1901) in 1872, based in an account by the prominent musician Bernardo Valentim Moreira de Sá (1853–1924).[43] The violinist Augusto Marques Pinto (1838–1888) hosted these private soirées and they were attended by Moreira de Sá, by the scholar Joaquim de Vasconcelos (1849–1936), and by other local musicians.[44] In this sense, Wagner's initial reception in Portugal was not exclusively dependent on staging. It also relied on private performances by professional musicians and on the dissemination of the composer's theoretical works.

The Real Teatro de S. Carlos presented operas by Portuguese composers.[45] However, these performances were sporadic. The presence of an Italian company and the role Italian opera played in the entertainment market made life more complicated for local composers. For example, when the opera *L'arco di Sant'Anna* was staged in 1868, some singers refused to learn it because it would not be performed anywhere else.[46] Even though the opera relied on

---

[38] *Illustração portugueza*, 1 Mar. 1909, 278.

[39] *Illustração portugueza*, 1 March 1909, 280.

[40] Paulo Osório, "Wagner em S. Carlos," in *Illustração portugueza*, 1 March 1909, 281–288; 8 March 1909, 289–295; 15 March 1909, 329–333; 22 March 1909. 353–358.

[41] Hans von Wolzogen, *Thematischer leitfaden durch die musik zu Rich. Wagner's festspiel Der ring des Nibelungen* (Leipzig, E. Schloemp, 1876).

[42] *Contemporânea*, March 1923, 137–141.

[43] *Contemporânea*, March 1923, 138.

[44] *Contemporânea*, March 1923, 138.

[45] Teresa Cascudo, "A década da invenção de Portugal na música erudita (1890–1899)," *Revista portuguesa de musicologia*, 10 (2000), 196–208.

[46] Benevides, *O Real Theatro de S. Carlos*, 324; Luísa Cymbron, "Francisco de Sá Noronha e L'Arco di Sant'anna: para o estudo da ópera em Portugal (1860–70)," master's thesis (Universidade Nova de Lisboa, 1990).

Italian models it was composed by Francisco de Sá Noronha (1820–1881) and would not enter the standard repertoire. As in other countries, many operas by local composers staged in the S. Carlos were inspired by Portuguese historical novels and dramas. *L'arco di Sant'Anna* was based in the novel *O arco de Santana*, by Almeida Garrett. Miguel Ângelo Pereira wrote *Eurico*, a work based on the novel *Eurico, o presbítero*, by Alexandre Herculano to be staged in 1870. *Fra Luigi di Sousa* was composed by Freitas Gazul and premièred in 1891. It was based in the drama *Frei Luís de Sousa*, by Almeida Garrett. This shows the importance of Romantic historicism for Portuguese opera composers, and indicates a complex relation between Portuguese subjects (albeit inspired by French models) and Italian operatic conventions.[47] Nevertheless, the historical drama dominated the Portuguese stages from the late 1830s and remained an important model throughout the century. There was a renewed interest in the genre in the 1880s, which was transformed to suit the new idea of the cultural nation-state, a tendency that is associated with a revival of Romanticism.[48] With the rise of the historical drama, factual rigor became significant in the appreciation of theatrical plots and of the *mise-en-scène*. This is reflected in some reviews of Meyerbeer's *L'Africaine*, an opera that draws on Portuguese history, and had several historical inaccuracies and inconsistencies.[49]

Toward the end of the 19th century, the Portuguese Augusto Machado (1845–1924) wrote operas that were performed in S. Carlos. After studying in Paris, Machado returned to Portugal, where he presented three operas and several operettas. His opera *Laureanne* is based in George Sand's drama *Les beaux messieurs de Bois-Doré*. It premièred in Marseille in 1883 and was staged in Lisbon the following year. In S. Carlos *Laureanne* was performed in Italian and the spoken dialogue was substituted for recitatives. This reveals the prominence given to Italian conventions in this theater, even when the repertoire was changing. Antonio Ghislanzoni (1824–1893) wrote the libretto for *I Doria* premièred in S. Carlos in 1887, and in the following year, *Mario Wetter* (libretto by Ruggero Leoncavallo) was staged. In addition to

---

[47] Luísa Cymbron, "Entre a tradição italiana, a reforma garrettiana e as motivações políticas— os compositores de ópera na Lisboa de meados do século XIX," in Luísa Cymbron, *Olhares sobre a música em Portugal no século XIX* (Lisbon: Edições Colibri/CESEM, 2012), 1–38.

[48] Luiz Francisco Rebello, *O teatro naturalista e neo-romântico (1870–1910)* (Lisbon: Instituto de Cultura Portuguesa, 1978), 41–54.

[49] Glória Bastos and Ana Isabel de Vasconcelos, *O teatro em Lisboa no tempo da Primeira República* (Lisbon: Museu Nacional do Teatro, 2004), 100; Gabriela Cruz, "*L'Africaine*'s Savage Pleasures: Operatic Listening and the Portuguese Historical Imagination," *Revista portuguesa de musicologia*, 10 (2000), 151–180.

Figure 2.1 A serrana, by Alfredo Keil [postcard], Lisbon: Tabacaria Costa, early 20th century, private collection. Postcard of Nabor, a character of the opera *A serrana*, by Alfredo Keil.

his work as composer, Machado co-directed the Real Teatro de S. Carlos between 1889 and 1892.[50]

The painter and composer Alfredo Keil (1850–1907) saw three of his operas performed in the Real Teatro de S. Carlos between 1888 and 1899: *Donna Bianca* (inspired by a poem by Almeida Garrett), *Irene* (premièred in Turin's Teatro Regio and published in Italy), and *Serrana* (an adaptation of Camilo Castelo Branco's short story *Como ela o amava*).[51] *Serrana*, one of several collaborations between Keil and Henrique Lopes de Mendonça, became the first opera to be later published in Portuguese, and was put forward as a national opera several years after it was first performed.[52] Nevertheless, it was initially performed in Italian in the S. Carlos. Figure 2.1 is one of a series of postcards published by the Tabacaria Costa that were inspired in the opera. Each card reproduces the opera's sets and

---

[50] António de Sousa Bastos, *Carteira do artista; apontamentos para a historia do theatro portuguez e brazileiro* (Lisbon: Antiga casa Bertrand, José Bastos, 1899), 242.

[51] Alfredo Keil, *Donna Bianca: drame lyrique en quatro parties et un prologue* (Paris: G. Hartmann, [1888–1890]); *Irene: leggenda mistica (dramma lirico) in quattro parti* (Lipsia: Stamperia Musical di C. G. Roder, [1893–1896]).

[52] César Fereal, Henrique Lopes de Mendonça, and Alfredo Keil, *Serrana: drama lyrico em três actos* (n.p.: n.p., 1899).

includes one character in his or her stage costume. It also contains a few bars of music associated with the depicted character and a portrait of the composer. The postcard in Figure 2.1 depicts the rocky scenery of Act 3 and the character Nabor (played by the bass Di Grazia), who sings his aria "Padre Nosso" after burying the protagonist Pedro.

Due to its affiliation with *verismo*, especially in depicting a vernacular rural community by using popular customs and "popular melodies," *Serrana* is now presented as a fundamental contribution to a nationalist opera.[53] However, its initial reviews did not depict *Serrana* as having a nationalist flavor.[54] The press wrote extensively on *Serrana*, reprised in the Coliseu dos Recreios two years after its première.[55] For example, the magazine *O branco e negro* reviewed the piece and presented it as a "new Portuguese opera," but did not mention nationalist underpinnings.[56] The article concentrated in the plot and the performance of the main singers (who, despite the Italian libretto, sang a few verses in Portuguese), complimenting Keil's work and pointing to a change in his style.[57] The opera was an attempt by Keil to establish himself in the entertainment market in Lisbon by adopting a style different from the Franco-Italian repertoire that was predominant in the S. Carlos. Some ten years later, in 1909, *Serrana* was given its première in Portuguese, and following this performance, *Ilustração portuguesa* published an article stating that Keil's opera presented a "genuinely national subject" and highlighted the composer's desire to create a Portuguese opera.[58] Keil did not set out to compose a "nationalistic" opera, but this review indicates a shift in the way the work was seen and attributed to the patriotism of the composer. The episodic staging of operas by Portuguese composers in the S. Carlos had an interesting case in 1907, with the première of *Amore e perdizione* by João Arroio (1861–1930). It was inspired by Camilo Castelo Branco's novel *Amor de perdição* published in 1862. The opera was performed in Hamburg in 1910 and Schott published its German edition.[59]

---

[53] Luís Raimundo, "Para uma leitura dramatúrgica e estilística de Serrana de Alfredo Keil," *Revista portuguesa de musicologia* 10 (2000), 227–274.

[54] Cascudo, "A década da invenção de Portugal," 205–206.

[55] *A arte musical*, 15 March 1899, 42–43; Colyseu dos Recreios and Empreza Santos, *Opera lyrica A Serrana: argumento* (Lisbon: Typ. Almeida, Machado, 1901). Shelfmark PTBN: M.9 A., National Library of Portugal.

[56] *O branco e negro*, 26 March 1899, 3.

[57] *O branco e negro*, 26 March 1899, 2–3.

[58] *Illustração portugueza*, 5 April 1909, 425.

[59] Alberto Pimentel, *Notas sôbre o Amor de Perdição* (Lisbon: Guimarães, 1915), 138–155; João Arroyo, *Liebe und Verderben: Lyrisches Drama in 3 Akten nach der Portugiesischen Novelle C. C. Branco's* (Mainz: Schott, 1909).

The idea of a national opera parallels the effort to create a national theater throughout the 19th century. In this process, the Real Teatro de S. Carlos was sometimes portrayed as an obstacle to the local theater as its Italian leanings favored the transnational repertoire instead of promoting Portuguese works. Also, governmental policy endowed the S. Carlos with greater subsidies than any other theater, namely, the Teatro Nacional D. Maria II. The press kept the public aware of the need for a real Portuguese theater. For example, the writer António Pedro Lopes de Mendonça (1825–1865) stated in 1847 that the opening of the "Italian theater" compromised the development of a national theater.[60] In 1853, Luís Augusto Palmerim (1825–1893), who became director of the Conservatório Geral de Arte Dramática in 1878, pointed out the absence of Portuguese plays by the followers of Almeida Garrett, the foremost Romantic playwright and an important theater reformer, and the predominance of translations.[61] The predominance of French plays in the Teatro de D. Maria II is mocked in Manuel Roussados' *revista Fossilismo e progresso,* where its personification speaks in an odd mixture of Portuguese and French.[62] Therefore, a duality between national theater and imported models was also present in the spoken theater, complicating the association between the S. Carlos with transnationalism and the D. Maria II with nationalism.

Along these lines, Eça de Queirós wrote a substantial article about Lisbon's theaters.[63] He stated that theatrical activity was condemned due to the decay of the audience's "spirit and intelligence" and to the economic situation of the theaters themselves.[64] Queirós stressed the role translations played in the Teatro Ginásio, the Teatro do Príncipe Real, and the Teatro da Rua dos Condes, where the performances and the scenic apparatuses lacked quality; and noted that the operettas and *zarzuelas* in the Teatro da Trindade were performed by poorly trained actors/singers.[65] Queirós stressed the lack of dramatic literature, the public's own inertia, economic difficulties, and the shortcomings in the training of actors.[66] He suggested a model whereby the Teatro D. Maria II would stage drama, the Teatro da Trindade would perform comic operas, and a third theater—which would be a merger of the Teatro da

---

[60] *A Revolução de Setembro,* 26 October 1847, 1

[61] *A Revolução de Setembro,* 11 July 1853, 1–2, nº 3378, 12 July 1853, 1–2, and nº 3383, 18 July 1853, 1.

[62] Manuel Roussado, *Fossilismo e progresso: revista* (Lisbon: Typographia Rua da Condessa nº3, 1856), 108–109.

[63] Ramalho Ortigão and Eça de Queirós, *As farpas: crónica mensal da política, das letras e dos costumes* (Lisbon: Typographia Universal, 1872), 48–72.

[64] Ortigão and Queiróz, *As farpas,* 49.

[65] Ortigão and Queiróz, *As farpas,* 49–50.

[66] Ortigão and Queiróz, *As farpas,* 51–52.

Rua dos Condes, the Teatro do Príncipe Real, and the Teatro Variedades—would perform popular theater at cheap prices.[67] He attacked the Real Teatro de S. Carlos as providing entertainment for the upper social stratum that was subsidized by the government whereas the D. Maria II did not get such generous support from the public revenue. Thus, an Italian repertoire that was seen as sensual and decadent was favored to the detriment of national theater.[68] However, despite his criticism, Eça de Queirós was a frequent visitor to the S. Carlos and his works contain extensive references to this theater.[69]

Operetta and *Zarzuela*

The Real Teatro de S. Carlos dominated the opera performances in Lisbon, and a strong association is made between this space and its repertoire. Moreover, the theater kept its reputation as a venue where the high society went to be seen and to enhance their social prestige, even when other places were staging opera. The existence of popular theater, which was mostly unsubsidized, was precarious. This is illustrated by the constant change of the firms that managed the theaters. Debt and uncertainty were part of everyday life on the popular stage, and the instability of the first part of the 19th century took its toll on the leisure market. The opening of new venues to accommodate a larger audience also meant that competition was intensified. Thus, uncertainty was pervasive for this segment of entertainment. Even so, there was some permanence. Some genres were predominantly associated with particular theaters, albeit less rigidly than in the Real Teatro de S. Carlos. For example, operetta found in the Teatro da Trindade a special place for its performance. Moving from opera to operetta and *zarzuela*, Lisbon accommodated several theaters where these genres ruled. Like opera, these shows have a coherent story and include music and dance. However, the *ariosos* and recitatives were replaced with spoken dialogue, and everyday situations formed an important part of their plots. I use the term "operetta" to include plays where spoken dialogue, music, and song have prominent roles, also known locally as *ópera cómica* (comic opera), *ópera burlesca* (burlesque opera), *comédia musical* (musical comedy), or *comédia lírica* (lyrical comedy). Their strategy was to communicate with a wide audience through satire and song, and the text was key to their success. To maximize its impact, this text was performed in the audience's language and the situations had to be adapted so they could easily be understood. Thus, imported works were adjusted to the local context and performed in Portuguese.

---

[67] Ortigão and Queiróz, *As farpas*, 58.
[68] Ortigão and Queiróz, *As farpas*, 59–72.
[69] Maria Filomena Mónica, *Eça de Queiroz* (Melton: Tamesis, 2005).

Associated with the leisure industry of the Second Empire and with the rise of a boulevard culture, the operetta was initially cultivated in Paris by people like Hervé and Offenbach.[70] Therefore, the urban development led by Haussmann in Paris was reflected in new forms of entertainment for a growing audience. The operetta is "a light opera with spoken dialogue, songs and dances," or "a comic opera of little importance."[71] As mentioned above, the transformations of Lisbon's urban landscape fostered new venues for sociability and entertainment. Nevertheless, most theaters were still concentrated in areas traditionally associated with shopping and entertainment, like Chiado or Trindade. *Opéra comique* and *zarzuela* had been featured in Lisbon in the first half of the 19th century, but the establishment of new theaters created a space for performance of recently imported genres from Paris, like the operetta and the *revista*. A marker of this change is the première of Offenbach's *La Grande-Duchesse de Gérolstein* in the Teatro do Príncipe Real on the 29 February 1868.[72] The play was translated by the playwright Eduardo Garrido (1842–1912) and performed in Portuguese as *A Grã-duquesa de Gérolstein*.[73] Its première was a success and the Teatro Ginásio premièred *As georgianas* (*Les géorgiennes*) in October, also translated by Garrido.[74] However, an Offenbach operetta, whose title in Portuguese is *O Tio Braz*, was translated and premièred in the Teatro Ginásio as early as 1859.[75] It was later performed in other theaters. Nevertheless, it was staged before the peak of Offenbach's international success. Moreover, most theaters that staged operetta in Lisbon on a regular basis had not yet been established.

The entrepreneur Francisco Palha translated and presented *Barba-Azul* (*Barbe-bleue*) in the Teatro da Trindade in June 1868, the space that would become primarily associated with operetta.[76] This première fell between the

---

[70] Richard Traubner, *Operetta: A Theatrical History* (London: Routledge, 2003); Vanessa R. Schwartz, *Spectacular Realities: Early Mass Culture in Fin-de-Siècle Paris* (Berkeley: University of California Press, 1998); Kracauer, Siegfried, *Jacques Offenbach and the Paris of His Time* (New York: Zone Books, 2002); Jean-Claude Yon, *Jacques Offenbach* (Paris: Gallimard, 2000).

[71] Andrew Lamb, "Operetta," *Grove Music Online*, ed. L. Macy. <www.oxfordmusiconline.com>, accessed 6 November 2012 and Sousa Bastos, *Diccionario*, 102.

[72] Carvalho, *Eça de Queirós e Offenbach*.

[73] *O Occidente*, 20 January 1913, 14–15; Eduardo Garrido, *A Grã-duqueza de Gérolstein: ópera burlesca em três actos e quatro quadros* (Lisbon: Typographia Universal de Thomaz Quintino Antunes, 1868).

[74] Sousa Bastos, *Carteira do artista*, 85–86, Eduardo Garrido, *As georgianas: ópera burlesca em três actos* (Lisbon: Typographia Universal de Thomaz Quintino Antunes, 1868).

[75] Sousa Bastos, *Diccionario*, 303. This is Mendes Leal's translation of an Offenbach operetta that was impossible for me to identify.

[76] Bastos, *Diccionario*, 303, Francisco Palha, *Barba azul: ópera burlesca em 3 actos e 4 quadros* (Lisbon: Typographia Franco Portugueza, 1868).

performances of Offenbach's operettas in the Teatro do Príncipe Real and in the Teatro do Ginásio mentioned above. Then, local versions of operettas and zarzuelas were frequently staged in the main hall of the Teatro da Trindade.[77] Making fun of the institutions and of the stereotypes of the Second Empire was an important part of Offenbach's work. This critical position is echoed in Portugal, and the imagery of his operettas was frequently used in Lisbon's satirical press. Rafael Bordalo Pinheiro's *O António Maria* and *A paródia* published caricatures depicting politicians as characters of Offenbach's operettas, especially *A Grã-duquesa de Gérolstein*.[78] Furthermore, in *As farpas*, Eça de Queirós stated that Portugal's fundamental laws seem to have been drawn from *Barba-Azul*.[79] In a slightly altered version of his text, Queirós goes even further and states that the institutions in Portugal seem to have been drawn from Offenbach's operettas *Barba-Azul* and *A Grã-duquesa de Gérolstein*.[80] This clearly resonates with Kracauer, who argued that "the operetta would never have been born had the society of the time not itself been operetta-like."[81] Moreover, the social significance of Offenbach's operettas is reflected in the literature of its time, including the work of Eça de Queirós. For example, the couplets "A carta adorada ("Lettre adorée")," from *A Grã-duquesa de Gérolstein* were given a prominent role in the novel *O primo Basílio*, and the first scene of his posthumous novel *A tragédia da Rua das Flores* was set in the Teatro da Trindade during a performance of *Barba-Azul*.[82] Although the Real Teatro de S. Carlos continued as a space for the performance of foreign music, sometimes harming local production, the Portuguese theaters also relied heavily on imported materials. Plays were translated to supply a growing entertainment market and for the performers to be able to communicate effectively with their audience. This is evident in a sketch of the *revista Tim tim por tim tim*, where the local translators, who "had been studying French for over a month," were critically satirized.[83] France and Spain were the main sources of these imported repertoires, a fact that can be observed by the dominance of the operetta and the *zarzuela* in the Teatro da Trindade. Furthermore, Sousa Bastos refers to the conventions pertaining to intellectual property (including both text and

---

[77] Tomaz Ribas, *O Teatro da Trindade: 125 anos de vida* (Porto: Lello & Irmão, 1993).

[78] Carvalho, *Eça de Queirós e Offenbach*, Maria Virgílio Cambraia Lopes, *O teatro n'A Paródia de Rafael Bordalo Pinheiro* (Lisbon: Imprensa Nacional-Casa da Moeda, 2005).

[79] Ortigão and Queirós, *As farpas*, 51.

[80] Carvalho, *Eça de Queiróz e Offenbach*, 38.

[81] Siegfried Kracauer, *Jacques Offenbach and the Paris of His Time* (New York: Zone Books, 2002), 215.

[82] Carvalho, *Eça de Queiróz e Offenbach*, 38.

[83] Sousa Bastos, *Tim tim por tim tim: revista phantástica e de costumes em 1 prólogo, 3 actos e 12 quadros* (Lisbon: Livraria Popular de Francisco Franco, n.d.), 10.

music of theatrical plays) between Portugal and France and between Portugal and Spain (ratified in 1867 and in 1881, respectively).[84] These two countries were probably the most significant for the local theaters.

Furthermore, translating for the theaters was in the hands of experienced agents like entrepreneurs and playwrights.[85] People like Francisco Palha, António de Sousa Bastos, Eduardo Garrido, or Aristides Abranches (playwright and stage director, 1842–1912) translated a large number of plays. Some translations were set by different composers, as the vaudeville-operetta *Mam'zelle Nitouche* illustrates.[86] According to Sousa Bastos, the libretto was translated by Gervásio Lobato (journalist, writer and playwright, 1850–1895) and Urbano de Castro (journalist and writer, 1850–1920). Its Lisbon première was held in 1886 in the Recreios Whittoyne, a space that presented circus and theater, and was demolished for the construction of the Estação da Avenida. In these performances the libretto was not staged with Hervé's music but with a setting by Rio de Carvalho (1838–1907).[87] In the following year the same translation was staged using the music by Hervé in the Teatro da Trindade.[88] This shows that the same libretto was used as a literary source for several productions. These librettos were published and were seen as collectables at the time.

Although operettas and *zarzuelas* were staged in several theaters, the Teatro da Trindade was the most prestigious space for their performance. Operettas and *zarzuelas* that were premièred there became the standard repertoire of the genre. Then they would circulate in other theaters. The importance of the Teatro da Trindade in staging operettas in Portuguese is evident in the following selection of titles: *Barba-azul* (*Barbe-bleue*, by Jacques Offenbach in 1868),[89] *Fausto, o petiz* (*Le petit Faust*, by Hervé in 1870),[90] *Sinos de Corneville* (*Les cloches de Corneville*, by Robert Planquette in 1877),[91] *A Perichole* (*La*

---

[84] Sousa Bastos, *Diccionario*, 44, 148.

[85] Kathryn J. Oberdeck, "Contested Cultures of American Refinement: Theatrical Manager Sylvester Poli, His Audiences, and the Vaudeville Industry, 1890–1920," *Radical History Review* (1996), 40–91; Eduardo Noronha, "Visconde S. Luiz Braga," in *O grande Elias*, 21 January 1904, 1–2.

[86] Sousa Bastos, *Diccionario*, 300.

[87] Sousa Bastos, *Diccionario*, 300; Urbano de Castro and Gervásio Lobato, *Mam'zelle Nitouche: vaudeville em 4 actos* (Lisbon: Liv. Economica, n.d.).

[88] However, I could not locate Carvalho's score, which makes it impossible to compare both settings.

[89] For an article published in 1906 concerning the première of *Barba-azul* see *Illustração portugueza*, 9 April 1906, 197–199.

[90] Aristides Abranches, *Fausto, o petiz: opereta phantastica em 3 actos e 4 quadros* (Lisbon: Livraria Popular de Francisco Franco, n.d.).

[91] Sousa Bastos, *Sinos de Corneville: opereta original em 1 acto* (Lisbon: Liv. Economica, 1879).

périchole, by Offenbach in 1880),[92] *Orfeu nos infernos* (*Orphée aux enfers*, by Offenbach in 1880), *Boccaccio* (by Franz von Suppé in 1884),[93] *O moleiro d'Alcalá* (*Le meunier d'Alcala*, by Justin Clérice, in 1887—according to some sources, the world première was given in the Teatro da Trindade on 11 April)[94]—and *Vinte e oito dias de Clarinha* (*Les 28 jours de Clairette*, by Victor Roger in 1894). This series is strongly French; however, it also includes the Viennese operetta *Bocaccio*, which was one of the most successful theatrical shows performed in Lisbon, according to Sousa Bastos.[95]

Zarzuela performances were also regularly done in the Teatro da Trindade. The Portuguese audiences were very familiar with the genre as *zarzuelas* had been performed since the middle of the 19th century. However, these performances were episodic and were usually staged in Spanish. This changed in the last third of the century. Many *zarzuelas* were performed in Portuguese in the Teatro da Trindade because Francisco Palha's strategy was to stage comic operas in Portuguese. This allowed for better communication between stage and audience and helped increase profit. The *zarzuelas* staged in this theater include *Amar sem conhecer* (*Amar sin conocer*, by Gatzambide and Guarnieri in 1871),[96] *Amazonas do Tormes* (*Las amazonas del Tormes*, by José Rogel and translated by Passos Valente in 1872),[97] *Segredo d'uma dama* (*El secreto de una dama*, by Barbieri in 1873), and *O último figurino* (*El ultimo figurino*, by José Rogel in 1880).[98] These belong to the sub-genre *zarzuela grande*, the Spanish equivalent of French operetta. The *zarzuela grande* was developed in the 1850s by composers like Gatzambide or Barbieri as a way of revitalizing the genre in a politically charged period for Spain. It relied on a large narrative form, sometimes inspired by local history, and technically demanding musical numbers, revealing its indebtedness to opera.[99] Despite its success, the company

---

[92] A contemporary manuscript with a version of the text and staging directions belongs to the National Library of Portugal collection. Henri Meillac, Ludovic Halévy, and Jacques Offenbach, *A Perichole*: opera burlesca em 3 actos e 4 quadros. Shelfmark PTBN: COD. 11735.

[93] Garrido, *Boccacio: opera comica em tres actos, accommodada á scena portugueza* (Lisbon: Imprensa Nacional, 1884).

[94] *American Annual Cyclopaedia and Register of Important Events* (New York: D. Appleton, 1888), 523; Garrido, *O moleiro d'Alcalá: opera comica em 3 actos e 4 quadros* (Lisbon: Livraria Popular de Francisco Franco, n.d.).

[95] Sousa Bastos, *Diccionario*, 295–305; Traubner, *Operetta: A Theatrical History*, 98–142; Péter Hanák, *The Garden and the Workshop: Essays on the Cultural History of Vienna and Budapest* (Princeton, NJ: Princeton University Press, 1999), 135–147.

[96] Aristides Abranches, *Amar sem conhecer: zarzuela em 3 actos* (Lisbon: Livraria Popular de Francisco Franco, n.d.).

[97] Sousa Bastos, *Diccionario*, 295.

[98] Mariano Barranco, *Marron glacé: juguete en un acto y en prosa* (Madrid: Impr. de C. Rodríguez, 1883), back cover.

[99] Young, "Zarzuela," 52–53.

working in the Teatro da Trindade had to keep costs low. The financial constraints of this company are documented in the memoirs of the actor Isidoro: in the 1869 performances of *Barba-Azul* his gloves became so worn they began to discolor.[100]

The Italian composer Ângelo Frondoni (1812–1891) was closely associated with the Teatro da Trindade between its opening and 1873. He moved to Portugal in 1838 and was extremely active in the theatrical circuit.[101] Frondoni was especially associated with Italian repertoires and worked in several theaters until he was hired by Francisco Palha to become the musical director for the Teatro da Trindade. At this time, a musical director performed varied tasks that included conducting the performances, composing, and coaching the actors/singers. For example, in the years he worked in Trindade, Frondoni wrote music for plays such as *Gata Borralheira*,[102] *Rosa de sete folhas*,[103] and *Três rocas de cristal*.[104] Vieira claims that Frondoni could maximize the vocal potential of "singers with no voice" by writing according to their competence. He also was skillful in adapting the scores of other composers.[105] The lack of professional training of singers was a frequent handicap for most of the operetta and *revista* companies, like the one based in the Teatro da Trindade.[106] Adapting vocal scores was common practice, and operettas "were written for commercial ventures as income-producing entities."[107] This means that they had to meet the expectations of their audience, whatever these were. Thus, both text and music were adapted to suit them, displaying the plasticity of the genre. Some adaptations involved a profound reworking of the original version. Parody became a popular strategy to adapt operetta and *zarzuela* to different contexts. Moreover, this was a way of capitalizing on the success of the original show. People knew its plot and the parody played with their expectations. To draw a parallel between the operetta craze in Portugal and in Brazil, the Brazilian operetta *Orfeu na roça* (Orpheus on the farm) premièred in the theater Fénix Dramática in Rio de Janeiro in 1868. This happened in the same year when frequent performances of Offenbach's operettas began in Lisbon.

---

[100] Isidoro Sabino Ferreira, *Memorias do Actor Izidoro* (Lisbon: Imprensa de J.G. de Sousa Neves, 1876), 61–62.

[101] Ernesto Vieira, *Diccionario biographico de musicos portuguezes: historia e bibliografia da musica em Portugal*, vol.1 (Lisbon: Lambertini, 1900), 433–438.

[102] Joaquim Augusto de Oliveira, *A gata borralheira: mágica em 3 actos e 16 quadros* (Lisbon: Livraria Popular de Francisco Franco, n.d.).

[103] Ângelo Frondoni, *A rosa de sete folhas* (Lisbon: Lence & Viuva Canongia, 1870).

[104] Aristides Abranches, *As três rocas de cristal* (Lisbon: Carvalho, [1874]).

[105] Vieira, *Diccionario biographico de musicos portuguezes*, vol.1, 436.

[106] Ortigão and Queirós, *As farpas*, 50–51.

[107] Traubner, *Operetta: A Theatrical History*, x.

Orfeu na roça was written by the actor and playwright Francisco Correa Vasques (1839–1893) and consisted of a parody of the Orpheus myth.[108] The show was very successful in Brazil and was performed more than 500 times.[109] It used Offenbach's music but was adapted to the local context. The characters and the plot were also altered to emphasize their Brazilian character. As in the Portuguese case a play that used Greek myths to criticize Parisian society was transformed into a show that made fun of local customs and incorporated vernacular music. This flexibility shows the space occupied by the operetta in the leisure market of the time, contrasting with a perspective that cherished self-referent works of art. Therefore, popular theater was the opposite pole of Wagner's music dramas. If Italian opera was perceived as superficial entertainment, other repertoires achieved artistic status. Moreover, there was a tendency to make opera more elitist in the 19th century.[110] This may have reinforced the status of the Real Teatro de S. Carlos as an exclusive space frequented by the elegant society. On the other side of the equation the operetta and the *revista* became dominant in the popular theaters.

Creating and Performing Operetta in Portugal

Eça de Queirós argued that the Teatro da Trindade should be "the representative and creator of the national comic opera."[111] Despite the frequent demand to create a national theater and a national opera, defining "national" is complex. On the one hand, most genres staged in Lisbon were based in imported models, such as opera, the historical drama, the operetta, and the *revista*. Conversely, equating the national with the works of Portuguese authors is misleading. For example, the operas by Portuguese composers staged in the Real Teatro de S. Carlos were frequently presented by the media as part of a nationalist endeavor. However, these operas share the conventions of the transnational entertainment market, and some Portuguese composers were educated abroad. Performing plays in Portuguese is associated with patriotism and nationalism. Benedict Anderson places local languages at the center of his theory of nation-building. However, in a theatrical market that relied heavily

---

[108] Silvia Cristina Martins de Souza, "Um Offenbach tropical: Francisco Correa Vasques e o teatro musicado no Rio de Janeiro da segunda metade do século XIX," *História e Perspectivas*, 34/ January–June (2006), 225–259.

[109] Décio de Almeida Prado, *História concisa do teatro brasileiro: 1570–1908* (São Paulo: Edusp, 1999), 95.

[110] John Storey, "Inventing Opera as Art in Nineteenth-Century Manchester," *International Journal of Cultural Studies*, 9/4 (2006), 435–456.

[111] Ortigão and Queirós, *As farpas*, 58.

on imported conventions and translations, a straightforward correspondence between works in Portuguese and nationalism is elusive. Even if the librettos contained Portuguese subjects, Paris continued to supply the model for them to be staged. The reliance on local artists also plays an important part in the discourse concerning the "national." For example, a company of Portuguese opera singers was created at the beginning of the 20th century. It contrasted with the Italian company hired by the Real Teatro de S. Carlos, and it was clearly underpinned by a nationalist perspective. The company lasted only a few months and performed operas and operettas in the Teatro da Trindade in the season of 1908/1909.[112] Some of these plays were sung in Portuguese, including the Portuguese version of *Serrana*. *Serrana* was staged frequently, not because of a nationalist agenda but rather because its performance requirements were simple.[113] The opera starred Delfina Victor, a prominent actress/singer who was frequently recorded, and it was conducted by Luiz Filgueiras (1862–1929), a composer of operetta and *revista*.[114]

There was a tendency to create operettas with "national characteristics" in Portugal as early as 1864.[115] Nevertheless, the style of operettas by Portuguese playwrights and composers was varied and heterogeneous.[116] Moreover, the accumulation of roles by the same people was frequent in Lisbon's theatrical scene. Portuguese opera composers had steady jobs in institutions like the Real Conservatório de Lisboa or the Real Teatro de S. Carlos. Augusto Machado taught in the Conservatório and worked as *répétiteur* in the Real Teatro de S. Carlos, where he occupied a number of administrative positions.[117] Other theatrical composers were members of the orchestra of the S. Carlos, like Rio de Carvalho or Tomás del Negro.[118] In this sense, these people fall into the category of "integrated professionals" put forward by Howard Becker in his analysis of the "art worlds:"

> Integrated professionals have the technical abilities, social skills, and conceptual apparatus necessary to make it easy to make art. Because

---

[112] Tomaz Ribas, *O Teatro da Trindade*, 37.

[113] Raimundo, "Para uma leitura dramatúrgica e estilística de Serrana de Alfredo Keil," 227–274.

[114] *Illustração portugueza*, 5 April 1909, 425–430.

[115] Rebello, *O teatro naturalista e neo-romântico (1870–1910)*, 87–89.

[116] Luiz Francisco Rebello, "Opereta," in Salwa Castelo-Branco (ed.), *Enciclopédia da música em Portugal no século XX*, vol. 3 (Lisbon: Círculo de Leitores, 2010), 935–938.

[117] Benevides, *O Real Theatro de S. Carlos*, 325, Luísa Cymbron, "Machado, Augusto," *Grove Music Online*, ed. L. Macy,. <www.oxfordmusiconline.com>, accessed 5 November 2009.

[118] *O Occidente*, 20 November 1907, 255; Leonor Losa, "Joaquim Tomás del Negro," in Salwa Castelo-Branco (ed.), *Enciclopédia da música em Portugal no século XX*, vol. 3, 904.

they know, understand, and habitually use the conventions on which their world runs, they fit easily into all its standard activities.[119]

The idea of an articulated program for creating a national operetta is highly problematic due to the heterogeneity of this form. A foreign genre was nationalized and adapted differently throughout the last part of the 19th century. Nevertheless, a wider nationalist trend was emerging and musical theater played a key role in that process. Portuguese operettas started featuring characters or plots that were part of a shared memory. This is associated with a strategy by the impresarios to maximize profit, and was intensified with the rise of realism. Therefore, it resonates with the development of *zarzuela's genero chico* toward the end of the 19th century. The *genero chico* comprised short plays and was developed to suit the commercial needs of the theaters by allowing for several shows to be performed on the same day. With more than one session a day the box office profit could be increased. Moreover, the *genero chico* played a key role in Spanish nationalism because it relied on local characters and languages, as well as local music, like *seguidillas* or *jotas*. Thus,

> with the *genero chico*, *zarzuela* became mass consumer culture. In the 1890s, mass culture served the purpose of nationalism extremely well: a popular art form integrated people into the urban vision of the Spanish nation far better than elite forms had.[120]

This reveals the strong association between nationalism and realism. Indeed, the new forms of representation were central in presenting the vernacular in an aestheticized and sanitized form to urban theatergoers. Therefore, it shows the popular as an external low-other (the lower class) that raises both opposition and desire in bourgeois audiences.[121] Within this framework, *genero chico* aimed to realistically represent elements of Spain, and the music reinforced this association. Thus, the naturalization of the national bond through leisure is a characteristic of the Iberian countries at the end of the 19th century. However, they had significant differences, such as the strength of diverse regional identities in Spain that complicated a top-down version of nationalism emanating from Madrid. Therefore, the two countries followed a different path. The *zarzuela grande* of the 1850s and 1860s was an effort with nationalist underpinnings for Spanish composers to develop a local genre to compete with both Italian

---

[119] Howard S. Becker, *Art Worlds* (Berkeley: University of California Press, 2008), 229.
[120] Young, "Zarzuela," 199.
[121] Peter Stallybrass and Allon White, *The Poetics and Politics of Transgression* (Ithaca, NY: Cornell University Press, 1986), 193.

and French opera. Given its nationalist stance, it was perceived as a regional genre by the Portuguese audiences, who cherished a cultural affinity with the cosmopolitan Paris. The dominant show on Lisbon's stages was the musical revue, a spectacle that relied mostly on allegory and personification. Legal and economic constraints played a key role in the process, as well as the reliance of the *revista* in recent events. Because the *revista* accommodated a narrative that could be simultaneously local and cosmopolitan, staging patriotism took a particular form in the genre. This contrasts with the rise of realism, reflected in both opera and operetta.

The work of Augusto Machado is symptomatic of the intersection of styles and models that was Portuguese operetta. He set to music the adaptations of foreign librettos, like *O desgelo* or *A leitora da infanta* (premièred in the Teatro da Trindade in 1875 and 1893, respectively). This indicates the pervasiveness of imported models in the local scene. Nonetheless, Machado also wrote operettas with Portuguese subjects. *Maria da Fonte*, inspired by the mythical popular heroine associated with the revolt against Costa Cabral, premièred in the Teatro da Trindade in 1879.[122] He also created an operetta that was was inspired by motives from the Portuguese playwright Gil Vicente (1465–1537). *Tição negro* premièred in the Teatro da Avenida in 1902. Vicente was seen as the founding father of Portuguese theater, and staging an opera inspired in his style was a form of presenting local history and promoting "national" culture in a pleasurable context. The libretto was supplied by Henrique Lopes de Mendonça, an author then associated with the historical recovery of Portugal's past, who worked regularly with people like Alfredo Keil. Building a selective and nostalgic past that prized a purported golden era for Portugal (the Expansion) was part of a move that crystallized a populist discourse that is frequently revisited throughout Portuguese history.[123]

Moreover, Portuguese positivists played an important part in staging celebrations of the nation's greats as part of civic rituals. These public ceremonies were clearly inspired by Auguste Comte's Positivist Calendar (an alternative calendar based on secular humanism), and played an important role in encouraging nationalism.[124] In France, the centennials of the deaths of Rousseau and Voltaire in 1878 were commemorated as national feasts. They took place in the recently established Third Republic and were a way of associating the new regime with the revolutionary and enlightened ideals of the First Republic.[125]

---

[122] Augusto Machado, Maria da Fonte: Comédia em três actos, 1878. Shelfmark PTBN: A.M. 318, National Library of Portugal.

[123] Ernesto Laclau, *On Populist Reason* (London: Verso, 2007).

[124] Pierre Nora (ed.), *Les lieux de memoire*, vol. 1 (Paris: Gallimard, 1984).

[125] Jean-Marie Goulemot and Eric Walter, "Les centenaires de Voltaire et de Rousseau: Les deux lampions des lumières" in Nora, *Les lieux de memoire*, vol. 1, 381–420.

The French model was soon adapted to Portugal as the celebrations of the 300th anniversary of the death of Luís de Camões (1524–1580), the 500th anniversary of the Infante D. Henrique (1394–1460), and the 400th anniversary of Vasco da Gama's journey to India took place in 1880, in 1894, and 1898, respectively. Camões penned *Os Lusíadas*, an epic poem about the Portuguese voyages first published in 1572. D. Henrique is the son of King John I who played an important role in the Portuguese Expansion.[126]

When *Tição Negro* was staged, the periodical *Brasil-Portugal* dedicated three pages to the operetta. It published a very positive review of the piece, and complimented the librettist, the composer, the impresario (António de Sousa Bastos, whose activity will be discussed in more detail), and the performers. The periodical also published photographs of the operetta, and a voice and piano arrangement of "Alvorada."[127] Therefore, *Brasil-Portugal*, includes different products associated with the Portuguese theatrical circuit of that time: press review, photographs, and sheet music. Concerning sources, *Tição Negro* is an exception. We have access to the manuscript libretto, to the manuscript score, to a vocal and piano reduction, to the *coplas* (the printed lyrics of the sung parts), and to the sheet music of some extracts.[128] This contrasts with most works staged in the popular theater. There is a scarcity of sources for studying operettas and, especially *revistas*. Because the *revista* was first conceived as an annual review and comment on events of the recent past, the materials associated with its production were ephemeral. In popular music theater, most surviving sources are partial and consist of printed materials, especially *coplas* and sheet music. This renders the full reconstruction of a play impossible and led me to focus on understanding how these shows became part of the rituals of everyday life.

---

[126] Fernando Catroga, "Ritualizações da História," in Luís Reis Torgal, José Amado Mendes, and Fernando Catroga, *História da História em Portugal*, vol. 2 (Lisbon: Temas & Debates, 1998), 221–226.

[127] *Brasil-Portugal*, 1 February 1902, 391–393.

[128] Augusto Machado and Henrique Lopes de Mendonça, Tição negro: libreto, 1902. Shelfmark PTBN: A.M./C.5//96, National Library of Portugal, *Tição Negro*: orchestra, 1902. Shelfmark PTBN: A.M. 171, National Library of Portugal; *Tição negro: farça lyrica em três actos sobre motivos de Gil Vicente* (Lisbon: Neuparth & Carneiro, n.d.). Shelfmark PTBN: A.M. 348 A., National Library of Portugal; *Tição negro: farça lyrica em três actos sobre motivos de Gil Vicente* (Lisbon: Neuparth & Carneiro, [1902–1910]) [Alvorada, Ensalada]. Shelfmark PTBN: A.M. 383 A., National Library of Portugal; *Tição negro: farça lyrica em três actos sobre motivos de Gil Vicente* (Lisbon: Neuparth & Carneiro, [1902–1910]) [Coplas, Dueto]. Shelfmark PTBN: A.M. 287 A., National Library of Portugal; *Tição negro: farça lyrica em três actos sobre motivos de Gil Vicente* (Lisbon: Typ. Annuario Commercial, 1907).

It is possible to map recurrent topics in the Portuguese operettas of the time. However, these tendencies sometimes intermingle and overlap with each other. Some historic/literary plots were stories about important figures of Portuguese literature. This is the case of *Tição negro* and of *O poeta Bocage*. *O poeta Bocage* portrayed the life of the poet Manuel Maria Barbosa du Bocage (1765–1805). Its libretto was penned by Eduardo Fernandes (1870–1945) and the music was composed by Filipe Duarte (1855–1928). They were both prominent authors for the popular theater and the operetta premièred in the Teatro da Rua dos Condes on 22 October 1902.[129] An interesting example of the intersection between the historical and the popular is *Maria da Fonte*, mentioned above. The operetta by Augusto Machado narrated the story of the character who symbolized the popular revolt of 1846 against António Bernardo da Costa Cabral, (1803–1889).[130]

Some operettas concentrated on the "popular." In these cases, the staging of popular characters was essential for the plot, paralleling the *zarzuelas* of the *genero chico* of the late 19th century.[131] Therefore, the vernacular was adapted and staged to suit the taste of the audiences. However, unlike the *genero chico*, a significant number of Portuguese operettas have more than one act. The operetta *Intrigas no bairro*, by Luís de Araújo (1833–1908) and Eugénio Monteiro de Almeida (1826–1898) is a good example of this. The operetta premièred in the Teatro da Rua dos Condes on 24 October 1864, preceding by a few years the Lisbon premières of Offenbach's most successful operettas.[132] However, realism intensified the role played by the vernacular toward the end of the 19th century. This is illustrated by the operetta *A Severa*, a play that focuses on the urban low-other. Its plot was adapted from the play with the same name by Júlio Dantas (1876–1962) that premièred in the Teatro D. Amélia on 25 January 1901. The plot revolves around the real-life turbulent romantic involvement between the popular singer Maria Severa and Conde de Vimioso (the Count of Vimioso, renamed by Dantas as Conde de Marialva). Maria Severa Honofriana died "apoplectic and without sacraments" at twenty-six, and "enjoyed the maximum popularity in her life, the popularity of the brothel, that is, but her name was known to everyone, her voice envied by her companions, and her slang, original and picturesque, earned her the celebrity that

---

[129] Eduardo Fernandes, *O poeta Bocage: opereta em 3 actos* (Lisbon: Impr. Lucas, 1902).

[130] Câmara Municipal da Póvoa de Lanhoso (ed.), *História da coragem feita com o coração—Actas do congresso "Maria da Fonte—150 anos—1846/1996"* (Póvoa do Lanhoso: Câmara Municipal da Póvoa de Lanhoso, 1996).

[131] Lucy D. Harney, "Zarzuela and the Pastoral," *MLN*, 123/2 (2008), 252–273.

[132] Rebello, *O teatro naturalista e neo-romântico*, 87–88; Luís de Araújo, *Intrigas no bairro: paródia às óperas cómicas* (Lisbon: Livr. Económica de Domingos Fernandes, 1864).

lived until recently in the oral tradition."[133] The main characters were played by Ângela Pinto, described by her colleague Eduardo Brazão as "a madcap, but with an extraordinary talent," and Augusto Rosa.[134] Its narrative was based on a reconstruction in a vernacular setting, the district of Mouraria. Dantas uses the characteristic slang of Lisbon's popular characters to convey a realistic story. Moreover, to intensify this realism, the operetta uses fado frequently. This trait bears striking resemblance to contemporary Spanish *zarzuelas*, especially its *genero chico*, and reveals the parallels between the entertainment circuits of the two countries. [135]

In 2 January 1909, the operetta *A Severa* was staged in the Teatro Avenida. Its libretto by André Brun was set to music by Filipe Duarte, both integrated professionals in the theater. Duarte had studied violin, composition, and conducting in Lisbon's Conservatoire. Due to financial constraints, he performed with a group of ocarinas and began working in the popular theater, where he rose to popularity.[136] The protagonist of the operetta was played by Júlia Mendes (1885–1911), a famous performer who was associated with both fado and the popular stage. She started to sing as a child busker in Lisbon's streets and then worked in the theaters, where she became very popular. When she was at her peak Mendes had two fairground theaters bearing her name (in the Alcântara Fair and in the August Fair, in Parque Eduardo VII), where she performed.[137] *A Severa* received a positive review by *Ilustração portuguesa*, where the work of Dantas, Brun, and Duarte was complimented. The critic stated that Duarte's music "had moments of scintillating liveliness."[138] Furthermore, *Serões* highlighted the performance of Júlia Mendes and the "genuinely Portuguese" atmosphere of the play, reinforced by "parts of great melodiousness that honor the composer."[139]

The operetta is based on the original drama and scored for flutes, clarinets, oboe, bassoon, trumpets, French horns, trombones, timpani, percussion, violins violas, cellos, and double basses. After an instrumental overture, the

---

[133] Paróquia de Socorro: Livro de Registos de óbito 1833–1852, PT/ADLSB/PRQ/PLSB53/003/O10, 143v.; Luiz Augusto Palmeirim, *Os excentricos do meu tempo* (Lisbon: Imprensa Nacional, 1891), 285.

[134] Eduardo Brazão, *Memórias de Eduardo Brazão que seu filho compilou e Henrique Lopes de Mendonça prefacía* (Lisbon: Empresa da Revista de Teatro, 1925), 153.

[135] Júlio Dantas, *A Severa: drama em quatro actos* (Lisbon: M. Gomes, 1901).

[136] Rui Cabral Lopes, "Filipe Duarte," in Salwa Castelo-Branco (ed.), *Enciclopédia da música em Portugal no século XX*, vol. 2, 385.

[137] Hugo Silva, "Júlia Mendes," Salwa Castelo-Branco (ed.), *Enciclopédia da música em Portugal no século XX*, vol. 3, 769.

[138] *Illustração portugueza*, 15 February 1909, 208.

[139] *Serões*, March 1908, 255.

action starts in a *tasca* (cheap eatery) where the coach driver Timpanas, a popular character, finds the men singing "Life is two days/Let us search for some pleasures/to keep bother at bay/The wine, the gambling, and the women."[140] The focus on displays of masculinity is part of representing the vernacular. This is reinforced in the plot with a number of references to bullfighting made by aristocrats and by popular characters. Thus, fado, fairs, food, and bullfights played a key role in the loosening of class boundaries. This is reflected in the complicated romance between Marialva and A Severa (who carried "a knife in the garter").[141] The scandalous romance between a count and a woman of the people who was associated with a marginal lifestyle attracted the curiosity of bourgeois audiences and ends with her death. Music was used to convey more realism to the play. The first song of A Severa is a strophic fado that resembles the traditional *Fado menor*, a fado in minor mode with no fixed melody whose support is a repeated pattern that alternates tonic and dominant.[142] To reinforce the vernacular character of the operetta, its ninth number is a naturalist reconstruction of a fair where gypsies from Andalusia, itinerant merchants, and coach drivers interacted. In this setting, a blind busker sang. These marginal characters populated the imagination of the urban middle classes, and the fair was the place where people belonging to different social strata socialized.

> The bourgeoisie inherited, not just the symbolic terms of the old hierarchies, in the midst of which they had to carve out their own particular semantic sphere, but also the hierarchy of the places of production of those symbols, the court, the country house, the church on the one hand, and the marketplace, the tavern, and the fair on the other, each with its own rules governing interaction, the body and language.[143]

Finally, a pervasive feature in the Portuguese operettas is the satire of current matters and local customs. The plot of Alfredo Keil's operetta *Suzanna* revolves around a romantic couple and the girl's tutor.[144] The operetta was staged in the Teatro da Trindade in 1883 and, despite Keil's later effort to associate himself with a national music, *Suzanna* was set in Alsace, the homeland of the composer's mother, in 1815. *O brasileiro Pancrácio* was performed in the Teatro da Trindade in 1893 and depicted the return of a Portuguese who

---

[140] Filipe Duarte, *A Severa* [vocal score, uncataloged manuscript in the National Library of Portugal].

[141] Duarte, *A Severa* [vocal score].

[142] Filipe Duarte, *A Severa* [instrumental score, ff. 32v.–33r, and vocal score, uncataloged manuscripts in the National Library of Portugal].

[143] Stallybrass and White, *The Poetics and Politics of Transgression*, 195.

[144] *O Occidente*, 1 February 1883, 30.

became rich in Brazil. The libretto for this comedy of manners was written by Sá de Albergaria (1850–1921) and set to music by Freitas Gazul. The wealthy *brasileiro* (not the Brazilian, but the returning emigrant) became a stereotype in Portuguese everyday culture, a person whose richness was not reflected in cultural refinement.[145]

The theatrical exchange between Portugal and Brazil was very intense, and companies that performed operetta and *revista* circulated on both sides of the Atlantic. These tours of Portuguese companies in Brazil depended on local impresarios.[146] Furthermore, performers or technicians who worked and had risen to fame in Portugal traveled to Brazil where they further developed their careers.[147] The Spanish-born Pepa Ruiz (1859–1925) became a famous actress of operetta and *revista* in Portugal, and then moved to Brazil, where she participated in a large number of successful shows. Conversely, Brazilian plays and operettas were staged in Lisbon, sometimes with Brazilian artists. A good example of this is the operetta *Capital federal*, written by the playwright Arthur Azevedo (1855–1908) with most of the music supplied by Nicolino Milano (1876–1962). It was staged in Rio de Janeiro in 1897 and after a great deal of success in Brazil, *Capital federal* was premièred in the Teatro da Trindade in 1903.[148] The work was based on the Brazilian *revista O Tribofe* and caricatured the stereotypes of Rio de Janeiro's fin-de-siècle society. Its plot revolves around the family of a rich farmer that moved from Minas Gerais to Rio de Janeiro in search of their daughter's missing fiancée. Rio was then the federal capital of the Brazilian Republic that had been established recently, and the family came in contact with the developments introduced by modernization.[149] The music of the operetta incorporates local music genres that would later be disseminated by phonography, like the *lundu* and the *maxixe*. This indicates the adaptation of the cosmopolitan universe of the Parisian operetta to local audiences, an issue discussed above.[150]

---

[145] Maria da Conceição Meireles Pereira, "O brasileiro no teatro musicado português—duas operetas paradigmáticas," *População e sociedade*, 14–15/2 (2007), 163–179.

[146] Sousa Bastos, *Diccionario*, 41.

[147] Fernando Antonio Mencarelli, "A voz e a partitura: teatro musical, indústria e diversidade cultural no Rio de Janeiro (1868–1908)," Ph.D. thesis (Unicamp, 2003), 33–35,194–195.

[148] Pereira, "O brasileiro no teatro musicado português," 166; Larissa de Oliveira Neves, "As comédias de Artur Azevedo—em busca da história," Ph.D. thesis (Unicamp, 2006).

[149] Arthur de Azevedo, *A capital federal: opereta de costumes populares brasileiros* (Lisbon: Livraria Popular de Francisco Franco, n.d.).

[150] A. A. Bispo,"Luso-brasileirismo, ítalo-brasileiros e mecanismos performativos: representações teatrais e revistas: Nicolino Milano," *Revista Brasil-Europa* 107/3 (2007), http://www.revista.brasil-europa.eu/107/Nicolino-Milano.htm, accessed 12 November 2009.

A discussion about Portuguese operetta would not be complete without the works by the playwrights Gervásio Lobato (1850–1895) and D. João da Câmara (1852–1908), with music by Cyríaco de Cardoso (1846–1900).[151] Collaborative work was frequent in the popular theater:

> Operetta librettists frequently worked in teams, or even trios, as did many *vaudevillistes* in nineteenth-century France. If nothing else, several authors writing together would assuredly get the text written more quickly, in time for the composer to set it and for the manager to present it. In the highly competitive pre-radio and television era, speed was desirable.[152]

The trio wrote operettas that were frequently staged in Portuguese and Brazilian theaters from 1891. *O burro do Sr. Alcaide* was reviewed by some periodicals as a "fully national work" and as a "truly Portuguese operetta."[153] The play premièred in the Teatro da Avenida in 1891 and its action is set in the rural and coastal surroundings Lisbon in the late 18th century.[154] *O Ocidente*, where Lobato published his chronicles, stated that *O burro do Sr. Alcaide* was created by Portuguese people on Portuguese motifs with Portuguese music.[155] Moreover, the periodical argued that *O burro do Sr. Alcaide* did more to promote patriotism than the speeches of politicians. To reinforce its local character, it features popular characters, like the *saloia* (woman from the rural outskirts of Lisbon), the servant, or the fisherman. The overall positive reception of *O burro do Sr. Alcaide* illustrates the rekindling of the nationalist flame in the aftermath of the British Ultimatum of 1890. Nevertheless, *O burro do Sr. Alcaide* was described as a "kind of Portuguese *zarzuela*."[156] This may indicate the closeness of the work to a Spanish model, contrasting with the French cosmopolitan canon. It could also be a strategy of the journalist to give the readers a comparison they could relate to. Sousa Bastos contrasted *zarzuela* with French operetta by focusing on the use of local music in the former. Thus, Cardoso's music for *O burro do Sr. Alcaide* may explain this association. The local focus of the play was emphasized by Vieira, who stressed the distance between *O burro do Sr. Alcaide* and the "offenbachian obscenities" which were frequently performed in Lisbon's

---

[151] Rebello, *O teatro naturalista e neo-romântico*, 88.
[152] Traubner, *Operetta: A Theatrical History*, xiii.
[153] *O Occidente*, 11 September 1891, 203; *O António Maria*, 28 August 1891, 208.
[154] *O Occidente*, 10 January 1908, 6; Gervásio Lobato and D. João da Câmara, *O burro do senhor alcaide* (Lisbon: Livraria Popular de Francisco Franco, 1904).
[155] *O Occidente*, 11 September 1891, 203–204, 206.
[156] *O Occidente*, 11 September 1891, 206.

theaters.[157] In 1867 the actor Isidoro saw a performance of *La Grand-Duchésse de Gérolstein* in the Parisian Théâtre des Variétés. In his memoirs he recalled that the performers crossed "the limits of exaggeration ... and sometimes of licentiousness."[158] Thus, *O burro do Sr. Alcaide* was a play that respectable people could watch without feeling morally shocked.

Given that both *zarzuela* and French operetta are topical shows, why is the former seen as local and the latter as cosmopolitan? Many French operettas satirize Parisian everyday life in a way that Kracauer draws a parallel between them and the local newspapers by stating that "some of his operettas are merely the equivalent of music journalism."[159] Nevertheless, they were perceived as part of cosmopolitan entertainment. Thus, what is local in Paris becomes cosmopolitan to Portuguese audiences. This contrasts with Spanish *zarzuela*, a show whose topicality is always perceived as local. Maybe Spain is too close to Portugal for its everyday life to be received as cosmopolitan by the local audiences. It is clear that Paris represented the capital of entertainment, epitomizing cosmopolitan sophistication. The constant negotiation of boundaries between the local, the national, and the global levels is reflected in this confusion. Despite the ephemerality of the entertainment market, *O burro do Sr. Alcaide* had many performances and was frequently reprised in different theaters. Nevertheless, Fialho d'Almeida reviewed the operetta as "the most depressing evidence of the bestiality of our audiences, and of the subservience of the littérateurs to that low level of culture."[160] He chose to use *O burro do Sr. Alcaide* to criticize the Portuguese audiences and not the work's authors, who were catering to them.

The introduction of Act 2, "one of the most Portuguese of the entire play," and the following "popular song" were published as sheet music.[161] The song is performed in a dance that takes place in a beach in Oeiras, with fishermen and *saloias*. The song alternates two solo singers, a *saloia* and a fisherman, whose parts are interpolated by a choral refrain. Each character sings about things they are familiar with. Therefore, the dance is where vernacular characters with different lives share their experiences. The introduction and the popular song are based on an *ostinato* that stylizes popular dance and reinforces the character of the lyrics. The instrumental overture uses the *ostinato* pattern and is followed by a contrasting introduction that prepares the vocal part. This

---

[157] Vieira, *Diccionario biographico de musicos portuguezes*, vol.2, 422.

[158] Isidoro Sabino Ferreira, *Memorias do Actor Izidoro* (Lisbon: Imprensa de J.G. de Sousa Neves, 1876), 89.

[159] Kracauer, *Jacques Offenbach and the Paris of His Time*, 190.

[160] Fialho d'Almeida, *Vida Irónica* (Lisbon, Livraria Clássica Editora, 1914 [1892]), 337.

[161] *O Occidente*, 11 September 1891, 203; Cardoso, Lobato, Câmara, *O burro do Sr. Alcaide: ópera cómica: canções populares* (Lisbon: Lith. Da Rua das Flores [1890]).

Music example 2.1 Popular song from the beginning of Act 2 of *O solar dos Barrigas*. Cyriaco de Cardoso, Gervásio Lobato, and D. João da Câmara, *O burro do Sr. Alcaide: ópera cómica: canções populares* (Lisbon: Lith. R. das Flores, n.d.). Museu Nacional do Teatro.

music aims to emulate the form and the lyrics of the local vernacular songs. Thus, in *O burro do Sr. Alcaide* music reinforces the realism of the plot in a similar way that vernacular song is used in the *genero chico* of the *zarzuela*. Thus, a parallel between the Portuguese operetta and the *zarzuela* is understandable in this case.

The song has a verse-chorus form with a syllabic organization in which the refrain's melody contrasts with the verse. After seven repetitions, the instrumental introduction returns and gives way to a small coda. The long and repetitive character of many theatrical songs is well represented here. One has to be very careful in equating the sheet music with its orchestral counterpart. Nevertheless, given the utilitarian nature of this repertoire there are not many full manuscripts available and the sheet music provides a useful, yet simplified, resource.

Lobato, da Câmara, and Cardoso produced other stage works, like *O valete de copas, O solar dos Barrigas, Cócó, Reineta & Facada* (that was rewritten later as *Bibi & C.ª*),and *O testamento da velha*.[162] *O solar dos Barrigas* premièred on 4 September 1892 in the Teatro da Rua dos Condes, and *O António Maria* described it as a graceful work for which Cyriaco de Cardoso composed "fresh, popular, joyful" music.[163] As argued before, satirists sometimes associated

---

[162] *Cóco, Reineta & Facada* was unsuccessful, a factor that led to its reformulation. Vieira, *Diccionario biographico de musicos portuguezes*, vol.1, 423; Rebello, *O teatro naturalista e neo-romântico*, 88. For a review of the première of this play that reinforces this opinion see A *semana de Lisboa*, 9 April 1893, 119., *O Occidente*, 10 January 1908, 6, *O micróbio*, 18 August 1894, 49.

[163] *O António Maria*, 10 September 1892, 611–612.

Figure 2.2 Rafael Bordalo Pinheiro, Sessão agitada [caricature of an agitated session of the Portuguese Parliament as the *Solar dos barrigas*, in *O António Maria*, 29 January 1897, 6, Hemeroteca Municipal de Lisboa. An agitated session of the Portuguese Parliament.

operettas with Portuguese institutions. Thus, the expression *O solar dos Barrigas* (roughly translated as The Manor of the Bellies) was used to describe the Chambers of the Portuguese Parliament, especially after the elections of 1895. Figure 2.2 is a caricature by Bordalo Pinheiro of an agitated session in these houses.

O solar dos Barrigas featured groups of popular characters, like the *saloia* and the servant in a similar way as in *O burro do Sr. Alcaide*.[164] Nevertheless, and despite the association of its authors with a Portuguese operetta, one number of *O solar dos barrigas* consisted in a burlesque romantic duet in mock Italian.[165] The authors were clearly mocking Italian operatic conventions and their depiction of romantic couples.

To understand the way authors communicated with the audience I chose the *Duetto dos P.P.*, a song in P-language between Manuela and Ramiro.[166] P-language is a language game that obscures the understanding of the words by doubling all vowels, and inserting a 'p' between the doubled vowels. It is sung that way because they arrange to elope and do not want their conversation to be understood by others. After an instrumental introduction, the characters engage in a dialogue that is close to the spoken language, given the number of repeated notes. Moreover, the overall texture hints at a waltz-like character.

Then Ramiro puts forward his intention and they both sing the chorus in thirds and unisons. A short return to the initial dialogue form precedes the final chorus.

---

[164] D. João da Câmara and Gervásio Lobato, *O solar dos Barrigas* (Lisbon: Livraria Popular de Francisco Franco, n.d.), 3, 12.

[165] Câmara and Lobato, *O solar dos Barrigas*, 15–16.

[166] Cardoso, Lobato, Câmara, *O solar dos barrigas: Duetto dos P.P.* (n.p.: n.p., n.d.).

Music example 2.2 First part of Duetto dos PP from *O solar dos barrigas*. Ciríaco Cardoso, Gervásio Lobato and D. João da Câmara, "Duetto dos P.P." (n.p.: n.p., n.d.) Museu Nacional do Teatro, MNT: 36972.

In another play, *O valete de copas,* D. João da Câmara, Gervásio Lobato, and Cyriaco de Cardoso use a genre that was also cultivated in Portugal: the *mágica*. The plots of the *mágica* were associated with the supernatural, relied on illusionist apparatus, and disregarded veracity.[167] This genre was cultivated by people like Joaquim Augusto de Oliveira (1827–1904) or Eduardo Garrido and was frequently staged in Portugal and in Brazil.[168] However, Eça

---

[167] Sousa Bastos, *Diccionario*, 89.
[168] Vanda Freire, "Óperas e mágicas em teatros e salões do Rio de Janeiro e de Lisboa," in *Anais do XV Encontro Anual da ANPPOM* (Rio de Janeiro: UFRJ, 2005), 232–241.

Music example 2.3 Refrain of Duetto dos PP from *O solar dos barrigas*. Ciríaco Cardoso, Gervásio Lobato and D. João da Câmara, "Duetto dos P.P." (n.p.: n.p., n.d.) Museu Nacional do Teatro, MNT: 36972.

de Queirós described the *mágica* as "the fireworks of idiocy."[169] Apart from the *mágica*, the *comédia com música* (a comedy with a few musical numbers) was also successfully performed on Lisbon's stages.

A factor that influenced the success of the operettas mentioned above was the music by Cyriaco de Cardoso. Like most Portuguese operetta composers, Cardoso was deeply involved in the theatrical life of Porto, Lisbon, and Rio de Janeiro. Born in Porto, Cardoso gained prominence in the city's circuit as a cellist, conductor, and composer. After directing the orchestra of the Teatro de São João (Porto's most important theater), Cardoso created and managed an operetta company in the Teatro Baquet until the tragic events of 1888. On 20 March, around 120 people, including Cardoso's son, were killed in a fire that destroyed the theater. Until 1891 he directed an opera company in the Teatro de D. Afonso, having moved to Lisbon in the same year.[170] Cardoso premièred *O burro do Sr. Alcaide*, a work that boosted his popularity in the city's theatrical market and introduced him to the local audiences. During the theatrical

---

[169] Ortigão and Queirós, *As farpas*, 62.

[170] Vieira, *Diccionario biographico de musicos portuguezes*, vol.1, 420–424, and Sousa Bastos, *Diccionario*, 321.

season breaks, Cardoso traveled regularly to Brazil where he presented his works, following the practice of frequent circulation of theatrical companies and composers between both countries. According to Vieira, Cardoso composed exclusively "light music."[171]

The operetta *O fado* embodies important tendencies concerning nationalism in Portugal. Composed by Filipe Duarte, it was staged in the Teatro Apolo on 26 November 1910.[172] Because the republican regime renamed places that referenced the monarchy, the Teatro do Príncipe Real became the Teatro Apolo. The operetta *A Severa* had already been performed there the year before. Thus, the urban low-other was a ubiquitous presence in the music theater, and fado was used to mark it. The libretto was written by João Bastos (1883–1957) and Bento Faria (1875–1954), and the action takes place in mid-19th-century Lisbon. Because of its subject, the authors included a large number of popular characters, an aspect that was emphasized by the press. For instance, *A máscara* pointed out that the authors wanted to create a Portuguese operetta by choosing fado, "so Portuguese and so vibrant," as its main subject.[173] Nevertheless, the reviewers state that the libretto lacked fado's "lyricism and feeling," and that the plot was not good.[174] However, the music was praised as one of Duarte's best scores, despite his use of unnecessary repetitions.[175] Duarte was also criticized by his "mere transcription of certain popular tunes, without developing them or merging them in the overall score."[176] On the one hand, the direct use of popular fados was a marker of purported authenticity in a period when realism was prized. On the other hand, a composer was not a song collector. Thus, the reviewers saw the use of transcribed materials in a negative way at a time when realism was an important tendency. Vieira's comment on *O fado* contrasts with this review. He argued that Duarte "took as a subject the popular tune that gives the title to the play, and developed it with extreme skill to the audience's content."[177] Moreover, Vieira stated that Duarte was the most admired composer for the popular theater at the time of his writing, and prized his adaptability. Duarte was required to master the conventions of several genres because he was an integrated professional who "dedicated himself to a kind of popular music that was applied to popular plays with national subjects."[178]

---

[171] Vieira, *Diccionario biographico de musicos portuguezes*, vol.1, 420–424.
[172] Ernesto Vieira, *A musica em Portugal: resumo historico* (Lisbon: Clássica Editora, 1911), 44.
[173] *A mascara: arte, vida, theatro*, 11 April 1912, 178.
[174] *A mascara: arte, vida, theatro*, 11 April 1912, 178.
[175] *A mascara: arte, vida, theatro*, 11 April 1912, 179.
[176] *A mascara: arte, vida, theatro*, 11 April 1912, 179.
[177] Vieira, *A musica em Portugal*, 44.
[178] Vieira, *A musica em Portugal*, 44.

Music example 2.4 Start of "Fado do Colete Encarnado" from *O fado*. Filipe Duarte, "Fado do colete encarnado" (Lisbon: Neuparth & Carneiro, n.d.).

O fado is scored for piccolo, flutes, clarinets, oboe, bassoon, French horns, trumpets, trombones, timpani, percussion, violins, violas, cellos, and double basses.[179] It also requires an onstage sextet of two violins, viola, cello, double bass, and piano. The operetta includes the "Fado do colete encarnado," an example I have selected to show how popular repertoires are stylized in plays that focus on the vernacular.[180] The song begins with an instrumental introduction that is somewhere between the Portuguese guitar accompaniment the *Fado menor* mentioned above and the Alberti bass.

The fado is in an AB form with the A section in A minor and a B section is in A major. The lyrics refer to the Portuguese guitar and to an unsuccessful love where the female killed the singer's heart "with the dagger of betrayal." The A section has a chordal accompaniment that is repeated with two different lyrics, and then modulates to the B section. Moreover, it strives to mimic the fado singer's rhythmic flexibility over a steady accompaniment, a trait that was associated with the popular forms of the genre.

Section B contrasts with A in tonality, register, and texture. Its accompaniment is more dynamic and is closer to the Alberti bass. It ends with two bars

---

[179] Filipe Duarte, O fado [uncataloged manuscript in the National Library of Portugal].
[180] Filipe Duarte, "Fado do colete encarnado" (Lisbon: Neuparth & Carneiro, n.d.).

Music example 2.5 Refrain of "Fado do Colete Encarnado" from *O fado*. Filipe Duarte, "Fado do colete encarnado" (Lisbon: Neuparth & Carneiro, n.d.).

that emulate the Portuguese guitar again. Despite the reliance on repetition of theatrical songs, some of these songs present a strong contrast between sections.

Apart from the creative process, a central issue for the study of musical theater is staging. Because it is difficult to reconstruct it has been often overlooked, especially when popular genres are being examined. Nevertheless *Ilustração portuguesa* published a report called *O theatro por dentro* (The theater from the inside) in November 1908.[181] The articles described how a musical play was rehearsed and staged in the Teatro Avenida. They were written by André Brun and illustrated with Joshua Benoliel's photographs, and they constitute a valuable source for understanding the collaborative and complex process of performing musical theater in Lisbon. Thus, it is where the "art world" surfaces. For Becker, "art worlds consist of all people whose activities are necessary to the production of the characteristic works which that world, and perhaps others as well, define as art."[182] Disregarding the predominance of a discourse that separates art from entertainment, I will apply Becker's

---

[181] André Brun, "O theatro por dentro," *Illustração portugueza*, 2 November 1908, 20–28, 9 November 1908, 4–9.

[182] Becker, *Art Worlds*, 34.

theory of the art worlds to the popular music theater. The operetta and the *revista* were seen as entertainment, not art. Nevertheless, they share many similarities with theatrical genres that were perceived as art. Therefore, a value judgment of taste cannot be used to place the popular music theater outside the art world. Becker argues that "members of art worlds coordinate the activities by which work is produced by referring to a body of conventional understandings embodied in common practice and in frequently used artifacts."[183] Furthermore, "the same people often cooperate repeatedly, even routinely, in similar ways to produce similar works, so that we can think of an art world as an established network of cooperative links among participants."[184] Setting aside the value judgment that confers artistic status on a cultural product, this description clearly illustrates Lisbon's theatrical scene. A good example of this is the operettas by Gervásio Lobato, D. João da Câmara, and Ciríaco de Cardoso mentioned above.

The reportage follows the company of the Teatro Avenida during the preparation and staging of a play. The first sections present acting as a strenuous task and as a serious activity, detaching it from a bohemian lifestyle that is associated with some performers. Brun, himself starting what would be a successful playwrighting career, remarked that the audience only has access to the final stage of the complicated process of staging. A play begins with the author writing a text that was then rehearsed in sit-down readings. This progressed to blocking rehearsals and to walkthrough rehearsals. The maestro or *ensaiador de música* enters the picture after the performers have learned the text. He coaches the soloists and the chorus and, when they all know their parts, the ensemble rehearsals begin. These start at the piano but soon the performers will be accompanied by the orchestra. Figure 2.3 shows the company rehearsing a group number at the piano.

Then, only the rehearsals with sets and props and the dress rehearsal stand between the performers and the première. Brun described the nervous playwright standing behind the scenes and the small tweaks on the costumes and props when the play was first running. The audiences comprised the official critics (who always publish favorable reviews) and the unofficial critics (who always have a negative opinion that they express in the *botequim*—watering-hole). Benoliel's photographs add a visual aspect to the reportage by reproducing elements that were superficially dealt with by Brun, such as the dressing of the performers.[185]

---

[183] Becker, *Art Worlds*, 34.
[184] Becker, *Art Worlds*, 34–35.
[185] Brun, "O theatro por dentro," 2 November 1908, 20–28.

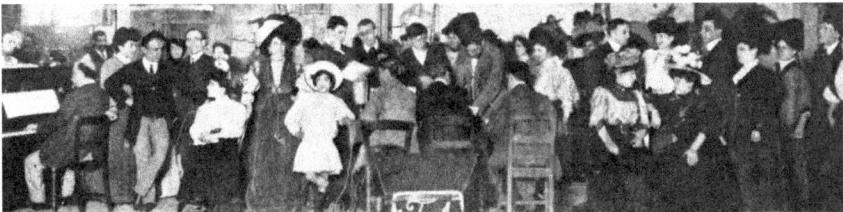

Figure 2.3 Joshua Benoliel, Um ensaio de junção, in *Illustração Portugueza*, 2 November 1908, 568, Hemeroteca Municipal de Lisboa. A group rehearsal in the Teatro Avenida.

Figure 2.4 Alberto Carlos Lima, Teatro Apolo—Bilheteira (previously Teatro do Príncipe Real), Lisbon, c.1910, Arquivo Fotográfico de Lisboa, Colecção Alberto Carlos Lima, PT/AMLSB/LIM/001096. The ticket office of the Teatro Apolo.

Brun also described the backstage, an area frequented by playwrights, scenographers, journalists, visitors, and admirers. The theater starts to get busy at half past seven in the evening, when the workers help the performers getting dressed in the dressing rooms. The actors, chorus girls, and extras arrive and begin dressing and putting on their makeup. At the same time, the technical staff corrects small problems and the orchestra tunes the instruments. After the last call, the *borlistas* (people who wanted free tickets) run to the ticket box to see if they can get in, and the performance starts. Figure 2.4 is a photograph of the hall of the Teatro do Príncipe Real (later Teatro Apolo) in the beginning of the 20th century, where the ticket office and a tobacconist were situated. In addition to cigars and cigarettes, the tobacconist sold newspapers, the *coplas* of the play, and tickets for the benefit shows of every theater, and rented binoculars. This illustrates the symbiotic relation between these stalls and the theater, which indicates that an articulated leisure market was in place at the time. Brun then described the backstage bustle during the performance, with the fast costume changes or the ongoing activity of the stage technicians. After the play finishes, the stage is cleaned, the performers leave their dressing rooms, and the theater is closed for the day. The reportage ends with the journalist's satirical take on badmouthing, an activity that he portrays as dear to the Portuguese people, and dearer to the Portuguese actors, whose backstage intrigues are also part of staging a play.[186]

An Archive on Popular Modernity: The Revue Theater and "The Nation"

The *revista* contrasts with opera, operetta, and *zarzuela* because it is structured in closed and heterogeneous numbers instead of having a narrative plot. It is "a topical, satirical show consisting of a series of scenes and episodes, usually having a central theme but not a dramatic plot, with spoken verse and prose, sketches, songs, dances, ballet and speciality acts."[187] Contrary to other genres, the *revista* does not have realistic intents and has an epic structure.[188] These plays comment on current events and are divided into unrelated sketches (*quadros*), which are linked by the *compère*. The *compère* is an always-on-stage character who comments on and links the sketches, creating a direct rapport with the audience. A discontinuous structure and the prevalence of allegorical and personified characters make the *revista* quite different from the naturalist theater of Lisbon.

The coexistence of realist and nonrealistic theatrical genres is an important characteristic of Lisbon's theatrical market. Plays by Ibsen or Strindberg had been staged by local and foreign companies since the 1870s.[189] Moreover, after the Lisbon performances of André Antoine (1858–1943) in 1903, two Portuguese companies were formed. The Teatro Livre (a direct translation from

---

[186] Brun, "O theatro por dentro," 9 November 1908, 4–9.

[187] Andrew Lamb, et al., "Revue," *Grove Music Online*, ed. L. Macy, <www.**oxfordmusiconline**.com>, accessed 5 December 2009. For an overview of the genre in Portugal during this period see Vítor Pavão dos Santos, *A revista à portuguesa* (Lisbon: O Jornal, 1978), 11–27.

[188] Luiz Francisco Rebello, *História do teatro de revista em Portugal*, vol. 1 (Lisbon: Publicações D. Quixote, 1984), 25. Rebello states that a few *revistas* had a plot, but they were rare.

[189] Rebello, *O teatro naturalista e neo-romântico*, 41–42.

the French name) and the Teatro Moderno (Modern Theater, a dissident group from the Teatro Livre) were inspired by his Théâtre Libre, which related realism and naturalism.[190] Like most theatrical ventures in Lisbon, these companies were precarious and only lasted for a few seasons. Naturalism and historicism were important tendencies for Portuguese theaters even when the allegorical *revista* was dominant. The importance of the naturalist paradigms in the local market is also reflected in the Real Teatro de S. Carlos, where *verismo* operas and Wagner's music were frequently staged. Although Wagner's works were not directly associated with naturalism, they relied heavily on illusionist stage apparatuses to realistically deliver their content, raising technical issues when performed in an Italian horseshoe-shaped theater like Lisbon's Real Teatro de S. Carlos. Nevertheless, a binary interpretation that places realism on one side and fantasy on the other is misleading given the success of the *mágica* and of the *revista*. The fragmentary and unrealistic features of the *revista* were a symptom of modernity and one of its major strengths. Its plasticity allowed the genre to rapidly incorporate the present (situations, characters, music, choreography, and visual presentation). Because it was based on current events, being able to rapidly incorporate the new was essential in the *revista*. Moreover, the genre was initially based on ephemerality and relied on current satire to be commercially successful. A precarious venture had to be in synch with modern society to stay afloat in a competing market. Therefore, accommodating rapid changes became a survival strategy for the *revista*. This is illustrated in the *revista Ó da guarda*. The play was a major success and was performed more than 250 times in the Teatro do Príncipe Real.[191] Its text was penned by Luiz Galhardo and Barbosa Junior, and set to music by Filipe Duarte and Luiz Filgueiras. For the critics of the magazine *Brasil-Portugal* the success of the *revista* was due to the continuous updating of its numbers by the authors who "are careful not to let their famous and beloved daughter age."[192] Moreover, a silent film was screened during the intermission of *Ó da guarda*. This was one of the earliest Portuguese narrative films. The film *O rapto de uma actriz* (The Abduction of an Actress) features the performers of *Ó da guarda* and its plot was associated with the *revista*. It follows the quest to find Lucinda do Carmo, who was taken from the theater. After a series of events that involved the police, the actress is returned to the theater, the curtain rises and the *revista* carries on.[193] Thus, the film was

---

[190] Rebello, *O teatro naturalista e neo-romântico*, 75–79.
[191] Sousa Bastos, *Diccionario*, 137–138.
[192] *Brasil-Portugal*, 1 October 1907, 272.
[193] Manuel Deniz Silva, "Música e cinema: 1 Do início do cinema à introdução do "sonoro" (18961930)," in Salwa Castelo-Branco (ed.), *Enciclopédia da música em Portugal no século XX*, vol. 3, 841.

devised to be a part of the narrative plot of the *revista*. Unfortunately *O rapto de uma actriz* has been lost.

The revue was imported from France in the middle of the 19th century and it commented on topical issues of the previous year.[194] Thus, it was a satirical review of recent events. The first Portuguese *revista* (*Lisboa em 1850*) was staged in the Teatro do Ginásio on 11 January 1851. Its authors were Francisco Palha and Latino Coelho (1825–1891). Palha would become the manager of the Teatro da Rua dos Condes and of the Teatro da Trindade, and Coelho, then a young officer, was on track to become a prominent intellectual.[195] The *revista* was predominantly staged in the Teatro do Ginásio during the 1850s. Its company performed important plays such as *O festejo dum noivado, Fossilismo e progresso* or *Os melhoramentos materiais* (in 1852, 1856, and 1860, respectively).[196] Because of the success of the genre, the Teatro da Rua dos Condes, the Teatro das Variedades, and the Teatro de D. Fernando also started to stage *revistas*.[197] The predominant strategy of the *revista* was to personify "even the most abstract things."[198] Therefore, its sketches relied on allegory and stereotypes. It also used metonymy in the narrative, so some characters stood for larger groups, condensing their traits in a satirical form. The process through which these characters were created reflected the fragmentary nature of reality, placing the *revista* as an important spectator of urban modern life. However, personifying or allegorizing characters was neither straightforward nor homogeneous and drew from different materials. Also, the *revista* relied frequently on stock characters such as policemen, maids, or members of parliament. Because of its fragmentary and modern nature, "the revue theater was to serve the new order as an important proving ground where the composite image of the New Japan [Portugal] could be crafted, displayed, and naturalized."[199] This is not to force a strict parallel between Portugal and Japan but to trace a relationship between revue theater and nationalism in both countries, illustrating the role played by popular entertainment in crafting a modern nation. Since nations

---

[194] Luiz Francisco Rebello, "Teatro de revista," in Salwa Castelo-Branco (ed.), *Enciclopédia da música em Portugal no século XX*, vol. 4, 1248–1253.

[195] Rebello, *História do teatro de revista em Portugal*, vol. 1, 55–56.

[196] Rebello, *História do teatro de revista em Portugal*, vol. 1, 231. See Manuel Roussado, *Fossilismo e progresso: revista* (Lisbon: Typographia Rua da Condessa nº3, 1856).

[197] For example, the *Revista do anno de 1859* premièred on 2 January 1860 in the Teatro da Rua dos Condes. Pedro Carlos d'Alcantara Chaves, *Revista do anno de 1859: scena com pretenções a comica e adubada com alguma musica original* (Lisbon: Viuva Marques & Silva, [1860]).

[198] Sousa Bastos, *Diccionario*,128.

[199] Jennifer Robertson, *Takarazuka: Sexual Politics and Popular Culture in Modern Japan* (Berkeley: University of California Press, 1998), 116.

are heterogeneous, a genre that fed on this heterogeneity became a site for promoting nationalism.

Fossilismo e progresso is a good example of how the narrative strategies of the *revista* worked. Moreover, it is one of the few plays whose full text is available to us.[200] Later *revistas* were printed partially, focusing on the sung *coplas*. *Fossilismo e progresso* premièred in the Teatro Ginásio in 1856 and its plot revolves around The Year 1855 and The Year 1856. They are both personified and become important characters in the *revista*. With the agreement of The Year 1855, the character Fossilism arranges the marriage of The Year 1856 with the Princesa Sensaboria (Princess Blandness). However, the character Progress aims to prevent this union and uses several tricks to do so. Nevertheless, his efforts are pointless and The Year 1856 rules with the Princesa Sensaboria after the death of The Year 1855. This story is interpolated with parallel narratives on current matters, like Lisbon's theatrical life or the tobacco monopoly. It is set in Lisbon, and some sketches feature popular characters of the city, like shoeshiners or peddlers, whose cries are used to convey realism to the action. Thus, an interesting relationship between allegory and realism is in place in the *revista*. Portugal is personified in the play as an old man who lives in the past and is afflicted with rheumatism. Thus, by choosing to marry the daughter of Fossilism, The Year 1856 delays the country's modernization and Progress has to wait for another year. The play uses satire to criticize the conservatism and backwardness of Portuguese society. Thus, comedy was a way of delivering a current message, and the mantra of the Regeneração revolved around progress and modernization. The company featured performers who would become prominent, like Taborda and Isidoro, and its music was adapted from the operas performed in the previous season of the Real Teatro de S. Carlos season by the composer Joaquim Casimiro Júnior (1808–1862).[201] Thus, the impresarios relied on music that was already known to the audience; a strategy that would soon change as original music became an important part of the show.

The *Revista de 1858* is also a good example of the early stage of the genre.[202] It was written by Joaquim Augusto de Oliveira and premièred in the Teatro Avenida on 1 February 1859.[203] The actor Isidoro was responsible for the *mise-en-scène* and, like *Fossilismo e progresso*, the music was adapted from recently

---

[200] Manuel Roussado, *Fossilismo e progresso: revista* (Lisbon: Typographia Rua da Condessa nº3, 1856).

[201] Isabel Gonçalves, "A música teatral na Lisboa de oitocentos: uma abordagem através da obra de Joaquim Casimiro Júnior (1808–1862)," Ph.D. thesis (Universidade Nova de Lisboa, 2012), 156.

[202] Joaquim Augusto de Oliveira, *Revista de 1858: em dois actos e dez quadros* (Lisboa: Escriptorio do Teatro Moderno, 1859).

[203] Oliveira, *Revista de 1858*, 4.

staged operas by Joaquim Casimiro Júnior. This reinforces the pervasiveness of opera in Lisbon and its adjustment to suit the needs of the popular stage. The prologue of the *revista* is set in Olympus, where the Roman gods are judging Lisbon, the main character of the play. The personified city then interacts with characters like the Provinces (revealing an opposition between the capital and the rest of the country), Commerce, and the Comet, who was sent by the gods. The three "theaters for laughing" in Lisbon are personified in a sketch, the Teatro Ginásio, the Teatro da Rua dos Condes, and the Teatro Variedades.[204] After a series of events, including a ghost hunt by the police, the Comet decides to stay in Lisbon instead of returning to Olympus, and the final apotheosis is a living tableau with Fame in its center.[205]

The "composite image" of Portuguese (mostly) urban society included, absorbed and metabolized everyday life, and translated it into an imaginary world whose tropes were recurrently revisited by the playwrights and composers. This created a set of shared conventions that were frequently staged in Lisbon. Moreover, the heterogeneity of its characters reflected the complexity of modern life. These could be events, laws, newspapers, musical genres, cities and regions, and so-called popular characters (paperboys, policemen, or *fadistas*). The *revista* also relied on theatrical activity, pointing to a certain degree of self-reference. For example, *Formigas e formigueiros* included a sketch in which the couplet, the scenery, and the *revista* were personified.[206] Furthermore, the *revista* included characters who were already known to the audience through other media. For example, Rafael Bordalo Pinheiro created Zé Povinho, a caricature that personified the Portuguese people. The character was introduced in 1875 in the newspaper *A lanterna mágica*. Later, Zé Povinho became part of several *revistas*. Other sources of imagery were Classic mythology, represented in the *Revista de 1858*, and exotic places. This imagery was a vehicle for the set and costume designers to create spectacular effects that complemented the text and the music of the plays to attract the audience. Therefore, the visual arts were also central in the theater, and prominent artists worked for the popular theater.

The impresario and playwright António de Sousa Bastos (1844–1911) transformed the *revista* from the 1870s onward. Bastos dominated the theatrical market in the last quarter of the 19th century, staging operettas and *revistas* in Portuguese and Brazilian theaters.[207] Additionally, he developed a model

---

[204] Oliveira, *Revista de 1858*, 67–68.

[205] Oliveira, *Revista de 1858*, 72.

[206] Eduardo Schwalbach, *Formigas e formigueiros: revista de costumes e acontecimentos em 3 actos e 9 quadros* (Lisbon: Livraria Popular de Francisco Franco, n.d.), 5–6.

[207] Rebello, *História do teatro de revista em Portugal*, vol. 1, 95–111.

that would prevail for a long period.[208] Apart from these activities, he wrote several works on Portuguese theater and created and wrote in periodicals like *O palco: hebdomário theatral*, *A arte dramática: folha instructiva, critica, e noticiosa* (1875–1878), and *Tim tim por tim tim: assumptos theatrais* (1889–1893). With these activities he was able to use the press to efficiently promote the plays he staged. This shows the diverse roles played by people in the Portuguese cultural market. The same individual could perform in the Real Teatro de S. Carlos, compose for the popular theater, and direct amateur *bandas*. The transformations of the *revista* undertaken by Sousa Bastos promoted actors/singers who eventually became icons of the musical theater of the time, like Pepa Ruiz and Palmira Bastos. Moreover, he hired prominent visual artists to create his stage sets and costumes, improving a profitable entertainment product.[209] Starting with *Coisas e loisas de 1869*, his successful activity spanned both sides of the Atlantic until his death. Nevertheless, his career had the ups and downs that were characteristic of a precarious market. Some of his most significant works were *Tim tim por tim tim* (a play that, according to Fialho d'Almeida had a tremendous success, 1889),[210] *Tam-Tam* (1891), *Fim de século* (1891),[211] *Sal e Pimenta* (1894),[212] *Em pratos limpos* (1897),[213] and *Talvez te escreva! . . .* (1901).[214] *Fim de século*, staged in Teatro da Rua dos Condes, was positively reviewed:

> The annual *revista* . . . deserves the most golden, the most enameled, the most complementary adjectives. Sprinkled with joy and lively grace, without filth in the dialogues and—a treat to the eyes!—picturesquely decorated and splendidly dressed. Certain passages, because of the liveliness of the wardrobe, of the brilliance of the props, of the turbulence of the music, and of the scenic disposition create the most surprising and unpredictable effect.[215]

---

[208] Roberto Ruiz, *O teatro de revista no Brasil: do início à I Guerra Mundial* (Rio de Janeiro: Ministério da Cultura, Instituto Nacional de Artes Cênicas, 1988).

[209] Rebello, *História do teatro de revista em Portugal*, vol. 1, 75.

[210] Fialho d'Almeida, *Actores e autores* (Lisbon: Livraria Clássica Editora, 1925), 85.

[211] *O António Maria*, 26 February 1892, 389–390.

[212] *O António Maria*, 17 September 1894, 79; Sousa Bastos, *Sal e pimenta: revista phantastica em 3 actos e 11 quadros* (Lisbon: Livraria Popular de Francisco Franco, n.d.).

[213] Sousa Bastos, *Em pratos limpos: revista do anno de 1896* (Lisbon: Costa Sanches, 1897).

[214] Sousa Bastos, *Talvez te escreva! . : revista em 3 actos e 12 quadros* (Lisbon: n.p., n.d.), and Rebello, *História do teatro de revista em Portugal*, vol. 1, 235. Concerning Sousa Bastos' entrepreneurial activity in Brazil see Fernando Antonio Mencarelli, "A voz e a partitura: teatro musical, indústria e diversidade cultural no Rio de Janeiro (1868–1908)," Ph.D. diss. (Unicamp, 2003), 132–137.

[215] *O António Maria*, 26 February 1892, 389–390.

This reveals the multidimensional world of the *revista*, a play that includes text, sets, props, wardrobes, music, and performers. It also points to the importance for the audience of the visual and auditory effects. Not all reviews of *revistas* are this complimentary, and many criticize the genre because its texts lacked literary value. Because the *revista* was a topical show, its texts were of the moment and not perceived as literary works.[216] Therefore, their negative reviews indicate a fundamental issue in the analysis of popular entertainment in the 19th century, the carving of a rift between art and entertainment. Nonetheless, the competence of the playwright Eduardo Schwalbach (1860–1946) was praised by the actor Augusto Rosa.[217] Schwalbach created an apparently homogeneous narrative from heterogeneous elements, a vital quality when writing for the theater, but especially for the *revista*, due to its diversity. Rosa's colleague Eduardo Brazão also praised Schwalbach's "pages of observation and irony, loose pages of a light and graceful humor."[218] In other cases, the success of the *revistas* was associated with its performers. The periodical *O António Maria* argued that *Em pratos limpos*, a revue staged in Teatro da Trindade, was successful because of its "spicy wit," of the performance of Palmira Bastos, who played a "variety of types," and of Rosa Vignon's proficiency in the *maxixe*, an Afro-Brazilian ballroom dance that was in fashion in the late 1800s and early 1900s.[219]

The *revista* was frequently presented as a minor theatrical genre in the reviews. Madureira pointed out that the intentions of the company of the 1903 *revista Beijos de burro* in the Teatro do Rato were not to rise to immortality, nor did its playwrights aim for the literary academy.[220] Its text was penned by Eduardo Fernandes (1870–1945) and Cruz Moreira (1862–1930), and the music was composed by Manuel Benjamim (1850–1933). Nevertheless, Madureira claims that the three acts of the play were "light, gracious, buzzing, and picturesque."[221] This contrasts with the company's lack of resources and with the unpretentiousness of the authors, as he also argued. The review states that *Beijos de burro* had "sufficient raciness to dispense with the reduction of the wardrobe," and that "with more vivacious music and less text in the first *quadro*" the play could become a model for a tired genre.[222] Furthermore,

---

[216] d'Almeida, *Actores*, 68–69; Sousa Bastos, *Diccionario*, 128.

[217] Augusto Rosa, *Recordações da scena e de fóra da scena* (Lisbon: Livraria Ferreira, 1915), 314.

[218] Eduardo Brazão, *Memórias de Eduardo Brazão*, 246.

[219] *O António Maria*, 20 May 1897, 5.

[220] Joaquim Madureira, *Impressões de theatro* (Lisbon: Ferreira & Oliveira, L.da, Editores, 1905), 358–359.

[221] Madureira, *Impressões de theatro*, 358–359.

[222] Madureira, *Impressões de theatro*, 358–359.

Madureira stated that most *revistas* "lowered to the mass grave of vulgar obscenity, or deteriorated in the pretentiousness of the flashy *mágica*" when they did not rely on politics or on personal caricature.[223] Most reviews give prominence to the text, to the performers, and to the visual aspects of the show. However, they tend to mention music in passing. This is because most journalists did not have musical training and had literary inclinations. Moreover, given the multimedia aspects of the *revista* the music was just another aspect of the spectacle. Nonetheless, these reviews are the first examples of popular music criticism in Portugal and show the development of a consumer culture under the sway of modern life.

The *revista Viagem à roda da Parvónia* was staged when Sousa Bastos dominated the theatrical circuit.[224] However, it contrasted with most *revistas*. It was described by Fialho d'Almeida as the "most literary and coherent of the Portuguese *revistas*" but also as a political pamphlet and not a theatrical play, a fact that helps us understand its interdiction after the première.[225] The play was written by Gil Vaz, the pseudonym of the poets Guilherme de Azevedo and Guerra Junqueiro, and performed in the Teatro do Ginásio in 1879. For the authorities, the *Viagem* attacked public morality, and the audience showed their disapproval of the play by stamping their feet.[226] However, Azevedo points to different reasons for the dismissal of the play. He argues that Portugal had been living in an "offenbachian regime" for fifteen years, both in politics and in the theater, and pointed out that the lack of a sophisticated stage apparatus made the satire seem bare.[227] Part of the audience "thought that it had paid too much to see too few legs," and took part in the general negative reaction by breaking the nearest benches.[228] Nevertheless, it should be noted that the full interdiction of a play was an extreme case. Despite the interdiction of the performances, its text was published "where the audience cannot stamp."[229] The republican inclinations of the authors could have fueled their reactions. At the time, republicanism was a small movement, and had elected its first members of parliament in 1878. Notwithstanding the republican association of the authors, political satire was not a monopoly of republicans. It was a pervasive

---

[223] Madureira, *Impressões de theatro*, 359.

[224] Guerra Junqueiro and Guilherme d'Azevedo, *Viagem à roda da Parvónia: relatorio em 4 actos e 6 quadros* (Lisbon: Off. Typ. da Empreza Litteraria de Lisboa, 1879).

[225] d'Almeida, *Actores*, 72–73.

[226] d'Azevedo, *Viagem à roda da Parvónia*, 11–12.

[227] d'Azevedo, *Viagem à roda da Parvónia*, 12–14.

[228] d'Azevedo, *Viagem à roda da Parvónia*, 15.

[229] Rebello, *História do teatro de revista em Portugal*, vol. 1, 80–81; d'Azevedo, *Viagem à roda da Parvónia*, 15.

trait of the *revista* and often present in this theatrical genre. Furthermore, the circulation of ideas of political transformation was frequent in the last years of the Constitutional Monarchy, recommending reforming the system or overthrowing it.[230] "New life was, and still is, the cry with one voice of all the living forces of the nation."[231]

An important restriction was imposed on the theater toward the end of the 19th century. In 1890, Minister of Justice Lopo Vaz issued a law that restricted the freedom of the press and prohibited personal caricature.[232] This law was published on 7 April 1890, following the turmoil of the British Ultimatum, and imposed heavy constraints on theatrical writers.[233] This law was passed when the popular theater in Lisbon was dominated by Sousa Bastos. Nevertheless, the *revista* thrived in the end of the 19th century, when plays by António de Meneses and by Francisco Jacobetty were successfully performed in Lisbon. The highlighting by Fialho d'Almeida of these new constraints points to the dominance of the burlesque caricature of individuals in the early *revistas*. Furthermore, he states that the limits imposed by this new law increased the reliance of its authors on "obscenities" and in spectacular stage apparatuses.[234] In spite of the restriction, the *revista* continued to include political satire in its sketches. On several occasions, people like João Franco were mentioned or portrayed indirectly. Nevertheless the genre was transformed as a consequence of this law, and started to privilege the critique of current matters and of social habits.[235] Thus, the so-called *revista de costumes* was a sanitized form of entertainment when compared with earlier examples of the genre. Nevertheless, comment on the ephemeral remained an important aspect of the *revista*. For example, a sketch about the Press Law of 11 April 1907 was part of the *revista P'rá frente*, premièred in the Teatro Avenida the same year. In this sketch, four newspapers (*O mundo*, *A vanguarda*, *O paiz*, and *A lucta*) were personified and complained about the law.[236] The same play includes a character named Boato (Rumor), who mentioned satirically the possibility of a republican revolution and alluded to a Zé Bacoco. Zé Bacoco was the nickname of José Luciano de Castro, head of the Progressive Party and several times head of government. This was not a direct reference to a person but was made in a way that the audience could easily

---

[230] Rui Ramos, *D. Carlos (1863–1908)* (Lisbon: Círculo de Leitores, 2006).

[231] Teixeira Bastos, *A crise: estudo sobre a situação política, financeira, económica e moral da nação* (Porto: Livr. Chardon, 1894), 112.

[232] Rebello, *O teatro naturalista e neo-romântico*, 94.

[233] d'Almeida, *Actores*, 81.

[234] Joaquim Madureira, *Impressões de theatro*, 359.

[235] Joaquim Madureira, *Impressões de theatro*, 359.

[236] Garcia and Costa, *P'rá frente: revista em 3 actos e 12 quadros* (Lisbon: Impr. Lucas, 1907), 11.

identify, showing the complex relation between laws and their enforcing.[237] *Ó da guarda* is a good example of the kind of satire directed at João Franco's government. The *revista* criticizes the government's reformist intentions, claiming that the outrage persisted. It also personified the monopolies that thrived by preying on the ignorant individual who "eats poorly, is ill-served and pays a lot."[238] A sketch shows a chorus of snitches who gather information and beat people up, even the "liberal bloc," with "tenderness, affection, and lots of love."[239] Furthermore, it satirizes progress and caricatures João Franco as the character Mexias who wants to put "everything in a dictatorship" for he is "very liberal."[240] Mexias is a phonetic corruption of Messiah in João Franco's accent, making him more recognizable to the audience.

In the last third of the 19th century, the *revista* had developed from a commentary on the previous year that was staged for a short period to a genre that was performed throughout the season. For example, the *revista* of 1884 *O micróbio* had more than 200 performances in the Teatro Chalet da Rua dos Condes. Rio de Carvalho set to music a text by Francisco Jacobetty and some of its numbers were published as sheet music.[241] Thus, Jacobetty could "rejoice for taking the entire Lisbon to the little theater Chalet of Avenida to see *O Micróbio*, and that for six months you could hear nothing but 'Tenho um cavaquinho/que me ganha o pão ...' in the squares and markets."[242] These lyrics belong to *Tenho um cavaquinho*, a song from the *revista* that was published as sheet music.[243] Extracting the song in sheet music form allowed its wide circulation in Lisbon, especially in the household parlor. One edition of sheet music is very interesting because it consists of a piano reduction of some numbers of the *revista* by its composer, Rio de Carvalho. Therefore, it points to the multiple roles theatrical composers had to perform and to the publisher's reliance on a repertoire that was already successful.

Jacobetty's adaptation of *La gran via* was performed in the Teatro Chalet do Rato in 1887.[244] It was based on the Spanish *revista* by Federico Chueca and Joaquín Valverde that had a huge success in Madrid in 1886. The Portuguese version was extremely successful, "dragging entire Lisbon to the Teatro do

---

[237] Garcia and Costa, *P'rá frente*, 7–8.

[238] Luís d'Aquino, Barbosa Júnior, and Filipe Duarte, *Coplas da revista Ó da guarda: em 3 actos e 12 quadros* (Lisbon: A Liberal, 1907), 9. 12.

[239] Aquino, Barbosa Júnior, and Duarte, *Coplas da revista Ó da guarda*, 15.

[240] Aquino, Barbosa Júnior, and Duarte, *Coplas da revista Ó da guarda*, 15.

[241] Rebello, *História do teatro de revista em Portugal*, vol. 1, 175.

[242] Júlio César Machado, "Jacobetty," in *Diário de Notícias*, 6 June 1889, 1.

[243] Francisco Jacobettty, Rio de Carvalho, *O Micróbio, musicas das coplas mais applaudidas: Tenho um cavaquinho, Tra la la* (Lisbon: Lith. Rua das Flores, n.d.).

[244] Sousa Bastos, *Carteira do artista*, 408.

Rato."[245] Contrary to the *zarzuela*, adapting a Spanish *revista* to the Portuguese stage was not frequent, given the local particularities of a genre that comments on current events. *La gran via* is a satirical take on the new urban developments in Madrid. These developments had a parallel in Lisbon's Avenida da Liberdade. Thus, Spanish and Portuguese authors staged the transformation of both Iberian capitals. Despite his work's structure in sketches, Sousa Bastos never uses the term *"revista"* when writing about *A grande avenida*. He prefers to call it a *"zarzuela* of mores."[246] This is probably because of the strong association between Spain and *zarzuela* in Lisbon's entertainment market.

The *revista* comprised both ephemerality and stability, as *Tim tim por tim tim* illustrates. This play was written by Sousa Bastos and set to music by Plácido Stichini. It premièred in the Teatro da Rua dos Condes in 1889 and was reviewed as a "good-humored composition, where the laughter bursts out, among allusions and gibes, that are lively, yet far from the obscene, matching the prudery of good society."[247] According to its author, *Tim tim por tim tim* was performed 109 times before packed houses, and was successfully reprised in other theaters in the following years.[248] The commercial success of the *revista* relied on its ability to remain pertinent. Because the genre commented on ephemeral events, the plays had to be updated. This displays a complex relation between ephemerality and fixedness that surfaced in the period when the *revista* became dominant.[249] A new act had to be created when *Tim tim por tim tim* was reprised in the Teatro da Avenida in 1890.[250] The following year the play was presented in the Teatro da Rua dos Condes. Thus, *Tim tim por tim tim* was "modernized and modified to suit the needs of 1891."[251] These transformations aimed to keep the "explosion of laughter provoked by *Tim-tim* in 1890, destined to last more years than the tobacco concession [a profitable monopoly attributed by the state]."[252] The play was staged in Rio de Janeiro in 1892 and became a success in Brazilian theaters, especially in São Paulo.[253] The cover of the ninth edition of the *coplas* for *Tim tim por tim tim* states that the *revista* had been performed around 4,000 times.[254] Even if this number

---

[245] Sousa Bastos, *Carteira do artista*, 264.
[246] Sousa Bastos, *Diccionario*, 298.
[247] *Pontos nos ii*, 28 March 1889, 101.
[248] Sousa Bastos, *Carteira do artista*, 115.
[249] Rebello, *História do teatro de revista em Portugal*, vol. 1, 96.
[250] *Pontos nos ii*, 17 April 1890, 128.
[251] *O António Maria*, 30 April 1891, 70.
[252] *O António Maria*, 30 April 1891, 70.
[253] Sousa Bastos, *Carteira do artista*, 115.
[254] Sousa Bastos, *Tim tim por tim tim: revista phantástica e de costumes em 1 prólogo, 3 actos e 12 quadros* (Lisbon: Livraria Popular de Francisco Franco, n.d.) [ninth edition].

Figure 2.5 Manuel Gustavo Bordalo Pinheiro, caricature of Sousa Bastos with the characters of the *revista Tim tim por tim tim* reprised in 1890, in *Pontos nos ii*, 17 April 1890, 128, Hemeroteca Municipal de Lisboa. Caricature of Sousa Bastos with the characters of the *revista Tim tim por tim tim* reprised in 1890.

is exaggerated, it points to enormous success in both sides of the Atlantic. Figure 2.5 is a caricature of the 1890 reprise of the *revista* with Sousa Bastos and the characters of the play.

The *revista* promoted several generations of actors, playwrights, visual artists, and composers throughout its history. The theatrical panorama was changing toward the end of the 19th century. Because the *revista* accommodated novelty rapidly it integrated new writers and composers, as well as subjects and musical styles. This was the heyday of Eduardo Schwalbach, as companies started to perform his *revistas*. The plays criticized current matters and social habits, and transcended the immediacy of the genre.[255] Since the *revista* became more perennial and the theatrical censorship was in place, its focus on recent events was mixed with more general subjects, like the humdrum of urban life. Schwalbach's *revistas de costumes* appeared from 1896 until 1901 and were very successful. These plays were *Retalhos de Lisboa* (music composed and coordinated by Freitas Gazul and Tomás Del Negro), *O reino da bolha* (music by Gazul and Del Negro), *Formigas e formigueiros* (by Gazul and Filipe Duarte), *Agulhas e alfinetes* (music by Filipe Duarte), and *O barril do lixo* (music by Filipe Duarte), and *Nicles!...* (music by Filipe Duarte).[256] *O reino da bolha* was reviewed in *O António Maria*, and its "extraordinary success" was attributed to the play being "one of the funniest *revistas* that had been staged in the last years."[257]

Nicles!... premièred in 1901 in the Teatro da Rua dos Condes. It coincided with the performances of *Talvez te escreva*... in the Teatro Avenida, a *revista* by Sousa Bastos and Luiz Filgueiras. *A paródia* reviewed both plays and found them excellent, with "heaps of fun."[258] It predicted they would be performed for a long time. However, these revues lacked criticism and the authors did not use "the speculum of their fine observation for the thorough examination of last year's events."[259] *A paródia* compares the reception of these *revistas* with other plays that were being performed, namely, *A Severa* and *Rosa engeitada*: "the audience grew accustomed to the violent emotions of the dramas in Mouraria, and does not want to go to a theater where the danger of being sewn by stabbings cannot be felt."[260] Nevertheless, selections of *Nicles!...* were published as sheet music and recorded by the wind band of the Guarda Municipal de Lisboa. It is scored for flutes, clarinets, oboe, bassoon, trumpets, French horns, trombones, timpani and percussion, violins, violas, cellos and

---

[255] Rebello, *História do teatro de revista em Portugal*, vol. 1, 121–122.

[256] Eduardo Schwalbach, *Retalhos de Lisboa: revista de costumes e acontecimentos* (Lisbon: Livraria Popular de Francisco Franco, n.d.); *O reino da bolha: revista de costumes e acontecimentos em 3 actos e 12 quadros* (Lisbon: Livraria Popular de Francisco Franco, n.d.); *Formigas e formigueiros: revista de costumes e acontecimentos em 3 actos e 9 quadros* (Lisbon: Livraria Popular de Francisco Franco, n.d.); *Agulhas e alfinetes: revista do anno de 1898 em 3 actos e 12 quadros* (Lisbon: Livraria Popular de Francisco Franco, n.d.); *O barril do lixo: revista de costumes e acontecimentos* (Lisbon: Livraria Popular de Francisco Franco, n.d.).

[257] *O António Maria*, 20 May 1897, 4.

[258] "A crise do theatro," *A Paródia*, 6 February 1901, 2.

[259] "A crise do theatro," *A Paródia*, 6 February 1901, 2.

[260] "A crise do theatro," *A Paródia*, 6 February 1901, 2.

double basses.²⁶¹ The orchestral manuscript does not include voices, and the conductor had to know the play very well. This means that the composer was often the conductor in the popular theaters. The play includes waltzes, polkas, marches (in the apotheosis of Act 1, for example), and gallops. Moreover, the score reveals the plasticity of the show, since the number 25 starts with a four-bar orchestral introduction with a mark to repeat "as many times as needed."²⁶² Thus, the interaction between the orchestra and the stage could vary in every performance.

In the 1900s the first plays of a new generation of dramatists were staged. People like Luís Galhardo or André Brun, who later became prominent writers, entered the theatrical circuit. Writing and composing for the theater remained virtually unaltered at this stage. Nevertheless, the death of prominent composers, like Cyriaco de Cardoso, and the arrival of new composers, like Luiz Filgueiras, transformed Lisbon's entertainment market. A new generation of writers and composers became extremely important in adapting the *revista* to the new demands of the Portuguese Republic.²⁶³ In this sense, the new regime fostered the association between patriotism and republicanism. Therefore, staging the republican nation became part of the plays, a tendency that is traceable in the apotheoses of the *revista*. The apotheosis is the final number of each act, where the magnificence of the staging was highlighted. Figure 2.6 shows the apotheosis of the first act of *Sol e sombra*. This *revista* was penned by Ernesto Rodrigues, Marçal Vaz, and Félix Bermudes, and its music was composed by Filipe Duarte and Carlos Calderon. It was performed in the Teatro Avenida in 1910 and its apotheosis caricatures several politicians as an orchestra. The photographer also allows us to have a glimpse of the dimensions of a theatrical orchestra.

The *revista* staged the current events of the new regime and incorporated Anglo-American musical styles in the 1910s and 1920s, like the fox-trot. The *revista* adjusted rapidly to the Republic, as *Agulha em palheiro* shows.²⁶⁴ This play premièred in the Teatro Apolo, the new name for the Teatro do Príncipe Real in 23 February 1911. Its authors were Félix Bermudes, Ernesto Rodrigues, and Marçal Vaz, and the music was composed by Filipe Duarte and Carlos Calderon. The *revista* included several moments where the republic is seen in a favorable way by its authors. For example, the play contains a sketch that mocks the expulsion of the religious orders from Portugal, a move

---

[261] Filipe Duarte, Nicles: Revista do anno 1900 [uncataloged manuscript in the National Library of Portugal].

[262] Duarte, Nicles

[263] Rebello, *História do teatro de revista em Portugal*, vol. 1, 137.

[264] Ernesto Rodrigues, Félix Bermudes, and Marçal Vaz, *Agulha em palheiro: revista de costumes portugueses em 3 actos e 10 quadros* (Lisbon: Imprensa de Manuel Lucas Torres, 1911).

Figure 2.6 An orchestra politica, apotheosis of the first act of the *revista Sol e dó*, Teatro Avenida, Lisbon, in *Illustração Portugueza*, 24 January 1910, 105, Hemeroteca Municipal de Lisboa.
The political orchestra, the apotheosis of the first act of the *revista Sol e dó*.

in which the republican anticlericalism surfaces.[265] The *revista* also contains a discussion that compares the flag of the monarchy with the new Portuguese flag. Despite falling outside the boundaries of this book, this play reveals how fast the new order was implemented in the theater. Some authors were staunch republicans during the monarchy and their new work reflected the end of censorship with the Republic. However, this did not last long as censorship was reinstated in 1912.

Structure and the Narrative in the *Revista*

The narrative strategies of the *revista* rely on specific modes of representation. The plays usually have three acts, and each act is divided in a varied number of closed and heterogeneous numbers (the *quadros*). These sketches consisted of a funny spoken dialogue between the characters, and many ended with a song that commented on their subject. The transitions between sketches had

---

[265] "A revista Agulha em Palheiro no Theatro Apollo," *Illustração portugueza*, 10 April 1911, 456.

to provide continuity in the *revista*. The task of the *compère* or the *commère* (if performed by a male or female actor, respectively) was to link the sketches. These always-on-stage characters were created when the genre was developed in France and were imported when the *revista* started to be performed locally. In Portugal, the role was usually performed by a male actor. The *compère* (or *compadre* in Portuguese) could be a stock character, like the man from the countryside who is strolling in Lisbon and is surprised with the things he finds. Nevertheless, the *compère* interacts with the characters and comments on what he experiences. Thus, he is not an external narrator, nor a *flâneur*. Because he was always on stage, the *compadre* had to establish a special rapport with the audience. Many unexpected things could happen in a performance of a *revista* and the audience reaction was unpredictable. Therefore, the *compère* was required to improvise and to trigger laughter rapidly. This was also a way to keep the interest of the audience when they were watching a *revista* they had seen several times. Each performance was unique and revealed the plasticity of the genre. Because of their talent to play the *compère*, some actors were especially associated with this comic role and performed it in several revues. For example, Alfredo de Carvalho (1855–1910) began his acting career in fairs and in provisional and improvised stages all around the country and later became famous for playing the *compère* in *revistas* such as Tim tim por tim tim, Tam-tam, Em pratos limpos, and Sal e pimenta.[266]

As seen above, the *revista* consists in a sequence of contrasting and loosely connected sketches, and the internal structure of the *quadros* relies on allegory. Moreover, they are often structured to display the binary opposition of characters, representing the oppositions associated with everyday life. The dialogues between Fossilismo and Progresso in the *revista* of the same name illustrate this tendency. To stage a conversation between opposites is to emphasize their differences, a strategy that was frequent in the *revista*. Thus, the discontinuity of the genre is also reflected in the way its characters are portrayed. This form of representation includes several dichotomies that are constitutive of modernity: the old and the new, the urban and the rural, the rich and the poor, and the local and the foreign. For instance, in his *revista Garotice & C.ª* (premièred in 1908) the republican Artur Arriegas personifies the Monarchy as the Ugly Girl and the Republic as the Pretty Girl, revealing the sometimes political character of these polar structures.[267]

---

[266] "A morte de um grande actor comico: Alfredo de Carvalho," in *Illustração portugueza*, 18 April 1910, 508–509.

[267] Rebello, *História do teatro de revista em Portugal*, vol. 1, 217.

A polarity concerning music is part of the *revista Tim tim por tim tim*. This play contains a sketch that personifies the Portuguese Song and the Brazilian Song with their particularities and colloquialisms.[268] *Tim tim por tim tim* was also performed in Brazil, since the works by Sousa Bastos were then frequently staged on both sides of the Atlantic. Hence, these personifications would be easily understood by the audiences of both countries. The Brazilian Song, *O Mugunzá*, reveals this transatlantic relation. It was performed by Pepa Ruiz in Act 2 of *Tim tim por tim tim*.[269] The music of *O Mugunzá* was composed by Francisco Carvalho, and the lyrics were penned by the comic actor Bernardo Lisboa. The song bears the subtitle is *lundu baiano* (lundu from Bahia). The *lundu* or *lundum* is an Afro-Brazilian dance that was integrated in Portuguese and Brazilian salon society in the 18th century. Later, it developed into a song, the *lundu-canção*, and became part of the urban entertainment market. Moreover, it was integrated in the *revistas* as a comic song. The *lundu* is a clear example of how the cultural practices of the low-others were appropriated and adapted to suit the routines of the aristocracy and the bourgeoisie. This ambivalent fascination with the lower classes is a pervasive feature in the development of a popular leisure culture.

However, the song's texture resembles a *maxixe*, the Afro-Brazilian dance that was incorporated in salon society at the time of the performances of *Tim tim por tim tim*. This shows how the vernacular was adapted for a bourgeois audience in post-colonial Brazil, where the local genres were transformed to suit the cosmopolitan conventions of popular music. Its sheet music does not offer a glimpse of how these pieces were performed on stage—and it was not expected to do so since its market was the bourgeois piano parlor. Nevertheless, *O Mugunzá* shows the difficulty that rises when naming music genres, especially when these are new. This common problem is also reflected on the sheet music. Sheet music was predominantly intended for domestic use. Furthermore, new genres were often marketed by using old labels to capitalize on the audience's *habitus*. To sell in quantity, they had to conform to the technical proficiency of a large audience. Hence, the norm was to publish a heterogeneous set of music as melody-driven transcriptions with a simplified accompaniment. Thus, opera, operetta, *revista*, and social dances were adapted to suit the conventions of the cosmopolitan commodity form. This means that sometimes their original score was altered substantially. Therefore, depending on its performance *O Mugunzá* could sound more like a *lundu-canção* or more like a *maxixe*.[270]

---

[268] Bastos, *Tim tim por tim tim*, 11–12.

[269] Francisco Carvalho and Bernardo Lisboa, *O mugunzá: lundu bahiano* (Rio de Janeiro: Edições Buschmann & Guimarães).

[270] Carlos Sandroni, *Feitiço decente: transformações do samba no Rio de Janeiro, 1917–1933* (Rio de Janeiro: Jorge Zahar Editor/UFRJ, 2008), 61.

Music example 2.6 First part of "O mugunzá" from *Tim tim por tim tim*. Francisco Carvalho and Bernardo Lisboa, "O mugunzá: lundu bahiano" (Rio de Janeiro: Edições Buschmann & Guimarães).

Setting the song as a *maxixe* makes sense, given the rapid incorporation of fashionable styles in the *revista* and the need to communicate with both Brazilian and Portuguese audiences. In this sense, the *maxixe* would be easily acknowledged by the Brazilian audiences. In Portugal things would have been slightly different. Even if the genre had not crossed the Atlantic, the song would be immediately recognized as Brazilian. This is because of the lyrics, of the singer's costume, and of her body language. Moreover, the song seems to be about cooking a Brazilian sweet, the *mugunzá*: "To make a good *mugunzá*/One has to put all the caring/*Jeitosa* like me there isn't/ A pure *baiana* doesn't say no." This is clearly a sexual innuendo, a mechanism that was frequently employed in the *revista*, reinforced by the double meaning of the word *jeitosa* as both skillful and attractive.

To understand the communicative strategy of the *revista* one has to know its conventions. Musically, many of them were topological, since the composer used signals to characterize people and situations. For example, a character from the urban working class was probably associated with fado whereas a peasant would be represented with a *chula*, a popular dance from the north of Portugal. Therefore, the use of elements that could be easily recognized by the audience to situate characters was very important. This is especially true when dealing with a genre that relied on internal diversity, like the *revista*. Music, costumes, and gestures were used to establish rapport with the audience and to enhance plot realism in a predominantly allegorical genre.

The theatrical exchange between Portugal and Brazil remained lively. The *revista Fado e Maxixe*, which was performed in the Teatro Condes between 1909 and 1910, was written by the Portuguese André Brun and the Brazilian João Phoca (the pseudonym of writer José Baptista Coelho); its music was composed and adapted by Luz Júnior, then the impresario of the theater and the stage director was Baptista Coelho. The revue was based on sketches that commented on the everyday life of Lisbon and of Rio de Janeiro, The *revista* received positive reviews from the press, with *Brasil-Portugal* praising the verve and the powers of observation of its authors, and stating that the music was suitable and would easily please the audience.[271] Furthermore, it staged popular music of both countries, and the last sketch included "all of the dances that are used in Rio de Janeiro during the Carnival."[272]

In 1900 Eduardo Schwalbach's *O barril do lixo* was staged in the Teatro Condes. The *revista* includes a sketch that deals directly with music and politics, and features two songs: the "Hino da Carta" and "A Portuguesa." The "Hino da Carta" was the national anthem of the Portuguese monarchy. "A Portuguesa" is a march by Henrique Lopes de Mendonça and Alfredo Keil that was composed in the aftermath of the British Ultimatum of 1890. Because of its patriotic poem it was soon appropriated by the republicans. This association was so strong that "A Portuguesa" was played by the marching bands of the failed republican revolt of 31 January 1891, and it was adopted as the anthem of the Portuguese Republic in 1911. Schwalbach was the inspector of the Conservatório Real de Lisboa, a position accessed through royal appointment. He associates the "Hino da Carta" with stately events, such as gala receptions, parades, or bullfights. This contrasts with "A Portuguesa," a song Schwalbach identifies with the Portuguese people, incarnated by Bordalo Pinheiro's Zé Povinho, a caricature of a man that personifies the Portuguese people.[273] This split between the official anthem and a march of the "people"

---

[271] *Brasil-Portugal*, 1 January 1910, 368.

[272] "As revistas do anno actualmente em scena nos theatros de Lisboa," *Illustração Portugueza*, 24 January 1910, 105.

[273] Eduardo Schwalbach, *O barril do lixo*, 6–7.

indicates the political significance of "A Portuguesa" in the last years of the monarchy.

Gender played an important role in the *revista*. Contrary to the Japanese Takarazuka revue, performed by companies constituted exclusively of male actors who had to cross-dress to perform feminine roles, the Portuguese companies employed both men and women.[274] Nevertheless, *revistas* included cross-dressing characters that were especially used with comical intent. In Eduardo Schwalbach's *Retalhos de Lisboa e Porto*, a revista performed in Porto in 1897, a male actor played a burlesque caricature of Sarah Bernhardt.[275] This parody is based on the inversion of roles, since Sarah Bernhardt was known for her performances of cross-dressing parts. Thus, a satirical approach to her career was made with a man dressed as a woman, like the negative of a photograph. Furthermore, in a version of *Tim tim por tim tim* performed in Brazil, Pepa Ruiz performed eighteen roles, some of them cross-dressed.[276] Instead of mocking an actress, this revealed the variety of characters that Pepa could play. In a system that relied on its stars for profit, concentrating the audience's attention in one lead actress was an intelligent way to market the play. As the *revista* relied on the burlesque depiction of stock characters, the genre included the stereotypical views of the feminine as they circulated in popular discourse. In *Em nome do padre* Câmara Lima includes a duet between two female characters, the hysteric and the neurasthenic.[277] The *revista* premièred in the Teatro da Trindade in 1908 and this sketch illustrates how popular perceptions of current medical matters were presented. This staging was clearly exaggerated, as shown by its satirical and sometimes misogynistic vein. At this time, Parisian cabarets performed songs about hysteria and epilepsy, conditions that somehow had grabbed popular imagination. These pathologies were staged, which added a "new repertoire of movements, grimaces, tics, and gestures" to the shows.[278] However, these gestures were inspired by scientific observation and by psychological experimentation.[279] Nevertheless, it is impossible to infer from the *coplas* of *Em nome do pai* the gestures made by its performers. The peak and rapid decline of hysteria as a social pathology toward the end of the 19th century coincides with a period when bourgeois cultures "produced a

---

[274] Jennifer Robertson, "Theatrical Resistance, Theaters of Restraint: The Takarazuka Revue and the "State Theater" Movement in Japan," *Anthropological Quarterly*, 64/4 (1991), 165–177.

[275] Rebello, *História do teatro de revista em Portugal*, vol. 1, 80–81.

[276] Rebello, *História do teatro de revista em Portugal*, vol. 1, 96–97; d'Almeida, *Actores*, 84–85.

[277] Câmara Lima, *Em nome do padre…: revista de costumes e acontecimentos* (Lisbon: Typographia de Palhares e Cª, 1908), 16–17.

[278] Rae Beth Gordon, "From Charcot to Charlot: Unconscious Imitation and Spectatorship in French Cabaret and Early Cinema," *Critical Inquiry*, 27/3 (Spring 2001), 515.

[279] Gordon, "From Charcot to Charlot," 515.

compensatory range of peripheral 'bohemias' which afforded 'liminoid' symbolic repertoires of a kind approximating to those of earlier carnival forms," an issue that will be addressed below.[280] Thus, as ideas concerning hysteria circulated, the focus on the unconscious opened the gate to new behavioral patterns in Western societies.

In terms of popular perceptions of gender, *Agulhas e alfinetes* includes a musical duet between two conceited women, revealing the association between bourgeois women and superficiality. It also indicates the expansion of a consumer culture, an issue that will be discussed in other chapters of this book. The *Duetto das vaidosas* shows a young woman and an older woman competing about their qualities to attract men. The young woman praised her tallness and her figure that resembles that of a grown woman. The older woman prizes her "juvenile looks."[281] The first section is in an AA form, and accelerates for the refrain after a fermata when the lyrics reference Cupid. It alternates with a refrain, which is based on onomatopoeic sounds that mimic the sound of sheep bells, and reflects the lyrics.

The exposure of the female body in a way some people described as pornographic was an important aspect of the *revista*. The reduced costumes, the racy choreography, and the double entendre dialogues reinforced this view.[282] For example, the "Capa da moda" (Fashionable cloak), a number from the *revista Nicles! . . .* , is a song that explores a double entendre of a sexual nature. The lyrics compare the cloak to a candle extinguisher which was able to extinguish the candle of a sexton, and the love of a seducing cousin.[283] This illustrates the mechanisms on which the *revista* relied, and which were heavily criticized by many writers. In *Crónicas imorais* (Immoral chronicles), the writer Albino Forjaz de Sampaio derogates the sexual character of the *revista*, which is reflected in its atmosphere, in its *coplas*, and in the bare legs of the female performers.[284]

The *revista O anno em três dias* premièred in the Teatro do Príncipe Real in 1904. Its third act includes the "Coplas do Kodack" [sic], a song in ABA form performed by Gomes, an actor known for his comic roles. As the title implies, it narrates the activity of photographing. However, the song describes a man taking opportunistic photographs of a "coquette blonde," and of other women

---

[280] Stallybrass and White, *The Poetics and Politics of Transgression*, 188.

[281] Eduardo Schwalbach and Filipe Duarte, *Agulhas e alfinetes: Duetto das vaidosas* (Lisbon: Neuparth & Comp., n.d.).

[282] Rebello, *História do teatro de revista em Portugal*, vol. 1, 34, Bastos, Diccionario, 128, d'Almeida, *Actores*, 92.

[283] Schwalbach and Duarte, *Agulhas e alfinetes*.

[284] Albino Forjaz de Sampaio, *Chronicas immoraes* (Lisbon: Livraria Cálssica Editora, 1908), 98.

Opera, Operetta, and Revista 135

Figure 2.7 A female character of the *revista Sol e Sombra* in costume, Teatro do Príncipe Real, Lisbon, in *Illustração Portugueza*, 24 January 1910, 107, Hemeroteca Municipal de Lisboa. A female character of the *revista Sol e Sombra* in costume.

whose skirts accidentally rise when blown by the wind or when they are adjusting their garters. This song reveals the rapid incorporation of the novelties of modern life in the *revista* and the kind of racy humor on which the genre often relied.[285] The exhibition of the female body was part of a commercial strategy to attract male audiences; in many types of popular entertainment, commodification of the bodies of female performers circulated in a varied set of products. Illustrated periodicals, theatrical postcards, and photographs show how images of the actresses' bodies entered the bourgeois home. Figure 2.7 is part

---

[285] Machado Correia, Acácio Antunes, and Filipe Duarte, *O anno em três dias: Coplas da lavadeira/Coplas do Kodack* (Lisbon: Salão Neuparth, n.d.).

of a magazine article that includes an image of an actress of the *revista Sol e sombra* in a scanty stage costume.

However, attracting male audiences was not the sole purpose of these revues, as in the Victorian music hall, "female entertainers forcefully presented the woman's perspective to a mixed audience."[286] Therefore, the heterosocial character of the audiences allowed for the multivocality associated with the popular theater.[287] This complicates a simplistic perspective in which male writers directed their plays to a predominantly male audience, a tendency that resonates with Lisbon's entertainment market. Nevertheless, the overwhelming majority of writers and composers who worked for the popular theater were men.

Despite the prominence given to characters who stand in opposition to each other, the *revista* employed other strategies. In some cases a parallel is made between the personified characters. In *O anno em três dias*, Correia and Antunes compare the Portuguese *fadista* with the Brazilian *capanga* (henchman).[288] The Portuguese character plays his Portuguese guitar and his Brazilian counterpart plays the *violão*. This is recognition of the people who live at the margins of the urban life in modern cities (the low-other), and is a chance to show less well-known forms of urban music. It was fashionable to incorporate the vernacular in transnational entertainment. This sketch also illustrates the relevance of the transatlantic relationship between Portuguese-speaking theatrical scenes. Thus, a single *quadro* points in multiple directions, a strength that made the *revista* the dominant show in the popular theater.

Many sketches are based on a dialogue between two characters who are polar opposites. These are sometimes punctuated with a collective chorus. Nevertheless, the *revista* also includes small ensemble numbers. In these *quadros*, each character takes turns in presenting his or her views. Sometimes they are competing with one another, and the *quadro* usually ends with a chorus where all characters sing the same text. The final number of each act of the *revista* was designed to create a scene of great spectacle and dazzling effect.[289] To achieve an impressive effect in a number that included music, dance, and a great number of characters who crowded the stage, the set, costumes, and lighting had to be magnificent. Given the heroic character of some of these finales and the need to include a large number of people with several levels of dancing skills, the march was frequently used in the final number of the *revista*.

---

[286] Judith R. Walkowitz, *City of Dreadful Delight: Narratives of Sexual Danger in Late-Victorian London* (Chicago: University of Chicago Press, 1992), 45.

[287] Walkowitz, *City of Dreadful Delight*, 45.

[288] Machado Correia and Acácio Antunes, *O anno em três dias: revista phantastica* (Lisbon: Instituto Geral das artes graphicas, 1904), 19–20 and 33–34.

[289] Soua Bastos, *Diccionario*, 14–15.

Music, Sources, and Orchestras

Because the *revista* is organized in closed numbers it uses a disjointed and fragmentary narrative of current events. Music was a way to depict characters and situations. It could also be used to give continuity and to emphasize stylistic breaks in the show. Music played an important role in the discontinuous narrative of the *revista* and enhanced a show whose aim was to be both entertaining for the audience and profitable for the company. Furthermore, the music used in the *revista* was not only an indication of modernity; it manufactured and presented that same modernity. The *revista* was pivotal for the introduction of musical styles such as the *maxixe* or the cakewalk in Portugal. To study theatrical genres that relied on topical issues presents methodological obstacles. The materials were conceived with utilitarian purposes. Therefore, they would probably not be used more than one season. This means that very few complete scores of *revistas* have survived, and it is problematic to assume that these survivors are representative of the genre. Nevertheless, I will use an example from the National Library of Portugal as a case study to display some features of the show.

The full manuscript score of the *Revista do anno de 1879* contains forty-one *quadros* divided into three acts.[290] The text was written by Sousa Bastos and set to music by Júlio Soares (1846–1888). The show is scored for a small orchestra and includes a plan of the numbers that includes parts of the text. As an autograph of the composer, the manuscript is particularly useful for understanding how music was written for the *revista*. The score is clearly a work in progress, displaying many changes, corrections, and cuts, illustrating the constraints of staging a play that deals with such dynamic topics. There are important issues pertaining to this *revista*. First, Soares was not a prominent composer for the music theater. He was a double bass player who worked in theatrical orchestras in Lisbon.[291] This makes him an integrated professional, according to Becker's terminology. Second, Sousa Bastos wrote the revue at a time when his plays were dominating Lisbon's theatrical scene. Third, the revue uses dances that were pervasive in the history of the genre, namely, the march and the waltz, and it relied on stock characters. Finally, the *revista* has a sketch set in Lisbon where the railways and Progress are personified. These were current matters at a time when new plans for the city were being implemented.

---

[290] António de Sousa Bastos and Júlio Soares, Revista do anno de 1879, 1880. Lisbon, National Library of Portugal, Shelfmark PTBN: M.M. 1071.

[291] Vieira, *Diccionario biographico de musicos portuguezes*, vol. 2 (Lisbon: Lambertini, 1900), 330–331.

The music of the *revista* was generally written for a small orchestra. The size of the instrumental group playing in the theater varied according to the show and the size of the venue.[292] The orchestra of the Real Teatro de S. Carlos was very different from the groups working in small theaters, like the Teatro da Alegria. Even so, the sources we have describing theatrical orchestras are scarce and not very reliable. The records of the Associação Música Vinte e Quatro de Junho are valuable for studying the activity of professional musicians in Lisbon,[293] but current data suggest that small theaters hired musicians who were not part of this association.[294] Looking at the constitution of theatrical orchestras in 1890, Leitão related the records of orchestral activity in Lisbon's theaters to the comment of Sousa Bastos,[295] who stated that theaters that accommodated spoken genres could discard the orchestra altogether or keep a small ensemble, like a sextet.[296] The musicians hired by the Teatro da Rua dos Condes and by the Teatro do Príncipe Real varied around this number.[297] Bastos recommended an orchestra of at least twenty people to perform operettas and *zarzuelas*.[298] This was roughly the same number of musicians working in the Teatro da Trindade.[299] However, the orchestra of the Real Coliseu de Lisboa had around forty musicians and also performed operettas and *zarzuelas*. Most were members of the orchestra of the Real Teatro de S. Carlos, whose season had already finished when these plays were staged in the Coliseu.[300] This shows the importance of Lisbon's opera house as a supplier of skilled musicians for other activities. Bastos states that an orchestra of a lyric theater should have around eighty elements.[301] The orchestra of the Real Teatro de São Carlos fluctuated between thirty-seven and eighty musicians.[302] However, the formation stabilized with around sixty instrumentalists toward the end of the 19th century, reflecting the financial condition of the country.[303] With the economic crisis and the withdrawal of government support for the theaters, there was a significant reduction

---

[292] Sousa Bastos, *Diccionario*, 102.

[293] Vieira, *Diccionario biographico de musicos portuguezes*, vol.1, 339–346.

[294] Leitão, "A ambiência musical e sonora da cidade de Lisboa no ano de 1890," master's thesis (Universidade Nova de Lisboa, 2006), 55–56.

[295] Leitão, "A ambiência," 49–62.

[296] Bastos, *Diccionario*, 102.

[297] Leitão, "A ambiência," 53–55.

[298] Sousa Bastos, *Diccionario*, 102

[299] Leitão, "A ambiência," 52–53.

[300] Leitão, "A ambiência," 60–61.

[301] Sousa Bastos, *Diccionario*, 102.

[302] Ernesto Vieira, "Orquestra," in Ernesto Vieira, *Diccionario musical* (Lisbon: Lambertini, 1899), 393.

[303] Vieira, "Orquestra," 393.

in the number of musicians.[304] The scarcity of reliable employment and the frequent mobility of musicians around venues in Lisbon indicate the hardships felt by the leisure market, a trend especially noticeable in the theaters where *revista* was performed. Given the precarious nature of these ventures, musicians were recruited according to the financial resources of the company and in keeping with the repertoire that was programmed for a season. Unsubsidized theatrical activity in Lisbon was volatile at this time.

The discontinuous, self-contained sketches of the *revista* were connected by a thin thread woven by the *compère*, and their varying subject matter allowed the use of music from a wide array of contexts. This practice of using both local and cosmopolitan music made the *revista* a mosaic of modernity and greatly enhanced the appeal of the show to the audience.

Musical numbers called fado often appeared in these revues. Bastos described fado as a "popular song and narrative . . . that much pleases when introduced in popular plays, mainly *revistas*."[305] At the turn of the century fado was frequently performed on the popular stages by the singers/actors of the commercial companies.[306] They were the first recording artists of the genre, and not the people who performed the vernacular form of the songs in the taverns and courtyards of the poor districts.

Including fado in a *revista* blends the ideas of "popular" and "national" in Portugal. For example, the *revista* O *tutti-li-mundi* included "O fado do Zé Povinho" (Zé Povinho's fado).[307] As stated earlier, a *revista* often included a character that portrayed the Portuguese people. Zé Povinho was a personification that circulated outside the stage in newspaper cartoons and ceramic sculptures, and was rapidly integrated in the *revista* as a character easily recognizable by the Portuguese audiences. *O tutti-li-mundi* premièred in the Teatro Condes in 1881 and "O fado do Zé Povinho" was sung by Marcelino Franco. Its piano reduction consists of an AABB form with an Alberti bass accompaniment.[308] The piece was included in the *Cancioneiro de músicas populares*, the most comprehensive collection of Portuguese traditional music.[309] The music

---

[304] Luísa Cymbron, "As orquestras dos teatros de ópera em Lisboa e no Porto durante o século XIX," in Luísa Cymbron, *Olhares sobre a música em Portugal no século XIX*, 113.

[305] Sousa Bastos, *Diccionario*, 63. This insistence by the author on the term "popular" is an element to notice.

[306] Rui Vieira Nery, *Para uma história do Fado* (Lisbon: Público/Corda Seca, 2004), 23–27 and 37–40.

[307] António de Sousa de Meneses, *O tutti-li-mundi: revista do ano de 1880* (Lisbon: Imp. Cruz, 1881); Francisco Alvarenga, *O fado do Zé Povinho: cantado pelo actor Marcelino Franco no Tutti himundi, revista do anno de 1880* (Lisbon: Lence &Viuva Canongia—Lith. R. das Flores, 1881).

[308] Alvarenga, *O fado do Zé Povinho*.

[309] César das Neves and Gualdino de Campos, *Cancioneiro de músicas populares*, 3 vols. (Porto: Tip. Ocidental—Empresa editora César, Campos & Cª, 1893, 1895, 1898).

is exactly the same but the collected version has different lyrics. "O fado do Zé Povinho" is probably a popular theatrical song that became part of oral tradition. Having a theatrical song collected in a work that focused on traditional music reveals a porosity between the stage and the streets. Nevertheless, it is odd that the collected version conforms with the sheet music even in the use of the Alberti bass. This may suggest the reliance of the collectors on sheet music, and certainly indicates a haziness between commercial and folk songs: an urban entertainment market that produces sheet music and an ethnology that relies on oral tradition interpenetrate each other.

The *coplas* of the *revista Na ponta da unha!* contain the "Fado da Severa" and the "Fado da Rosa Enjeitada."[310] This play was staged in the Teatro Condes in 1901, and its authors were Alfredo Mesquita, Câmara Lima, and Dias Costa. The dramas *A Severa* and *A Rosa Enjeitada* were performed in Lisbon in 1901. *A Severa* is the play that was the basis of the operetta mentioned above.[311] D. João da Câmara's *A Rosa Enjeitada* is a "populist *feuilleton*" that comprised a love triangle between popular characters, and premièred in the Teatro do Príncipe Real.[312] Both plays displayed the vernacular, a tendency that was mentioned above. The *quadro* of *Na ponta da unha!* neither focused on fado nor on the "popular," but on Lisbon's theatrical circuit. Thus, it is possible to extract several layers from this: the role played by the *revista* as a commentator on reality, the use of the vernacular song in the theater, and the importance of the theaters in providing subjects to the *revista*.[313]

The *revista P'rá frente* also contained fado. It was written by Camanho Garcia and by Aires Pereira da Costa, and set to music by Tomás del Negro and Carlos Calderon. In the beginning of the play the Portuguese guitar was described as a "poor and unfortunate" instrument that depended solely on fado.[314] This association has been pervasive throughout the history of the genre. Further into the play, a sketch personifies three types of fado, the Velho Fado, the Fado Rigoroso, and the Fado Liró. The Velho Fado (Old Fado) has a four-line stanza, in which both couplets are repeated, a convention that is still associated with the so-called traditional fados.[315] The Fado Rigoroso (Rigourous Fado) uses the phonetics of Lisbon's *fadistas* and mentions the

---

[310] Alfredo Mesquita and Dias Costa, *Na ponta da unha!: revista em 3 actos e 12 quadros* (Lisbon: Livraria Popular de Francisco Franco, n.d.), 11.

[311] Júlio Dantas, *A Severa: drama em quatro actos* (Lisbon: M. Gomes, 1901).

[312] Rebello, *O teatro naturalista e neo-romântico*, 65.

[313] For a photograph in costume of the actresses who performed Severa and Rosa Enjeitada see *Brasil-Portugal*, 1 February 1902, 399.

[314] Camanho Garcia and Aires Pereira da Costa, *P'rá frente: revista em 3 actos e 12 quadros* (Lisbon: Impr. Lucas, 1907), 3.

[315] Garcia and Costa, *P'rá frente*, 13.

knife brawls of these marginal individuals.[316] According to Pimentel, the "Fado Rigoroso" was the same as the "Fado Corrido," believed to be one of the oldest fados.[317] Finally, the "Fado Liró" (freely translated as Elegant Fado— "liró" was a slang word of the time for elegant or smart), is described as a "more elegant" type associated with the aristocracy.[318] The *quadro* indicates differentiated patterns of consumption associated with several types of fado. It is consistent with sources that point to the transformations of the genre to suit audiences other than marginal characters of Lisbon's popular districts. Figure 2.8 depicts several characters of *P'rá frente*, including the personification by Júlia Mendes of the Fado Rigoroso holding his guitar. This set of photographs illustrates the variety of the *revista*.

In this sense, fado was associated by the authors of the *revista* with both the lower segments of society and with the aristocracy. Given that the *revista* was frequented by a wide range of people, it became a prominent, yet contested, site for the presentation and naturalization of the "popular." Therefore, incorporating fado, a genre associated with the extremes of the social spectrum, indicates its ubiquity in Lisbon—and this is intensified by its frequent performance on the popular stage, attended by an audience that was socially heterogeneous. A song named "Fado Liró" was part of *A.B.C.*, a very successful *revista* dealing with patriotic propaganda[319] that was staged in the Teatro Avenida.[320] Its music was composed by the same Del Negro and Calderon who set to music a large number of plays. In *A.B.C.*, "Fado Liró" is sung by the soloists and chorus and the lyrics place this aristocratic fado as "high-life slang."[321] However, there are several songs called "Fado Liró." Approximately at the same time, the Brazilian composer Nicolino Milano traveled to Lisbon and worked in the Teatro Avenida. He then composed what became his most successful song, "Fado Liró."[322] This one and the song in *A.B.C.* had different lyrics, and Milano's fado was not the song included in this *revista*. Moreover, the *coplas* and the reviews of the play did not acknowledge Milano. Nevertheless, he was working at the Teatro Avenida when *A.B.C.* was staged, and he took this *revista*

---

[316] Garcia and Costa, *P'rá frente*, 13–14.

[317] Alberto Pimentel, *A triste canção do sul: subsídios para a história do fado* (Lisbon: Livraria Central, 1904), 281.

[318] Garcia and Costa, *P'rá frente*, 14.

[319] Rebello, *História do teatro de revista em Portugal*, vol. 1, 145.

[320] Acácio de Paiva and Ernesto Rodrigues, *A.B.C.: Revista em 3 actos e 12 quadros* (Lisbon: Impr. Lucas, 1908).

[321] Paiva and Rodrigues, *A.B.C.*, 9–10.

[322] A. A. Bispo, "Luso-brasileirismo, ítalo-brasileiros e mecanismos performativos: representações teatrais e revistas: Nicolino Milano," *Revista Brasil-Europa* 107/3 (2007), http://www.revista.brasil-europa.eu/107/Nicolino-Milano.htm, accessed 12 November 2009.

Figure 2.8 Photographs of performers of the *revista P'rá Frente* in stage costumes, Teatro Avenida, Lisbon, in *Illustração Portugueza*, 4 November 1907, 598, Hemeroteca Municipal de Lisboa. Photographs of performers of the *revista P'rá Frente* in stage costumes.

to Brazil in 1909. Since the *revista* was always changing to accommodate novelty, it is not impossible that Milano's song replaced the original "Fado Liró."

What is interesting about this is the prevalence of fado as the symbol for urban popular songs that were in the process of being legitimized and promoted through the entertainment market. The *mágica* (plays involving the supernatural) also included songs named "fado," as the "Canção de Belphogor (Fado)" illustrates. *O cabo da caçarola* was written by Joaquim Augusto de Oliveira (the foremost author of *mágicas*) and by the impresario Salvador Marques.[323] It was staged in the Teatro Avenida in 1901 with music by Filipe Duarte. The song had a narrative form and the characters interacted with a chorus. Nevertheless, it gives predominance to the demon Belphogor, who varies the melodies every time he sings. The examples in this chapter show the difficulty of seeing fado as a song that uses a specific form. Nonetheless, it is significant that so many theatrical songs use "fado" in their title or subtitle. This is not surprising since "fado" was a synonym for popular song at the time. With the correspondence between the pervasiveness of fado and the promotion of Portugal as a nation, the role of music in the *revista* helps us to frame this issue. If fado became an important song in the structure of the *revista*, other genres were no less important. The *Revista do anno de 1879*, which used the march and the waltz, also includes sections named Tango and Gallop.[324] Tango, then perceived as an African dance, was played when black characters from the Portuguese colonies entered the stage. Here, the music reinforces the plot. The Gallop, a dance that was frequently used by Offenbach, re-created the sound of the train, a modern technology. *Vistorias do Diabo*, a *revista* by Francisco Jacobetty staged in the Chalet da Rua dos Condes, uses the music of Angel Rubio's zarzuela *La salsa de Aniceta* in a song.[325] *Na ponta da unha!* features the "Habanera da Cocotte" as well as the "Fado da Severa" and the "Fado da Rosa Enjeitada." *A.B.C.* has a number in French called "La Masseuse," performed together with sketches that promoted patriotism.[326] In André Brun's articles concerning the staging of a musical play discussed above, Benoliel photographed a group of dancers practicing a "cake-walk" (Figure 2.9)[327] This reference to a black American genre that was recently introduced in Europe is surprising.[328] Nevertheless, a transnational market for commodified "modern"

---

[323] Joaquim Augusto de Oliveira, Salvador Marques, and Filipe Duarte, *Canção de Belphogor (Fado)* (Lisbon: Salão Neuparth, n.d.).

[324] Sousa Bastos and Júlio Soares, Revista do anno de 1879.

[325] Francisco Jacobetty, *Coplas das vistorias . . . do Diabo* (Lisbon: Eduardo Roza, 1884), 4.

[326] Paiva and Rodrigues, *A.B.C.*, 15.

[327] Brun, "O theatro por dentro," *Ilustração* portugueza, 2 November 1908, 20.

[328] H. Wiley Hitchcock and Pauline Norton, "Cakewalk," *Grove Music Online*, ed. L. Macy, www.oxfordmusiconline.com, accessed 5 December 2009; Jody Blake, *Le Tumulte Noir*:

Figure 2.9 Joshua Benoliel, Ensaiando um *"cake-walk,"* in *Illustração Portugueza*, 2 November 1908, 563, Hemeroteca Municipal de Lisboa. A company practicing a cakewalk in the Teatro Avenida.

music facilitated the circulation of new repertoires. Moreover, Benoliel's photograph shows the importance of choreography in the musical theater. Due to the lack of sources, this book will not deal with stage movement, but given the frequent reference to the chorus girls, dance was also a form of capturing the audience's attention.

The *revista Favas contadas* was written by Câmara Lima and Filipe Duarte for the Teatro Avenida. In 12 January 1907, the play was staged there for the first time. Duarte's score calls for flutes, clarinets, oboes, bassoons, trumpets, French horns, trombones, timpani and percussion, violins, violas, cellos, and double basses.[329] There is also an incomplete voice and piano manuscript that appears to be a copy used in rehearsals. This reinforces the statements in Brun's article mentioned above, showing that the vocal rehearsals were accompanied with the piano. The play starts with an instrumental overture followed by a female chorus that introduces a number that is close to speech. The "Coplas da Sciencia infusa" (*coplas* of the Infused Science) personifies and satirizes local science. It also includes political references to members of parliament and to the loans of the Portuguese Treasury. Political allusions are made in another

Modernist Art and Popular Entertainment in Jazz-Age Paris, 1900–1930 (University Park: Pennsylvania State University Press, 1999), 15.

[329] Filipe Duarte, Favas contadas: Revista de costumes e acontecimentos em 3 actos [uncataloged manuscript in the National Library of Portugal].

number, where the character Gira mentions that the Portuguese assets were being sold and that the country did not have enough money to "make a blind man play," a Portuguese saying.

International politics are also part of this *revista*. Russia is personified and characterized with a military march that mentioned the Russo-Japanese War. It is followed by a duet between Spain and Portugal that focuses on developing a closer relationship between the countries, now that Spain had lost both Cuba and Puerto Rico to the United States of America. France is portrayed as being the "head of the world." The sketch is followed by a funny duet between Virtue and Vice stating that they are merged in modern life. Then, a woman is going to her husband's workplace to ask for a promotion that he had requested three years before. This mocks a situation that was frequent in Portuguese public office. A collective number presents politics as the force that caused the decay of Science, Art, Literature, Agriculture, Commerce, and Industry. These are personified and are the protagonists of the sketch. A strophic chorus of popular characters then sing in thirds and in a register close to declamation. Other numbers include a Revolutionary Maid who complains about her employers, a trio where the corset is associated with coquetry, an Italian song, a chorus of snitches, and a trio of cocottes. *Favas contadas* reflects the multiple events and situations that were part of the everyday life of a European city. Thus, it had many registers whose effect was maximized through music. The score is varied and includes strophic forms, songs with refrain, and narrative moments. It embodies the heterogeneity of the genre and mixes foreign influences with local styles. The critic of *Ilustração Portuguesa* called *Favas contadas* a model to follow for the rebirth of the *revista*.[330] The genre had become decadent because of political constraints and its growing reliance on pornography.[331] The review emphasized the success the *revista* had enjoyed ten years before, in the heyday of Schwalbach's activity, and it placed *Favas contadas* as a worthy successor. Moreover, it complimented Câmara Lima for his double entendres and malice, which hint at current events through irony. The exuberance of its staging was highlighted in the article and the role of the actor and director José Ricardo was praised. The review reproduced a small part of a sketch and included photographs of the play. Moreover, it noted the investment of the company of the Teatro Avenida in this staging to compensate for its distance from the main entertainment circuit.[332] This perception of isolation is significant because the Teatro Avenida was situated in the newly developed Avenida da Liberdade, showing that the urban transformation was not evenly reflected in the leisure

---

[330] *Illustração Portugueza*, 21 January 1907, 90.
[331] *Illustração Portugueza*, 21 January 1907, 90.
[332] *Illustração Portugueza*, 21 January 1907, 92.

market. In evaluating Filipe Duarte's music, the journalist was succinct, stating that "the music alone is sufficient to guarantee the success" of the *revista*.[333] This is a typical review, where the music is perceived as an organic part of the show, along with stage design, lighting, costume design, text, and performance.

Representing the Nation in the *Revista*: Multivocality and Modernity on Stage

The structure and content of the *revista* can be related to theories of nationalism and modernity. This section articulates the variety of the information presented in this chapter and sets the stage for Chapter 4 and Chapter 5, where the material associated with the entertainment market (sheet music, gramophone records, phonograph cylinders, player piano rolls, *coplas*, and postcards) is analyzed. The work of Richard Middleton is very helpful in explaining the logic between the local and the global.[334] He points to the movable place the "national" might occupy in this model as both the "non-local" and the "not-global."[335] At first this may seem to be a negation of "national," but then it shows that the "national" can combine both of these characteristics. This is especially helpful when dealing with the *revista*, where local songs and dances were presented alongside international ones. In this sense, the construction of the "national" is a process where a plurality of visions of the nation are performed, contested, and naturalized. In another model, Middleton introduces the ideas of "tradition" and "modernity" and relates them with the "global" and the "local."[336] This presentation becomes crucial when dealing with the *revista* because it displays the problem of locating the "national" in a local/global polar system, making way for its placement as a complementary space. Conversely, it poses an interesting situation: despite incorporating both local (or, sometimes, promoted as "national") and transnational music, the repertoires were considered "modern" at the time, hence my categorizing of the *revista* as an archive, or a repository, of popular modernity. With this proposition, one question arises: which space does the "national" occupy in Middleton's last elaboration? In my work, I believe the "national" does not occupy a fixed and determined space in the system, but it is a logic that is embedded in the process. This logic appears in either the foreground or the background due to the constraints of

---

[333] *Illustração Portugueza*, 21 January 1907, 92.

[334] Richard Middleton, "Afterword," in Ian Biddle and Vanessa Knights (eds.), *Music, National Identity and the Politics of Location* (Aldershot: Ashgate, 2007), 195.

[335] Middleton, "Afterword," 195.

[336] Middleton, "Afterword," 195.

both modernity and nationality, situating the "national" as a contingent and contested place between the local and the global. Therefore, the fleeting notion of the nation is embedded in the transience of modern life.

Lacan's distinction between pleasure and *jouissance* is extremely useful when addressing the *revista*. For Chiesa, "*jouissance* is "pleasure *in* pain." More specifically, this is always equivalent to the "*jouissance of object petit a*, which is a remainder of the Real which tears holes in the symbolic structure."[337] Therefore, *jouissance* is located beyond Freud's pleasure principle, due to its inherently masochistic status. For Lacan "the function of the pleasure principle is, in effect, to lead the subject from signifier to signifier, by generating as many signifiers as are required to maintain at as low a level as possible the tension that regulates the whole functioning of the psychic apparatus."[338] Thus, the pleasure principle works within the symbolic order, "the collection of codes and distinctions embodied in language and culture."[339] Furthermore, "it is pleasure that sets the limits on *jouissance*, pleasure as that which binds incoherent life together."[340] Relating his theory to theater, it becomes possible to draw a parallel between the idea of pleasure as a path from signifier to signifier and the intrinsically heterogeneous nature of the *revista* (itself a discontinuous path between signifiers). Therefore, pleasure in the *revista* is contained and delimited within the symbolic order. This creates a space that, although seemingly and fleetingly liberated (which can relate to Victor Turner's concept of *communitas*), contributes to the homeostasis of the system.[341] The *revista* A.B.C. defined the genre as "the relief for the Zé Povinho, the greatest freedom that is allowed to him."[342] This not only emphasizes the role of the *revista* as an entertainment for the "people," but also stresses its almost liberating character, that, although circumscribed, traced the boundaries of the social conventions. The political role played by popular entertainment is emphasized by Kracauer in his study of Offenbach's operettas as "the most definite form of revolutionary protest" in the French Second Empire, given the powerlessness of the left wing and the political inactivity of the bourgeoisie.[343]

---

[337] Lorenzo Chiesa, "Lacan with Artaud: fouis-sens, jouis-sens, jouis-sans," in Slavoj Žižek (ed.), *Lacan: The Silent Partners* (London: Verso, 2006), 353.

[338] Jacques Lacan, *The Ethics of Psychoanalysis, 1959–1960* (New York: Routledge Chapman & Hall, 1992), 119.

[339] Lewis A. Kirshner, "Rethinking Desire: The *Objet petit a* in Lacanian Theory," *Journal of the American Psychoanalytical Association*, 53/1 (2005), 86.

[340] Jacques Lacan, *Écrits: A selection* (London: Routledge, 2001), 244.

[341] Victor Turner, *The Ritual Process: Structure and Anti-Structure* (Hawthorne, NY: Aldine de Gruyter, 1997), 132.

[342] Rebello, *História do teatro de revista em Portugal*, vol. 1, 145.

[343] Kracauer, *Jacques Offenbach and the Paris of His Time*, 324.

When studying the theater from an anthropological stance, the works of Victor Turner and Richard Schechner are of great importance. Turner points to the role theater plays in modern societies as a mechanism of self-reflexivity, which is especially appropriate when studying the *revista*.[344] Moreover, "industrial pre-electronic societies tend to stress theater which assigns meanings to macroprocesses—economic, political, or generalized familial problems."[345] In this sense, despite the small scale of Portuguese industrialization and its concentration in very specific sectors and places, we can perceive the role the stage could play in this process of assigning meanings to both the macroprocesses of nation-building and of modernity. This can be seen clearly when dealing with the *revista* as a commentator on reality, indicating the role the theater played in the process of self-reflection enacted in Portuguese society. Furthermore, Turner associates theater with ritual. His elaboration of Van Gennep's work distinguishes between liminal and liminoid phenomena, placing the theater in the latter category.[346] For Turner, liminality is associated with events of a compulsory nature within a society (like rites of initiation, for example) and is a state in which the actors are "neither here nor there; they are betwixt and between the positions assigned and arrayed by law, custom, convention, and ceremony."[347] "Liminoid phenomena, on the other hand, flourish in societies of more complex structure, where, in Henry Maine's terms, 'contract has replaced status' as the major social bond, where people voluntarily enter into relationships instead of being born into them."[348] In modern societies, Turner argues, both types of phenomena (liminal and liminoid) coexist and "the liminoid is more like a commodity—indeed, often is a commodity, which one selects and pays for—than the liminal, which elicits loyalty and is bound up with one's membership or desired membership in some highly corporate group."[349] Therefore, he associates the voluntary experience of theatergoing with the *liminoid*.

However, Turner classifies satire (the most prevalent aspect of the *revista*) as pseudo-liminal because, although it has a critical stance, "its criterion of

---

[344] Victor Turner, "Are There Universals of Performance in Myth, Ritual, and Drama?," in Richard Schechner and Willa Apel, *By Means of Performance* (Cambridge: Cambridge University Press, 1997), 8.

[345] Turner, "Are There Universals of Performance in Myth, Ritual, and Drama?, 8.

[346] Victor Turner, *The Ritual Process: Structure and Anti-Structure* (Hawthorne, NY: Aldine de Gruyter, 1997); Victor Turner, "Frame, Flow and Reflection: Ritual and Drama as Public Liminality," *Japanese Journal of Religious Studies*, 6/4 (1979), 465–499.

[347] Turner, *The Ritual Process: Structure and Anti-Structure*, 95.

[348] Turner, "Frame, Flow and Reflection," 492.

[349] Turner, *From Ritual to Theater: The Human Seriousness of Play* (NY: PAJ Publications, 1982), 55.

judgement is usually the normative structural frame of officially promulgated values."[350] Consequently, instead of inverting the status quo (as in the liminal phases), satire subverts it, but from the standpoint of, and maintaining, the official system.[351] It is precisely because of the prominence of subversion instead of inversion that I associate Lacan's concept of pleasure and not his idea of *jouissance* with the *revista*. Therefore, the prevalence of the pleasure principle is precisely what allows the subversiveness of satire in the *revista* to maintain the homeostasis of the system, instead of the transgressive and disruptive action of *jouissance*. This reinforces the prevalence of the Symbolic (even with the workings of different, even competing, sets of symbols), preventing the fall into the unruly realm of *jouissance*. For example, the exposure of the female body in the *revista* is a symptom of this tendency. The reduced costumes, the choreographic settings, and the double entendre dialogues can be interpreted as devices that displayed and yet contained the physical sensuousness associated with the female body within its accepted boundaries. Nevertheless, pleasure, promoted not only as an escape for the audience but also as a factor associated with the loosening of social conventions (related to the liminoid state Turner associates with the theatrical performance), acts as a facilitator for the composite image of the modern nation to be naturalized and internalized. Consequently, the depiction of patriotism and modernity in the entertainment market is a process of commodifying the nation and making its consumption pleasurable for the audience. Moreover, Turner's theorization of the symbolic can be useful for understanding the process of personification and allegory associated with the *revista*. For him, symbols "exhibit the properties of condensation, unification of disparate referents, and polarization of meaning."[352] In this framework, "a single symbol, in fact, represents many things at the same time: it is multivocal, not univocal. Its referents are not all of the same logical order but are drawn from many domains of social experience and ethical evaluation."[353] Furthermore, "symbols are multi-vocal, manipulable, and ambiguous precisely because they are initially located in systems, classified or arranged in a regular, orderly form."[354] Consequently, the personifications and allegories in the *revista* could not only be manipulated but could also be interpreted and decoded in multiple ways. The recurrence of stock characters throughout the history of the genre points precisely to the plasticity associated with this process.

---

[350] Turner, *From Ritual to Theater*, 40–41.
[351] Turner, *From Ritual to Theater*, 40–41.
[352] Turner, *The Ritual Process: Structure and Anti-Structure*, 52.
[353] Turner, *The Ritual Process: Structure and Anti-Structure*, 52.
[354] Victor Turner, "Symbolic Studies," *Annual Review of Anthropology*, 4 (1975), 146.

Mencarelli associates the Brazilian *revista* of the late 19th century with "one of the first attempts in the process of constitution of mass culture" due to the wide spectrum of its audience, relating this dissemination with its polysemic and open-ended structure that allowed for different readings of relevant topics in the actuality being displayed.[355] I will go further and argue that the inherently polysemic character of the *revista* promoted the widening of its audience (making it a profitable business enterprise) and the presentation of a symbolic order in which traces of the modern nation were embedded. This contrasts with Young's perspective on *zarzuela*, in which the association of Spanish nationalism with the *genero chico* could become a liability for both if the trends of the entertainment market relied less on local culture.[356] In Portugal the ability for the *revista* to integrate distinct, and sometimes conflicting, elements of everyday modern life makes its association with nationalism more subtle and open-ended. Thus the symbolic nation is one of the many layers that are included in the genre, and its relationship with the stage varied across this period, from the overt promotion of patriotism to a barely noticeable subtext (if detectable at all). Thus, the nation creates a dynamic that binds culture, memory, and place. In this process the selection of national symbols had to be twofold: they had to be sufficiently recognizable for the "people" to attach to them and they had to be ambiguous enough to be continuously re-encoded to broaden their meaning.[357] Furthermore, the importance of a personal investment in the identification and construction of collective identities complicates a perspective that emphasizes the role of the cultural elite in an almost univocal process of nation-building.[358] Therefore, the symbolic multivocality of the *revista* places it as a narrative that preserves "the scope to become a theater of new, unforeseen constellations" and in which "the stamp of the definitive is avoided," a characteristic Walter Benjamin associates with southern European cities.[359]

---

[355] Fernando Antonio Mencarelli, "A cena aberta: a interpretação de 'Bilontra' no teatro de revista de Arthur Azevedo," master's thesis (Unicamp, 1996), 24.

[356] Young, "Zarzuela," 199.

[357] Slavoj Žižek, *For They Know Not What They Do* (London: Verso, 2008); Stuart Hall, "Encoding/Decoding" in Centre for Contemporary Cultural Studies (ed.), *Culture, Media, Language: Working Papers in Cultural Studies, 1972–79* (London: Hutchinson, 1980), 128–138.

[358] Yannis Stavrakakis and Nikos Chrysoloras, "'(I Can't Get No) Enjoyment': Lacanian Theory and the Analysis of Nationalism," Psychoanalysis, *Culture & Society*, 11/2 (2006), 144–163.

[359] Walter Benjamin and Asja Lacis, "Naples," in Walter Benjamin, *Reflections: Essays, Aphorisms, Autobiographical Writings* (New York: Schocken Books, 2007), 166.

3

Song Collection in Portugal

Between Domestic Entertainment and Scientific Objectivity

The study of folklore played an important role in nation-building across Europe, and Portugal was no exception. Representing the vernacular became important in Lisbon toward the end of the 19th century. Fascination with the vernacular inspired many artists, and the portrayal of the low-other (the lower classes) became an integral part of entertainment. However, most representations of this low-other were distorted when they appeared in a theatrical play or an art exhibition. Therefore, "what is socially excluded or subordinated is symbolically central in the formation of desire."[1] This does not mean that the rural other was not part of everyday urban life; the porosity between the country and the city in a nation that was predominantly rural was very real. Many authors argued that the rural culture needed salvaging because it became endangered with urbanization. Nevertheless, the gap between the rural and the urban is open to question, especially in a period when "the leisure and literary habits of the middle classes encouraged the burlesque mimesis of rural customs and the systematization of the fantasized images of rural life created via this mimesis."[2] This is symptomatic of an ongoing process that entailed both industrialization and urbanization.[3] Therefore, a study that reflects the urban/rural dichotomy in which song collectors worked is very problematic at this stage. This is also reflected in the historical study of fado that emphasized its

---

[1] Peter Stallybrass and Allon White, *The Poetics and Politics of Transgression* (Ithaca, NY: Cornell University Press, 1986), 152.

[2] António Medeiros, "Imperialist Ideology and Representations of the Portuguese Provinces during the Early Estado Novo," in Sharon R. Roseman and Shawn S. Parkhurst (eds.), *Recasting Culture and Space in Iberian Contexts* (New York: SUNY Press, 2008), 87.

[3] Raymond Williams, *The Country and the City* (New York: Oxford University Press, 1975); John Comaroff and Jean Comaroff, "Images of Empire, Contests of Conscience," in Comaroff and Comaroff, *Ethnography and the Historical Imagination* (Boulder, CO: Westview Press, 1992), 192.

specificity as the music of the urban low-other. However, the term "fado" was used almost indiscriminately across the country to mean popular songs.

As a counterpoint to the pessimism concerning the future of European culture in the late 19th and early 20th centuries, the search for an "authentic" culture was carried out by scholars. This often created an imagined other, the "illiterate folk or peasants, supposedly untouched by modern civilization or transformation, whose 'natural' culture stands in contrast to anything implicated in urban life and affected by commercial interests."[4] This naive perspective did not rely on direct observation. In the early days, most scholars had little contact with the "peasants" who created popular culture; they used "the people" as an empty signifier that occupied an important space in their ideological apparatus,[5] holding the heterogeneous elements of nation-building in place. The study of rural music was a secondary concern of Portuguese ethnology. Nevertheless, the results of this work were published and became part of the entertainment market. *Chulas* and *corridinhos* (a regional dance of the Portuguese south) were staged in theatrical plays and published as sheet music. Therefore, music from rural areas became known by the urban middle classes, in the theaters and in their homes. This sanitization of the "people" on Lisbon's stages is evident in a piece about Lisbon's poor published in 1908.[6] The article argued that the plays *A Severa* and *Rosa Enjeitada* revealed good observation and well-delineated characters, but the representations were stylized.[7] Therefore, they fell short of portraying the actual living conditions of the people who were characterized. The piece intends to give "the perfect idea of those streets," reinforced with photographs that emphasize the precarious nature of the "filthy life of the population of those districts," the "wretched with no permanent abode who spend their miserable life in the uncertainty of next day's dinner."[8] This is the type of imaginary construction of the "other" on which popular entertainment relied and shows how the vernacular was presented to audiences.

This contrasts with the work carried out by scholars who were influenced by positivism and aimed to show the "real lives" of the rural population. Most of them worked and lived in cities, where their findings were published and

---

[4] Julie Brown, "Bartók, the Gypsies, and Hybridity in Music," in Georgina Born and David Hesmondhalgh (eds.), *Western Music and Its Others: Difference, Representation, and Appropriation in Music* (Berkeley: University of California Press, 2000), 131.

[5] João Leal, *Etnografias portuguesas (1870–1970)*, 102; Ernesto Laclau, *On Populist Reason* (London: Verso, 2007), 171.

[6] Luís da Câmara Reys, "A miséria em Lisboa," *Serões: revista mensal ilustrada*, November 1908, 334–342.

[7] Reys, "A miséria em Lisboa," 335.

[8] Reys, "A miséria em Lisboa," 336, 338–339, 342.

shared with the general public. Some of the collected songs were then adapted to the urban popular stage and their sheet music entered the bourgeois parlor. This reveals the paradox on which the study of folklore relies, that their ruralist content was created, established, and reproduced in an urban context.[9] Although the country's rural life as presented on the stage was often not realistic, even these representations helped with the spread of nationalism in Portugal by creating a broader awareness among the urban population of all parts of Portuguese life, thus binding the parts of the nation closer together.

Cultural identity and traditional music can be traced back to Herder's *Volkslied*, a term that fuses both ideas.[10] Herder linked national consciousness to popular traditions and believed that "the oral tradition contained the essence, or soul, of a nation."[11] Therefore, folk culture is used as a symbol of nationalism and played an important role in creating and reproducing national identities. In Portugal, the interest in collecting songs was initially associated with literary Romanticism, which perceived and constructed "the people" as the repository of the nation's cultural substrate.[12] This situates "the people" in "an anterior temporal space, within but not fully of the present."[13] The Spanish Miguel de Unamuno also had an ahistorical vision of the "deep people."[14] This people was the "common mass to all castes, its protoplasmatic matter" before they were differentiated and divided by class and by historical institutions.[15] Moreover, Unamuno claimed that the official forms of culture, especially the periodicals, ignored the "silent life of the millions of men without a history that, everyday and in all countries of the globe, get up at sunrise, and go to the fields to carry on with their obscure and silent labor, both daily and eternal."[16] This intra-historical life, "silent and continuous like the living seabed, is the

---

[9] Jorge Freitas Branco and Salwa Castelo-Branco (eds.), *Vozes do povo: a folclorização em Portugal* (Oeiras: Celta Editora, 2003), 7.

[10] Philip Bohlman, "Traditional Music and Cultural Identity: Persistent Paradigm in the History of Ethnomusicology," *Yearbook for Traditional Music*, 20 (1988), 31–33.

[11] John Francmanis, "National Music to National Redeemer: The Consolidation of a "Folksong" Construct in Edwardian England," *Popular Music*, 21/1 (2002), 2.

[12] Salwa Castelo-Branco and Manuela Toscano, "'In Search of a Lost World': An Overview of Documentation and Research on the Traditional Music of Portugal." *Yearbook for Traditional Music*, 20 (1988), 159.

[13] Janet Sorensen, "Alternative Antiquarianisms of Scotland and the North," *Modern Language Quarterly*, 70/4 (2009), 416.

[14] Miguel de Unamuno, "Sobre el marasmo actual de España," in Miguel de Unamuno, *En torno al casticismo: cinco ensayos* (Madrid: Residencia de Estudiantes, 1916), 214.

[15] Miguel de Unamuno, "Sobre el marasmo actual de España," in Miguel de Unamuno, *En torno al casticismo: cinco ensayos* (Madrid: Residencia de Estudiantes, 1916), 214.

[16] Unamuno, "La tradición eterna" in Unamuno, *En torno al casticismo* (Madrid: Residencia de Estudiantes, 1916), 40–41.

substance of progress, the real tradition, the eternal tradition, not the lied tradition that tends to retrieve from the past buried in books, and papers, and monuments, and stones."[17] Thus, this hidden people was seen by Unamuno as the key to regenerating Spain in a critical period. This idea is paralleled in Portugal with the new ethnological currents that developed toward the end of the 19th century. Early Portuguese ethnology was mainly concentrated on texts and relied on a Romantic ethos, foregrounding the lyrics as the primary concern of popular song collection. This emphasis relegated music to the background. In spite of this, many transcriptions of traditional music were published from the last third of the 19th century onward. These were often presented in contrast to the publications associated with the urban entertainment market and claim a purported authenticity that stands in opposition to fado and to the theatrical songs that were dominant. A strong reaction toward this dominance was not limited to the urban/rural dichotomy. The split between art and entertainment that was taking place also reflected this. Therefore, the popular stage was simultaneously too artistic and not artistic enough for some people. The distinction between art and entertainment was a consequence of "an intense dislike of the market conditions that turned art into a commodity."[18] In this separation, popular music was seen as a business in which profit, and not artistic accomplishment, was the main concern.[19]

The transcription of Portuguese traditional music between 1872 and the 1920s was concentrated in three main categories: harmonizations of collected melodies; arrangements of these melodies for choruses, *bandas*, or orchestra; or exact transcriptions of the melodies.[20] The techniques used in transcribing these materials often seemed alien to the folk music itself. While the study of rural populations relied on the notion of scientific objectivity, in which the agency of the collector is effaced, most transcriptions of traditional music were made using the conventions of published sheet music in their harmonization and instrumentation. Therefore, the music was arranged for solo piano, for voice and piano, as well as for ensembles, and became part of Lisbon's soundscape. Traditional music crossed into the piano room, the bandstands, and the popular stage. The first known publication of Portuguese traditional music is the *Álbum de músicas nacionais portuguesas* (Album of Portuguese National

---

[17] Unamuno, "La tradición eterna," 41.

[18] Derek B. Scott, *Sounds of the Metropolis: The 19th-Century Popular Music Revolution in London, New York, Paris and Vienna* (Oxford: Oxford University Press, 2008), 88.

[19] Scott, *Sounds of the Metropolis*, 88.

[20] Castelo-Branco and Toscano, "In Search of a Lost World", 168; Salwa Castelo-Branco, "Etnomusicologia," in Salwa Castelo-Branco (ed.), *Enciclopédia da música em Portugal no século XX*, vol. 2 (Lisbon: Círculo de Leitores, 2010), 421–422.

Musics) by João António Ribas (1799–1869). He was a prominent violinist and music dealer working in Porto, where this work was published in 1857.[21] Some years later, Neves e Melo published his groundbreaking volume of "popular musics and songs collected from the tradition."[22] In the 1890s the *Cancioneiro de músicas populares*, the largest collection of traditional Portuguese music, was published in Porto.[23]

The *Cancioneiro*, a three-volume work coordinated by César das Neves (1841–1920) and Gualdino de Campos (1847–1919) contains a large number of songs—from original compositions to songs drawn from Portuguese rural and urban contexts as well as songs from abroad.[24] It consists of vocal and piano arrangements and was sold in installments published fortnightly. Thus, the *Cancioneiro* reflected a nationalist ideology by adjusting what were predominantly rural songs to the taste of urban audiences, thus making the urban citizens more aware of the country's rural dwellers.[25] The collection illustrates the trend of shaping the vernacular to suit the conventions of the entertainment market. In this work, the prevailing urban musical form was an important principle for selecting the repertoires collected in rural areas. Despite including songs from many regions, the *Cancioneiro* includes only transcriptions for solo voice and piano, glossing over the vocal polyphonic practices of several areas (like Alentejo or Minho).[26] The collectors selected and arranged the traditional music to conform to the widespread format of sheet music. Each song was dedicated to an aristocratic or bourgeois woman or girl. This indicates the intended audience for the publication, primarily the female public.[27] Despite its placement between strict ethnographic collection and the entertainment market, the *Cancioneiro* contains important information and reveals the ambiguous place occupied by traditional music at that time. Neves supervised the musical component and Campos was in charge of the texts. In the *Cancioneiro* they included the name of the collector, the date and place of the collection, or

---

[21] João António Ribas, *Album de musicas nacionaes portuguezas: constando de cantigas e tocatas usadas nos differentes districtos e comarcas das províncias da Beira, Traz-os-montes e Minho* (Porto: C. A. Villa Nova, 1860).

[22] Adelino das Neves e Melo, *Musicas e canções populares colligidas da tradição* (Lisbon: Imprensa Nacional, 1872).

[23] César das Neves and Gualdino de Campos, *Cancioneiro de músicas populares*, 3 vols. (Porto: Tip. Ocidental—Empresa editora César, Campos & Cª, 1893, 1895, 1898).

[24] Maria do Rosário Pestana, "César das Neves," in Salwa Castelo-Branco (ed.), *Enciclopédia da música em Portugal no século XX*, vol. 3, 909–910.

[25] Pestana,"César das Neves," 909–910.

[26] Susana Sardo, "Música popular e diferenças regionais," in Mário Ferreira Lages and Artur Teodoro de Matos (eds.), *Portugal: Percursos de Interculturalidade*, vol. 1 (Lisbon: ACIDI, 2008), 421.

[27] Sardo, "Música popular e diferenças regionais," 421.

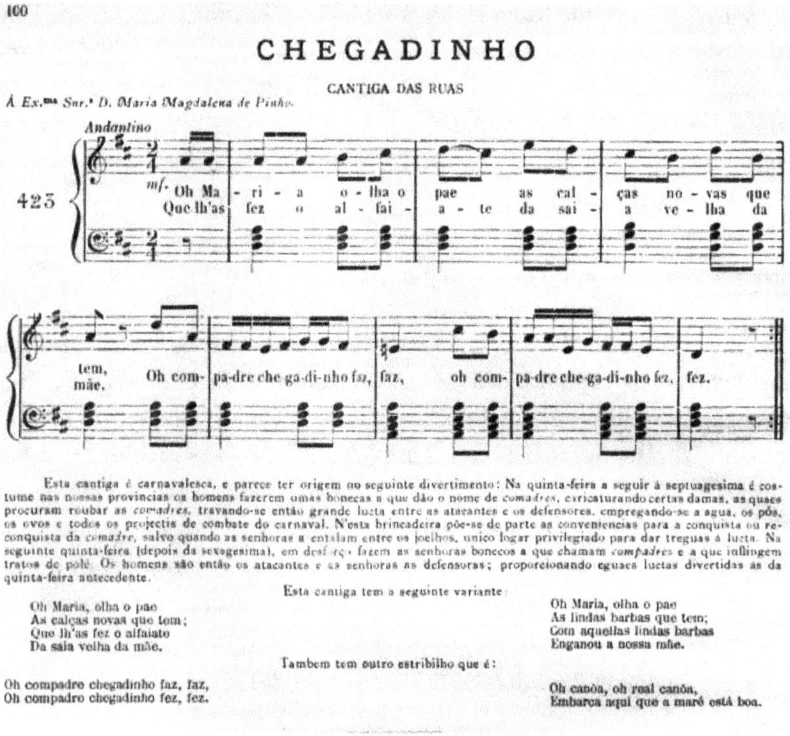

Esta cantiga é carnavalesca, e parece ter origem no seguinte divertimento: Na quinta-feira a seguir á septuagesima é costume nas nossas provincias os homens fazerem umas bonecas a que dão o nome de *comadres*, caricaturando certas damas, as quaes procuram roubar as *comadres*, travando-se então grande lucta entre as atacantes e os defensores, empregando-se a agua, os pós, os ovos e todos os projectis de combate do carnaval. N'esta brincadeira põe-se de parte as conveniencias para a conquista ou reconquista da *comadre*, salvo quando as senhoras a entalam entre os joelhos, unico logar privilegiado para dar treguas á lucta. Na seguinte quinta-feira (depois da sexagesima), em desforço fazem as senhoras bonecos a que chamam *compadres* e a que infligem tratos de polé. Os homens são então os atacantes e as senhoras as defensoras; proporcionando eguaes luctas divertidas ás da quinta-feira antecedente.

Esta cantiga tem a seguinte variante:

Oh Maria, olha o pae
As calças novas que tem;
Que lh'as fez o alfaiate
Da saia velha da mãe.

Oh Maria, olha o pae
As lindas barbas que tem;
Com aquellas lindas barbas
Enganou a nossa mãe.

Tambem tem outro estribilho que é:

Oh compadre chegadinho faz, faz,
Oh compadre chegadinho fez, fez.

Oh canôa, oh real canôa,
Embarca aqui que a maré está boa.

Figure 3.1 Musical transcription of *Chegadinho,* in César das Neves and Gualdino de Campos, *Cancioneiro de músicas populares,* vol. 3 (Porto: Tip. Ocidental – Empresa editora César, Campos & Cª, 1898), 100, Biblioteca Nacional de Portugal, MPP-21-a-1_3. Musical transcription of *Chegadinho.*

of the first source in which the song appeared. To illustrate this information, Figure 3.1 is the transcription of a "street song," the "Chegadinho."

The "Chegadinho" is connected with Carnival, and the authors describe the accompanying choreography which involves men and women fighting for dummies. The men make dummies that caricature the women and the dance consists of people trying to steal the dummies from each other. The following week, the gender roles are reversed. The women make the dummies and the men try to steal them. They also throw projectiles associated with the Carnival, like eggs, water, or powders. Thus, the *Cancioneiro* is also an important source for studying dance. Neves and Campos were not the only collectors involved with the work. For example, the song "Trolha d' Afife" had been included in *Álbum de músicas nacionais portuguesas,* by João António Ribas. "Trolha d' Afife" was collected by Ribas in 1850, and the melody is set over an Alberti bass.[28] This reflects the arrangement of a regional melody in the conventions of the transnational sheet

[28] Neves and Campos, *Cancioneiro,* vol. 1, 74–75.

music of the middle of the 19th century. Therefore, the *Cancioneiro* is a patchwork of repertoires, collectors, and regions. It is also a work that represents different historical times. "Batalha de Alcácer Quibir" is a song that commemorates an event from the nation's deep past.[29] It tells of the Battle of Alcácer-Quibir (or Ksar El Kebir) fought in northern Africa in 1578, where the Portuguese king D. Sebastião presumably perished, creating a crisis that culminated with the union of the two Iberian kingdoms from 1580 to 1640. The piece was collected from Miguel Leitão de Andrada's book *Miscellanea do sitio de N. S^a. da Luz do Pedrogão Grande*, published in 1629 and republished by the Imprensa Nacional in 1867.[30] Neves reduced a song in which the three voices were written separately and in C clefs to a two-stave piano setting, a strategy he describes in his critical commentary.[31] Despite its strophic form and narrative stance, aspects that seem to place the song within popular balladry, Neves argues that its contrapuntal features indicate a non-popular, composed origin for the song.[32] This shows how popular culture was seen by collectors as sometimes preserving vestigial traces of erudite cultural creations of the past.

Neves and Campos identified the collectors of the pieces, using the prestige (or social capital, to use Bourdieu's terminology) of these collectors to promote the *Cancioneiro*. Another promotional strategy was finding eminent scholars to write prefaces for the collections. For example, the volume *Canções populares da Beira*, organized by Pedro Fernandes Tomás (1853–1927), had an introduction by Leite de Vasconcelos, a leading ethnographer of the time.[33] The *Cancioneiro de músicas populares* also used this strategy. Each volume had a foreword by a personality associated with Porto, the city where Neves and Campos worked. In the preface to the first volume, Teófilo Braga compared the abundance of study of the lyrics with the lack of research on the music. He attributed this shortage to most ethnologists' lack of musical training. A major issue in the collection was to transcribe songs while preserving the "naive simplicity of the melodies" and their "spontaneous naturality."[34] The strong association between text and music was seen by Braga as a product of the "mental syncretism of the races."[35] This situates the traditional songs within

---

[29] Neves and Campos, *Cancioneiro*, vol. 2, 1–3.

[30] Miguel Leitão de Andrada, *Miscellanea do sitio de N. S^a. da Luz do Pedrogão Grande* (Lisbon: Matheus Pinheiro, 1629), 230–231; Andrada, *Miscellanea* (Lisbon: Imprensa Nacional, 1867).

[31] Neves and Campos, *Cancioneiro*, vol. 2, 2.

[32] Neves and Campos, *Cancioneiro*, vol. 2, 2.

[33] Pedro Fernandes Tomás, *Canções populares da Beira: acompanhada de 52 melodias recolhidas para piano* (Figueira da Foz: Lusitana, 1896).

[34] Teófilo Braga, "As melodias portuguesas," in Neves and Campos, *Cancioneiro*, vol. 1, v.

[35] Braga, "As melodias portuguesas," vol. 1, v.

an ethnogenealogical interpretation of history. He traced this strong association back to the Rigveda, a work he believed was made by the Aryan ancestors of the Portuguese.[36] Braga also discussed medieval and early modern songbooks, arguing that the popular melodies held traces of the far past. This argument not only creates an unbroken line in the history of Portuguese poetry but also posits "the people" as the sources of this historical past. His claim was made in a critical period for Portugal, a country "threatened by decadence" where revivification of the "national genius is dependent on the vitality of its tradition."[37]

The prominent art historian and archeologist Sousa Viterbo (1845–1910) introduced the second volume of the *Cancioneiro* by praising the work and the service it provides to "Portuguese nationality."[38] He studied the link between science and folklorism, which walks "hand in hand to the fields, collecting, a little by chance, the flowers that spontaneously blossomed at their feet."[39] Viterbo argued that the *Cancioneiro* should be used as a source for comparing the aesthetic manifestations of different peoples. He also pointed to the influence of the theater and of the church in Portuguese traditional songs. Viterbo argued that these songs might also have been influenced by the cultures of the Jews and Moors who had settled in the Iberian Peninsula.[40] This view was followed by Alberto Pimentel in his work on Portuguese songs, where he traced a north/south divide based on ethnicity. The second volume of the *Cancioneiro* contains a long preamble by César das Neves, in which he discussed the "primitive music of the crude people," initially focused on rhythm. To illustrate, he looked at the ensembles of percussionists and bagpipers that played in the religious feasts in the north of Portugal.[41] Neves characterized different types of songs by their subject and by their instrumentation, pointing to the diversity that is found in Portugal.[42] He drew a historical account of the Portuguese popular song, showing that the dominant role played by theatrical music and the alleged stagnation of traditional music were symptoms of national decadence.[43] Thus, the charge of Portuguese decadence permeates several parts of the *Cancioneiro*, which aims to rescue this traditional music from oblivion.

[36] Braga, "As melodias portuguesas," vol. 1, v.
[37] Braga, "As melodias portuguesas," vi–vii.
[38] Sousa Viterbo, "Cancioneiro de músicas populares," in Neves and Campos, *Cancioneiro*, vol. 2, v.
[39] Viterbo, "Cancioneiro de músicas populares", vol. 2, v.
[40] Viterbo, "Cancioneiro de músicas populares," vol. 2, vi.
[41] Neves, "Preambulo," in Neves and Campos, *Cancioneiro*, vol.2, xi–xiii.
[42] Neves, "Preambulo," vol. 2, xiii–xv.
[43] Neves, "Preambulo," vol. 2, xv.

Manuel Ramos, a journalist with several publications on music, introduced the last volume of the series. The text is predominantly focused on how traditional music should be used as thematic material for art music. He began by praising the Pre-Raphaelites and their use of the English popular culture to create a national style.[44] Ramos then focused on music, and examined the work of Russian, Scandinavian, and Bohemian composers associated with nationalism.[45] He turned to the Iberian Peninsula and traced an account of Portuguese music in the 19th century, associating this period with the rise of a nationalist movement. This includes composers like Francisco de Sá Noronha, João Arroio, Ciríaco de Cardoso, Viana da Mota (1868–1948), Victor Hussla (1857–1899), Alexandre Rey Colaço (1854–1928), and Alfredo Keil. Among these, Viana da Mota was a prominent pianist who had a career abroad but had already composed works that used Portuguese popular music. He returned to Portugal during the First World War and was instrumental in reforming the country's musical life. Hussla was a German violinist born in St. Petersburg who moved to Portugal. He taught in several institutions and directed orchestras. As a composer he used materials from the collection published by João António Ribas in his *Rapsódias portuguesas*. This shows how nationalism permeated Portuguese culture in the end of the 19th century. Rey Colaço wrote many small pieces for piano, including fados. In his preface, Ramos emphasized the role that traditional music should play in the renewal of Portuguese music, enumerated the collections of local popular songs, and argued for some of these materials to become part of the curricula of primary schools.[46] Therefore, the *Cancioneiro* points to the multiple uses of folklore, reflecting its four major trends:

> an ideology of nationalism, an ethnographic emphasis on surveying social context, an ethical dimension that involves the preservation of music thought to be traditional and endangered throughout the world, and an educational aspect in which the music becomes part of the public school curriculum and is offered to adults as well.[47]

If the first three aspects are predominant in the study of Portuguese folklore, implementing the last point was a complicated task. Given the scarcity

---

[44] Manuel Ramos, "Cancioneiro de Músicas Populares," in Neves and Campos, *Cancioneiro*, vol. 3, v.

[45] Ramos, "Cancioneiro de Músicas Populares," vol. 3, v–vi.

[46] Ramos, "Cancioneiro de Músicas Populares," vol. 3, vii–viii.

[47] Jeff Todd Titon, "Knowing Fieldwork," in Gregory Barz and Timothy J. Cooley, *Shadows in the Field: New Perspectives for Fieldwork in Ethnomusicology* (Oxford: Oxford University Press, 2008), 29.

of public education, singing traditional songs in the classroom was extremely limited. Moreover, a network of public schools working under a national curriculum was an important part of republican propaganda. Therefore, traditional music constituted a repository of melodies for composers to draw upon, a part of domestic entertainment, and could become an educational tool in which patriotism is embedded.

Phonography, the Effacement of the Collector, and the Market

Collections of traditional songs were part of the publishing business in the dawn of the 20th century. They were part of the commercial entertainment market, and Vieira reports that some constituted an "abusive commercial exploitation" of traditional music.[48] Nevertheless, a scientific approach was developed not only for selecting the repertoire but also to the methods used when collecting to avoid the earlier tendency of transcribing traditional music with commercial intent. Therefore, effacing the collector became important in Portuguese ethnology. The collector is always "a witness who intervenes between us and the performance and colors the record of it with some of his or her own ideas and assumptions."[49] In 1902 the Council of Musical Art of the Lisbon Conservatoire released a circular that aimed to systematize the way folk songs were collected throughout the country.[50] The document requested the cooperation of all people who were interested in the musical traditions of Portugal to create "the most faithful and complete" collection of Portuguese folklore.[51] It was signed by Eduardo Schwalbach, then inspector of the Conservatório Real de Lisboa. The document said that collection of traditional music would enhance a better understanding of the Portuguese people and would assist in developing the country's art music. The circular noted that some songs had been "modernized" when they were collected.[52] It said that the variants of the same song should be mapped, and songs should be collected "by simply recording the melodies as they are presented by the people," "without the slightest personal intervention of the collector who can disturb them."[53] Thus, the collector should retreat to invisibility in the

---

[48] Vieira, *Diccionario*, vol. 2, 254.

[49] Vic Gammon, "Folk Song Collecting in Sussex and Surrey, 1843–1914," *History Workshop Journal*, 10/1 (1980), 62.

[50] "Cancioneiro popular portugues," *Revista do Conservatorio Real de Lisboa*, May 1902, 15–16.

[51] "Cancioneiro popular portugues," 15.

[52] "Cancioneiro popular portugues," 15.

[53] "Cancioneiro popular portugues," 15–16.

process. Nevertheless, he or she would impose meaning on and organize the repertoires. These methods contrast with those used in producing the bulk of the previously published songbooks, which predominantly consisted of tonal harmonizations. In the new methodology, music had to be collected "directly from the people" and must include the place of collection, the events where the songs were performed, or the instruments used. This illustrates a shift from a Romantic folklorism that was directed to transcriptions to be played in the piano parlor and toward a purist framework where the unharmonized melodies would be prized.[54] Unfortunately, the impact of the circular was not substantial and most transcriptions that fitted its aims were not made until after 1910. Nevertheless, some collectors did change their method for collecting music. Pedro Fernandes Tomás did not harmonize the melodies he published in 1913 and removed the harmonizations included in *Canções populares da Beira* when the book was republished in 1923.[55]

In 1907 Leite de Vasconcelos published an article about popular poetry and music, "Canções do berço" (Songs of the cradle).[56] It includes transcriptions of traditional melodies that fit this new paradigm and were published without harmonization. A leading scholar working on music was an exception in the ethnological climate of the time. Vasconcelos discussed cradle songs in Portugal, and placed them in an interethnic framework. He traced these songs in Portugal back to the Renaissance and included illustrations of cribs from several Portuguese regions, reflecting his growing interest in material culture. The core of the work consists of a long set of poems collected in various regions by Vasconcelos and others.[57] Many were taken "directly from the people's mouth."[58] He organized the texts in four main categories: prelude, lullabies, songs of the cradle, and songs that have distinctive characteristics. The "prelude" contains poems that express the care the mother has toward her children. It explains the significance and the origin of the lyrics. The songs were learned from previous generations of mothers and showed the role women played in the transmission of culture in the home. This role is shared by women from different parts of the social spectrum and will be studied in detail in the next chapter. The "lullabies" were performed with the mother holding the child, and the "songs of the cradle" were sung while the child is being rocked in

---

[54] "Cancioneiro popular portugues," 16.

[55] Pedro Fernandes Tomás, *Velhas canções e romances populares portugueses* (Coimbra: França Amado, editor, 1913); Castelo-Branco and Toscano, "In Search of a Lost World," 161.

[56] Leite de Vasconcelos, "Canções do berço: segundo a tradição popular portuguesa," *Revista Lusitana*, 10/1–2 (1907), 1–86.

[57] Leite de Vasconcelos, "Canções do berço," 23–24.

[58] Leite de Vasconcelos, "Canções do berço," 23–24.

the cradle. The last category comprised songs with an unusual meter or stanza length, songs that include Mirandese or Spanish words, proverbs, and sayings as well as poems that, despite not being originally designed to lull children, were used for this aim.[59] Vasconcelos argued that the differences between the lullabies and the songs of the cradle are mostly theoretical and that the same songs could be used in both contexts.[60] The journal article "Canções do berço" also includes an appendix containing lyrics that were collected after the work was paginated, an extensive commentary on the materials, and the transcription of several regional songs.

Tomás Borba (1867–1950), who taught harmony in Lisbon's Conservatoire, was trained in the Azores before studying music and letters in Lisbon. He was a Catholic priest and an important music educator. He was also influenced by the Council of Musical Art's circular on the correct way to collect folk music. Following its directives, he published in *Ilustração Portuguesa* a study of Portuguese traditional songs and dances that used unharmonized transcriptions. In it he discussed monophonic and polyphonic songs and dances, such as fados, peddlers' cries, dances from the north, *modas* from Alentejo (generic name for popular music of the region), songs from Coimbra, and music from the Azores.[61] This work includes ethnographic photographs and emphasizes the diversity of Portuguese traditional music. Borba compared music from several parts of the country and discussed modal variations, traditional instruments, the introduction of the accordion in rural areas, and the music associated with Portuguese feasts. Also, he showed the interpenetration of cultures when describing the music imported from the Portuguese migrants in Brazil, which became part of the local dances. In describing the songs from Coimbra, he argued that they had so much energy because the music circulated between the students and the "people."[62] Students gathered in Coimbra from the entire country and gave "popular melodies their final coat of paint."[63] Thus, as a professional musician, Borba had a more dynamic approach to traditional music than most collectors, who were still trying to find the authentic Portugal.

The use of portable sound recording technologies transformed the way music was collected and studied. It greatly enhanced collecting and safeguarding a culture that would soon be lost. Nevertheless, it was seldom used in Portugal. In the introduction to *Velhas canções e romances populares portugueses*, the art

---

[59] Leite de Vasconcelos, "Canções do berço," 13–14, 19–22.
[60] Leite de Vasconcelos, "Canções do berço," 13–14, 19–22.
[61] Tomás Borba, "Dansas e cantos populares da nossa terra," *Illustração Portugueza*, 23 December 1907, 833–838.
[62] Borba, "Dansas e cantos populares da nossa terra," 838.
[63] Borba, "Dansas e cantos populares da nossa terra," 838.

critic António Arroio (1856–1934) strongly supported using sound recording as a way to avoid the collector's intervention in the materials.[64] Promoting technological devices as guarantors of mechanic objectivity transfers the role of the mediator from a human to a machine. *Velhas canções e romances populares portugueses* was published by Pedro Fernandes Tomás in 1913 and, despite falling outside the boundaries of this book, contains important information concerning the new processes and methods for song collecting in Portugal. In the introduction, Arroio stated that he had done field recordings.[65] If this is true, it is the first mention of the phonograph in song collection. Regrettably, there is no further evidence of these phonograms nor of the dates of the recordings.[66] To complicate this issue, several songs from the *Cancioneiro de músicas populares* were recorded and released by the Companhia Franceza do Gramophone. This illustrates the ambiguous status of traditional music, caught in the space between the entertainment market and ethnology.

The rise of a scientific approach to a number of disciplines played an important role in creating the Portuguese nation-state. The efforts of Portuguese scholars were predominantly focused on language and race, the two main routes of tracing ethnicity. In addition, studies of traditional music were carried out by people like Leite de Vasconcelos, Pedro Fernandes Tomás, and César das Neves.[67] This was evidence of a wider process, mostly undertaken by republican scholars like Consiglieri Pedroso, Teófilo Braga, or Adolfo Coelho. It aimed to ground Portugal firmly in science and to dissociate it from a genealogy that associated Portugal with the ruling dynasty. Therefore, it established a competing notion of nationality that emanated from their republican beliefs. For this to be realized, the origins of "the Portuguese people" had to be grounded in archaeology, physical anthropology, philology, folklore studies, linguistics, and history. However, idolizing "the people" was seen by Fuschini as a form of propaganda furthered by the republican press, arguing that "while others prostrate themselves in front of the king, they worship the people, exploiting their passions and their crass ignorance."[68] The market for the vernacular continued to grow, and although this music was collected from "the people," it shared the conventions of sheet music or of the gramophone record. In this

---

[64] António Arroio, "Introducção," in Pedro Fernandes Tomás, *Velhas canções e romances populares portugueses*, xxiv–xxv; Lorraine Daston and Peter Galison, "The Image of Objectivity," *Representations*, 0/40 (1992), 81–128.

[65] Arroio, "Introducção," xxiv.

[66] Castelo-Branco and Toscano, "In Search of a Lost World," 161.

[67] Étienne Balibar, "The Nation Form," in Etienne Balibar and Immanuel Wallerstein, *Race, Nation, Class: Ambiguous Identities* (London: Verso, 2000), 96.

[68] Augusto Fuschini, *O presente e o futuro de Portugal* (Lisbon: Companhia Typographica, 1899), 330.

way, the vernacular was sanitized, creating "'safe' ways for middle-class city dwellers (and the respectable working class) to enjoy the proletarian pleasures of noisy public behavior."[69] Despite the focus of folklorists on rural cultures, both urban and rural styles were transformed to fit the market for cultural goods. This is also true of fado, the music of the urban low-other. Therefore, repertoires found their common ground in the entertainment market, complicating an essentialist perspective that relies on a clear separation between the urban and the rural or between the ethnological and the entertaining. Both ethnology and the entertainment market reflected and influenced a growing public awareness of national and regional identities in Portugal, thus facilitating the spread of patriotism.

The Urban Low-Other and Fado

Fado stands out as the most international Portuguese genre in the 21st century. However, its association with nationalism was complicated. As stated above, many collections of traditional music were published as a wholesome alternative to the dominant role fado and theatrical songs played in Portugal. This shows the opposition between "authentic" folk songs and composed popular entertainment. Lisbon's fado consisted predominantly of narrative forms that integrated the fleeting everydayness, and embodied modern life. Therefore, its lyrics reflected the tendencies of the time, such as the rise of socialist and anarchist propaganda. Moreover, new writers and poetic forms were incorporated in the genre. Contrasting different compositions named "fado" adds a new layer of complexity to this issue and emphasizes the ubiquity of fado in Lisbon's society. Important historical works about its history were published in the first decade of the 20th century. Pinto de Carvalho (1858–1930) published his *História do fado* in 1903.[70] In the following year, Alberto Pimentel (1849–1925) published *A triste canção do sul: subsídios para a história do fado*.[71] These works have different perspectives on fado and soon became important sources for studying the genre. This places the writing of music histories as part of a wide nationalist project that involves the construction of a common musical heritage. In this sense, "far from being a neutral exercise in facts and basic truths, the study of history, which of course is the underpinning of

---

[69] Simon Frith, *Performing Rites: On the Value of Popular Music* (Cambridge, MA: Harvard University Press, 1998), 34.

[70] Pinto de Carvalho, *História do fado* (Lisbon: Empreza da História de Portugal, 1903).

[71] Alberto Pimentel, *A triste canção do sul: subsídios para a história do Fado* (Lisbon: Livraria Central, 1904).

memory, both in school and university, is to some considerable extent a nationalist effort premised on the need to construct a desirable loyalty to and an insider's understanding of one's country, tradition, and faith."[72]

Carvalho argued that national characters and customs are best found through a country's popular songs, which resonates with the Herderian view of popular culture. He placed the origins of fado in the 1840s, a song by sailors that became part of the *habitus* of the marginal *fadista* in Lisbon. For Ortigão

> The *fadista* does not work nor has capital that represents an earlier accumulation of labor. He lives from the expedients of exploiting his fellows. He usually is supported by a public woman whom he beats systematically. Has no fixed abode. He lives in the tavern, in the gambling den, in the game of quoits, in the brothel, and in the police station. He is completely atrophied by inactivity, by the sleepless nights, by the overuse of tobacco and alcohol. He is anemic, cowardly, and stupid. He has a cough and a fever; his chest is concave, the arms are frail, the legs are bent, the womanlike hands are thin and pale, sweaty, with the bum's long fingernails, the fingers burnt and blackened by the cigarette; the hair is fetid, floured with dust and dandruff, shining with lard. The tools of his trade are a guitar and a Holy Christ, the name they use for the large switchblade.[73]

At this time, fado was associated with a lifestyle of drinking, smoking, and brawling in dark and unclean places, which were frequently linked to prostitution. Carvalho embarked on a historical reconstruction of the Lisbon district of Mouraria to examine the mythology associated with A Severa, the popular singer from Mouraria discussed in Chapter 2. He described the taverns and the *hortas*, the clothes of women *fadistas*, and their social lives.[74] For him, fado had two stages. The "popular and spontaneous stage" lasted until 1868–1869, when fado was performed by Lisbon's popular segments. The "aristocratic and literary phase" started when fado became incorporated into the city's salons.[75] In the late 1860s the Portuguese guitar rose to prominence in salon performances and the piano was relegated to popular entertainment venues.[76] Therefore, a straightforward connection between the piano and the bourgeois

---

[72] Edward W. Said, "Invention, Memory, and Place," *Critical Inquiry* 26/2 (2000), 176.

[73] Ramalho Ortigão and Eça de Queirós, *As farpas: crónica mensal da política, das letras e dos costumes*, vol. 2 (Lisbon: Typographia Universal, 1878), 32–33.

[74] Carvalho, *História do fado*, 45–69.

[75] Carvalho, *História do fado*, 79.

[76] Carvalho, *História do fado*, 79.

parlor in Portugal has to be carefully studied. This is also true with the link between the Portuguese guitar and the marginal characters of Lisbon's alleys. Carvalho discussed the conventions associated with the lyrics and the music of fado. He drew a chronology of its performers and argued that the genre was cultivated outside Lisbon. It also reflected political and social change, and republican, anticlerical, and socialist fados enlarged the repertoire. Political fado can be traced back to 1848, when the political turmoil was deeply felt and reflected in the lyrics of popular songs.[77] The *História do fado* includes a list of fados and extensive reproductions of their lyrics. It is still a valuable source for fado historiography, especially when addressing the relationship between popular music and national character and how the vernacular was appropriated.

A triste canção do sul: subsídios para a história do fado shows fado to be a song that represents the entire south of Portugal. By making this claim, Pimentel ignored the plurality of the musics in the region, giving prominence to an urban popular genre by disregarding rural songs. He published *As alegres canções do norte* in 1904. In this work Pimentel based the differences between the character of northern and southern music in Portugal on ethnicity and on the environment.[78] Furthermore, he opposed "spontaneous" choral singing by peasants in the north to a soloist-inflected song of the cities.[79] This essentializes the urban/rural dichotomy as well as the north/south divide. To frame his perspective Pimentel quoted a substantial section of the entry "Fado" in the musical dictionary published by Ernesto Vieira.[80] Vieira dismissed possible Arab origins of fado, a theory defended by Teófilo Braga, and limited its original practice to Lisbon. Later, the influx of migrant students from Lisbon to Coimbra carried fado to this city. To emphasize the specificity of fado Pimentel contrasted it with the music performed in the rural surroundings of both Lisbon and Coimbra. For him, the spread of fado throughout the country resulted from a fad that was not able to fully absorb the regional songs.[81] Pimentel reproduced fado lyrics throughout the book, and, contrary to Carvalho, included musical transcriptions. The spread of the genre is illustrated with the large number of publications containing fado lyrics and music.[82] These formed a heterogeneous set, from amateurish transcriptions to piano sheet music, showing the

---

[77] Carvalho, "O triste fado," *Illustração portugueza*, 11 February 1907, 170.

[78] Pimentel, *As alegres canções do norte* (Lisbon: Livraria Viúva Tavares Cardoso, 1905); José Manuel Sobral, "O Norte, o Sul, a raça, a nação—representações da identidade nacional portuguesa (séculos XIX–XX)," *Análise social*, 39/171 (2004), 271.

[79] Pimentel, *A triste canção do sul*, 33–34.

[80] Ernesto Vieira, "Fado," in Ernesto Vieira, *Diccionario musical* (Lisbon: Lambertini, 1899), 238–239.

[81] Pimentel, *A triste canção do sul*, 21–22.

[82] Pimentel, *A triste canção do sul*, 68–70.xxxxx

ubiquity of fado in different social settings. Pimentel discussed song lyrics and poetic techniques, and A Severa. Finally, he included a survey of fados in which three main branches are predominant: sheet music, theatrical plays, and the *Cancioneiro de músicas populares*. This shows a unified vision of fado, still undivided by contexts of performance or by formal and musical aspects. However, relying on commercial printed music as a source for some sort of authenticity of fado is a naive approach. Perhaps Pimentel was not searching for authenticity and his work falls in a different category from the books by Portuguese ethnologists. Nevertheless there is an attempt to establish a chain of authenticity in fado from a very early stage. "While music can never belong to us (as myths of authenticity would wish), belonging to a music (making ourselves at home within its territory) is distinctly possible."[83] This is certainly the case of fado in Lisbon, whose retrospective association with a reflective nostalgia, the "longing and loss, the imperfect process of remembrance," was built in the 20th century and served as a major marketing strategy.[84]

Pimentel's main contribution to the history of fado is *A triste canção do sul*. Nevertheless, he made references to the genre in other works. In his earlier *Fotografias de Lisboa* (Photographs of Lisbon), a series of small articles, Pimentel included a chapter on fado.[85] Interestingly, the title of the book reveals the rising importance of photography as an accurate representation of reality. *Fotografias de Lisboa* portrayed everyday life in Lisbon and was published in 1874. Pimentel pointed to the relevance of fado as a popular genre and placed the Portuguese guitar as its most important instrument. In support of this, the renowned guitarist João Maria dos Anjos published a method for the Portuguese guitar in the end of the 19th century.[86] This illustrates its rising popularity, resonating with the perspective put forward by Pinto de Carvalho. Pimentel characterized the appropriation of fado by other social strata as an "invasion of the people's rights," emphasizing the unsuitability of the piano to accompany vernacular genres.[87] He also placed fado as the "anthem of misfortune/disgrace (*desgraça*), the romance of the obscure sorrows, the epic poem of the people."[88] Thus, Pimentel changed his views on fado between *Fotografias*

---

[83] Richard Middleton, "Musical Belongings: Western Music and Its Low-Other," in Georgina Born and David Hesmondhalgh (eds.), *Western Music and Its Others: Difference, Representation, and Appropriation in Music* (Berkeley: University of California Press, 2000), 78.

[84] Svetlana Boym, *The Future of Nostalgia* (New York: Basic Books, 2001), 41; Richard Elliott, *Fado and the Place of Longing: Loss, Memory and the City* (Aldershot: Ashgate 2010).

[85] Pimentel, "A guitarra," in Pimentel, *Fotografias de Lisboa* (Lisbon: Frenesi, 2005), 73–78.

[86] João Maria dos Anjos, *Novo methodo de guitarra* (Lisbon: Livraria de António Maria Pereira, 1889).

[87] Pimentel, *A triste canção do sul*, 77.

[88] Pimentel, *A triste canção do sul*, 73.

de Lisboa and *A triste canção do sul*. This can be related to the new developments in the Portuguese social sciences, namely, the rekindling of interest in ethnicity in the 1890s.

Both Pimentel and Pinto de Carvalho limited the discussion of fado to Lisbon and Coimbra. However, the *Cancioneiro de músicas populares* includes songs named "Fado" that were collected in places like Porto, Figueira da Foz, Cascais, Leça, Cinfães, Tancos, or Azores. This heterogeneous universe can be explained by the polysemic use of the term "fado." In the dictionary by Cândido de Figueiredo, fado is a "popular song, generally allusive to the everyday life of working people."[89] Hence, "fado" has to be understood as a generic term for popular song, despite the endeavor to present it as a musical genre within a circumscribed historical and geographic context. In *A relíquia*, a novel by Eça de Queirós published in 1887, protagonist told a concocted story that happened in his pilgrimage to Jerusalem, in which an English woman with whom he was romantically involved played the piano and sang fados (the term Queirós uses) and theatrical songs.[90] In a study of the music of the Azores, Longworth, Dames, and Seemann pointed out that "fado" was used to name popular songs and dances in this region.[91] Therefore, one must discuss the narrative in which fado was created in Lisbon and then migrated to Coimbra by pointing out the existence of popular songs with this name in several parts of the Portuguese territory. Moreover, "the word 'fado' is used with a singular meaning in Portugal which seems to have absolutely no connection with the musical form."[92] Drawing from an Anglophone parallel, fado is the "the laborer's song of fate" and what "the Portuguese indiscriminately call 'fados' is what we designate as serenades, ballads, jigs, and sailor's hornpipes."[93] Nevertheless, there is a link between fado and Portuguese identity, a cultural trope that is frequently repeated. For Moore, "A musically inclined Portuguese (and most Portuguese are musically inclined) can instantly tell whether a song is a 'fado' or not; though he cannot sucessfully explain it to any one who is not a born Portuguese."[94]

The republican publicist João Chagas published his ideas on fado in the periodical *O berro*. Writing under the pseudonym Ivan, he reflected on the recent death of Augusto Hilário, a singer of the Coimbra tradition.[95] For Chagas, fado

---

[89] Figueiredo, *Nôvo diccionário*, vol. 1, 595.
[90] Eça de Queirós, *A relíquia* (Porto: Typ. de A. J. da Silva Teixeira, 1887), 395.
[91] M. Longworth Dames and E. Seemann, "Folklore of the Azores," *Folklore*, 14/2 (1903), 145.
[92] Isabel Moore, "Portuguese Folk-songs," *Journal of American Folklore*, 15/58 (1902), 165.
[93] Moore, "Portuguese Folk-songs," 165–166.
[94] Moore, "Portuguese Folk-songs," 165.
[95] João Chagas, "O fado (palavras d'um revoltado)," *O berro*, 12 April 1896, 3.

was the embodiment of Portuguese fatalism. The Portuguese people had created fado to define and to express themselves.[96] This makes a direct association between the music and the character of the people who perform it. "The people began singing fado on the day they began to suffer. Not being able to penetrate the unknown reason of their sorrows, they attribute it to their fortune, and from that superstition they make the *romancero* of their misfortune."[97] Thus, fado reflects the psychological character of the Portuguese, and Chagas proposed to substitute it with songs that make the people "sing like the birds, the songs of dawn," instead of a funeral chant.[98]

> Fado is the refrain of their madness. The soul of the people babbles like this for many centuries, wandering, delirious, the same song, and the same melopoeia. Let us search for its soul if it is being held captive, let us free it if it is abducted and, in a new song, let us make them to forget, to lose the memory of what it was and what they have been through.[99]

Chagas saw a need to find songs that foster a new attitude, revealing the people's real soul, a soul that had been submerged by fado. Therefore, collecting traditional music was a way of denying the psychological attitude embodied in fado. As stated above, this work was undertaken by scholars, many of them of republican persuasion.

This negative view of fado resonates with the work of Rocha Peixoto (1868–1909). It embodied the despondency of the end of the 19th century, when a generally favorable view of popular culture gave way to a more pessimistic perspective that presented some of its traits as symptoms of Portuguese decadence.[100] Peixoto's interest in the "ethnic psychology" of the Portuguese is present in the essay "O cruel e triste fado" (The Cruel and Sad Fado). The piece was written in 1890, in the aftermath of the British Ultimatum, and was revised by the author in its final version in 1897. Then, ethnic psychology became a "strategic domain for the demonstration of the decadence of Portugal and of the Portuguese people."[101] Thus, he took for granted the idea of decadence and used fado as a metaphor for the Portuguese situation. "Fado" condenses fatalism, a trait he presented as a characteristic

---

[96] Chagas, "O fado," 3.
[97] Chagas, "O fado," 3.
[98] Chagas, "O fado," 3.
[99] Chagas, "O fado," 3.
[100] Leal, *Etnografias Portuguesas*, 56.
[101] Leal, introduction to Rocha Peixoto, "O cruel e triste fado," *Etnográfica*, 1/2 (1997), 332.

of the Portuguese temperament and the popular songs, a link that has been prevalent in the genre since its early stage.[102] "The only people in the world who sing fado has in it the flagrant and clear expression of its tendencies, of its sentimentality, and of its understanding; the fate, the chance, the luck that presides our destiny, that determines our actions, and that explains the more varied aspects of our existence."[103] Therefore, fado is both fate and the songs of fate, an idea that has had a broad circulation until now. Peixoto related Portuguese history to the lack of initiative of its people, a trait that is embodied in fado, a song he believed to "dramatically express the substance of the national soul."[104] Peixoto focused on the abandonment of the country by its own people in detriment of the richness of the colonies, echoing Oliveira Martins in this point. "Never were the Portuguese people occupied with the large revolutions in the sciences and in the arts, and they were never united by the self aware and altruistic feeling of nationality."[105] The reliance on fate situates the decadence of Portugal in its people. For Peixoto, "fado is Portuguese, it is an entire mentality, it is an entire History," and reflected the temperament of the Portuguese.[106] Therefore, the genre stood for local identity of a people who were portrayed as "filthy, loafer, hypocrite, and crook."[107] Peixoto described a group of men singing a typical fado as representing the temperament of the Portuguese. Fado was a "charmless melopoeia, without elevation, without freshness, without ingenuity" that embodied national misery.[108]

At the same time, fado became a vehicle for the spread of class ideology for the working class.[109] This usually took place in voluntary societies, taverns, cheap eateries, and parties. "The people of Lisbon, limited to the streets and to the city's taverns and, once in a while, rarely, to the *hortas* of the outskirts, find in the guitar, in the songs of Fado, their best distraction."[110] Fado singers and poets like João Black (João Salustiano Monteiro, 1872–1955), Francisco Viana (1885–?1945), Fortunato Coimbra, José Carlos Rates (1879–1945), or Avelino de Sousa (1880–1946) performed for workers regularly, spreading their political beliefs throughout the country.[111] João Black was also an important

---

[102] Leal, *Etnografias Portuguesas*, 43.
[103] Peixoto, "O cruel e triste fado," 332
[104] Peixoto, "O cruel e triste fado," 332–336.
[105] Peixoto, "O cruel e triste fado," 334.
[106] Peixoto, "O cruel e triste fado," 334–335.
[107] Peixoto, "O cruel e triste fado," 335–336.
[108] Peixoto, "O cruel e triste fado," 335–336.
[109] Rui Vieira Nery, *Para uma história do Fado* (Lisbon: Público/Corda Seca, 2004), 37–40.
[110] Pimentel, *A triste canção do sul*, 26.
[111] *A voz do operário*, 17 November 1907, 3.

journalist, who wrote in *O Século* (from 1892) and published a column about fado's lyrics ("A carteira de um operário") in *A voz do operário* between 1905 and 1920.[112] Avelino de Sousa was a typographer and dedicated most of his life to promoting fado. Typographers were a very active set of workers, especially when it comes to publishing periodicals. Because their work required them to be literate, they sometimes became the spokesmen for the other workers. Published in 1912, his *O fado e os seus censores* is an important source for studying the polemics that fado expressed.[113] The book includes articles in which de Sousa defended fado against the attacks conducted by some detractors. These had been initially published in *A voz do operário*, a newspaper with a significant circulation. His argument relies on a moralistic perspective, associating fado with progressiveness and with the political education of the illiterate people. Responding to the connection of fado with marginal and degenerate milieus and performers, de Sousa juxtaposes its practice to respectable, honest, and hardworking citizens.[114] The association between fado and Lisbon's marginal sectors is captured by Rafael Bordalo Pinheiro in Figure 3.2. In a series depicting the popular characters of Lisbon he drew a caricature of a singer and a guitarist who seem to be performing. Their attire and expression illustrate the link between fado and marginality, echoing the description made by Ortigão and reproduced above.

João Black, Avelino de Sousa, and Carlos Harrington (1870–1916) were the most distinguished performers associated with the working class.[115] The way these performers promoted political ideals through fado helped the genre to spread, associating music with the indoctrination of the workers. In 1892, Carlos Harrington published a book in which he recorded the poems of his improvisations.[116] Most consist of the *quadra glosada em décimas*, a form I will explain below. In his work, most poems focus on love, except for "Desgraçada! . . ." This poem has a political message and analyzes the motives that lead poor women to prostitution.[117] Denouncing the helplessness of the poor is a frequent trope in working-class perspectives, and is reflected in fado. Several poems by Harrington were published in a booklet that was probably issued

---

[112] Pedro Félix, "João Black," in Salwa Castelo-Branco (ed.), *Enciclopédia da música em Portugal no século XX*, vol. 1, 144; António Alberto Ramos, "A memória de João Black e o fado como canção de protesto," *Sítios e Memórias*, 2 (1997), 63–68.

[113] Avelino de Sousa, *O fado e os seus censores: artigos colligidos da Voz do Operario: Crítica aos detractores da canção nacional* (Lisbon: Avelino de Sousa, 1912).

[114] Maria Filomena Mónica (ed.), *A formação da classe operária portuguesa: antologia da imprensa operária, 1850–1934* (Lisbon: Fundação Calouste Gulbenkian, 1982).

[115] *O Fado*, first published in Lisbon, 16 April 1910.

[116] Carlos Harrington, *Improvisos (Fados)* (Lisbon: Typographia Costa Braga, 1892).

[117] Harrington, *Improvisos*, 55–56.

TIPOS DE LISBOA, — por R. BORDALLO PINHEIRO.

—Os fadistas. (O cantador.)

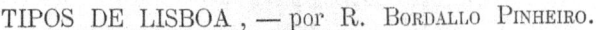

Figure 3.2 Rafael Bordalo Pinheiro, Tipos de Lisboa: os fadistas, in *El mundo cómico*, 28 September 1873, 1. Lisbon typical characters: the *fadistas*.

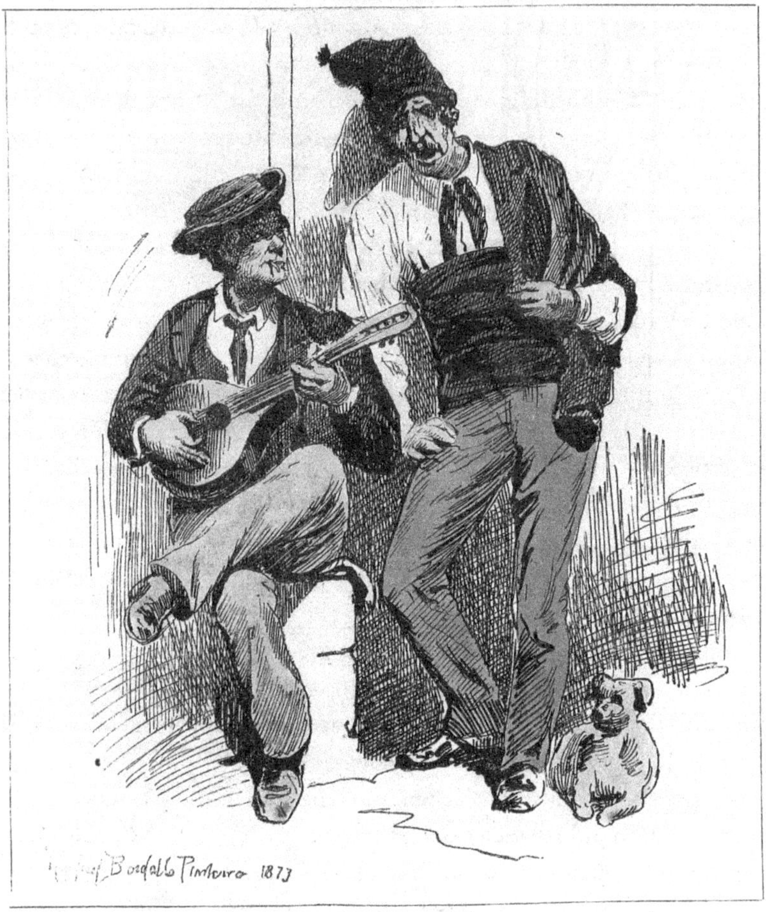

without the author's supervision.[118] This publication includes poems with a two-line *mote* (motto) and only one ten-line stanza. The lines of the *mote* correspond to the fourth and tenth lines of the stanza, respectively. Harrington also uses the *quadra glosada em quadras*, in which a four-line *mote* is developed in four four-line stanzas. The book contained a fado that presents the genre as the expression of the "national soul," a trope that is still revisited frequently.[119]

[118] Harrington, *Versos de Carlos Harrington, para guitarra, orchestra ou piano* (Lisbon: Impr. Lucas, 1907).

[119] Harrington, *Versos de Carlos Harrington*, 8.

Later, Harrington directed *O Fado*, a periodical about the genre that was published in 1910.

An example of a socialist fado was published in Carvalho's *História do fado*. It is a *quadra glosada em décimas*, in which a four-line *mote* is developed in four ten-line stanzas with a rhyming structure abbaaccddc that finishes with the corresponding line of the *mote*. The *mote* is: "First of May, alarm, alarm!/ Soldiers of freedom/Forward, to destroy/Borders and property."[120] The first stanza is developed in an encouraging tone, reflecting the messianic role of the revolution. "Down with the vile capital/Enemy of equality" is part of the next stanza, where the poem enumerates Portuguese socialists like José Fontana and Antero de Quental.[121] Next, it denounces the wealth produced by exploitation and calls for the "walls of oppression" to be destroyed. The poem condemns militarism and issues a call to "show the vile society" a "beautiful positivism."[122] "The earth belongs to all humanity/All it encloses belongs to everyone/There cannot be in it/Neither borders nor properties."[123]

Artur Arriegas had already been a successful playwright in Lisbon when his first book on fado appeared. He was an active republican and promoted fado in periodicals such as *A canção de Portugal: o Fado* and *O faduncho* (established in 1916 and 1917, respectively).[124] *A canção da minha terra: fados* includes a preamble by the playwright D. João da Câmara (1852–1908)in which he states the importance of the city as a topos for poetry.[125] Most poems are about love, but "O caçador" (The Hunter) reflects the republican views of the author.[126] At this time, most references to hunting made by republicans had King D. Carlos I in mind. For them, the king carried on with his hobbies while the nation was falling apart. This is also the subject of a cartoon by the republican artist Tomás Júlio Leal da Câmara (1876–1948) that was published in the French periodical *L'assiette ao beurre* and reproduced here as Figure 3.3.[127]

The cartoon was published when D. Carlos was visiting Paris officially and depicts the monarch's favorite activities: horseback riding, bullfighting, fishing, traveling as frequently as possible, eating, and sleeping. Leal da Câmara illustrated several books and worked for republican periodicals, such as *A corja: semanario de caricaturas* (1898) or *A marselheza: supllemento de*

---

[120] Carvalho, *História do fado*, 261.
[121] Carvalho, *História do fado*, 262.
[122] Carvalho, *História do fado*, 262.
[123] Carvalho, *História do fado*, 262.
[124] Artur Arriegas, *A canção da minha terra: fados* (Lisbon: Impressão C. do Cabra, 1907); Artur Arriegas, *A trova portugueza: Fados e canções* (Lisbon: Barateira, 1922).
[125] Arriegas, *A canção da minha terra*, 11–13.
[126] Arriegas, *A canção da minha terra*, 51–52.
[127] *L'assiette au beurre*, 25 November 1905,

Figure 3.3 Leal da Câmara, Les occupations du roi, in *L'Assiette au beurre*, 25 November 1905, 557. The King's occupations.

caricaturas (1897–1898). Political reasons made him leave the country in 1898 to work in Spain, France, and Belgium, only to return to Portugal after the fall of the monarchy.[128]

Returning to Arriegas, he directed the comic periodical *O Casmurro*, where he published his poems frequently. They were usually in the *quadra glosada em décimas*, and one of them tells the story of a woman who "had lived in vast salons/between lights and glitters" and was later "reduced to the dark hunger and to the cold/because beauty had gone away."[129] The disgraced woman occupies a special place in moralistic lyrics, associating greed and social aspirations with moral decay. This is echoed in another *quadra glosada em décimas*, whose *mote* is "Once you dressed in wool/Now silk is your robe;/Some people say you have risen/But I say you've dropped! . . ."[130] The poem tells the story of a village girl who woke up early to herd and feed the cattle, ate simple food, and wore cheap fabrics. Then she married an aristocrat and traded an honest and serious life for a life of luxury and vice, representing her fall in the eyes of the poet. Apart from its moralistic content, this poem is interesting because it is based on a *mote* that was given to Arriegas by another person. Moreover, he proposes to develop in the newspaper every *mote* sent by readers, providing there are rhymes for them. This reveals the virtuosity that was required of fado poets and singers, whose ability to develop the same *mote* in several stanzas was prized. The *fadista* João "Patusquinho" was able to spend "three and four nights singing about the same subject, and he could sing twenty or more songs with just one *mote*."[131] "Patusquinho" was a serious contender in the *canto a atirar*, a contest between *fadistas* who took turns in improvising lyrics over a strophic accompaniment. In the *canto a atirar* the singers frequently taunted each other.[132]

Fado also told everyday stories and, in some cases, in a funny way. Arriegas wrote a poem about a leopard that ran away from Lisbon's zoo, making fun of the incompetence of the Municipal Guard that was sent to catch it.[133] It is a *quadra glosada em décimas* and the story begins with a *mote* that flatters the aim of the Municipal Guard. This is an ironic reference since a guard was almost shot by his colleagues. The fado also mentions the courtship between guards and maids, a trope that had wide circulation at the time. The leopard escapes and

---

[128] Victor Santos, *Leal da Câmara—um caso de caricatura: a sátira na atitude política portuguesa* (Sintra: Câmara Municipal de Sintra, 1982).

[129] Artur Arriegas, "Fadinhos," *O Casmurro*, 5 June 1905, 2.

[130] Arriegas, "Fadinhos," *O Casmurro*, 31 July 1905, 2.

[131] Pinto de Carvalho, *História do fado*, 163.

[132] Pinto de Carvalho, *História do fado*, 163, 80.

[133] Arriegas, "Fadinhos," *O Casmurro*, 12 August 1905, 2.

panic breaks out. Then, the Municipal Guard shows up "to save humankind" and chases the animal fiercely. They shot "as if they were blind," and almost injured a fellow guard.[134] Arriegas then suggested that the guards should be sent to fight the Cuamatas, a people from the south of Angola who were at that time fighting the Portuguese. The agreement of 1886 drew the border between Portuguese Angola and German South-West Africa (now Namibia). The Cuamatas resisted the Portuguese occupation fiercely and a large military operation ensued. This fado illustrates how poets incorporated current matters in their lyrics. In a single song Arriegas was able to connect the urban courtship rituals of the working class, leisure venues (the zoo), and Portuguese colonial policy, merging distinct aspects of everyday life. Therefore, it becomes possible to understand how narrative songs permeated the entertainment market and how they were used to comment on recent events, a process that also was the basis for the *revista*. It is no coincidence that Artur Arriegas worked in both areas.

The Celtic North, the Semitic South, and the Colonies

When a country is formed, it is generally made up of numerous ethnic groups. These groups must begin to share a common culture if they are to be molded into a nation. This means they have to be "represented in the past or in the future as if they formed a natural community, possessing of itself an identity of origins, culture and interests which transcends individuals and social conditions."[135] The attempt to homogenize the Portuguese population under the umbrella of a unified popular culture was a crucial trend for nation-building. However, the way scholars saw popular culture was transformed toward the end of the 19th century, as they began to prize internal diversity and the heterogeneity of communal culture. This was used to add the layer of regional between the national and the local. Nevertheless, some writers took an extreme position, arguing that the variety between regions was associated with ethnic differences within Portugal. The republican politician from Porto, Basílio Teles (1856–1923), developed a theory that related the people from the north of Portugal with the Aryans and the southerners with the Semitic populations.[136]

---

[134] Arriegas, "Fadinhos," *O Casmurro*, 12 August 1905, 2.

[135] Étienne Balibar, "The Nation Form," in Étienne Balibar and Immanuel Wallerstein, *Race, Nation, Class: Ambiguous Identities* (London: Verso, 1991), 96.

[136] José Manuel Sobral, "Race and Space in the Interpretation of Portugal: The North-South Division and Representations of Portuguese National Identity in the Nineteenth and Twentieth

This view was shared by the historian Alberto Sampaio (1841–1908) and by Alberto Pimentel and was reflected in their work. This reveals the competing views about Portugal that were circulating. On the one hand, the link between the Lusitanians and the Portuguese had surfaced again. On the other hand, some scholars denied that common ancestry. Therefore, "by denying a shared ethnic identity among the Portuguese, Teles also put in question the national myth linking the Portuguese to the Lusitanians, an idea that had experienced a revival since the last decades of the nineteenth century."[137]

These views were well received among northern writers as they embraced an ideology that supported the racial superiority of the north toward the south. This is especially clear in *As alegres canções do norte*, a book by Alberto Pimentel. By transferring the theories developed by Teles to music, Pimentel opposes a Semitic south, whose spirit is embodied in fado, to a north where a distinct ethnic and natural background made the "joyful songs" thrive. *As alegres canções do norte* associates the popular songs performed in the Portuguese north with a Galician background. It is interesting to see how Pimentel associated the south with only one song and the north with several. The ethnic divide proposed by Teles and Pimentel resonates with the theories of Manuel Murguía (1833–1923). Murguía was a Galician journalist and historian who presented local culture as a product of the Celtic heritage in the northwest of the Iberian Peninsula.[138] He based his evolutionism on a biological and historical difference between the peoples of the Peninsula, a point that would later be dismissed by Unamuno. Thus, theories of nationalism tend to be as heterogeneous as the nations themselves.

The songs from Minho were described by Pimentel as "vibrant with villager joy or with choreographic vigor."[139] He later argued that these songs were also performed in Lisbon's theaters, albeit stripped of their nature and, therefore, "dampened."[140] This illustrates the integration of rural songs in the urban entertainment market as discussed earlier. The songs could be used in operettas to intensify their realism and in *revistas* as a way of depicting characters. They could also be used to evoke memories in the audience members, especially if these individuals had migrated from the north to work in Lisbon. The migration from rural areas to Lisbon in the 19th century included many people

---

Centuries," in Sharon R. Roseman and Shawn S. Parkhurst (eds), *Recasting Culture and Space in Iberian Contexts* (NY: SUNY Press, 2008), 214–216.

[137] Sobral, "Race and Space in the Interpretation of Portugal," 218.

[138] Pimentel, *As alegres canções do norte*, 21; Sobral, "O Norte, o Sul, a raça, a nação," 271. See also Manuel Murguía, *Historia de Galicia*, vol. 1 (Lugo: Imprenta de Soto Freire, Editor, 1865).

[139] Pimentel, *As alegres canções do norte*, 7.

[140] Pimentel, *As alegres canções do norte*, 7.

from Minho, and this is something the people who worked for the theaters knew well. The songs from Minho were related to a type of social organization, the religiousness of the peasants, the prevalent type of family institution, and ethnicity.[141] For Pimentel, the social fabric in Minho relied on small property owners who worked their own land and were ethnically related to the Galicians. It contrasted with the Semitic origin of the *saloio*, the peasant of the rural outskirts of Lisbon. The joyful character of the songs of the north was seen as a result of a system of "mesological, physical, and moral factors."[142] Moreover, the joyful character of the music is carried into the everyday life of the region. This view of the peasant from Minho was heavily romanticized. People living far away from the capital, with its industry and politics, were seen as the bearers of the idyllic authenticity of popular culture. This idea of the authentic was reinforced when Pimentel praised the beauty of both solo and choral songs of the peasants from Minho, presenting the latter as a quasi-spontaneous phenomenon.[143]

The poetry of the popular songs reflects the life of the peasants and the role played by nature and religion in it. The lyrics are divided into several groups. The first group includes songs that refer to plants. The poems of the second group include animals, especially birds. The third group includes names of rivers, of hills, of settlements, of saints associated with popular festivities, and of the habits and customs that permeate rural everyday life.[144] Pimentel also studied the dances of the northern songs, and included a large number of transcriptions. If singing formed part of the daily routine of the northern peasants, dancing was associated with their leisure, especially on Sundays and on religious festivities.[145] Figure 3.4 represents a traditional dance from Santo Tirso, in the north, performed by two farmers in their traditional costumes. This image is also featured in early 20th century postcards, which reinforces the role played by these products in building and disseminating the imagery of rural Portugal.

For Pimentel, the northern "choreographic songs" had a leaping character and, like agricultural chores, were an affirmation of stamina.[146] These songs included singing, sometimes in dialogue form, and contrasted with the dances that were performed in the cities. He argued that the dances from the outskirts of Lisbon were based on a "monotonously Arabic dragging of the feet."[147] The

---

[141] Pimentel, *As alegres canções do norte*, 8–22.
[142] Pimentel, *As alegres canções do norte*, 27.
[143] Pimentel, *As alegres canções do norte*, 33–34.
[144] Pimentel, *As alegres canções do norte*, 35–67.
[145] Pimentel, *As alegres canções do norte*, 69.
[146] Pimentel, *As alegres canções do norte*, 71.
[147] Pimentel, *As alegres canções do norte*, 71.

Figure 3.4 N.A., Dança de camponezas do norte do paiz, in *Illustração Portugueza*, 23 December 1907, 837, Hemeroteca Municipal de Lisboa. A peasant dance of the north of Portugal.

dances from the north followed the same choreographic pattern, and Pimentel enumerated them while discussing their origin.[148] The transcriptions he included have harmonizations and transcriptions of the melodic line. Pimentel described and analyzed dances such as the *Caninha verde*, the *Malhão*, the *Chula*, the *Vira*, and the *Marrafa*, and placed them as a form of resistance and protest against what he designates as the "invasion of urbanism."[149]

---

[148] Pimentel, *As alegres canções do norte*, 73.
[149] Pimentel, *As alegres canções do norte*, 74–101.

The work by Pimentel is permeated by the urban/rural binary. He saw the urban world as a nefarious influence that decharacterizes and corrupts the rural people, and criticized the "country girls who, with the vain intention of imitating aristocratic conventions, dance the polka or the waltz, especially when played by a *banda* or at a piano."[150] This reveals the porosity of boundaries between the country and the city and how some activities were predominantly associated with a particular mix between gender and class. Also, it shows that the appropriation of the vernacular was not one-sided. On the one hand, bourgeois country girls reproduced the trends of the urban entertainment market. On the other hand, the theaters staged music that was associated with the rural areas. Thus, an interesting dynamic is in place in the way repertoires circulated from the city to the country, and from the fields to the stage. The essentialism in which Pimentel relied resonates with the work of Ortigão. He described Viana do Castelo, a city in Minho, as a place without the "idiotic hats" that "crowned absurd hairstyles," a result of the "pathology of fashion" lived in the cities.[151] Moreover, Viana was free from "the pianos fiercely rattled by innocent maidens, immolated by their parents to the musical Minotaur commonly known as the Carpentier Method."[152] Thus, Lisbon was overcrowded with the "poor key-switching girls, whose ears were inaccessible to all notions of tuning and time, and whose fingers were refractory to technical agility and to the vibrancy of talent."[153] This traces a boundary between the country and the city based on fashion and on playing the piano, activities associated with the bourgeois urban female. Pimentel argued that this boundary had been violated, thus contaminating "the people" with urban habits. In *As alegres canções do norte* he pointed to the role music played in the festivals of the region. The section on popular pilgrimages and feasts places these events in context and includes several photographs, extracts of lyrics, and musical transcriptions. Pimentel studied two important manifestations of popular religiosity: Christmas and St. John's Day (held on 23–24 June). Despite basing his assumptions on an ethnic division of the country, a view that was not widely shared, the work carried out by Pimentel was an attempt to systematize and integrate popular song in the wider context of cultural practices through a system in which several binaries are operating, namely north/south, Galician/Semitic, and urban/rural.

However, this split between the urban and the rural is very problematic. On the one hand, it essentializes both spaces in a way that does not account for the

---

[150] Pimentel, *As alegres canções do norte*, 100.

[151] Ramalho Ortigão, *As farpas*, vol.1 (Lisbon: Livraria Clássica Editora, 1948), 38.

[152] Ortigão, *As farpas*, 38. For the method see Mademoiselle Charpentier, *Méthode de piano* (Paris: Firmin-Didot, 1875).

[153] Ortigão, *As farpas*, 38.

porosity between them. Conversely, seeing the rural world as the site where an "authentic" popular culture needs to be safeguarded from urbanization tends to overlook such trends as internal migration. The itinerant musicians illustrate this relation. Groups of wandering musicians were frequently seen in Portuguese towns and villages, performing songs from successful comic operas, associated with the urban stage.[154] Therefore, in a time when ethnologists were developing and promoting an essentialist view of Portugal's rural areas, street musicians were shattering the boundaries between the urban and the rural. In this sense, they played an important role in the spread of theatrical repertoires from urban to rural spaces, and extended their audience.

Racial aspects were important for authors like Teles, Pimentel, Sampaio, and Murguía. Their work concentrated on the Iberian Peninsula and pointed to an alleged superiority of northerners, even though their views were not shared by many. However, racism permeates the work of several people who studied the Portuguese colonies. For example, Oliveira Martins describes the black as an "adult child" and the black race as "anthropologically inferior, frequently closer to the anthropoid, and unworthy of being called human."[155] This illustrates a rigid hierarchy in which races other than the Aryans (or Indo-Europeans) are perceived as inferior, a strategic move that both naturalized, in the biological sense of the term, and legitimated Portuguese colonialism.[156] Nevertheless, there were contrasting views on the subject. António Francisco Nogueira published *A raça negra sob o ponto de vista da civilização da África* in 1880. The work studies race in the Portuguese African colonies and portrays the "Negro race" as an "indispensable element in the civilizing process we [the Portuguese] have to carry in Africa."[157] Moreover, "the Negro needs to be aided in his evolution towards civilized life."[158] This places the whites as "the necessary element for direction and progress" and the colonized blacks as "the active instrument of labour."[159] The variety of perspectives concerning the Portuguese colonies contributes to the questioning of a binary opposition between nation-building and empire-building anthropologies. The popular culture of the metropolis was the main concern for most ethnologists.

---

[154] *O Occidente*, 25 November 1896, 258–259.

[155] Oliveira Martins, *O Brazil e as colonias portuguezas* (Lisbon: Livraria de António Maria Pereira, 1888), 284.

[156] Valentim Alexandre, "Questão nacional e questão colonial em Oliveira Martins," *Análise Social*, 31/135 (1996), 201.

[157] António Francisco Nogueira, *A raça negra sob o ponto de vista da civilização da África; usos e costumes de alguns povos gentilicos do interior de Mossamedes e as colonias portuguezas* (Lisbon: Typographia Nova Minerva, 1880), 7.

[158] Nogueira, *A raça negra sob o ponto de vista da civilização da Africa*, 11.

[159] Nogueira, *A raça negra sob o ponto de vista da civilização da Africa*, 209.

Nevertheless, the work carried out by explorers and scientists in the colonies should not be overlooked. The history of Portuguese anthropology contained elements of both traditions, but paid more attention to nation-building. Thus, "the construction of an Other in the colonial world was part of the process of constructing the Same in the homeland."[160]

The Problems of Naming: Popular Music and Light Music

The polysemic character of the term "popular" has to be put into context. Ethnography and song collecting played a key role in defining the sphere of the *música popular* in its specific terms. Scholars like Braga identified it with the "melodies of the people," music that was predominantly associated with the country's rural areas.[161] Therefore, *música popular* (the "spontaneous" or "authentic" music of "the people") would now be called traditional or folk music. In Cândido do Figueiredo's Portuguese dictionary, the definition for "popular" is "relative to the people; proper of the people; agreeable to the people; esteemed by the people, democratic."[162] This evidences the term's ambiguous usage and polysemic character. One interesting word in this definition is "democratic." Figueiredo defined "democrat" as "the one who belongs to the popular class or who does not like aristocracy."[163] He also used the term "democracy" to describe a "social class that includes the proletariat and the smallest population."[164] This is a symptom of the ongoing intellectual debate on the incorporation of the popular masses into the Portuguese political reality of the end of the 19th century.[165] Consequently, it becomes possible to draw an analogy between *música popular* and the scientific approaches that, by studying "the people," contributed to its integration as part of the political discourse.[166]

---

[160] Miguel Vale de Almeida, "Anthropology and Ethnography of the Portuguese-Speaking Empire," in Prem Poddar, Rajeev S. Patke, and Lars Jensen, *A Historical Companion to Postcolonial Literature: Continental Europe and Its Empires* (Edinburgh: Edinburgh University Press, 2008), 436.

[161] Teófilo Braga, "As melodias portuguesas," in César das Neves and Gualdino de Campos, *Cancioneiro de músicas populares*, vol. 1 (Porto: Typographia Occidental, 1893), v.

[162] Cândido de Figueiredo, *Nôvo diccionário da língua portuguêsa* (Lisbon: Livraria Tavares Cardoso & Irmão, 1899), vol. 2, 344.

[163] Figueiredo, *Nôvo diccionário da língua portuguêsa*, vol. 1, 389.

[164] Figueiredo, *Nôvo diccionário da língua portuguêsa*, vol. 1, 389.

[165] Jorge Freitas Branco, "A fluidez dos limites: discurso etnográfico e movimento folclórico em Portugal," *Etnográfica*, 3/1 (1999), 27.

[166] Freitas Branco, "A fluidez dos limites," 27.

Nevertheless, this contrasts with the definition of popular music in the Anglophone world. The current form of understanding popular music can be traced back to the 18th and 19th centuries.[167] Popular music is associated with features that were symbiotically interrelated, such as the increase in the number and size of audiences, the new public institutions for music education, and the new channels for the spread of music.[168] This new area carved a rift between art, the "emergent canonic repertory of 'classics,'" and entertainment, the "low-class, 'trivial' genres."[169] Nevertheless, an essentialist definition of "popular" is highly problematic. Drawing from a Lacanian-Žižekian perspective, Middleton argued:

> However "popular music" is articulated, whatever we try to make it mean, the people as subject is embedded somewhere within it, and with an emotional charge that will apparently just not go away. We need to account for that investment as well as the (necessary) mutability of content. And here the word itself must come to the fore. Žižek's position is grounded, more broadly, in an anti-descriptivist theory of naming. Names ("the people," "music," "popular music"), he argues, do not acquire meaning through reference to given properties but through a "primal baptism" followed up in a "chain of tradition."[170]

The "popular" can also be a space in the market for cultural goods. Nevertheless, equating between market choice and popular culture is problematic because popularity would be "consumption as measured by sales figures and market indicators."[171] However, this is not directly applicable to the Portuguese context, at a time for which the quantitative data concerning the theatrical and musical activities in Lisbon is scarce and unreliable. Nevertheless, the opposition between art and entertainment was circulating in Portugal, albeit with a different terminology. Vieira stated that Cyriaco de Cardoso wrote only *música ligeira* (light music).[172] He attributed this to Cardoso's lack of formal training

---

[167] Richard Middleton, "Popular Music: I. Popular Music in the West, 1. Definitions," *Grove Music Online*, ed. L. Macy, <http://www.oxfordmusiconline.com>, accessed 5 June 2014. [168] Middleton, "Popular Music: I. Popular Music in the West, 1. Definitions."

[169] Middleton, "Popular Music: I. Popular Music in the West, 1. Definitions."

[170] Richard Middleton, *Voicing the Popular: On the Subjects of Popular Music* (London: Routledge, 2006), 34. See Slavoj Žižek, *The Sublime Object of Ideology* (London: Verso, 2008), 98–99.

[171] Simon Frith, *Performing Rites: On the Value of Popular Music* (Cambridge, MA: Harvard University Press, 1998), 15.

[172] Ernesto Vieira, *Diccionario biographico de musicos portuguezes: historia e bibliografia da musica em Portugal*, vol. 2 (Lisbon: Lambertini, 1900), 424.

and to his work for the popular stage.[173] This clearly shows that a recognized difference between *música ligeira* and *música clássica* (classical music, the term Vieira used throughout his dictionary) was in place at the time.

Naming is the preferred mechanism for the organization and unification of a heterogeneous object, and has retroactive effect on the object.[174] Naming becomes the enunciation and arrangement of reality. By considering the thought of both Gramsci and Lacan in the works of Laclau, it is possible to expand the idea of naming from an operation that is exclusively taxonomical toward a perspective in which "the production of meaning is simultaneously an operation of power."[175] According to Bourdieu,

> In the symbolic struggle over the production of common sense, or, more precisely, for the monopoly of legitimate naming, that is to say, official i.e.,— explicit and public—imposition of the legitimate vision of the social world, agents engage the symbolic capital they have acquired in previous struggles, in particular, all the power they possess over the instituted taxonomies, inscribed in minds or in objectivity, such as qualifications.[176]

The problematic segmentation between *música ligeira* and *música popular* (literally, popular music) is reflected in the local market for cultural goods. Thus, we can trace a historically situated association between *música popular* with what was perceived to be "proper to the people" and between *música ligeira* with what was considered "agreeable to the people." In this sense, *música ligeira* consisted of the products of the urban entertainment market, where theatrical music was dominant. Naturally, the associations stated above are not mutually exclusive, as the definitions may (and many times do) overlap each other. Being "proper to the people" is not incompatible with being "agreeable to the people." Nevertheless, there were preferential meanings of the term "popular" according to the context in which it was used. Therefore, *música ligeira* designated what is now called popular music, displaying the shift of the meaning of "popular" throughout the 20th century, especially after its placement within

---

[173] Ernesto Vieira, *Diccionario biographico de musicos portuguezes: historia e bibliografia da musica em Portugal* (Lisbon: Lambertini, 1900), 424.

[174] Ernesto Laclau, "Ideology and Post-Marxism," *Journal of Political Ideologies*, 11/2 (2006), 109.

[175] James Martin, "The Political Logic of Discourse: A Neo-Gramscian View," *History of European Ideas*, 28/1–2 (2002), 26.

[176] Pierre Bourdieu, "The Social Space and the Genesis of Groups," *Theory and Society*, 14/6 (1985), 731.

the culture industries.[177] The division of the market for cultural goods has thus been present in public discourse since at least the second half of the 19th century. This division is associated with the differentiation of some social groups in a period when both the universe for these goods and the numbers of its intended consumers were rapidly expanding. According to Scott, "the field of the popular that opened up in the 19th-century was one in which different classes and class fractions fought over questions of intellectual and moral leadership (in Gramscian terms, hegemony)."[178] This indicates an area in which distinct and competing notions of the "popular" were operating, and shows that essentializing its character is misleading.

---

[177] For various discussions of the definition of popular music see Roy Shuker, *Understanding Popular Music* (New York: Routledge, 1994); Peter Manuel, *Popular Musics of the Non-Western World: An Introductory Survey* (Oxford: Oxford University Press, 1990); Richard Middleton, *Studying Popular Music* (Milton Keynes: Open University Press, 1990); Simon Frith, *Popular Music: Critical Concepts in Media and Cultural Studies*, vol. 2 (London: Routledge, 2004), 3–4; Keith Negus, *Popular Music in Theory: An Introduction* (Middletown, CT: Wesleyan University Press, 1996).

[178] Scott, *Sounds of the Metropolis*, 9.

4

Programs, Postcards, *Coplas*, and Sheet Music

Introduction

The music theater generated goods such as programs, postcards, *coplas*, and sheet music. These were bought and sold throughout the country, indicating the role played by the popular stage in the spread of modern music. Selling images, texts, and sounds was an ongoing trend in the transnational entertainment market. Musical styles such as French operetta or the Viennese waltz spread rapidly because they were designed to be exchangeable among cultures and appealed to a large market where they were understood both by locals and wider audiences.[1] In Portugal, the theater was the focal point for making and performing songs and dances that were then made available to a broader audience in various forms. Librettos, sheet music, and recordings were bought and sold by a heterogeneous set of people, comprising a complex and dynamic market in which the spaces where everyday life takes place intersected.

Domestic Space, Class, Gender, and the Piano

"The mould of our society girls varies very little. They all know long and short stitch, how to play *La Sonnambula* and *Il trovatore* on the piano, to make crochet covers, to parrot childish funny sentences in two or three languages, to dance the lancers quadrille, and to criticize their close *friends*."[2] The nature of domesticity was important for the development of the Portuguese entertainment

---

[1] Derek B. Scott, *Sounds of the Metropolis: The 19th-Century Popular Music Revolution in London, New York, Paris and Vienna* (Oxford: Oxford University Press, 2008), 44.

[2] Maria Amália Vaz de Carvalho, *Mulheres e creanças: notas sobre educação* (Porto: Joaquim Antunes Leitão e Irmão, 1880), 139.

market during the late 19th and early 20th centuries. As in other countries, the bourgeois woman incarnated a form of domesticity that relied on the idea of personal achievement. Thus, female domestic life included activities such as collecting, embroidering, reading, and domestic music making. The dominant instrument in the home was the piano, which, to a certain extent, embodied bourgeois culture. It occupied a unique place in everyday life, and musical soirées were much more than public displays of amateur artistry. They opened the doors of the domestic space where Victorian notions of privacy reigned. The piano embodied and reflected the refinement of the household.

"Domestic" was defined as "relative to the home, to the intimate life of the family; related with the running of the home; familial."[3] Therefore, domesticity binds space, family, and intimacy together. At the same time it reflected modernity, as similar transnational cultural practices were found throughout Europe and the Americas. The international bibliography has tended to concentrate on Anglophone and Francophone contexts. Given the influence of Parisian culture in Portugal, the locals developed a strong relationship with cosmopolitan forms of entertainment. This was not confined to the theaters, since novels, newspapers, sheet music, and piano methods traveled from France and found their way into the parlors and libraries of the Portuguese. Teachers, fortune-tellers, hairdressers, and booksellers used French names, and some actually were of French descent. A French name was symbolic with cosmopolitan prestige. The link with Britain is not so direct, even if Portugal was closely associated with it. There is a strong relationship between the royal families of Britain and Portugal. The husband of D. Maria II, D. Fernando de Saxe-Coburgo-Gotha, was first cousin to Queen Victoria and to Prince Albert. Moreover, royal palaces were built or refurbished according to the paradigms of Victorian privacy. The Palácio da Pena, in the Romantic landscape of Sintra, stands out as a good example of this tendency. The Portuguese selectively appropriated cultural aspects that were associated with cosmopolitanism and mixed them with local elements. Some striking parallels between Portugal and other European and American countries reinforce the assumption that there was a broad transnational circulation of cultural goods.

A definition of the domestic that connects space, people, and social bonds is very important for studying how cultural goods circulated in Portugal. The vast majority of the sheet music business was concentrated on the piano, the prevalent instrument for Lisbon's bourgeoisie and aristocracy. The piano was common in many households in Portugal during the 19th century. This

---

[3] Cândido de Figueiredo, *Nôvo diccionário da língua portuguêsa*, vol. 1 (Lisbon: Livraria Tavares Cardoso & Irmão, 1899), 461.

is illustrated by the frequent advertising in the local press by stores that sold pianos and printed music. The piano had "established itself as a mark of prosperity and cultural sophistication in middle-class homes everywhere in the Western world . . . and it remained the most diffused household status symbol until well into the twentieth century."⁴ It became a symbol of social status that merged both economic capital and cultural capital.⁵

> The piano, lodging itself in the public concert, the salon and the bourgeois home, was to become the single most potent symbol of that [mercantile music] culture. It drew to itself both a modern technology that would in due course translate craft to industry, and a new social order that would translate economic success to cultural and political status.⁶

Purchasing a piano represented a significant investment of capital, and learning how to play it required a large investment of time. Therefore, the piano was only available to people who had a considerable amount of money and time to invest in leisure. This is a distinctive status marker of the economically privileged. It was especially visible in the routines of bourgeois women and children. Maria Amália Vaz de Carvalho argued that "we must, however, warn that the monomania of the piano, as it is inoculated and propagated, is a scourge, a fearsome scourge, and nothing more."⁷ This shows the importance of the piano in Portuguese salon culture, perceived by her as a negative influence for people who live in a false feeling of luxury.⁸ In her work on educating women and children, Carvalho asserted that music is a powerful tool as long as its "far reach, its moralizing influence" is understood.⁹ Hence, she valued the rational aspects of music while warning of its frivolous side associated with the standard education of the bourgeois woman, which considered the piano as another dimension of "elegant teaching."¹⁰ This complicates the prevailing opinion that was in place, which saw the masculine as rational and the feminine as emotional. If education were improved,

---

⁴ Peter Ward, *A History of Domestic Space: Privacy and the Canadian Home* (Vancouver: University of British Columbia Press, 1999), 64.

⁵ Pierre Bourdieu, "The Forms of Capital," in Mark Granovetter and Richard Swedberg (eds.), *The Sociology of Economic Life* (Boulder, CO: Westview Press, 2001), 50.

⁶ Jim Samson, *Virtuosity and the Musical Work* (Cambridge: Cambridge University Press, 2004), 22.

⁷ Carvalho, *Mulheres e crianças*, 50.

⁸ Carvalho, *Mulheres e crianças*, 33.

⁹ Carvalho, *Mulheres e crianças*, 52.

¹⁰ Carvalho, *Mulheres e crianças*, 52.

the piano will stop being the scourge and the plague of the casual soirées, the torment of the close neighbors, the nightmare of the husbands, the martyrdom of the performers. It will not reign exclusively as it has until now, as that despotic and terrible instrument. We will not say of the *well educated* girls: *she plays admirably*, suggesting that she plays the wretched *piano*.[11]

Learning and practicing the piano were ways for women to acquire cultural capital. In its basic state this form of capital is "linked to the body and presupposes embodiment."[12] Acquiring this capital relies on an investment of time by the person who achieves it, and cannot be accumulated through delegation.[13] Therefore, the piano became important in the Victorian idea of self-achievement and became entrenched in the idea of culture that was associated with the bourgeois.In the broader world, things were also changing. During the ancien régime, keeping a skilled orchestra was perceived as a marker of prestige for the court. This was the case of the Portuguese Orquestra da Real Câmara (Royal Chamber Orchestra), an ensemble established in Lisbon in the 18th century. Patrons used economic capital to enhance their prestige. This could be done through delegation, as they paid musicians to entertain their social circles. Public concerts and domestic music making were evidence of an important transformation. On the one hand, ensembles could be sponsored by voluntary societies and perform in public venues such as concert halls, a trend that could reflect a larger independence of music from patrons. Conversely, domestic music making valued the acquisition of personal skills. For Bourdieu,

> The work of acquisition is work on oneself (self-improvement), an effort that presupposes a personal cost (*on paie de sa personne*, as we say in French), an investment, above all of time, but also of that socially constituted form of libido, *libido sciendi*, with all the privation, renunciation, and sacrifice that it may entail.[14]

This shows that bourgeois ideas of self-sacrifice for achievement were circulating. However, mapping the bourgeois raises important questions. The ever-changing dynamics of social space and the processes through which practices are internalized complicate a straightforward definition of class. Bourdieu expanded the Marxian definition of class by emphasizing its

---

[11] Carvalho, *Mulheres e creanças*, 52.
[12] Bourdieu, "The Forms of Capital," 48.
[13] Bourdieu, "The Forms of Capital," 48.
[14] Bourdieu, "The Forms of Capital," 48.

relational aspects.[15] For Marx, class is the role a group develops within the processes of production. Thus, it is defined by the place people occupy in the productive system. To overcome Marx's focus on substance, Bourdieu places class as a category that is constructed. For this analysis to be effective, one has to understand Bourdieu's concepts of field and *habitus*. Field is "understood as a space of objective relations between positions defined by their rank in the distribution of competing powers or species of capital."[16] Therefore, class can be studied as a space in which "shared dispositions result from the internalization of shared conditions of existence."[17] This shows Bourdieu's implicit acknowledgment of homophily as the predominant relation when creating social networks.[18] Thus, he situates "the *habitus* into a relatively homogenous, self-contained and reproducing region of social space."[19] However, Lisbon's entertainment market shows that actual practice was not this simple. The Real Teatro de S. Carlos was the space frequented by people who shared social standing and dispositions but the popular theater attracted a varied mixture of people that could change every night.

Nevertheless, this tendency to constitute homogeneous groups is evident in the literature. In his novel *Os Maias*, Queirós points out that the women who feature in the periodicals are the same who attend the horse races, performances at the S. Carlos, and entertainments in the houses of the aristocracy.[20] Figure 4.1 shows a benefit concert held in the Real Teatro de São Carlos as seen from the stage. Visible are the audience in the boxes and in the stalls as well as the Royal Box, illustrating the role played by this theater as a gathering place of the city's elegant society.

Homophily was also not exclusive to the upper strata of Lisbon's population, as Fialho d'Almeida documented: "Isolated, or in small groups, on inflexible hours, we see those sleepless creatures emerging from the gateways of the houses, and entering and leaving the cafés, the billiard houses, the gambling dens, the houses of prostitution, and the hard liquor taverns."[21] Whatever the

---

[15] Pierre Bourdieu, "The Social Space and the Genesis of Groups," *Theory and Society*, 14/6 (1985), 723–744.

[16] Pierre Bourdieu and Loïc Wacquant, *An Invitation to Reflexive Sociology* (Oxford: Polity Press. 1992), 113.

[17] Wendy Bottero, "Relationality and Social Interaction," *British Journal of Sociology*, 60/2 (2009), 414.

[18] Bottero, "Relationality and Social Interaction."

[19] Bottero, "Relationality and Social Interaction," 409.

[20] Eça de Queirós, *Os Maias: episódios da vida romântica* (Porto: Livraria Chardron/Casa Editora Lugan & Genelioux Successores, 1888), vol.1, 421.

[21] Fialho d'Almeida, *Lisboa galante* (Porto: Livraria Civilisação, 1890), 214.

Figure 4.1 N.A., O Real Theatro de São Carlos—Vista da sala de espectáculo, in *O Occidente*, 1 July 1893, 149. Hemeroteca Municipal de Lisboa. The Real Teatro de São Carlos—a view of the hall.

status of a group, people of like interests and abilities tended to coalesce as a social group.[22] The *habitus* are "systems of durable, transposable dispositions, structured structures predisposed to function as structuring structures."[23] Therefore, the embodiment and internalization of hierarchical relations forms

---

[22] Pierre Bourdieu, "La parenté comme représentation et comme volonté," in Pierre Bourdieu, *Esquisse d'une théorie de la pratique, précédé de Trois études d'ethnologie kabyle* (Paris: Éditions du Seuil, 2000), 173.

[23] Pierre Bourdieu, *Outline of a Theory of Practice* (Cambridge, MA: Cambridge University Press, 1977), 72.

the basis of Bourdieu's theory of subject formation, "in which socialized individuals actively reproduce those social relations."[24]

If public spaces were the place to promenade social status, domesticity played a key role in transmitting cultural capital.[25] Middle-class women were essential to the dissemination of cultural capital in Britain's homes of the 19th and 20th centuries.[26] First, rearing children was perceived as a woman's responsibility, which gave her a major role in educating the subsequent generation.[27] This stresses the importance of informal learning in the domestic space, a process in which a *habitus* is internalized by children. Second, various signals that marked the socio-cultural status of the entire household were expected to be embodied by middle-class women.[28] These markers included some proficiency in music. Finally, "women had a critical part in transmitting cultural competence by embodying it in their own person, their dress, deportment and behaviour."[29] For Carvalho, living in society took more from women than from their husbands. This reveals that women were in charge of a significant part of the family's relations, and that there was a visible asymmetry of gender roles. While the man was "the arm, the support, the pillar," the woman had to be "the watchfulness, the economy, the continuous vigilance, the dispenser and regulator of the family's material comforts."[30] "Women, especially married women, represented embodied cultural capital; they were arbiter and proof of distinction (or of its vulgar other)."[31] Gunn associated new forms of domestic consumerism with suburbanization in Victorian and Edwardian Britain. There, the notion of a suburban culture that entailed home-centered consumerism emerged. Even though suburbanization had no parallel in Portugal, these values can be linked to Lisbon's redevelopment and to the new ways urban space was being constructed.[32] The important role women played in the home-centered consumerism cannot be understated, especially when it comes to the transmission of cultural capital. The so-called separate spheres doctrine associated domestic space with the feminine during the 18th and 19th centuries. According to this formula, "adult males should dominate a family's relationship to the outside or

---

[24] George Steinmetz, "Bourdieu's Disavowal of Lacan: Psychoanalytic Theory and the Concepts of 'Habitus' and 'Symbolic Capital,'" *Constellations*, 13/4 (2006), 450.

[25] Bourdieu, "The Forms of Capital," 48.

[26] Simon Gunn, "Translating Bourdieu: Cultural Capital and the English Middle Class in Historical Perspective," *British Journal of Sociology*, 56/1 (2005), 55.

[27] Gunn, "Translating Bourdieu," 55.

[28] Gunn, "Translating Bourdieu," 55.

[29] Gunn, "Translating Bourdieu," 55.

[30] Carvalho, *Mulheres e creanças*, 22.

[31] Gunn, "Translating Bourdieu," 55.

[32] Gunn, "Translating Bourdieu," 53.

public world while adult women properly should take direction of the domestic world."[33] Thus, the home was the woman's realm, where she reared her children, entertained guests, and catered to her husband's needs. There was a pervading idea that "a woman's sphere of influence was the home, that her life ought to be one of quiet fulfillment of her duties, out of the public eye."[34] Therefore, "women were not to sully themselves with the dirty work of the masculine sphere, the public arena."[35] Thus, the separate spheres doctrine drew a line between the public and the private. Limiting women to the physical boundaries of the home (and its extension, the garden) as well as to particular domestic activities was omnipresent in Lisbon society, and is well documented.[36] Writers associate domestic tasks with purportedly feminine qualities (like sensitivity, frailty, and susceptibility, for instance), and place the woman in a complementary, yet backstage role to the one played by the "head of the family."[37] This resonates with Carvalho's statement that "the parlor woman lives for everyone but for herself."[38] Nevertheless, the role played by aristocratic and bourgeois wives in their homes did not include menial chores such as cooking and cleaning. These tasks were carried out by hired servants. In the novel *O primo Basílio*, the servant Juliana blackmails her mistress Luísa into performing her chores by threatening to disclose to Luísa's husband the adulterous nature of the wife's relationship with Basílio.[39] Some maids helped the courtship of well-to-do girls by carrying letters, by acting as confidant, and by deceiving their parents. As payment, the maid "earns indulgence for her faults, gains a lawyer who, by fear of sympathy, defends her cause, and, if needed rebels against maternal authority for her love."[40] The maid also gains "someone who assists her in her work!"[41] Thus, a mutually beneficial relationship between bourgeois and working women could be established within the household.

A wealthy marriage was seen as the best path to securing financial stability and, consequently, the material welfare of Portuguese bourgeois women.[42]

---

[33] Woodruff Smith, *Consumption and the Making of Respectability, 1600–1800* (London: Routledge, 2002), 175.

[34] Julia Eklund Koza, "Music and the Feminine Sphere: Images of Women as Musicians in Godey's Lady's Book, 1830–1877," *Musical Quarterly*, 75/2 (1991), 108.

[35] Koza, "Music and the Feminine Sphere," 108.

[36] Maria de Fátima Outeirinho, "A mulher: educação e leituras francesas na crónica de Ramalho Ortigão," *Intercâmbio* (1992), 148–161.

[37] Outeirinho, "A mulher."

[38] Carvalho, *Mulheres e crianças*, 22.

[39] Eça de Queirós, *O primo Bazilio: episódio doméstico* (Porto: Livraria Chardron, 1878), 422–4.

[40] Carvalho, *Mulheres e crianças*, 220–1.

[41] Carvalho, *Mulheres e crianças*, 221.

[42] Ramalho Ortigão and Eça de Queirós, *As farpas: crónica mensal da política, das letras e dos costumes* (Lisbon: Typographia Universal, 1872) 79–82.

Therefore, the social function of the Portuguese aristocratic and bourgeois women would be circumscribed to the family. This excluded them "through habits or laws, from politics, from industry, from commerce, and from literature."[43] *O primo Basílio* focuses on the social life of the lower segments of Lisbon's bourgeoisie and of an adulterous relationship, and it is not by chance that its subtitle is *episódio doméstico* (domestic episode). In the cultural and educational climate of the time, the woman belonging to the privileged sectors of society was "confined to the world of feeling."[44] Queirós portrays the bourgeois woman as being primarily associated with sensation, a cultural trope that was circulating in several European and American contexts. This devaluation of rationality and focus on immediacy was reflected in leisure activities such as reading dramas and novels, or attending the theater.

The satirical content of the periodical *As farpas* has to be put into context when discussing gender. The publication sometimes relied on exaggerations of stereotypes and on ironic caricature. Nevertheless, both Queirós and Ortigão shared these views. And male writers were not the only ones who divided spaces and activities according to gender. For instance, Carvalho believed that the ideal role of a woman was to be an "honest companion" to her husband, the holder of household authority, and to cater to his happiness and the happiness of their children.[45] These views were disseminated and reinforced in several periodicals aimed at women, people who were also the intended readership of the works by Carvalho.[46] To place this discussion in a wider context, both Ortigão and Carvalho refer to Jules Michelet, a prominent French historian. This illustrates the pervasiveness of French culture in Portugal and the complexity of discussing gender,[47] revealing the dialectic between local and cosmopolitan contexts that was present at the time.

To add another layer to this subject, historians have criticized the strictness of the separate spheres doctrine, arguing that it was not a reflection of concrete realities but a projection of an idealized society.[48] This separation between masculine activities that were carried on outside the home and female domesticity is problematic when dealing with living space in the Victorian period.

> Victoria's reign had been marked by an increasing volume and an increasing awareness of sound—from the shriek and roar of the railway

---

[43] Ortigão and Queirós, *As farpas*, 67.
[44] Ortigão and Queirós, *As farpas*, 86.
[45] Outeirinho, "A mulher," 151.
[46] Outeirinho, "A mulher," 151.
[47] Outeirinho, "A mulher," 151.
[48] Amanda Vickery, "Golden Age to Separate Spheres? A Review of the Categories and Chronology of English Women's History," *Historical Journal*, 36 (1993), 383–414.

to the jarring commotion of urban streets, and from the restrained tinkling of the drawing-room to the hushed property of the middle-class parlour.[49]

At the time, a significant number of middle-class professionals "divided their time between increasingly distinct arenas of home and office."[50] The literature scholar John Picker studied writers and artists who had to work at home, and to whom street noises were a nuisance. These people "lacked a separate, official workplace that affirmed their vocational status."[51] Thus, the study, a room associated with masculine activities, was added to the household and played an important role in this economy of work, leisure, and gender.

This duality surfaces very clearly in a passage of *O primo Basílio*, where Jorge takes Sebastião to his study to have a private conversation. The study consisted of "a small room with a tall glass-fronted bookshelf" in which there was a pile of *Diários do Governo* (the official publication of the Portuguese government).[52] The presence of the *Diário do Governo* indicates that the room was a workplace for Jorge, a mining engineer. Nevertheless, Luísa also had access to the study, which complicates the differentiation between masculine and feminine spaces. It was in the same study that Luísa wrote the letter containing elements that could prove the adulterous nature of her relationship with Basílio. This letter was then seized by the servant Juliana and used to blackmail Luísa.[53] The division between male-dominated and female-dominated rooms is also part of *Os Maias*. In this novel, Afonso da Maia, the grandfather of the protagonist Carlos da Maia and a rich proprietor, spends most of his time in the study. This room was an important setting for male social life, along with the billiard room, where men played cards, smoked, drank, and talked.[54]

If domesticity is seen as feminine and the piano formed the basis of domestic music making, the piano and the feminine are linked. "The first concern of every vain or illustrated mother, intelligent or mediocre, is that her daughters learn how to play the piano."[55] This did not go unnoticed in Portuguese literature, and Fialho d'Almeida satirically remarked that women entered

---

[49] John M. Picker, *Victorian Soundscapes* (Oxford: Oxford University Press, 2003), 111.

[50] Picker, *Victorian Soundscapes*, 52–53.

[51] John M. Picker, "The Soundproof Study: Victorian Professionals, Work Space, and Urban Noise," *Victorian Studies*, 42/3 (2000), 428.

[52] Queirós, *O primo Bazilio*, 57–64.

[53] Queirós, *O primo Bazilio*, 233–255.

[54] Queirós, *Os Maias*, vol.1, 149–156.

[55] Carvalho, *Mulheres e crianças*, 50.

photographic studios to be portrayed at the piano "with the eyes facing the sky, like yielded Saint Cecilias."[56]

> The piano was pre-eminently a woman's instrument. Nineteenth-century notions of middle-class femininity highly valued musical ability and held skilled piano playing supreme cultural accomplishment, along with a fine singing voice. But even indifferent capacity was valued as a sign of female gentility and cultivation. In an age when families made their own music women held a central place in home and community entertainment, very often as pianists.[57]

Several musicologists have also related the piano almost exclusively to females. Gender was embedded in the piano, "an object to be looked at beyond being heard or played upon," and was an important part of this way of seeing.[58] Moreover, it had the extra-musical role of working as "the visual-sonoric simulacrum of family, wife, and mother" in the home.[59] In his description of an 1801 model of a pianoforte, Leppert states that the cupboard design marks the piano as middle class—prestigious as a grand yet modest, even a bit severe. It also marks the piano as feminine: the objects it might properly hold, apart from printed music or smaller instruments are bric-a-brac. The move toward practicality and the feminization of the domestic piano quickly concatenated in the eyes of manufacturers. Thus small pianos, early in the nineteenth century, were made to double as sewing tables.[60]

The doubling of the piano as a sewing table illustrates the role played by the instrument and its relationship with class, gender, and space. The object concentrated two activities that were a staple of female bourgeois domesticity, playing the piano and sewing. Both were expressions of the cultural capital that was developed inside the home. This resonates with Portugal, as embroidery, crochet, and playing the piano were part of the standard education of society girls. Nevertheless, associating the piano with the bourgeois woman was a more nuanced and complex process.[61] The piano became part of the

---

[56] Fialho d'Almeida, *Pasquinadas (jornal d'um vagabundo)* (Porto: Livraria Chardron, Lello & Irmão, 1904), 22–23.

[57] Ward, *A History of Domestic Space*, 65.

[58] Richard Leppert, "Sexual Identity, Death, and the Family Piano," *19th-Century Music*, 16/2 (1992), 105.

[59] Leppert, "Sexual Identity, Death, and the Family Piano," 105.

[60] Leppert, "Sexual Identity, Death, and the Family Piano," 115.

[61] Richard Leppert, "The Female at Music: Praxis, Representation and the Problematic of Identity," in Leppert, *Music and Image: Domesticity, Ideology and Socio-cultural Formation in Eighteenth-Century England* (Cambridge: Cambridge University Press, 1988), 147–175.

strategies of distinction of the bourgeoisie because it was associated with a set of values that included frugality.[62] Thus, the double role of the piano/sewing table merged leisure/work in the same item.[63] "Ideologically, the pairing was brilliant in its self-confirmation of the association of the instrument with women and women with domesticity."[64]

Leppert's views can be adapted to other periods. The form of the piano was already established in the mid-19th century. Nevertheless, the link between the piano, domesticity, and the feminine was not limited to the instrument's configuration. It can be transferred to the repertoire. However, this move is not a simplistic shift to a repertoire-based discussion because the association of some repertoires with femininity was already in place in earlier periods, and instrument manufacturers, composers, and publishing houses articulated their efforts and contributed to institute and to reinforce these gender and class stereotypes.

As stated above, work on the segmentation of musical genres according to gender has been predominantly carried out within Anglo-American contexts. Nevertheless, various traits of this discussion were present in Portugal. In the Victorian period "certain musical styles were considered unsuitable or even unnatural for women composers."[65] This was a consequence of an articulation between 19th-century social theory, the new scientific approaches to gender and sexuality, and the spread of an aesthetic dichotomy between the sublime and the beautiful.[66] Also, there were important constraints to the career development of female composers. The imposed pressures women were subjected to on social, economic, and educational levels played a key role in the gendering of the repertoire.[67] The purported existence of feminine and masculine qualities in music, their hierarchical distribution, and their supposed biological foundation also affected male composers, especially when their work was placed in comparative terms "with the less elevated output of women."[68] This discussion of gender roles and abilities was widely circulating throughout Western culture at the time and is illustrated by the formulation that the woman was "confined to the world of feeling" mentioned above.[69] This has musical resonances,

---

[62] Leppert, *Music and Image*, 156.

[63] Leppert, *Music and Image*, 156.

[64] Leppert, *Music and Image*, 156.

[65] Derek B. Scott, "The Sexual Politics of Victorian Musical Aesthetics," *Journal of the Royal Musical Association*, 119/1 (1994), 91.

[66] Scott, "The Sexual Politics of Victorian Musical Aesthetics," 91.

[67] Scott, "The Sexual Politics of Victorian Musical Aesthetics," 91.

[68] Scott, "The Sexual Politics of Victorian Musical Aesthetics," 91.

[69] Ortigão and Queirós, *As farpas*, 86.

since female composers were associated with emotionality in a period when rationality, then seen as a masculine category, was prized.

The polarity between the sublime and the beautiful enclosed a binary male/female logic that was supported by the psychiatry of the time.[70] Consequently, aesthetic theories based on a bifurcation between the sublime and the beautiful had a direct translation in music. The sublime was "typified by qualities such as the awesome, solemn, pathetic, colossal, lofty and majestic" and the beautiful was "typified by qualities of the graceful, charming, delicate, playful and pretty."[71] This distinction associated the masculine with the sublime and the feminine with the beautiful. Consequently, this division aimed to exclude women from writing music that was perceived as untrue to the female nature.[72] This was not exclusive to Britain, given the professionalization of female musicians in the United States of America and their growing autonomy from the stereotypical "piano girl."[73] Tick put forward a division that associates the female composer with lyricism and melodiousness and with "smaller forms, like songs and piano pieces."[74] This reinforces the pervasive link that was made between women and frivolity, an association that was reflected in the music business.

The opera *Haydée* in Portugal is an interesting yet exceptional example of an opera written by a woman and performed in Portugal. It was composed by Felicia Lacombe Casella, a French-born musician who was the sister of the pianist/composer Louis Lacombe (1818–1884).[75] She had studied singing and piano in the Paris Conservatoire before going to Portugal with her husband and co-performer, the cellist Cesare Casella.[76] Thus, Felicia had familiar ties to two virtuosos. Placing women in a system of kinship with male musicians was often used to promote their works. This reveals the asymmetry of the gender relations of the time, and the prevalence of gender stereotypes. Felicia and Cesare had international careers, and their itinerancy was characteristic of the virtuoso performer of the first half of the 19th century. Nevertheless, they lived in Porto, in Lisbon, and in the Azores in the years that surrounded the composition of *Haydée*.[77] The opera was inspired by Dumas' *The Count of Monte*

---

[70] Scott, "The Sexual Politics of Victorian Musical Aesthetics," 99.

[71] Scott, "The Sexual Politics of Victorian Musical Aesthetics," 99.

[72] Scott, "The Sexual Politics of Victorian Musical Aesthetics," 99.

[73] Judith Tick, "Passed Away Is the Piano Girl: Changes in American Musical Life, 1870–1900," in Jane Bowers and Judith Tick, *Women Making Music: The Western Art Tradition, 1150–1950* (Urbana: University of Illinois Press, 1986), 325–348.

[74] Tick, "Passed Away Is the Piano Girl," 337.

[75] Ernesto Vieira, *Diccionario biographico de musicos portuguezes: historia e bibliografia da musica em Portugal*, vol.1 (Lisbon: Lambertini, 1900), 238–239.

[76] Vieira, *Diccionario*, 238–239.

[77] Vieira, *Diccionario*, 238–239.

Cristo and premièred in the Teatro de S. Sebastião (in S. Miguel, Azores) in 1852. It had a Portuguese libretto, and the orchestra was conducted by Cesare Casella and relied on amateur musicians from the local *bandas*.[78] The subsequent year, *Haydée* was staged in the Teatro de D. Maria II, and Felicia sang the leading role. This is very atypical in four different ways: an opera written by a female composer, a composer performing her own theatrical work, a libretto in Portuguese, and an opera performed in the Teatro de D. Maria II—a house that was almost exclusively dedicated to drama.

The Real Teatro de S. Carlos offered mostly opera in Italian by established composers. Moreover, the performers were predominantly Italian. Thus, an opera performed in Portuguese had to be performed by another company in a different setting. *Haydée* was dedicated to the King D. Fernando, which may have contributed to its being staged in a major theater and not in a less prestigious venue. Lisbon's performance of *Haydée* was the object of a *feuilleton* about famous women artists by Lopes de Mendonça.[79] Despite the author's praise of Felicia Lacombe Casella, the article concentrated on French female writers whom Mendonça admired. Apart from the printed version of the libretto of *Haydée*, the National Library of Portugal holds one piano piece and one song composed by Felicia Lacombe Casella. These genres were far more consonant with the association between women and "light" music than opera.

A patriarchal discourse that associates femininity with "light music" (or "trivial music" to borrow the expression coined by Dahlhaus) was also reflected in the music publishing business of the time.[80] These topics surface in Portuguese novels like *O primo Basílio* and *Os Maias*, by Eça de Queirós and *Amanhã!*, by Abel Botelho. In *O primo Basílio*, female characters are associated with the piano in several passages. Luísa sings and plays the piano in the parlor. She performs a poem by Soares dos Passos (a writer associated with late-Romanticism), the finale of *La traviata*, and the "Fado do Vimioso."[81] This shows the varied repertoire that was performed in the home; supplying this market constituted the core of the music publishing business, as it provided operatic reductions, fado, and parlor songs.[82] The compositions mentioned above are vocal pieces, reinforcing the argument that singing and playing the

---

[78] João Silva, O diário "A Revolução de Setembro" (1840–1857): Música, poder e construção social de realidade em Portugal nos meados do século XIX, master's thesis (Universidade Nova de Lisboa, 2007), 152–153.

[79] *A Revolução de Setembro*, 25 June 1853, 1–2.

[80] Carl Dalhaus, *Nineteenth-Century Music* (Berkeley: University of California Press, 1991), 311–319.

[81] Queirós, *O primo Bazílio*, 19.

[82] Derek B. Scott, *The Singing Bourgeois: Songs of the Victorian Drawing Room and Parlour* (Aldershot: Ashgate, 2001).

piano were part of the skills expected of aristocratic and bourgeois women. Therefore,

> young middle-class women often took special pains to develop their keyboard skills because prospective suitors commonly regarded a musical education as especially attractive in a wife. For this reason the piano could play an important part in a woman's courtship strategies, to say nothing of those of parents anxious to advance their daughters' marital interest.[83]

These abilities were key to the cementing of social relations, such as an advantageous marriage, an aspect that resonates with the analysis of the condition of the Portuguese woman by Eça de Queirós. This strategy was also used in Portugal. Carvalho argued that the married woman could "close the piano, throw away the pencil and the paints, abandon sewing and embroidering, and fall in the *dolce far niente* without being afraid of maternal reproaches."[84] In *Lisboa em camisa*, a novel by Gervásio Lobato, the civil servant Justino Antunes had married an eighteen-year-old girl who "could play the piano like a charm, embroider with gold thread, and sing *La Traviata* in Italian."[85] Thus, acquiring basic skills in music and needlework was used to secure a good marriage.

The repertoire Luísa performed throughout *O primo Basílio* is varied, but it is mostly associated with the feminine. She and her friend Leopoldina sing and play Italian songs, waltzes, opera and operetta transcriptions, and fado.[86] These are clearly "light music," where an association between melodious sensuousness and emotional immediacy prevailed. Therefore, these repertoires are situated at the opposite pole from a music that prizes "masculine" and "intellectual" characteristics, such as structural complexity, harmony, and counterpoint.[87] Moreover, a little girl is heard playing Thécla Badarzewska's piece "La prière d'une vierge" on a piano near Luísa's house, with a "vagrant Sunday sentimentalism."[88] Thus, the link between woman and sentimentality was made from an early age, resonating with Bourdieu's theory of *habitus*. The repertoire played by the character Sebastião contrasts with the music performed by Luísa. Sebastião had manifested a precocious inclination for music that

---

[83] Ward, *A History of Domestic Space*, 65; Craig H. Roell, *The Piano in America, 1890–1940* (Chapel Hill: University of North Carolina Press, 1989), 25–26.

[84] Carvalho, *Mulheres e creanças*, 241.

[85] Gervásio Lobato, *Lisboa em camisa* (Lisbon: Empreza Litteraria de Lisboa, 1882), 9.

[86] Queirós, *O primo Bazilio*, 60–63.

[87] Tick, "Passed Away Is the Piano Girl," 337.

[88] Queirós, *O primo Bazilio*, 34.

encouraged his mother to engage a piano teacher for him.[89] When asked about his musical prowess at an informal gathering, the Conselheiro Acácio compared Sebastião with Thalberg or Liszt.[90] Although this comparison is exaggerated, it relates Sebastião with the male virtuoso, clearly distinguishing him from Luísa or Leopoldina. Nevertheless, he is depicted playing a nocturne by Chopin, a composer associated by Tick with the feminine.[91] On the one hand, this indicates that a straightforward segmentation of repertoires according to gender is complex. On the other hand, it reveals the importance of Chopin's pieces in the musical soirées. Moreover, the Portuguese music publishing business was dominated by opera, operetta, and parlor songs. Thus, Chopin's nocturnes seem to inhabit a more elevated place in the hierarchy of musical taste. The association between the piano and young women from privileged strata is also made by Abel Botelho in *Amanhã!*. He depicted Adriana, the "patrician daughter of the owners of the house" and of the factory, playing the piano.[92] However, taking piano lessons was not exclusive to young females. For example, a painting by Columbano Bordalo Pinheiro portrays his young nephew, Manuel Gustavo Bordalo Pinheiro, struggling with a difficult passage while practicing the piano.[93]

Nevertheless, a strong association between the woman and the piano persisted. Figure 4.2 is a photograph of the actress and singer Medina de Sousa looking over her daughter's shoulder while she practices the piano. Medina de Sousa had a remarkable career in the music theater in Portugal and in Brazil, and recorded for the Gramophone Company. Moreover, she played the lead role in the Portuguese version of *Serrana* that was staged in Rio de Janeiro in 1910.[94] The photo was taken in a domestic setting that emphasizes intimacy. However, the room has a large photograph of Medina de Sousa and several flower bouquets that were probably given to her after one of her performances. This is used to remind the viewer of the status of the singer. Moreover, the photograph shows that prominent female artists also prized familial domesticity, contrasting with the stereotypes of the popular performer that were circulating at the time.

In *Os Maias*, the character Cruges is described differently. He was probably inspired by Augusto Machado and by Jaime Batalha Reis, who belonged to

---

[89] Queirós, *O primo Bazilio*, 152.

[90] Queirós, *O primo Bazilio*, 152.

[91] Queirós, *O primo Bazilio*, 65; Tick, "Passed Away Is the Piano Girl," 337.

[92] Abel Botelho, *Amanhã!* (Porto: Livraria Chardron, 1902), 81–87.

[93] Columbano Bordalo Pinheiro, *Trecho difícil*, 1885. Inventory number CMAG: 928, Casa-Museu Dr. Anastácio Gonçalves (Lisbon).

[94] 'A "Serrana": opera portugueza de Alfredo Keil,' in *O paiz*, 2 September 1910, 1–2.

Figure 4.2 Alberto Carlos Lima, A actriz cantora Medina de Sousa, early 20th century, Arquivo Fotográfico de Lisboa, Colecção Alberto Carlos Lima, PT/AMLSB/LIM/003278. Medina de Sousa, actress and singer.

the group of intellectuals in which Queirós circulated.[95] The appreciation of Cruges for German composers was likely drawn from Batalha Reis, who studied in a German school in Lisbon. Cruges expresses his admiration for composers like Bach, Beethoven, Mozart, and Wagner, who were associated with masculine qualities.[96] Furthermore, he performs Mendelssohn, Chopin, and, most notably, Beethoven's "Pathétique" sonata.[97] Nevertheless, this should not be directly associated with gender. Cruges was a conductor, composer, and pianist. Therefore, he was a music professional in contrast to the dilettantes of the novels by Queirós. In this context, the character admires the technical proficiency of Austro-German composers. Nevertheless, the composers he holds in high regard were associated with both "masculine" and "intellectual" qualities, reflecting a hierarchy of taste and its implications on matters such as technique and gender. Thus, Cruges is presented as the "serious" (and male) musician who operates in a different space from the amateur practitioners,

---

[95] Mário Vieira de Carvalho, *Eça de Queirós e Offenbach* (Lisbon: Edições Colibri, 1999), 95–100.

[96] Queirós, *Os Maias*, vol. 1, 292–294.

[97] Queirós, *Os Maias*, vol. 2, 361–362.

despite sharing some social circuits with them. Gender is important here because women were seen as singers and actresses but not as professional composers or pianists.

In conclusion, a number of characteristics were predominantly associated with everyday domestic and, therefore, feminine activities. Nevertheless, the association between them and gender proves to be elusive and complex. Furthermore, significant transformations were beginning to appear. The lower strata of the bourgeoisie and of the white-collar proletariat started to have disposable income. They bought pianos and financed lessons for their children. Since the piano was a marker of social status, it is not surprising that aspiring sectors would partake in this form of embodying and displaying cultural capital. Moreover, the operetta and the *revista* expanded an entertainment market in which the place for music was changing. The theater entered the piano parlor with its marches, waltzes, and fados.

Librettos, Programs, Posters, and Postcards

The trade in goods such as *coplas* (booklets containing the lyrics of the songs from the *revistas*) or sheet music promoted the domestic consumption of theatrical repertoires, expanding their range. In this sense, the circulation of different goods helped theatrical music become a ubiquitous presence in everyday life. This brings to the foreground the complex interaction between continuity and change in the repertoire. The same musical piece had to be accommodated to its intended context, audience, and medium. Adapting music to be performed in heterogeneous settings sometimes transformed it substantially. This is illustrated by the piano pieces inspired by theatrical melodies. Because they were intended to circulate among a large audience, the pieces had to be compatible with the skill of the average pianist. In the case of phonography, significant changes had to be made to the sonic materials themselves for the music to record well. Librettos of the operettas and the *coplas* of the *revista* had a significant circulation inside and outside the theater. These booklets exist in several formats with varying degrees of completeness and are a very important source for the study of popular theater. Their status as collectables adds some permanence to the precarious nature of performances. In most cases, the librettos and *coplas* are small-sized brochures that contain the text of the play. Sometimes, they contain its full text; in other cases, the dialogues are only partially reproduced. Many contain only the songs, which complicates a complete reconstruction of the plot. Nevertheless, they allow a partial understanding of the narrative. Some booklets also contain important information about the play such as the theater or theaters where it had been performed, the people involved, and the date of its première.[98] Unlike the *revista*, the publication of operetta librettos started simultaneously with their regular performance in Lisbon. This is illustrated with the publishing of the librettos of the three operettas by Offenbach that premièred in Lisbon in 1868 (*As georgianas, Barba-azul*, and *A Grã-duquesa de Gérolstein*). Indeed, Eduardo Garrido's translation of Offenbach's *La Grande-Dûchesse de Gérolstein* was printed at least four times by two different publishers in 1868 and 1869.[99] Although it is not possible to determine the circulation of these books, the reprinting of this libretto clearly shows that Offenbach's operettas were important in Portugal and is a further indication that such booklets were widely circulated in the local entertainment market.[100] In a large number of cases, the operetta librettos were published when the play was performed. Nevertheless, there is a stable body of librettos that were recurrently printed. They constitute evidence of the role librettos played as collectables for their intended consumers, even without the immediacy of a performance. A collection of librettos and *coplas* was a way to archive one's experience. Moreover, given the frequent reprises of the pieces, the same booklet could be used on several occasions. Of course this is more effective with the operetta than with the *revista*. The operetta was more stable, while new sketches were frequently devised for the *revista*. Eduardo Garrido's translation of *Les cloches de Corneville* was reprinted several times between 1879 and the beginning of the 20th century, and the libretto of the 1891 operetta *O burro do senhor alcaide* was published at least six times before 1904.[101]

When moving from the librettos of operettas to the *coplas* of *revista* one must address their particular characteristics. Operettas offered a coherent plot with music. Therefore, their printed text is similar to the opera libretto. This means that, in their revivals, operettas generally used the same text. The reprise of the operetta *Os sinos de Corneville* by the Nicolau da Silva Group used the translation by Garrido that was performed in the play's première in

---

[98] Eduardo Fernandes, *O poeta Bocage: opereta em 3 actos* (Lisbon: Impr. Lucas, 1902).

[99] Eduardo Garrido, *A Grã-duqueza de Gérolstein: ópera burlesca em três actos e quatro quadros* (Lisbon: Typographia Universal de Thomaz Quintino Antunes, 1868); Eduardo Garrido, *A Grã-duqueza de Gérolstein: ópera burlesca em três actos e quatro quadros* (Lisbon: Typographia Universal de Thomaz Quintino Antunes, 1869); Eduardo Garrido, *A Grã-duqueza de Gérolstein: ópera burlesca em três actos e quatro quadros* (Lisbon: P. Plantier, 1869). This last libretto states it is a second edition.

[100] Eduardo Garrido, *As georgianas: ópera burlesca em três actos* (Lisbon: Typographia Universal de Thomaz Quintino Antunes, 1868); Francisco Palha, *Barba azul: ópera burlesca em 3 actos e 4 quadros* (Lisbon: Typographia Franco Portugueza, 1868).

[101] Gervásio Lobato and D. João da Câmara, *O burro do senhor alcaide* (Lisbon: Livraria Popular de Francisco Franco, 1904).

1877.[102] This happened in the Teatro Ginásio in 1900. The early *revista* was based on loose episodes of the previous year. It was not staged during the entire season since it was only performed in the first months of the following year. Consequently, printing the text of a play that was staged for a relatively short period and which would not be revived would not have been a good business opportunity for publishers. Therefore, it is not surprising to find that the frequent publication of the texts of the *revistas* started only around the 1880s, when the genre became a year-round entertainment.[103] As the *revista* dealt with current events, these plays were frequently transformed throughout their performance history. This happened when *Tim tim por tim tim* was revived in the Teatro da Avenida in 1890. The *revista* had premièred in the Teatro da Rua dos Condes the year before and the *coplas* were then published. Given its success, the publisher Alfredo da Costa Braga issued several versions of the *coplas*, including a luxury edition that contains a photograph of the lead actress Pepa Ruiz.[104] However, an entire new act was devised for the new production.[105] Therefore, to market goods associated with a changing repertoire, a publisher had to be able not only to deal with these transformations but also to maximize profit in these volatile circumstances. For example, when *Tim tim por tim tim* was revived in the season 1898–1899, an "expanded" edition of the *coplas* was printed.[106] This is also true for the successful *revista Ó da guarda*, premièred at the Teatro do Príncipe Real in 1907, when the reprint of its *coplas*, presented as Figure 4.3, reflected the play's new sketches.

Printing librettos and *coplas* was important to several publishing houses. The Livraria Popular de Francisco Franco published a large collection of "*coplas* of various comic operas." It contains librettos and *coplas* of operettas, *vaudevilles, mágicas, revistas*—a body of texts that became a fundamental source for the study of theatrical activities in Portugal. The Livraria was established in Lisbon in 1890, in the heyday of the *revista* and became an important publisher of cheap books.

---

[102] Eduardo Garrido, *Os sinos de Corneville: opera-comica em 3 actos e 4 quadros*. Shelfmark PTBN: COD. 12136, National Library of Portugal.

[103] Luiz Francisco Rebello, *História do teatro de revista em Portugal*, vol. 1 (Lisbon: Publicações D. Quixote, 1984), 85.

[104] António de Sousa Bastos, *Coplas, tangos, fados e córos de: "Tim Tim Por Tim Tim: revista do ano de 1888" de Sousa Bastos: Edição de luxo, ornada com o retrato da actriz Pepa* (Lisbon: Typographia de Alfredo da Costa Braga, 1889).

[105] *Pontos nos ii*, 17 April 1890, 128; António de Sousa Bastos, *Tim tim por tim tim: revista do anno de 1888* (Lisbon: Typographia de Alfredo da Costa Braga, 1889).

[106] Sousa Bastos, *Tim tim por tim tim de 1898: coplas, fados, córos e tangos* (Lisbon, Libanio & Cunha, 1898).

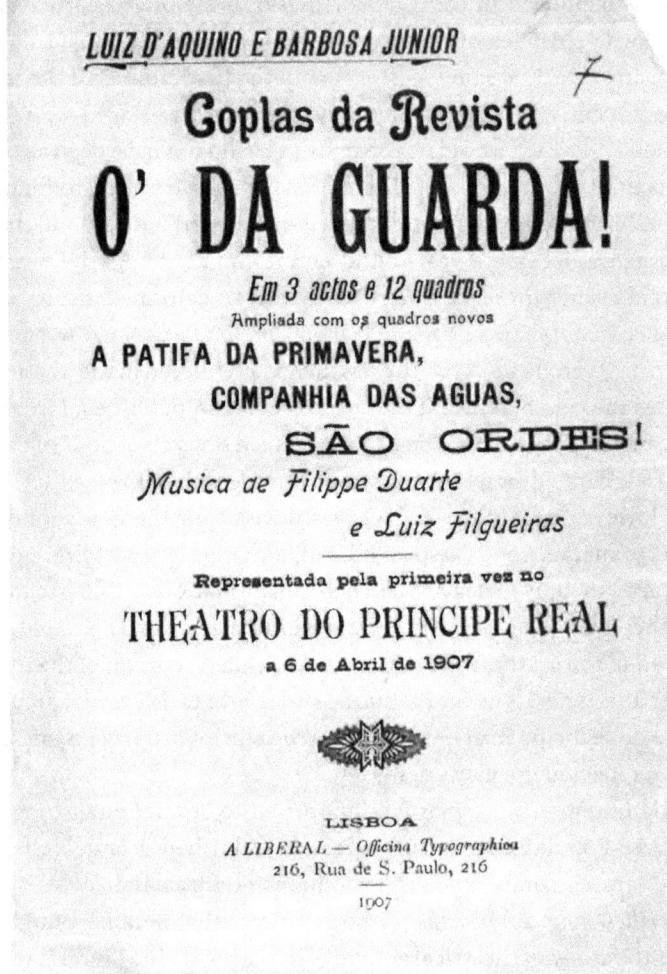

Figure 4.3 Front cover of the *Coplas da revista Ó da guarda: em 3 actos e 12 quadros* (Lisbon: A Liberal, 1907). Biblioteca Nacional de Portugal, l-9162-7-v. Front cover of the *Coplas da revista* Ó *da guarda: em 3 actos e 12 quadros*.

The libretto and the *coplas* stand out as sources for the plots of theatrical plays. For other types of information one must rely on the program. It is valuable because it lists the people who worked in a specific play. The fleeting nature of theatrical materials associated with perishable shows such as the operetta and the *revista* has already been discussed. The program for a set of performances illustrates the ephemeral nature of some theatrical enterprises and repertoires. Unlike librettos, not many theatrical programs have survived. Nevertheless, it is possible to trace a few common traits from this small sample. The program for the *revista Beijos de burro* (premièred in the Teatro

Chalet do Rato in 1903) includes the names of the characters and the performers who played them as well as the title of the sketches.[107] In other cases, such as the first performances of the operetta *O solar dos barrigas*, the program lists its technical and artistic personnel.[108] The program for the *revista Raios X*, reproduced as Figure 4.4, identifies the authors, and then lists the characters and the performers who played them, as well as the titles of its numbers. Apart from identifying the personnel involved in a production, the program also played an important role in advertising the shows,[109] even though its inadequate distribution reduced the medium's efficiency.[110] Nevertheless, for the unsubsidized companies, in which the popularity of the performers was important in attracting audiences, the program could play a significant role as a part of a wider marketing plan devised by the impresarios. This was usually accompanied with advertisements in periodicals, which aimed to reach the largest number of people possible.

Halftone printing and photography promoted substantial transformations in the advertising market in the last third of the 19th century. Hence, a new form of representation became widely available. It reflected a tendency to create icons, a trend that became extremely important in theatrical advertising. Technology is an agent for changing our perception of the world.[111] Although Kittler examined the transformation of the discourse networks from 1800 to 1900, he paid little attention to the relationship between text- and image-based communications, despite focusing on a period of intense change in this relationship. As technology developed, marketing a show required new media, and this iconographic shift marks an important change in the relationship between image and audience. On the one hand, it promotes proximity between distant elements. On the other hand, it increases the distance between them by reinforcing the aura of the symbol. In this dialectical motion "the aura opens up distance only the more effectively to insinuate intimacy."[112] Therefore, images that were circulating in the press and on the

---

[107] *Beijos de burro* [program], Lisbon (Teatro Chalet do Rato), [1903]. Shelfmark MNT: 17092, National Theater Museum (Lisbon), *Raios X* [program], Lisbon, (Teatro da Trindade), [1904/1905]. Shelfmark MNT: 112557, National Theater Museum (Lisbon).

[108] *O solar dos barrigas* [program], Lisbon (Teatro da Rua dos Condes), 1892. Shelfmark MNT: 29871, National Theater Museum (Lisbon).

[109] Sousa Bastos, *Diccionario do theatro portuguez* (Lisbon: Imp. Libânio da Silva, 1908), 116–117.

[110] Sousa Bastos, *Diccionario*, 116–117.

[111] Friedrich A. Kittler, *Gramophone, Film, Typewriter* (Palo Alto, CA: Stanford University Press, 1999).

[112] Terry Eagleton, *Walter Benjamin or Towards a Revolutionary Criticism* (London: Verso, 2009), 39; Walter Benjamin, *The Work of Art in the Age of Mechanical Reproduction* (London: Penguin Books, 2008).

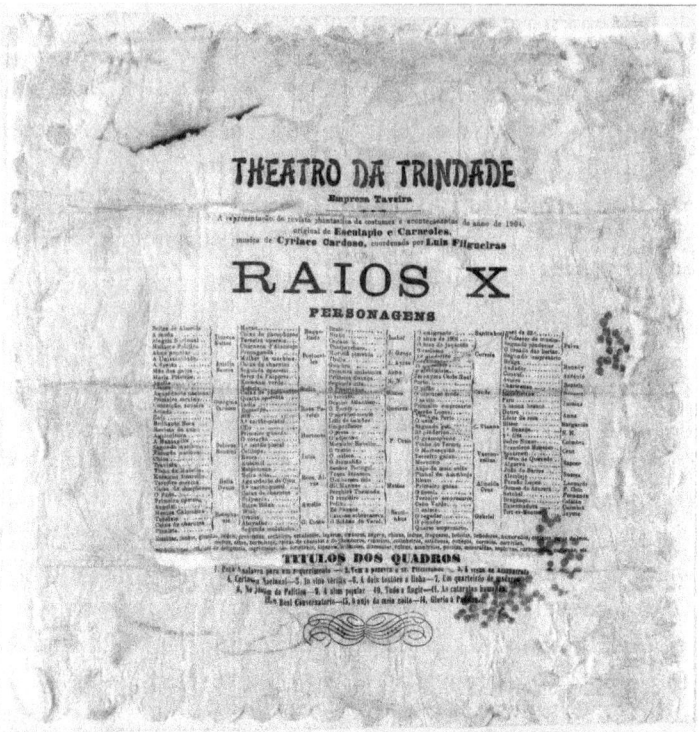

Figure 4.4 Program of the *revista Raios X*, Teatro da Trindade, Lisbon, 1904, Museu Nacional do Teatro, MNT 112557. Direção-Geral do Património Cultural/Arquivo de Documentação Fotográfica. Program of the *revista Raios X*, Teatro da Trindade, Lisbon, 1904.

street walls signaled the simultaneous presence and absence of theatrical performers in spaces that ranged from the domestic intimacy of a parlor to the bustle of Lisbon's busy thoroughfares. Benjamin relates aura in photography to a correspondence between object and technology, emphasizing the relation between the photographer and the technique.[113] Hence, "aura and photography are not simply cast as mutually exclusive opposites but are in fact engaged in a complex process of interaction."[114] Photography soon became an important mechanism for constructing a collective memory. For example, the photographs of Joshua Benoliel (1873–1932) have been widely used in illustrating publications about the Portuguese 20th century. Hence, the wide circulation of pictures began to play an important role as an organizer of a

---

[113] Walter Benjamin, "Little History of Photography," in Walter Benjamin, *Selected Writings*, vol. 2, 1927–1934 (Cambridge, MA: Harvard University Press, 1999), 507–530.

[114] Carolin Duttlinger, "Imaginary Encounters: Walter Benjamin and the Aura of Photography," *Poetics Today*, 29/1 (2008), 80.

visual collective memory. "Memory and its representations touch very significantly upon questions of identity, of nationalism, of power and authority."[115] Photography further enhanced the circulation of this iconographic heritage by crystallizing everyday images into icons, a turn that became fundamental for the spread of two products that were used to advertise the theater: the poster and the postcard.[116]

Posters were an efficient medium for advertising theatrical shows throughout Portugal.[117] They started as "small and simple" but became "huge, printed in colors and illustrated with scenes of the plays" by the beginning of the 20th century.[118] They were distributed in Lisbon and in Porto by special agencies hired by the theatrical companies.[119] In other places they were probably distributed by the promoter of the shows. Although few of these posters have survived, a sign of their functional and ephemeral status, they played an important role in advertising theatrical shows in public spaces. Thus, the posters simultaneously reflected and were a reflection of an iconographic shift.[120] The posters are heterogeneous. The poster for the forty-eighth performance of *Pontos nos ii*, a *revista* of 1885, is scarce in both images and information.[121] It contains the place, date, and time of the show as well as its title and authors. It advertises new *coplas* that had recently been included in the *revista*. In other cases the posters, like the programs, named the people involved in the performance. The poster for the *revista A.B.C* in the Teatro Avenida includes the same information as the poster from *Pontos nos ii*. It adds catchy slogans, like "colossal turnouts," "stunning props," or "laugh the entire evening" to the listing of people involved.[122] The poster claimed that "clergy, nobility, and commoners, monarchists, republicans, and socialists are all fellows when it comes to *ABC*."[123] This slogan uses the social divides in Portuguese society as a way of promoting the show. Therefore, it resonates with the multivocality of the genre. In some cases, like *O tutti-li-mundi*, the poster includes the names of the characters and the performers who play them, the sketches that comprise

---

[115] Edward Said, "Invention, Memory, and Place," *Critical Inquiry* 26/2 (2000), 176.

[116] Roland Barthes, *Camera Lucida* (London: Vintage Books, 2000), 6, 13.

[117] Sousa Bastos, *Diccionario*, 34.

[118] Sousa Bastos, *Diccionario*, 34.

[119] Sousa Bastos, *Diccionario*, 34.

[120] Sally Charnow, "Commercial Culture and Modernist Theatre in Fin-de-siècle Paris: André Antoine and the Théâtre Libre," *Radical History Review*, 77 (2000), 60–90.

[121] *Pontos nos ii* [poster], Lisbon, Chalet da Rua dos Condes (1886), PT-ADPRT-COL-CDAC-017-034-01677, Porto District Archive.

[122] *ABC* [poster], Lisbon, Teatro Avenida (1908), PT-ADPRT-COL-CDAC-017-034-01699, Porto District Archive.

[123] *ABC* [poster].

the *revista*, and the musical numbers each act contains.[124] This is also the case of the poster for *Tim tim por tim tim* that is reproduced in Figure 4.5. It includes the place and time of the play as well as a list of characters and the people who perform them, the musical numbers, the titles of the numbers, and other agents involved in the production, such as authors, set designers, props, hairdressers, or stage technicians.[125] Unfortunately, the poster is torn and does not include the theater where the *revista* was performed, the Teatro da Avenida. Another form of advertising with posters is the partial reproduction of the texts of one or more sketches, giving the audience a juicy glimpse of the show.[126] However, Sousa Bastos warns the audience to be careful with the posters because they all start by proclaiming the great success the play has had even when this did not correspond to the truth.[127]

The poster for the 1902 performances of *Tição negro* in the Teatro Avenida is a good example of an advertising tool with artistic intentions.[128] The plot of this "lyrical farce" drew upon elements associated with the Portuguese playwright Gil Vicente (1465–1537) in a period when historicist and naturalistic trends played an important role in the theatrical market. Consequently, the poster reflected this trend and catered to the needs of advertising a theatrical production with historical claims, containing the same information one would expect to find in a program: a list of the performers and the characters they played, the musical numbers, and the technical staff.[129] The poster was printed in very large dimensions and emulated the aesthetics of the period in which the play is set. This is reflected in language that emulates Gil Vicente's style, in the lettering, and in an illustrated strip that recalls late medieval motives.[130]

Photographic reproduction was crucial in the development of the illustrated postcard as a modern collectable, reflecting the processes of urbanization, industrialization, and the spread of literacy during the 19th century as well as the communication of personal travel experience.[131] Postcards emerged in the last third of the 19th century, and sending them

---

[124] *O tutti-li-mundi* [poster], Lisbon, Teatro da Rua dos Condes (1881), PT-ADPRT-COL-CDAC-017-034-01728, Porto District Archive.

[125] *Tim tim por tim tim* [poster], Lisbon, Teatro da Avenida (1889), PT/ADPRT/COL/CDAC/005/002/01708, Porto District Archive.

[126] *A grande avenida* [poster], Lisbon, Teatro do Rato (1887), PT-ADPRT-COL-CDAC-017-034-01706, Porto District Archive.

[127] Sousa Bastos, *Diccionario*, 138.

[128] *Tição negro* [poster], Lisbon, Teatro Avenida, [1902]. Shelfmark MNT: 18062, National Theater Museum (Lisbon).

[129] *Tição negro* [poster].

[130] *Tição negro* [poster].

[131] Brenda Darnet, *Cyberpl@y: Communicating Online* (Oxford: Berg, 2001), 161.

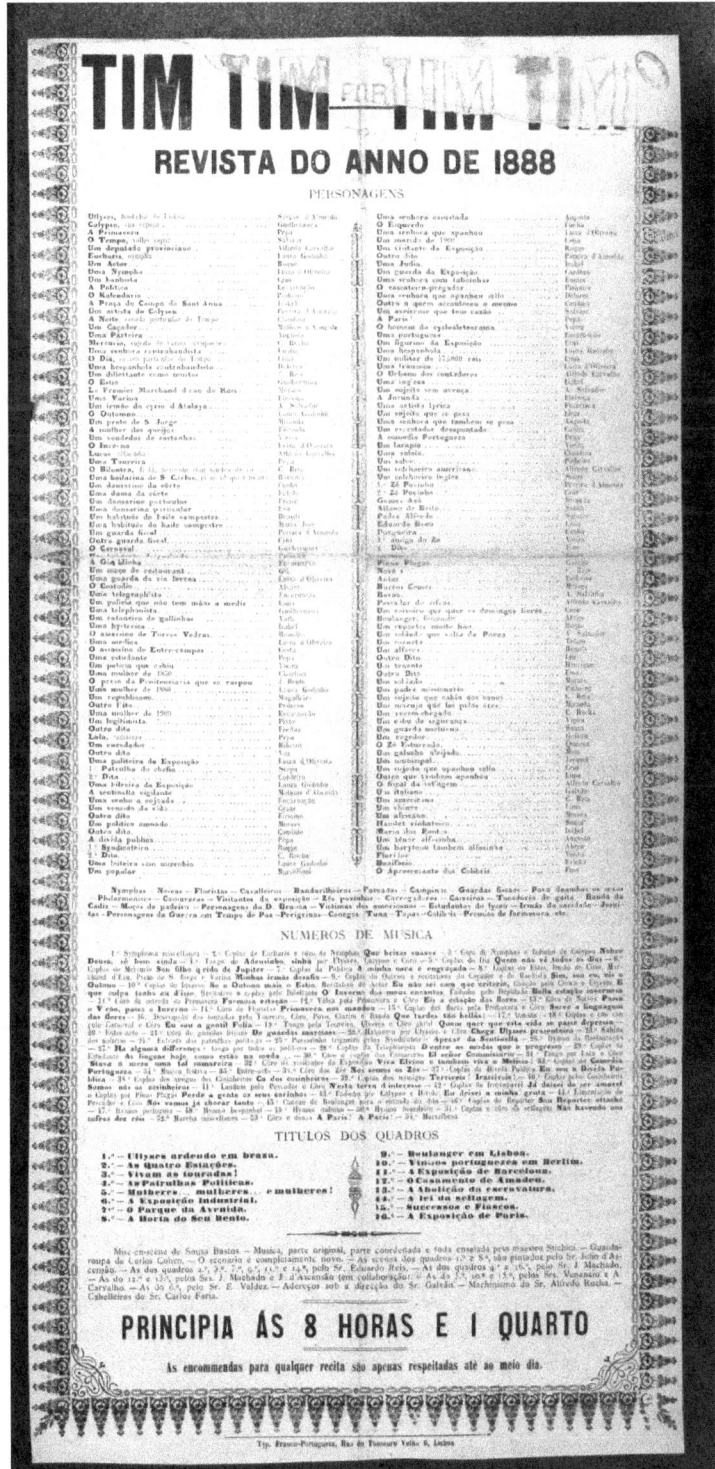

Figure 4.5 Poster for *Tim Tim por Tim Tim: revista do ano de 1888*, Lisbon, Typographia Franco-Portugueza, [1891], Arquivo Distrital do Porto, PT/ADPRT/COL/CDAC/005/002/01714. Poster for *Tim Tim por Tim Tim: revista do ano de 1888*.

soon became part of people's routines, a practice that advertisers were aware as early as 1878, the first year Portuguese postcards were sold.[132] The standardization of both the card's dimensions and its layout were key to the widespread circulation of the illustrated postcard, "a sign of the rise of the culture of the image."[133] Rapid adoption of the "divided back" postcard in the first decade of the 20th century stands out as an important development. The image now occupied one entire side of the card, emphasizing the iconographical shift mentioned above. Postcard writing, as well as letter writing (apart from commercial correspondence), was considered a feminine activity, a trait that reinforced "the association of the feminine with the trivial, the picturesque, the ephemeral."[134] This is also true in Portugal, where letters played an important role in courtship strategies. The wife recollects her "fake lyricisms of a single woman, the letters she wrote making style and copying sentences of the great lovers that the tale and the novel immortalize" with a slight embarrassment.[135] Conversely, the postcard was associated with collecting, then perceived as a masculine activity. "If . . . collection is generally theorized as a masculine activity, the postcard constitutes an interesting exception to these laws of gendering: it is the very example of the feminine collectable."[136] Postcards were also used to advertise theatrical activity. Not unlike posters, few postcards are preserved and available, since most of them are in the hands of private collectors. Nevertheless, advertisements of postcard sellers were regularly published in the press.[137] An important maker and seller of postcards was Tabacaria Costa, a tobacconist in downtown Lisbon, whose shop windows and staff are photographed in Figure 4.6. In the image it is possible to see the outlet's large offering.

Postcards representing theatrical activities became widely common in the beginning of the 20th century. The Portuguese theatrical postcard falls into two main categories: close-ups of the performers in costume, and entire scenes of a play. *Vénus* is a Portuguese version of *Frau Venus*, a German play by Oscar Blumenthal and Ernst Pasqué that premièred in the Teatro de D. Amélia in 1905. The adaptation was made by Acácio Antunes and Augusto Machado.[138]

---

[132] Rosamond B. Vaule, *As We Were: American Photographic Postcards, 1905–1930* (Boston, MA: David R. Godine, 2004), 47–52; David M. Henkin, *The Postal Age: The Emergence of Modern Communications in Nineteenth-Century America* (Chicago: University of Chicago Press, 2007).

[133] Naomi Schor, "Collecting Paris," in John Elsnera and Roger Cardinal, *The Cultures of Collecting* (Cambridge, MA: Harvard University Press, 1994), 263.

[134] Schor, "Collecting Paris," 262.

[135] Carvalho, *Mulheres e creanças*, 242.

[136] Schor, "Collecting Paris," 262.

[137] *O Occidente*, 20 February 1905, 40.

[138] *O Occidente*, 10 January 1906, 2–3.

Figure 4.6 Alberto Carlos Lima, Tabacaria Costa, Lisbon, early 20th century, Arquivo Fotográfico de Lisboa, Colecção Alberto Carlos Lima, PT/AMLSB/LIM/ 001055. Tabacaria Costa, an important postcard publisher in Lisbon.

The play generated a series of postcards on which Palmira Bastos is portrayed in several stage costumes. The series also includes some collective scenes of the play.[139] Figure 4.7 is a postcard that depicts a group of characters of *Vénus*, the American Women. The star on their hats indicates their nationality, and their costume seems to represent sophistication.

What is interesting about theatrical postcards is that they rely on the same conventions used by periodicals when printing theatrical photographs. For example, the issue of *O Ocidente* that published the review of *Vénus* contained a set of stage photographs that are similar to the printed postcards.[140] They were taken by the same photographer, which indicates that there were not many photographers working in Lisbon at that time. Given the similarity of the theatrical postcards with other goods we can say that different products shared the same strategies of representation. The resemblance of the photographs published in the periodicals, in the advertisements, and on the postcards contributes to spreading not only the medium but also the aesthetic and

---

[139] *Venus* [postcards], [1906]. Shelfmarks PTBN: P.I. 63 P., PTBN: P.I. 64 P., PTBN: P.I. 65 P., PTBN: P.I. 66 P., National Library of Portugal; J. Fernandes, *Vénus: Americanas* [postcard], Lisbon, Pap. Typ de Paulo Guedes e Saraiva, [1906]. Shelfmark PTBN: P.I. 5755 P., National Library of Portugal.

[140] *O Occidente*, 10 January 1906, 5.

Figure 4.7 Coimbra: O gaiteiro—costume dos arrebaldes [postcard], Coimbra, Papelaria Borges,?Early 20th century, ETH-Bibliothek Zürich, Bildarchiv, Fel_ 028588-RE. Group of bagpipers and percussionists from the outskirts of Coimbra.

ideological models embedded in it. This seems to be a frequent practice at the time, since the same was made with the operetta *Tição negro*.[141] Associating the strategies of representing and advertising with collectables was extended to the *revista*. For instance, a set of colored postcards from *O anno em três dias* was made in which several female performers in costume are portrayed individually.[142] This demonstrates that photography intensified the way the female body was commodified as part of an advertising strategy for the popular theater. Moreover, it reveals a still underdeveloped star system. Given the reliance of the unsubsidized companies on famous performers to attract audiences and to increase revenue, photographs of the main performers became an important part of their advertising. Their ubiquity is well documented in periodicals, in postcards, in the librettos, and on the covers of sheet music.

The development of sound recording influenced the postcard tangentially, and a machine to record phono-postcards, "the biggest wonder of the century," was advertised in *Ilustração Portuguesa*.[143] It resembles an early gramophone

[141] *Tição negro* [postcard], Lisbon: Union Postale Universelle, [1902]. Shelfmark PTBN: A.M./C.3//6, National Library of Portugal.

[142] *O anno em três dias* [postcards]. Shelfmarks MNT: 32135, MNT: 32179, MNT: 32271, and MNT: 32388, National Theater Museum (Lisbon).

[143] *Illustração Portugueza*, 19 November 1906, back cover.

that writes directly on the card and shows that sound technologies were used as dictating machines. This was part of the Edison company's strategy, when a scientific approach to office management was implemented in the United States.[144] Because these postcards had to be prepared for handling in a regular postal service and they were not intended to be mass produced or reproduced, the weight and the frailty of shellac currently in use was inadequate. Therefore, lighter materials like celluloid were used either to make records or to coat the postcard so that the sound could be stored.[145] The machine and its cards were sold by José Santos Rocha, a postcard and stamp dealer who was also a tobacconist. Nevertheless, these goods do not seem to have circulated widely, probably because of their cost and of their technological demands.

The postcard had uses other than advertising. The reliance of Portuguese ethnology on texts changed toward the end of the 19th century. It began to include art, architecture, technologies, and forms of economic and social life.[146] This reflects a more complex view of popular culture in the 1890s, in which evolutionist theories played a key role. This shift is clear in the work of Rocha Peixoto (1868–1909), a scholar who developed his work in Porto and strove to establish a scientific basis for Portuguese culture. He used natural history and physical anthropology to determine the ethnicity and the "ethnic psychology" of the Portuguese.[147] His work epitomizes the new trends in the study of popular culture. In a posthumous text that was possibly written in 1908, Peixoto discussed the role played by illustrated postcards as subjects for ethnography.[148] This demonstrates the wide circulation of these items as souvenirs, showing the role that tourism began to play in Portugal. Peixoto discussed how technological innovations and the mass production of postcards might have been articulated with ethnological practices.[149] Moreover, he presented them as an "iconic statement" of the epoch.[150] This happens because postcards were mass produced, a relatively new development. Peixoto pointed to the coexistence of two types of postcards that represent popular customs.

---

[144] David Morton, *Sound Recording: The Life Story of a Technology* (Santa Barbara, CA: Greenwood Press, 2004), 43–54.

[145] Emilien Jean Baptiste Brocherioux, Paul Joseph Tochon, Alfred Fortier, Leon Victor Marotte, "Composition for Sound-records," U.S. Patent 842,070, 22 January 1907.

[146] João Leal, *Etnografias portuguesas (1870–1970): cultura popular e identidade nacional* (Lisbon: Publicações D. Quixote, 2000), 43.

[147] Augusto Santos Silva, "O Porto em busca da Renascença (1880–1911)," *Penélope: revista de história e ciências sociais*, 17 (1997), 54–55; Leal, Etnografias portuguesas, 89–90.

[148] Rocha Peixoto, "A arqueologia e a etnografia nos bilhetes postais," *Etnográfica*, 4/1 (2000), 185–188.

[149] Peixoto, "A arqueologia e a etnografia nos bilhetes postais," 186.

[150] Peixoto, "A arqueologia e a etnografia nos bilhetes postais," 186.

Some reproduce a scene in a faithful way while the others "sacrifice reality" for aesthetic purposes.[151] He valued authenticity, which points to the role that realistic depiction played in both science and the arts. For Barthes,

> the photograph possesses an evidential force, and ... its testimony bears not on the object but on time. From a phenomenological viewpoint, in the Photograph, the power of authentication exceeds the power of representation.[152]

It is easy to understand why photography was perceived as a guarantor of objectivity in the era of positivism, just by supposedly obliterating the subject behind the camera.[153] Thus, "the photograph profess[es] to be a mechanical analogue of reality, its first-order message in some sort completely fills its substance and leaves no place for the development of a second-order message."[154] Peixoto discussed the postcards he considered to have ethnographic and archaeological value both in Portugal and abroad. He praised a collection published in Coimbra by Papelaria Borges. I was able to track two of these postcards that include musical scenes. The first postcard is reproduced as Figure 4.8 and portrays a group of musicians from the rural areas near Coimbra.[155] The group comprises a bagpiper, two percussionists (on snare and bass drum, respectively) and male onlookers.

The second postcard I found shows a *serenata* (serenade), a musical event that was part of the student life of the University of Coimbra. Five male students wearing their traditional academic robes are portrayed playing a Portuguese guitar a Spanish guitar and what appears to be a mandolin.[156] These postcards depict realism, a feature that is prized by Peixoto throughout his text, and not a conventional aestheticization of the popular. Thus, the photographic postcard worked as an advertisement, as a collectable, and as an ethnographic artifact. It embodied new forms of communication, of domesticity, and of commodification.

---

[151] Peixoto, "A arqueologia e a etnografia nos bilhetes postais," 186.

[152] Barthes, *Camera Lucida*, 88–89.

[153] Lorraine Daston and Peter Galison, "The Image of Objectivity," *Representations*, 0/40 (1992), 81–128.

[154] Barthes, "The Photographic Message," in Barthes, *Image-Music-Text* (New York: Hill and Wang, 1978), 18.

[155] *Coimbra, o gaiteiro, costume dos arrabaldes* [postcard], Coimbra, Pap. Borges, [1904]. Record number Fel_028588-AL-RE, ETH-Bibliothek Zürich, Bildarchiv, Feller Collection.

[156] *Coimbra, Uma serenata d'estudantes* [postcard], Coimbra, Pap. Borges, [1904]. Record number Fel_028589-AL-RE, ETH-Bibliothek Zürich, Bildarchiv, Feller Collection.

Programs, Postcards, Coplas 217

Figure 4.8 Rafael Bordalo Pinheiro, Illustration for the *cançoneta* "Meios de Transporte," in Rio de Carvalho and Alfredo de Moraes Pinto, *Meios de transporte: cançoneta original* (Lisbon: Liv. Económica de F. Napoleão de Victoria, 1887), 10. Biblioteca Municipal de Mafra. Illustration for the *cançoneta* "Meios de Transporte."

Sheet Music and the Theater

A widespread market for sheet music began in Portugal in the 19th century and was concentrated in the urban centers. This parallels other countries, reflecting how printed music became part of the domestic routines of the aristocracy and the bourgeoisie. An important part of domestic music making relied on musical literacy. The number of prospective buyers of sheet music had risen toward the end of the 19th century. Then, the lower strata of the bourgeoisie could afford to buy pianos and to finance piano lessons as part of an investment in the education of their children.[157] Therefore, the notion of the piano as a reflection of accumulated cultural capital had a deep impact on publishing. The spread of printing technologies and instruments was part of a business model that flourished until the middle of the 20th century, lasting until recorded music and radio became dominant.[158]

---

[157] José Rodrigues Miguéis, *A escola da paraíso* (Lisbon: Estúdios Cor, 1960).
[158] Leonor Losa and João Silva, "Edição de música. 1. Geral," in Salwa Castelo-Branco (ed.), *Enciclopédia da música em Portugal no século XX*, vol. 2 (Lisbon: Círculo de Leitores, 2010), 391–392.

The Parisian *magasins de musique* had a major influence on the Portuguese music scene. In the middle of the 19th century stores were established that traded in instruments and sheet music.[159] The goods they traded reveal the role domestic music played in this period, since most of them were directed to this market. Apart from selling pianos and sheet music these stores also supplied instruments for the emerging *bandas*. Some were established by people of German or Italian descent, like Eduardo Neuparth (founder of the Armazém de Música e Instrumentos de Eduardo Neuparth) or João Baptista Sassetti (founder of Sassetti e Comp.ª). Their business model relied on a pre-industrial organization that depended on the articulation between the sale of printed music and the instruments for its reproduction. Thus, new industrial processes of printing and of instrument-making reinforced the symbiotic relationship between these goods, enhancing the possibilities of success for the retailers. With new processes that reduced production costs and time, the instruments and the sheet music became more readily available to a wider audience. The press reflected this trend as more space was allocated to advertising these products. Paid advertisements were part of the strategy of some firms, intensified by rising competition.

Nevertheless, print was not the only form in which written music circulated before the advent of phonography. For example, copying music by hand was still important in the transitional period of the middle of the 19th century, when cheap printing processes were not yet universally available in Portugal. Musicians often worked as copyists for several institutions, music stores included. This is evidenced by the large quantity of hand-copied scores that have survived until today. These include manuscripts whose calligraphy resembles the printed product as well as very rudimentary reproductions. The approaches used indicate a varied universe of copyists, processes, and objectives. In this sense, copyists played a role in the spread of repertoires. Furthermore, music copying helps us to understanding how the repertoires were selected, appropriated, and organized by amateur musicians to suit their needs.

Most imported goods came from France and Brazil, reflecting the importance of the popular music theater of these countries in the local Portuguese scene. However, some Portuguese companies published their own sheet music. This is especially visible with the large amount of local music that was published at the time, especially songs from the theater. Companies like the Armazém de Música e Instrumentos de Eduardo Neuparth or Sassetti e Comp.ª, the Armazem de musica, piannos, instrumentos e lythografia de J. I. Canongia & Comp.ª, the Armazém de Muzica de João Cyriaco Lence,

---

[159] Losa and João Silva, "Edição de música. 1. Geral," 391–392.

Salão Mozart, Armazem de Muzicas e Pianos Lambertini & Irmão, and the Armazem de Musicas e pianos de Matta Júnior fit this profile. Some of these names changed through time and reflected what was happening in the companies. For instance, in 1849 Lence and Canongia started a business association that lasted a number of years and underwent several name changes.[160] Nevertheless, the relationship between stores and publishers was not exclusive. Music outlets also traded in music printed by other publishers, a tendency that is demonstrated by the stamps of the dealers. For example, a piece of sheet music by Neuparth could have a stamp of Salão Mozart, indicating that it was sold there. There were also companies that traded in musical instruments and sheet music without becoming themselves publishers. Nonetheless, a significant volume of the printed music business was concentrated among the publishers mentioned above. In other cases, the trade of sheet music, pianos, and organs was made by generic import-export dealers such as the Casa Suéca de Adolpho Engestrom, who also imported sugar, coffee, wines, and liquor.[161]

Although music printing implies a degree of specialization, other companies also published sheet music. Nevertheless, this was done on a much smaller scale. The Livraria Popular de Francisco Franco issued librettos and *coplas* as well as the sheet music of a few theatrical numbers. It was common for the back cover of sheet music to advertise similar goods from its publisher. Less frequently, it advertised related products by other publishers, showing that a symbiosis between different companies and goods was established in the entertainment market. For instance, the sheet music of the "Duetto das vaidosas," a song from the *revista Agulhas e alfinetes*, was published by Neuparth and advertised the *coplas* of the same *revista*, which were published by the Livraria Popular de Francisco Franco.[162] Thus, the *coplas* and sheet music were perceived as complementary and not as competing goods, and the sales of one product could benefit from the commercial success of the other. An important characteristic of the music publishing business in Portugal is the accumulation of roles. In many cases, publishers were active musicians and teachers who had a direct knowledge of Lisbon's entertainment market. Thus, they were integrated professionals. For instance, Augusto Neuparth was an orchestra musician and taught at the Lisbon's Conservatoire.[163] Joaquim Ignacio Canongia Júnior was the son of a professional clarinetist and worked as a music copyist

---

[160] Ernesto Vieira, *Diccionario biographico de musicos portuguezes: Historia e bibliografia da musica em Portugal*, vol. 2 (Lisbon: Lambertini, 1900), 26–27.

[161] Augusto Massano, et al., *O Elvense: Numero brinde aos senhores assignantes em 1894* (Elvas: Typographia d'O Elvense, 1894), 44.

[162] Eduardo Schwalbach and Filipe Duarte, *Duetto das Vaidosas* (Lisbon: Neuparth e C.ª, n.d.).

[163] Vieira, *Diccionario*, vol. 1, 203–204.

and as a prompter in the Real Teatro de S. Carlos before establishing his publishing business.[164] A comparable case occurred in Brazil during the same period. The Porto-born pianist Arthur Napoleão moved to Brazil in 1868 and established his music store in Rio de Janeiro after touring around the world as a virtuoso. The company was initially named Narciso & Arthur Napoleão; it published music and traded on musical instruments. Thus, there is a striking similarity between the music stored in Portugal and in Brazil. Furthermore, this is an indication that the commodification of music was a transnational process.

The sheet music business was heterogeneous and included different types of fashionable music. Local and imported repertoires were frequently renewed, to create a stable number of sales for a long period of time. This focus on publishing transient repertoires encouraged a quick turnover and relied on strategies of planned obsolescence.[165] Therefore, "fashion" and "modern" were terms that were frequently used in advertising. This strategy allowed the stores to widen the scope of their business and to promote a continuously changing set of similar goods. Thus, a steady sales volume was assured. Furthermore, planned obsolescence forced the renewal of the repertoires and created a strong dynamic in the entertainment market. Nevertheless, one can discern differentiated degrees of transience and permanence. If an opera was frequently performed, the publishers would release works associated with it for a large period of time.

The bulk of the sheet music consisted of pieces that were already known to the audiences through other media, especially the theater. This practice was similar in other countries, showing that the commodification of music was transnational and relied on a profitable set of similar works being frequently published. Products like librettos, *coplas*, sheet music, or phonograms had a very close relationship with the theater. Therefore, the changing market for theatrical performances was the primary source for the music printing business in Portugal well into the middle of the 20th century. The link between the stage and music publishing is intensified because several music publishers worked as performers, prompts, or copyists in the theater. The opera, operetta, and *revista* were the major supplier of content for this market. For example, Lence & Viúva Canongia published a piano reduction of a piece from the play *O marido mata a mulher?*.[166] It was published as a polka, showing the porosity

---

[164] Vieira, *Diccionario*, vol. 2, 121–127.

[165] Jacques Attali, *Noise: The Political Economy of Music* (Minneapolis: University of Minnesota Press, 1985), 68.

[166] Carlos Augusto Pereira Bramão, *O marido mata a mulher? Polka da comedia do mesmo titulo para piano* (Lisbon: Lence & Viúva Canongia, 1872).

between theatrical music and social dance, a ubiquitous trend in the entertainment market.

Given that the theater was an important source for publishers, the changes in the repertoire of the Real Teatro de S. Carlos were directly reflected in the printed music business. Therefore, pieces from French operas were published from the 1860s onward. The local success of Gounod's operas, especially *Faust*, was mirrored in the growing amount of sheet music based on them. These fell into two major categories: adaptations for voice and piano of opera arias, and works for solo piano that were based on the melodies of the opera. There were people who specialized in arranging operatic pieces. Joaquim de Almeida (d. 1874) arranged a large number of operatic pieces for piano, published by Lence & Canongia and by Sassetti.[167] These included a set of twelve fantasias for piano inspired by operas.[168] Vieira noted that Almeida's arrangements were well received among pianists who were "not very demanding in artistic nor original features."[169] This illustrates that amateur performers were the target of music publishers and demonstrates the problematic association between these repertoires and the intellectualizing discourse about music. Nevertheless, Vieira's statement has to be put in context. Sheet music was predominantly used for playing pieces in the home of its buyers that were presented through other media. Thus, the originality of the arrangements is not the best measure to evaluate them. Printed music relied on amateur music making, and the publications had to cater to a public with different levels of musical skills. Amateur musicians were looking for music they were already familiar with and were able to recognize. Sheet music could not exclude consumers based on technical proficiency nor on unfamiliarity, and Almeida's "artistic undemanding" and "unoriginal features" were not pitfalls but strengths that catalyzed the success of his arrangements.

A causal relation between theatrical performance and printed music seems to be operating. However, Gounod's *Faust* complicates this perspective. Two arias of the opera were arranged for voice and piano. They were published in Italian, the language in which the opera was performed in the S. Carlos, and their suggested date of publication is 1859, the year in which the opera premièred in Paris. This seems to be a mistake since the opera was not premièred in the Real Teatro de S. Carlos until 1865 and was performed for thirty-six times that season.[170] Thus, the sheet music of "Parlatele d'amor" ("Faites-lui mes

---

[167] Vieira, *Diccionario*, vol. 2, 19–20.
[168] Joaquim d'Almeida, *Fausto de Gounod* (Lisbon: Lence & Viúva Canongia, [1873]).
[169] Vieira, *Diccionario*, vol. 2, 19–20.
[170] Mário Moreau, *O teatro de S. Carlos: dois séculos de história*, vol. 1 (Lisbon: Hugin Editores, 1999), 89.

aveux") and of "O ciel! quanti gioielli!" ("O Dieu! que de bijoux") raises two distinct possibilities.[171] The first possibility is that they were printed later than 1859 and around the time the opera premièred in Lisbon. This is supported by the fact that Sassetti published the pieces with Italian lyrics. Nevertheless, the international success of *Faust* started in 1862, after the première of a revised version of the opera.[172] The second possibility is that these arias were already part of a transnational sheet music repertoire and were published in Lisbon before the opera's première. If this is true, the relationship between the stage and the music publishers was not then one of direct causality but a more nuanced process. Of course, this also shows the huge methodological problem of articulating the products of Lisbon's theatrical market. The lack of accurate dating for some items, especially sheet music and recordings, complicates a chronological study of the leisure markets.

The policy of many publishers relied on printing the successful pieces performed in Lisbon's theatrical market. Thus, the prominent role played by operetta was reflected in a large number of publications.[173] Nonetheless, works inspired by Offenbach's operettas were published before his heyday in Lisbon, the late 1860s. Philippe Musard's (1792–1859) "La couturière," a waltz based on Offenbach's melodies, was published by Canongia and by Sassetti in the 1850s.[174] As expected, the 1868 premières of *A Grã-duquesa de Gérolstein*, *As georgianas*, and *Barba-azul* stimulated interest among publishers and created publishing momentum. This tendency was not limited to Lisbon, and pieces inspired by Offenbach's *La Grande-Duchesse de Gérolstein* were published in Coimbra and Porto during the 1860s and 1870s.[175] Given the complementary relationship between the theater and music publishing, sheet music mirrored the performance of operettas by Portuguese composers. The performance of these plays started in the 1860s. Yet the bulk of the sheet music held in the National Library of Portugal is from later works. This may indicate that the interest in publishing these pieces started later in the century. However, one

---

[171] *Fausto: musica di Carlo Gounod* (Lisbon: Sassetti, [1859]), shelfmarks M.P. 1302//2 V. and M.P. 1302//1 V., respectively.

[172] Steven Huebner, "Gounod, Charles-François," *Grove Music Online*, ed. L. Macy, <www.oxfordmusiconline.com>, accessed 10 July 2010.

[173] Luiz de Freitas Branco, *Comemoração do centenário da "Casa Sassetti"* (Lisbon: Sassetti & C.ª, 1948).

[174] Philippe Musard, *A costureira* (Lisbon: J.I.Canongia [1853] ; Musard, *La couturière: valse sur des motifs d'Offenbach* (Lisbon: Sassetti, [1855–60]).

[175] *Les grands succès de l'opéra: collection choisie de morceaux célèbres des opéras anciens et modernes: couplets des lettres dans La Grande Duchesse de Gerolstein pour piano* (Porto: C A Villa Nova, n.d.) ; F. S. L. Macedo, *Morceau sur l'opéra La Grande Duchêsse de Gérolstein de J. Offenbach* (Coimbra: Litografia de Macedo e Filho, n.d.).

must note that the collections of public institutions tend to rely on donations. Thus, the earlier period of the Portuguese operetta may not be represented in these collections because of the way they were formed. Nevertheless, far more sheet music from the popular theater can be found as we progress toward the end of the century. Many songs from the operetta *O solar dos Barrigas* were published as sheet music.[176] The operetta premièred in 1892 but the sheet music cannot be dated accurately. Even so, its presence points to the success of the operetta, which had regular revivals. The sheet music of a number from *O burro do Sr. Alcaide* was printed in the Litografia da Rua das Flores, and Neuparth published extracts of Augusto Machado's *Tição negro*.[177] These are reductions for voice and piano of some of their songs.

Piano pieces that used the melodies from the popular theater were also published. For example, Augusto Neuparth published a fantasia based on motives from Alfredo Keil's operetta *Suzanna*.[178] These pieces help us understand the relationship between the stage and the culture of domesticity. Sassetti published a piano arrangement of Offenbach's *Orphée aux enfers* made by Johann Strauss II.[179] Similarly, von Suppé's *Boccaccio* was arranged by the same Johann Strauss and published in Porto by Costa Mesquita.[180] The dance component of these pieces is revealing. On the one hand, dance was embedded in the operetta. On the other hand, the arrangement of operetta extracts as quadrilles indicates the superimposition of two entertainment forms that were part of "the nineteenth-century popular music revolution."[181] Johann Strauss II was a leading composer of dance music who wanted to establish his career in the

---

[176] Ciríaco Cardoso, Gervásio Lobato and D. João da Câmara, *O solar dos Barrigas: opera comica: Duetto e trovas populares* (n.p.: n.p., [c.1892–1894]). The National Theater Museum holds the pieces "Valsa" (n.p.: n.p., n.d., shelfmark MNT: 36969), "Carta" (n.p.: n.p., n.d., MNT: 36970), "Coplas dos foguetes" (n.p.: n.p., n.d., shelfmark MNT: 36971), "Dueto dos P.P." (n.p.: n.p., n.d., MNT: 36972), and "Coro das velhas" (n.p.: n.p., n.d., MNT: 36973).

[177] Cyriaco de Cardoso, Gervásio Lobato, and D. João da Câmara, *O burro do Sr. Alcaide: ópera cómica: canções populares* (Lisbon: Lith. R. das Flores, n.d.); Augusto Machado and Henrique Lopes de Mendonça, *Tição negro: farça lyrica em três actos sobre motivos de Gil Vicente* (Lisbon: Neuparth & Carneiro, [1902–1910]), Nº 15 [Alvorada, Ensalada]. Shelfmark PTBN: A.M. 383 A., National Library of Portugal; Machado and Mendonça, *Tição negro: farça lyrica em três actos sobre motivos de Gil Vicente* (Lisbon: Neuparth & Carneiro, [1902–1910]) [Coplas, Dueto]. Shelfmark PTBN: A.M. 287 A., National Library of Portugal.

[178] Guilherme Ribeiro, *Suzanna: opera comica num acto: fantasia brilhante* (Lisbon: Augusto Neuparth, [1883]).

[179] Johann Strauss, *Orphée aux enfers: quadrille-cancan sur l'opera de J. Offenbach: pour piano* (Lisbon: Sassetti, n.d.).

[180] Johann Strauss, *Boccacio: quadrilha para piano: Opera comique de F. Suppé* (Porto: Costa Mesquita, [1882]).

[181] Scott, *Sounds of the Metropolis*, 38–57.

Viennese operetta. Thus, for him to arrange pieces by successful operetta composers was not unusual. In this context, sheet music for amateurs merged the stage on which operettas were performed with the dance hall. Also, this fusion occurred in the piano room of the home, demonstrating the role domesticity played in this complex relationship between repertoires and contexts.

As in the case of the operetta, printing music of the *revistas* gained prominence in the last decades of the 19th century. Most publications of *revista* consisted of songs. This contrasted with the operetta, in which songs were paralleled in the printed music business by instrumental works, such as the fantasia or the potpourri. Nevertheless, the publisher from Porto Costa Mesquita printed a quadrille by Francisco Alves Rente, which was based on motives of the *revista Etcoetera e tal*.[182] The *revista* premièred in 1882 in the Recreios Whittoyne, a large circus that was torn down when the Avenida da Liberdade was built. The *revista* occupied a dominant position in the theatrical circuit by the turn of the century, as evidenced in the spread of a large quantity of musical pieces from these entertainments. Thus, in the same way the *revista* dominated Lisbon's stages, its songs reigned over the family piano. "Music from the most applauded *coplas* of the *revista*" *O micróbio* was published,[183] establishing a connection between the stage success of some sketches and their publishing. Although it was not possible to date it accurately, a large quantity of sheet music from the *revistas* performed between 1867 and 1910 was published, such as *O tutti-li-mundi, Pontos nos ii, Sal e pimenta, Retalhos de Lisboa,* and *O anno em três dias*.[184] In addition to songs from the operetta or the *revista*, detached songs were performed on Lisbon's stages. These were the *cançonetas*. The genre was imported from France, like the operetta and the *revista*, and consisted of "small scenes for one character that are divided in *coplas*, and are intersected

---

[182] Francisco Alves Rente, *Quadrilha sobre os principais motivos da revista do anno Etc e tal* (Porto: Costa Mesquita, n.d.).

[183] Francisco Jacobetty and Rio de Carvalho, *O microbio: revista de 1884 de F. Jacobety: músicas das coplas mais applaudidas: tal qual a família ... pegue-lhe ... pegue-lhe* (Lisbon: Lith. R. das Flores, n.d.); Francisco Jacobetty and Rio de Carvalho, *O microbio: revista de 1884 de F. Jacobety: músicas das coplas mais applaudidas: tenho um cavaquinho ... tra la la ... : redução para pianoforte* (Lisbon: Lith. R. das Flores, n.d.).

[184] Francisco Alvarenga, *O fado do Zé Povinho: cantado pelo actor Marcelino Franco no Tutti himundi, revista do anno de 1880* (Lisbon: Lence &Viuva Canongia—Lith. R. das Flores, 1881); Rio de Carvalho, Júlio Rocha, and Baptista Machado, *O Tournure é cousa boa: para piano* (Lisbon: Lith. R. das Flores, n.d); Rio de Carvalho, Júlio Rocha, and Baptista Machado, *Fado alfacinha: para piano* (Lisbon: Lith. R. das Flores, n.d.); Freitas Gazul, *Sal e pimenta: revista de Sousa Bastos* (Lisbon: Lith. R. das Flores, 1894); *Retalhos de Lisboa: revista do anno de 1895: O amanhã fado cantado pelo actor Queiroz* (Lisbon: Lith. R. das Flores, n.d.); Filipe Duarte, Acácio Antunes, and Machado Correia, *O anno em 3 dias: coplas da lavadeira* (Lisbon: Neuparth & Carneiro, 1904).

with spoken sections."[185] This type of song was performed during the intermission of the main play. Bastos points out that some *cançonetas* had been very successful in Lisbon. Presented side by side with the play, *cançonetas* were used to attract the audience, as their performances were advertised.[186] For Dias, the *cançoneta* played a political role in France before 1789 and was later integrated in the café-concert by losing its political stance and by becoming voluptuous.[187] Acording to the journalist Carlos Malheiro Dias, the Portuguese *cançoneta* was a hybrid development that didn't catch on in the local environment, and the *revista* was unable to popularize the genre.[188] Nevertheless, given the amount of surviving *cançonetas* there is substantial evidence to contradict this statement. A large set of recordings were made under the name *cançoneta*, which points to its relevance for the recording industry. The 1908 catalogue of the Companhia Franceza do Gramophone includes a large number of *cançonetas* by Baptista Diniz (1859–1913), the successful author of *revistas* such as *O século XIV, À procura do badalo, Zás traz,* and *Da Parreirinha ao Limoeiro*.[189] The lyrics of *cançonetas* were also published, a practice that parallels the printing of the libretto and of the *coplas*. The division of the *revista* into independent sketches facilitated the inclusion of the theatrical *cançoneta* in its narrative. To add another interpretative layer to this discussion, the word *cançoneta* had several meanings. Although the *cançoneta* was often framed as a theatrical song, the term literally means "little song" and was also used to name pieces that were not presented in theaters. These *cançonetas* were possibly intended for domestic music making and paralleled the Victorian drawing-room ballad.

The Materiality of Sheet Music

The expression "sheet music" can be traced back to the United States in the 1830s; its wider use began in the 1850s.[190] Because of the large number of broadsides and ballads that were printed, "sheet music" was used to differentiate publications that included music notation from materials that contained

---

[185] Bastos, *Diccionario*, 32–33.

[186] Rui Leitão, A ambiência musical e sonora da cidade de Lisboa no ano de 1890, master's thesis (Universidade Nova de Lisboa, 2006), 41–42.

[187] Carlos Malheiro Dias, *Cartas de Lisboa: terceira série (1905–1906)* (Lisbon: Livraria Clássica Editora, 1907), 223–225.

[188] Malheiro Dias, *Cartas de Lisboa*, 223–225.

[189] Companhia Franceza do Gramophone, *Novo catalogo de discos portuguezes* (Lisbon: n.p., 1908), 2–5.

[190] Calvin Elliker, "Toward a Definition of Sheet Music," *Notes, Second Series*, 55/4 (1999), 839–840.

exclusively printed words.[191] The classification of printed music reflected the gap between art and entertainment that was being carved in the 19th century: Songs, arias, choruses, and instrumental pieces exhibiting the tendencies of musical legitimacy, sophistication, formalism, development, and substance—whether European or American—comprise "musical works." Conversely, songs that are unimportant, unsophisticated, formless, hackneyed, and short-American vernacular songs published as separate entities for quick sale-comprise "sheet music."[192]

Thus, the classification of printed music required an aesthetic judgment. However, this distinction would not endure toward the end of the 19th century. Then, music associated with both opposite poles of the repertoire ("European art songs" and "American vernacular songs") were widely represented in the sheet music catalogues.[193] This complicates a definition of sheet music based on the repertoire. "Sheet music consists of musical notation printed on sheets of paper that remain intentionally unattached and unbound at the time of sale."[194] Therefore, what defined sheet music was its material form.

The most frequent term used in Portugal to designate printed music is *músicas* (musics). It was a generic name used to categorize a varied set of publications that contained musical notation. This was made regardless of genre and editorial format. Sometimes, the expression *folhas de música*—the direct translation of "sheet music"—is employed. Most surviving Portuguese music publications of the time are sheet music. They were intentionally unbound and included one or two small pieces. Shorter works were usually produced as a single folio, but if the extent of the work demanded it, a half-sheet or even a second folio could be inserted.[195] Usually, neither the half-sheet nor the second folio were fastened.[196] A few were grouped and bound by their buyers, which indicates a tendency to compile and organize the music according to the owners' criteria. This illustrates how a personal or familiar informal archive of sheet music was created.

Sheet music covers are important to understand the strategies of advertising employed by the publishers as well as the dominant forms of representation. Some illustrate the relationship between sheet music and other cultural goods. Newspapers and magazines, postcards, posters, and sheet music covers were a clear sign of the spread of the printed image. This highlighted

---

[191] Elliker, "Toward a Definition of Sheet Music," 838.
[192] Elliker, "Toward a Definition of Sheet Music," 847.
[193] Elliker, "Toward a Definition of Sheet Music," 848–849.
[194] Elliker, "Toward a Definition of Sheet Music," 857.
[195] Elliker, "Toward a Definition of Sheet Music," 849.
[196] Elliker, "Toward a Definition of Sheet Music," 849.

the commodity-in-display, a major tendency of modern consumer culture. Unamuno noticed this trend while vacationing in Portugal in July 1908. He saw stationers that sold postcards with pictures of D. Carlos I and of Prince D. Luís Filipe, of their shooters Manuel Buíça and Alfredo Costa, and of the new King D. Manuel II.[197] He had even found a brand of liqueur whose labels featured prominent republicans.[198] The printed image spread to sheet music covers. In many cases, the cover contained important information about the repertoire, its publishers, and its sellers. It might also include an illustration that evoked the context of the song or portrayed the artists who performed it. When the pieces were taken from theatrical shows the covers usually represented scenes of the play. The cover of the pieces from the *Tição negro* depicts a scene that includes two characters from the play.[199] The sheet music of "Fado Roldão" and "O fado do Zé Povinho" reinforces this. The first shows a singer/guitarist on top of a murder in a popular setting and was published by the Livraria Popular de Francisco Franco.[200] The murder was part of the plot of the play that included "Fado Roldão," *José João* by Eduardo Fernandes, premièred in the Teatro do Príncipe Real in 1896. It was inspired by *Juan José*, a realist play of social critique by the Spanish playwright Joaquin Dicenta, performed in Madrid's Teatro De La Comedia the year before. This reinforces the link between the Portuguese and the Spanish theatrical markets. Although the song was claimed to be original, Alberto Pimentel noted a strong resemblance between "Fado Roldão" and "Hija del Guadalquivir," a song collected in the *Cancioneiro* published by Neves and Campos.[201] The collectors had stated that it was impossible to trace the melody but it was widely disseminated in Portugal in its many variants.[202] Pimentel explained this resemblance as a "natural coincidence," due to the flow of music that relied on oral transmission in the early era of sound recording. The cover of "O fado do Zé Povinho" portrays the popular character Zé Povinho and was published by Lence & Viuva Canongia.[203] In cases where several pieces were extracted from the same play, the same front cover illustration was often

---

[197] Miguel de Unamuno, *Por tierras de Portugal y de España* (Madrid: V. Prieto, 1911), 48.

[198] Unamuno, *Por tierras de Portugal y de España*, 48.

[199] Augusto Machado and Henrique Lopes de Mendonça, *Tição negro: farça lyrica em 3 actos sobre motivos de Gil Vicente* (Lisbon: Neuparth & Carneiro, n.d.), shelfmark PTBN: A.M. 348 A. of the National Library of Portugal.

[200] *Fado Roldão: cantado na peça José João no Theatro do Príncipe Real* (Lisbon: Livraria Popular de Francisco Franco, n.d.).

[201] Alberto Pimentel, *A triste canção do sul: subsídios para a história do Fado* (Lisbon: Livraria Central, 1904), 282–3.

[202] César das Neves and Gualdino de Campos, *Cancioneiro de músicas populares*, vol. 1 (Porto: Typographia Occidental, 1893), 153–154.

[203] Francisco Alvarenga, *O fado do Zé Povinho: cantado pelo actor Marcelino Franco no Tutti himundi, revista do anno de 1880* (Lisbon: Lence & Viuva Canongia—Lith. R. das Flores, 1881).

used. In some cases minor changes were made. A common practice was to include a list of the numbers printed by the publisher on the cover and underline the title of the respective piece. With this system, the same printing plate could be used for several products. This is shown in the sheet music of some numbers from the operetta *O solar dos Barrigas*. In some theatrical pieces the front covers included an illustration of the person who performed it, sometimes with a sentence identifying and praising the performer. Also, the cover frequently mentioned the title of the play and the theater where it had been performed. The casts were key to attracting Lisbon's audience to a play, especially the most famous performers. Thus, printing their portraits was part of the publisher's advertising strategy. This shows an incipient star system that relied on iconography. The power of the performers to attract buyers is reinforced by publishing similar images in the press, on postcards, and on the cover of sheet music. In other cases the front covers did not reflect this association. Cervantes de Haro's cover for the "Fado Liró" (from the *revista A.B.C.*) portrays people wearing Portuguese regional costumes.[204] This number is included in a collection of Portuguese pieces for voice and piano and shared the set's cover illustration. Therefore, the regional costumes stood as the iconic representation of Portugal, as the graphic reinforcement of the idea of nationality. The back covers of sheet music were also used for advertising purposes. They usually comprised a list of similar works by the same publisher. This raised the awareness of prospective buyers and promoted the sale of other pieces.

The study of sheet music conventions helps us to understand the rapid spread of repertoires. These models tend to be transnational, forming common ground for a large number of musical styles across the Western world. To show the similarities and the differences between sheet music that was published in Portugal, I will compare two songs, "Meios de transporte" and "A Portuguesa." The theatrical *cançoneta* "Meios de transporte" was performed in the theaters of Lisbon and Porto by Lucinda do Carmo and Emília Eduarda, respectively.[205] The prominent composer Rio de Carvalho set to music a text by the journalist Alfredo de Morais Pinto (1851–1921). Its cover is not illustrated and the song does not comply with the most frequent format of sheet music. Theatrical *cançonetas* consisted of small scenes to be performed during the main play's intermissions. Therefore, their form relies on a long text that tells a story to the audience. "Meios de transporte" (translated as "Modes of Transport") depicts several episodes in which a woman interacts with various men when taking several means of transport (a train, a

---

[204] *Fado liró* (Lisbon: Neuparth & Carneiro, n.d.), shelfmark PTBN: C.N. 1669 A. of the National Library of Portugal.

[205] Rio de Carvalho and Alfredo de Moraes Pinto, *Meios de transporte: cançoneta original* (Lisbon: Liv. Económica de F. Napoleão de Victoria, 1887).

carriage, a horse, and a boat). The piece relies on comical double entendres that were probably performed with cheeky slyness. In the train episode, the woman shares the compartment with a priest and, after a brief period in a dark tunnel, she noticed his shoulder "smeared with cosmetic powder."[206] In another episode, so that she can avoid the bumps of the stagecoach, a passenger strongly grabs her waist and holds her in his lap.[207] The lyrics include an introduction to the story of four four-line stanzas. This is followed by four episodes individually devoted to each mode of transport. Because of the lyrics, the sheet music only includes the introductory episode. The lyrics for the other sections are published after the score in groups of four stanzas per page. This was very common when publishing strophic songs.[208] These four stanzas were divided into two groups of two, which are divided by an illustration by Rafael Bordalo Pinheiro or by Manuel Gustavo Bordalo Pinheiro. The drawings illustrate the lyrics, as shown in Figure 4.8. Here, the woman is pushed inside the stagecoach where she could not find a seat. The tendency to include the work of prominent visual artists on the covers of Portuguese sheet music continued well into the 20th century, a characteristic that was paralleled in other countries.

The musical structure of the piece is an AB strophic form preceded by an eight-bar piano introduction. Both A and B consist of two four-verse stanzas, and the piano is essential to emphasize the contrast between the sections. In section A (in 6/8 time), the piano supports the singer by alternating low notes in the left hand with chords in the right hand.[209] Section B is in 2/4 time, and the right hand of the piano doubles the melody and, in some parts, adds ornamental passages while the left holds the rhythm and harmony of the piece in place by alternating single low notes with chords.[210] The score consists of a three-staff system, in which the superior staff corresponds to the voice part and the lower two to the piano part. This is frequent in pieces in which the melody and the right hand piano part are different. In cases like "Meios the transporte" a three-staff system proves to be more practical. When the right hand of the piano duplicates the voice, the songs were published as a two-staff system. The two-staff format allows for the music to be performed both as a song and as a solo piano piece, a strategy that enlarged the number of prospective customers. This clearly demonstrates that these pieces were aimed at domestic performance.

The march "A Portuguesa" consists of a setting by Alfredo Keil of a poem by Henrique Lopes de Mendonça. The piece was performed on Lisbon's stages in

---

[206] Carvalho and Pinto, *Meios de transporte*, 8–9.
[207] Carvalho and Pinto, *Meios de transporte*, 11.
[208] Carvalho and Pinto, *Meios de transporte*, 8–15.
[209] Carvalho and Pinto, *Meios de transporte*, 5.
[210] Carvalho and Pinto, *Meios de transporte*, 6–7.

1890 and was rapidly associated with the reaction to the British Ultimatum. Moreover, it was arranged for various groups and ensembles and performed in the city's theaters as part of patriotic events and of *revistas*. When it was performed in the patriotic play *As cores da bandeira*, staged in the Teatro da Rua dos Condes on 19 March 1890, and in the Great Patriotic Concert, held in the Teatro de S. Carlos on 29 March 1890, the audience already knew it well.[211] *A portuguesa* had a patriotic tone, and its lyrics incited the people to march against the cannons. The march was soon appropriated by the republicans and used by the marching bands of the rebellious military units that took part in the Porto revolt of 31 January 1891. As a consequence, public performances of "A Portuguesa" by regimental bands were not allowed until the last years of the 19th century.[212] The association with the republican movement was so strong that "A Portuguesa" was adopted as the anthem of the Portuguese Republic in 1911, a place it still holds. Shortly after the Republic the march was issued in a variety of formats that included sheet music, sound recordings, and player piano rolls. The magazine *Serões* published a piano version of "A Portuguesa" in November 1910 with separate lyrics and photographs of its authors.[213] Thus, "A Portuguesa" was ubiquitous, and people could perform it in their homes, as the title of *Serões* (soirées) suggests.

The sheet music of "A Portuguesa" shares similarities with "Meios de transporte" but it also contains significant differences.[214] The cover contains the title of the march set over a white and blue background, the colors of the Portuguese monarchy. It also includes the stamps of Neuparth & C.ª and a stamp stating that it was free.[215] This is probably one of the scores of "A Portuguesa" that was distributed gratuitously soon after the British Ultimatum of 1890. Moreover, the score appears to be a cheap non-illustrated edition, perfect for free distribution. It consists of a three-staff system in which the voice part is written in the upper staff and the lower two staves are for the piano. As in the *cançoneta*, the march begins with a four-bar piano introduction. However, the refrain of "A Portuguesa" is written as a three-part choir in the upper staff. In this publication, reproduced in Figures 4.9 and 4.10, the verse of the march is set for solo

---

[211] Luiz Francisco Rebello, *O teatro naturalista e neo-romântico (1870–1910)* (Lisbon: Instituto de Cultura Portuguesa, 1978), 47; *Pontos nos ii*, 27 March 1890, 97.

[212] Manuscript note on the first page of Alfredo Keil and Henrique Lopes de Mendonça, A Portugueza-Marcha. Shelfmark PTBN: M.M 345//3, National Library of Portugal.

[213] *Serões*, November 1910, 397–400.

[214] Alfredo Keil and Henrique Lopes de Mendonça, *A Portugueza: marcha* (Lisbon: Neuparth & C.ª, n.d.), shelfmark PTBN: C.I.C. 78 A. held in the National Library of Portugal.

[215] Mónica Martins, Lina Santos, and Catarina Latino, "Hino Nacional," in Salwa Castelo-Branco (ed.), *Enciclopédia da música em Portugal no século XX*, vol. 2 (Lisbon: Círculo de Leitores, 2010), 617–618.

Figure 4.9 Alfredo Keil and Henrique Lopes de Mendonça, First page of the sheet music of "A Portugueza: Marcha," Biblioteca Nacional de Portugal, CIC-78-A.
First page of the sheet music of "A Portugueza: Marcha."

II

Desfralda a invicta bandeira
Á luz viva do teu céo!
Brade a Europa á terra inteira:
Portugal não pereceu!
Beija o sólo teu jucundo
O Oceano, a rugir d'amor;
E o teu braço vencedor
Deu mundos novos ao mundo!

Ás armas! sobre a terra, sobre o mar,
Pela patria luctar!
Contra os canhões marchar!

III

Saudae o sol que desponta
Sobre um ridente porvir;
Seja o echo de uma affronta
O signal do resurgir.
Raios d'essa aurora forte
São como beijos de mãe,
Que nos guardam, nos sustêm,
Contra as injurias da sorte.

Ás armas! sobre a terra, sobre o mar,
Pela patria luctar!
Contra os canhões marchar!

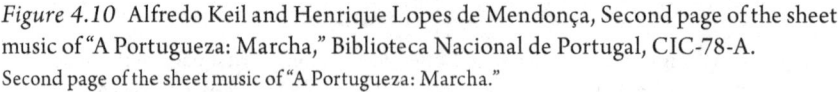

Figure 4.10 Alfredo Keil and Henrique Lopes de Mendonça, Second page of the sheet music of "A Portugueza: Marcha," Biblioteca Nacional de Portugal, CIC-78-A.
Second page of the sheet music of "A Portugueza: Marcha."

voice and contrasts with the choral refrain. Throughout the piece, the right hand of the pianist performs chords while doubling the voice and the left hand plays octaves and chords. Furthermore, the chordal texture and the repetitive accompaniment emphasize the character of the march. In "A Portuguesa," the score includes the first verse and the refrain, and the text of the two remaining verse-chorus structures is printed immediately after the music in a two-column format.

The two music examples are very different. "Meios de transporte" was destined to entertain the people who went to the theater and "A Portuguesa" aimed to boost patriotism. Nevertheless, they were both performed on Lisbon's stages, and their presentations as sheet music shared various features. To be available to domestic amateur performers—and thus make a profit—the repertoires had to be adapted to suit a transnational set of conventions that transformed music into a commodity that could be bought and performed in people's houses across the Western world.

5

The Mechanization of Everyday Life

Mechanical Instruments, Phonography, and Modernity

The integration of music recording into everyday life started in the last decades of the 19th century. The growing commodification of music occurred in a period when the "world economy was international rather than cosmopolitan."[1] This globalization introduced new products into Lisbon's market for cultural goods, spreading through established entertainment circuits and business models that were already in place. The stage provided artists for most recording companies, and Portugal was no exception. Technological novelties, like the player piano, the phonograph (which produced sound recorded on a cylinder), and the gramophone (which produced sound recorded on a flat, spinning disk) became part of the household furniture. Mechanical music transformed social routines and mirrored how domestic space was transformed in the early 20th century. The trade of these goods followed different business models. The Victorian era is associated with the transformation of what the Romantics considered a sublime experience "into a quantifiable and marketable object or thing, a sonic commodity, in the form of a printed work, a performance, or, ultimately, an audio recording."[2] Therefore, the commodification of music is associated with industrial and scientific developments that became part of the daily environment of people, creating a wider social and cultural panorama in which new forms of domestic entertainment and mass-produced goods were prized.

Mechanical instruments and phonography were the main categories associated with these novelties. Because of their particular aspects, each strand requires a particular form of analysis. The sound of mechanical instruments is "produced from a pre-programmed mechanical source [that is] operated either

---

[1] Eric J. Hobsbawm, *Nations and Nationalism since 1780: Programme, Myth, Reality* (Cambridge: Canto, 1992), 25.

[2] John Picker, *Victorian Soundscapes* (Oxford: Oxford University Press, 2003), 10.

without human participation ... or with musically unskilled human aid."[3] The heyday of these devices fell between 1890 and the early 1930s, when the player piano was predominant in the household.[4] The automated piano played a key role in the commodification of music given its positioning in the social practices of the time.[5] Tracking the acceptance of the player piano provides valuable information on the "broad transformation of the ways that music was made and experienced, helping to constitute it as a commodity in the sense we know it in today's market."[6] The story of the player piano can be traced back to the late 18th century. However, its mechanism was developed between the 1880s and the 1910s.[7] In Portugal the sources concerning this instrument are scarce. Nevertheless we can infer that such devices were traded in Lisbon by companies that were already known for selling musical instruments and printed music, like Neuparth & Carneiro. Because the player piano mechanism could easily be fitted to the piano already in the home, stores that sold pianos were the natural retailers for this good. The player piano was perceived as an added component of the traditional piano, and they were eager to expand their markets.[8] The advent of the player piano occurred when phonographic products were entering the local market, which would seem to set the player piano and the gramophone as competing technologies. However, things were far more complicated than that.

The spread of phonography follows a different model from the path of the player piano. It merged the transnational and the local levels differently and in a variety of degrees. The business models adopted by different phonographic companies were far from uniform, as the same goods were produced and sold differently according to the strategy of each company. At the dawn of the 20thh century the multinational recording companies established stores in Portugal that traded exclusively in their products.[9] These included

---

[3] Arthur W. J. G. Ord-Hume, "Mechanical Instruments," in John Shepherd et al., *Continuum Encyclopedia of Popular Music of the World*, vol. 2 (Performance and Production) (London: Continuum, 2003), 323.

[4] Ord-Hume, "Mechanical Instrument," *Grove Music Online*, ed. L. Macy, http://www.oxfordmusiconline.com, accessed 21 July 2010.

[5] Timothy D. Taylor, "The Commodification of Music at the Dawn of the Era of 'Mechanical Music,'" *Ethnomusicology*, 51/2 (2007), 281–305: Alfred Dolge, *Pianos and Their Makers* (Covina, CA: Covina Publishing, 1911), 131–162.

[6] Taylor, "The Commodification of Music," 283.

[7] Ord-Hume, "Player Piano," *Grove Music Online*, ed. L. Macy, http://www.oxfordmusiconline.com, accessed 21 July 2010.

[8] Taylor, "The Commodification of Music," 285.

[9] Leonor Losa, "Indústria fonográfica," in Salwa Castelo-Branco (ed.), *Enciclopédia da música em Portugal no século XX*, vol. 2 (Lisbon: Círculo de Leitores, 2010), 633–634; Geoffrey Jones,

the Companhia Franceza do Gramophone, associated with the Britain-based Gramophone Company and the France-based Pathé Frères. To establish themselves required a significant marketing effort, and the Companhia Franceza do Gramophone especially published flashy advertisements in local periodicals.[10] Smaller recording companies, such as Beka, Dacapo, Parlophone, Homokord, and Odeon, ventures that began to integrate with the German group Lindström from 1908, adopted a different business model.[11] They used established merchants as local agents, selling their products through the merchants' stores.[12] Also, they often traded in other goods that were perceived as technological novelties, such as bicycles, sewing machines, and optical equipment (such as binoculars).[13] This allowed them to capitalize on the association between phonography, a technological novelty that was a clear embodiment of modernity, and other innovations. This model lasted until the 1920s, when recorded sound began to be more exclusively the domain of the establishments that traded in instruments and in printed music.[14]

Mechanical Instruments, Data Storage, and Repertoires

Mechanical instruments played an important role in the dissemination of music in modern everyday life. When comparing the player piano with the phonograph, Taylor argued that the former, a "seemingly less sophisticated technology[,] provides a better site to address the question of the commodification of music."[15] This view is shared by Suisman, to whom "even more than the piano and the phonograph, it is the player piano that best symbolizes the close relation between music machines and industrial manufacturing—and not just by homology."[16] Taylor's main argument relates to the penetration of

---

"The Gramophone Company: An Anglo-American Multinational, 1898–1931," *Business History Review*, 59/1 (1985), 83.

[10] Losa, "Indústria fonográfica."

[11] Losa, "Indústria fonográfica," 633.

[12] Leonor Losa and Susana Belchior, "The Introduction of Phonogram Market in Portugal: Lindström Labels and Local Traders (1879–1925)," in Pekka Gronow and Christiane Hofer (eds.), *The Lindström Project: Contributions to the History of the Record Industry: Beiträge zur Geschichte der Schallplattenindustrie*, vol. 2 (Vienna: Gesellschaft für Historische Tonträger, 2010), 7.

[13] Losa and Belchior, "The Introduction of Phonogram Market in Portugal," 7.

[14] Losa, "Indústria fonográfica," 633.

[15] Taylor, "The Commodification of Music," 284.

[16] David Suisman, "Sound, Knowledge, and the 'Immanence of Human Failure,'" *Social Text*, 102, 28/1 (2010), 19.

the player piano in American households. It was rapidly integrated in everyday life, contrasting with the ways the phonograph was used as a form of domestic entertainment:

> For one thing, since the original player piano was a machine that attached to a piano, it had an easier time of becoming part everyday life since as many as half of all American homes already contained pianos by the mid-1920s. The phonograph, on the other hand, was slow to catch on; there was some debate about its usage, even whether or not it should be used for music; and its poor fidelity prevented it from becoming popular until well into the twentieth century.[17]

The player piano mechanism could be attached to an existing piano. The piano was already part of many households and was used just to make music. This contrasted with the phonograph that was used both as an office tool and as a supplier of recorded music. Situating the mechanical piano as the intermediate stage between the piano and the phonograph is problematic. Nevertheless, it connects an age when live music was the norm with a period when recorded sound took the lead. Elements like the ability to play the piano—and the time and effort required in learning to do so—were transformed with mechanization. Player pianos did not annul the possibilities of "regular" playing of the same instrument. Rather, they integrated the Victorian pride in self-achievement with the availability of recorded entertainment, a new manifestation of modernity. With this new device, humans went from music performers to machine operators, and the expertise involved in reproducing music was relocated to a mechanism.[18]

Early player pianos "consisted of what looked like a small cabinet which was wheeled up to the pianoforte, and from the back of which felt-covered hammers projected, which were adjusted to the keyboard."[19] Thus, they were external to the traditional piano. The mechanism was explained in an article in *O Ocidente*, a piece which reported the demonstration of a player piano in Lisbon, an event that was promoted by the firm Neuparth & Carneiro.[20] The instrument demonstrated was a 73-note Phonola. The Phonola was built by the German manufacturer Ludwig Hupfeld AG, and was launched in 1902. Like many of its competitors it used a pneumatic device to reproduce music

---

[17] Taylor, "The Commodification of Music," 284–285.

[18] Suisman, "Sound, Knowledge, and the 'Immanence of Human Failure,'" 22.

[19] G. C. Ashton Jonson, "Mechanical Piano-players," *Journal of the Royal Musical Association*, 42/1 (1915), 17.

[20] M. O., "O Phonola," *O Occidente*, 28 February 1905, 46.

Figure 5.1 O phonola applicado ao pianno e funcionnando, in "O Phonola," *O Occidente*, 28 February 1905, 46, Hemeroteca Municipal de Lisboa. The Phonola working while connected to a piano.

recorded earlier on music rolls.[21] The writer of the article described it as being similar to a harmonium, which has a pneumatic system in which a bellows is activated by foot pedals, explaining the process through which the hammers of the Phonola struck the keys of the piano.[22] Figure 5.1 reproduces the illustration from the article, showing that the Phonola could be easily fitted to any piano.

---

[21] Alfred Dolge, *Pianos and Their Makers*, 155; Rayner E. Lotz, "Hupfeld," *Grove Music Online*, ed. L. Macy, http://www.oxfordmusiconline.com, accessed 10 August 2010.

[22] M. O., "O Phonola," 46.

The figure shows a woman using the Phonola, reinforcing the link between the piano and feminine domesticity. However, the de-skilling of music through its mechanization disrupted the earlier forms of accumulating cultural capital, achieved by learning to read music and play the piano. Merchants would praise the immediacy of making music with the player piano, which saved their buyers the time and frustration required to master the instrument without the automatic player function. However, being able to play the piano retained its importance as a desired mark of self-achievement until the second half of the 20th century. The article in *O Ocidente* is clearly part of an advertising strategy by Neuparth & Carneiro to publicize the player piano. Instead of publishing an advertisement, they were able to include a review of the Phonola in the main pages of the magazine. The article included several promotional statements, and noted that the journalist had been invited by Neuparth & Carneiro to attend the demonstration. It was not coincidental that Neuparth & Carneiro was the exclusive agent of the Phonola in Portugal. The journalist pointed out that the Phonola did not require the "long and fastidious practice" of learning to play the piano,[23] an argument frequently used by manufacturers and dealers to promote automatic pianos.[24] Consequently, the advertisements of player pianos presented the de-skilling of music as a major strength. Nevertheless, the article makes clear that the Phonola was not completely self-sufficient and fully automated. It required human intervention for controlling its expressive devices.[25] Therefore, some degree of technical proficiency was required to reproduce musical pieces, and people were quick to discover that not all performances on the instrument were equal:

> The Pianola has a technique of its own. It is perfectly true that an absolute beginner having been shown how to use the levers can play an elaborate and difficult piece of music with a certain amount of effect, but to get a really artistic and musicianly rendering of a piece, you require to be a trained musician and to have thoroughly mastered the technique of the instrument.[26]

The commercial strategy of player piano manufacturers emphasized the ease with which the instrument could easily reproduce pre-prepared music, which marked an important distinction from the Victorian middle-class ideal of

---

[23] M. O., "O Phonola," 46.
[24] Taylor, "The Commodification of Music," 286.
[25] M. O., "O Phonola," 46.
[26] Jonson, "Mechanical Piano-players," 19.

individual achievement and creativity.[27] Reproducing flawlessly a vast number of difficult pieces was a major strength of the player piano but the quality of the performance depended on the degree of virtuosity the user employed to control its mechanisms.[28] Nevertheless, the impact of these controls on the performance was limited, since the player could only control tempo, loudness, and sustain. Therefore, they seem to be a way of not effacing totally the human aspect of the performance, creating a more interactive experience that contrasted with the passivity of listening to a gramophone record.

The first devices used in domestic settings and in concert halls were external and had to be wheeled up to a piano. The next step in the development of the player piano was "the placing of the mechanism inside upright pianofortes, which had the great advantage that the pianoforte could then be used as an ordinary pianoforte and played by hand."[29] Manufacturers devised strategies for the mechanism to be integrated in the instrument itself, keeping the appearance of the piano as a furniture item. By preserving its traditional shape, the piano retained its status both as a musical instrument and as a piece of bourgeois furniture.[30] This also happened with the talking machines, which had to blend in with the furniture of the living room.[31] Thus, the new player pianos articulated the role assigned to the traditional piano with the "modern" tendencies in which an automated mechanism reproduced music in domestic settings. Information concerning player pianos in Portugal is scarce, but these devices appear to have been introduced in the first decade of the 20th century. Therefore, this book can only study the first stage of their implementation. Most player piano rolls belong to a later period (like rolls with fados composed and performed by the singer of the Coimbra tradition António Menano), suggesting that the player piano gained importance in the 1910s and 1920s, a trend that was paralleled in several countries. Nevertheless, some undated rolls contain musical pieces from an earlier period, such as the march "A Portuguesa." Although they may fall outside the time frame of this book, they may nonetheless indicate the permanence and the significance of some piano rolls. Some of their boxes state that Abel Ferreira da Silva was the only Portuguese manufacturer of these goods during their unspecified date of production. The scarcity of sources on player pianos contrasts with the abundance

---

[27] Lisa Gitelman, "Media, Materiality, and the Measure of the Digital; or, the Case of Sheet Music and the Problem of Piano Rolls," in Lauren Rabinovitz and Abraham Geil (eds.), *Memory Bytes: History, Technology, and Digital Culture* (Durham, NC: Duke University Press, 2004), 207.

[28] Jonson, "Mechanical Piano-players," 19.

[29] Jonson, "Mechanical Piano-players," 17.

[30] Theodor W. Adorno, "The Ccurves of the Needle," *October*, 55 (1990), 51.

[31] Kyle S. Barnett, "Furniture Music: The Phonograph as Furniture, 1900–1930," *Journal of Popular Music Studies*, 18/3 (1996), 301–324.

Figure 5.2 The "piano with motor" sold in Casa Favorita, in the advertisement published in the front cover verso of *Branco e negro*, 5 April 1896, Hemeroteca Municipal de Lisboa. The "piano with motor" sold in Casa Favorita.

of materials associated with the phonographic industry. Therefore, a more detailed study of phonographs can help show how recorded sound became part of Portuguese everyday life.

Figure 5.2 is an advertisement for a keyboardless "piano with motor" sold by Casa Favorita.[32] This is one of the earliest references to mechanical instruments in Portugal. The Casa Favorita was owned by Santos Diniz and sold a variety of goods, such as mechanical instruments, gramophones, and toy carts.[33] Diniz was an early enthusiast of phonography and is discussed later in detail. The advertisement is for a Pianophon Orchestrion, a mechanical instrument whose hammers struck metal strings. Its music is stored in perforated folded books, and the timbre resembles both the mandolin and the piano. The instrument is presented as an affordable, durable, and user-friendly improvement over music boxes. The advert claims that its volume

---

[32] *Branco e negro: semanário ilustrado*, 5 April 1896, verso of the front cover.
[33] *Diário illustrado*, 7 May 1899, back cover.

was "capable of making 300 people in a room dance," and the instrument could be played night and day.[34]

The *Boletim da propriedade industrial* published the registration of the trademarks "Aeolian" and "Pianola" in 1903.[35] It contained applications filed during 1901, three years after the first commercial use of the Pianola trademark by the Aeolian Company.[36] The company was based in Meriden, Connecticut, and was represented in Portugal by G. J. C. Henriques.[37] The brand was also represented by Salão Mozart in the 1910s and 1920s.[38] As the name "Pianola" was being used by other dealers to advertise other player piano mechanisms, Salão Mozart published a notice stating that the name "Pianola" was registered by the Aeolian Company, Ltd., and its exclusive agent was Salão Mozart.[39] Even so, the word "Pianola" came to stand for all player pianos:

> Now what exactly is the Pianola? The word itself is really the trade name for the particular make of mechanical piano-player manufactured by the Aeolian Company, of New York, and the allied Company called the Orchestrelle Company, of 135, New Bond Street, London. Now I do not know whether these two companies take it as a compliment or consider it a nuisance, but the general public and the Press have adopted the term "Pianola" as a generic term for all mechanical piano-player devices.[40]

Pieces with Portuguese titles were included in the January 1911 issue of the *Bulletin of New Music for the Pianola Pianola-Piano, Orchestrelle and Aeolian Grand*.[41] All pieces of the "Foreign and special music" section have Portuguese titles, but they were probably Brazilian.[42]

The music for player pianos was usually stored on a paper roll or in a Z folded brochure that contained performance instructions as a sequential set of holes. The mass production of music rolls was articulated with the trade of

---

[34] *Diário illustrado*, 7 May 1899, back cover.

[35] Portugal, Ministério das Obras Públicas Comércio e Industria, *Boletim da propriedade industrial*, 2ª série—18º anno (Lisbon: Imprensa Nacional, 1903), 6 July 1901, 148.

[36] *Boletim da propriedade industrial*; "History of the Pianola—piano players," Pianola Institute (2008), http://www.pianola.org/history/history_pianoplayers.cfm, accessed 2 August 2010.

[37] *Boletim da propriedade industrial*, 148.

[38] *A capital*, 6 January 1914, 3.

[39] *O Domingo ilustrado*, 25 January 1925, 11.

[40] Jonson, "Mechanical Piano-players," 16.

[41] Aeolian Company, *Bulletin of New Music for the Pianola Pianola-Piano, Orchestrelle and Aeolian Grand* (New York: Aeolian Company, 1911).

[42] Aeolian Company, *Bulletin of New Music*, 14.

player pianos, and many of these rolls included pieces that were already known to the audience. This mirrors the market for sheet music and sound recordings. Manufacturing piano rolls shares striking similarities with the making of commercial sound recordings. To produce a large number of copies, a master roll, cylinder, or disc had to be made first. It was then replicated through an industrial process. Before the spread of technologies that punched the master rolls directly, the preparation of master rolls was manual. The musical editor drew and punched the master roll based on the sheet music, and then produced "fair copies."[43] The fair copies were known as stencils and were then replicated by automatic punching machines. Despite several innovations that made the automated production of music rolls easier, the manual process was not entirely abandoned. Furthermore, the forms of making music rolls served two very distinct purposes. The piano keyboard-operated punching machine facilitated the mass production of music rolls.[44] The reproducing piano, a "development of the ordinary player piano which, with special reproducing music rolls, can re-enact the original touch and expression of the recording pianist," worked as a music recording and reproduction device.[45] The former facilitated a quicker production of rolls in the music roll factories, while the latter was used to recreate professional performances at home.

The reproducing piano was invented in the first decade of the 20th century. The German firms M. Welte & Söhne and Ludwig Hupfeld AG played an important role in this development. The companies developed reproducing pianos such as the Welte-Mignon and the Masterspiel DEA, respectively. In the subsequent decade, two American manufacturers—the Aeolian Company and the American Piano Company—placed their devices on the market. The reproducing piano allowed for a more faithful capture and reproduction of aspects such as tempo and dynamics. Thus, it became possible to listen to a performance by a famous pianist without leaving the house. The manufacturers of the Welt-Mignon and the DEA hired famous pianists and composers to record the so-called hand-played rolls. These rolls were not made by punching holes directly in the master roll. Instead, the performance was traced on ink on a roll and the corresponding holes were subsequently punched by using the manual process described above.[46] Hupfeld had experimented with recorded piano

---

[43] "History of the Pianola—Music Roll Manufacture," *Pianola Institute* (2008), http://www.pianola.org/history/history_rolls.cfm, accessed 2 August 2010.

[44] H. P. Ball, "Perforated Device for Music-rolls," US Patent 778.835, 18 February 1902.

[45] Frank W. Holland and Arthur W. J. G. Ord-Hume, "Reproducing Piano: 1. History and Technical Development," *Grove Music Online*, ed. L. Macy, http://www.oxfordmusiconline.com, (10 August 2010); Dolge, *Pianos and Their Makers*, 57–58.

[46] "The Reproducing Piano—Welte-Mignon," Pianola Institute (2008), http://www.pianola.org/reproducing/reproducing_welte.cfm, accessed 2 August 2010.

rolls toward the end of 1905 and its Künstlermusikrollen (Artists Music Rolls) were readily available for the Phonola and for the Phonoliszt. The Phonoliszt is "an expression piano powered by an electric suction pump, with three levels of automatic dynamics, and variable speed crescendos between the levels."[47]

As explained, music rolls consist of a sequential and discontinuous set of instructions for the instrument to play a particular piece. The holes have a direct correspondence with the musical piece itself. Thus, the instructions are interpreted in strict order as the roll moves. The roll uses mutually exclusive and discontinuous values. There are only two possible, discontinuous, and exclusive conditions in the information recorded in a sheet of paper, where "the surface of the paper in any given area is either solid or not."[48] Then, the music rolls for the player piano are discontinuous storage media. A system in which the medium surface stores a code has been used in different sectors. Both the Jacquard loom and Charles Babbage's planned Analytical Engine used perforated paper as their input device.[49] This indicates a transectorial innovation that was used in different activities, namely mathematics, the textile industry, and music.[50] The complex relationship between the analogue and the digital was discussed by Barthes. His work about text and photography can very helpful if translated to recorded music:

> From the object to its image there is of course a reduction—in proportion, perspective, colour—but at no time is this reduction a *transformation* (in the mathematical sense of the term). In order to move from the reality to its photograph it is in no way necessary to divide up this reality into units and to constitute these units as signs, substantially different from the object they communicate; there is no necessity to set up a relay, that is to say a code, between the object and its image. Certainly the image is not the reality but at least it is its perfect *analogon* and it is exactly this analogical perfection which, to common sense, defines the photograph. Thus can be seen the special status of the photographic image: it is a message without a code; from which proposition an important corollary must immediately be drawn: the photographic message is a continuous message.[51]

---

[47] "The Reproducing Piano—Hupfeld DEA," Pianola Institute (2008), http://www.pianola.org/reproducing/reproducing_welte.cfm, accessed 2 August 2010.

[48] Richard Benson, *The Printed Picture* (New York: Museum of Modern Art, 2008), 274.

[49] Paul Thebèrge, *Any Sound You Can Imagine: Making Music/Consuming Technology* (Hanover, NH: Wesleyan University Press, 1997), 27–29.

[50] Thebèrge, *Any Sound You Can Imagine*, 27–29.

[51] Roland Barthes, "The Photographic Message," in Roland Barthes, *Image-Music-Text* (New York: Hill and Wang, 1978), 17.

Thus, language is a digital code that translates reality into a system of signification.[52] The main difference between analogue and digital is the code that stands between reality and its representation. Photography and phonography were embedded in similar cultural processes that experienced parallel developments toward the end of the 19th century. If photography is a visual analogue of reality, phonography is an auditory analogue of reality. Therefore, the code used in the player pianos is closer to language because it is a system that represents notes and dynamics and instructs the mechanism to perform actions that produce sound.

Sound recording involves the inscription of the music's "acoustic being in time."[53] There is a break between the sound waves themselves and storage media in which a code is present, like music notation. Therefore, "phonography captures not the code but the act, not the script but the voice, not the score but the performance."[54] This theoretical stance bears striking parallels with the theory of the image developed by Barthes. Then, it becomes possible to place early music recording within the wider context of the main historical narratives about sound:

> If both the player-piano and phonograph were forms of inscription, they diverged in what they inscribed—and this divergence illuminates the complementary ways the two technologies contributed to the underlying constitution of modern society. The phonograph inscribed and conveyed sound-in-time—that is, sound as the ephemeral vibrations in the air produced by a specific instance of musical labor (or other sound-making activity). The player-piano, by contrast, represented a system of sound-in-knowledge—that is, information and instructions on how to make music. It inscribed and conveyed how to perform, over and over, the labor required to produce certain predetermined sounds.[55]

A simplistic interpretation of the history of sound recording history from 1877 onward presents it as a sequential and teleological transition from analogue to digital technologies. However, the narrative pertaining to recorded music can only be multilayered and complex since competing technologies overlapped for a significant period. Hand-played rolls, cylinders, and flat records

---

[52] Roland Barthes, "Rhetoric of the Image," in Barthes, *Image-Music-Text*, 41.

[53] Eric W. Rothenbuhler and John Durham Peters, "Defining Phonography: An Experiment in Theory," *Musical Quarterly*, 81/2 (1997), 243.

[54] Rothenbuhler and Peters, "Defining Phonography," 243.

[55] Suisman, "Sound, Knowledge, and the 'Immanence of Human Failure,'" 23–24.

were being traded at the same time. Placing the player piano as an intermediate stage between the age of domestic music making and the age of phonography tends to oversimplify a complex process. Thus, a polar opposition between the embodiment of vocal and instrumental skills and "an atomised and passive form of musical experience" becomes very difficult to accept.[56] In addition, the coexisting music storage technologies were relevant in domestic entertainment and were symbiotically articulated with each other and with other music goods. Therefore, the technologies for the reproduction of sound and music that are materialized in the player piano and in the phonograph encapsulated two contrasting, yet complementary, tendencies of modernity.[57] On the one hand, the player piano embodies the rationalization of culture, labor, and knowledge, and displays the modern inclination toward "quantification, mechanization, automation, and digitization."[58] Conversely, the phonograph helped to reorganize the sensory perception of both space and time, a process that encapsulated a metaphysical transformation of human experience under the sign of modernity.[59]

Mechanical Instruments in the Streets of Lisbon

The sound of mechanical instruments was part of the auditory landscape of a 19th-century city. The spread of mechanical instruments and their integration in domestic music making starting in the 1880s is symptomatic of a cultural shift. This transition is associated with technological innovation, the development of auditory techniques, and the growing presence of mass-produced goods in the household.[60] However, the sounds of mechanical instruments in the streets were already heard in a remote past. The church tower's self-playing chiming clock became part of the European auditory landscape in the 14th century. It consists of several bells that are periodically struck through an automated device. Initially, it relied on pinned wheels that activated levers when rotating. These levers were connected to hammers that struck the bells.

---

[56] Max Paddison, "The Critique Criticised: Adorno and Popular Music," *Popular Music*, 2 (1982), 206. However, authors argued that this "passivity" is actively constructed by the subject. See Emilie Gomart and Antoine Hennion, "A Sociology of Attachment: Music Amateurs, Drug Users," *Sociological Review*, 46/S (1998), 220–247; Tia DeNora, *After Adorno: Rethinking Music Sociology* (Cambridge: Cambridge University Press, 2003), 91–93.

[57] Suisman, "Sound, Knowledge, and the 'Immanence of Human Failure,'" 24.

[58] Suisman, "Sound, Knowledge, and the 'Immanence of Human Failure,'" 24.

[59] Suisman, "Sound, Knowledge, and the 'Immanence of Human Failure,'" 24.

[60] Jonathan Sterne, *The Audible Past: Cultural Origins of Sound Reproduction* (Durham. NC: Duke University Press, 2003), 204.

If people wanted to change the tune, entire wheels had to be replaced.[61] This system was replaced in the 16th century with a cylinder that had removable pins, making the programming of the tunes easier. Then, the melodies that periodically intertwined with the town's auditory landscape could be changed with less effort.[62] Thus, the chiming clock became another instrument for spreading new melodies.

The sound of church bells is ubiquitous in Lisbon's auditory landscape because Lisbon has many churches. Like Benjamin's Naples the churches are "hidden, built in; high domes are often to be seen only from a few places, and even then it is not easy to find one's way to them, impossible to distinguish the mass of the church from that of the neighboring secular buildings."[63] If one goes to an elevated spot close to the city center, like the Jardim do Torel, one can hear the bells of at least half a dozen churches striking the time. Some do it every quarter of an hour, creating a curious sound effect because they are not perfectly synchronized, striking the time at slightly different points. Church bells imparted "a rhythm to the ordinary functions of the community," acting as an "auditory synchronizer" of everyday life.[64] Bells were used to summon people for mass, to punctuate religious and secular festivities, to mark the passing of time, and to sound alarm. Through the sounding of these many bells, "a subtle auditory rhetoric was developed" and integrated into the everyday life of Lisbon.[65] Maria Rattazzi's book *Portugal de relance* ("Portugal at a glance") consists of satirical letters about her stay in Portugal, and includes interesting passages on church bells. Originally published in French with the title *Le Portugal a vol d'oiseau*, it was translated into Portuguese and published in Lisbon around 1880.[66] *Portugal de relance* generated a fierce reaction and instigated the publication of works that disavowed the author's statements.[67] For Camilo Castelo Branco, *Portugal de relance* was an "indiscreet gossipy work" of a fake princess, whose "badmouthing is blatantly European."[68] The book is

---

[61] Teun Koetsier, "On the Prehistory of Programmable Machines: Musical Automata, Looms, Calculators," *Mechanism and Machine Theory*, 36 (2001), 592.

[62] Koetsier, "On the Prehistory of Programmable Machines," 592.

[63] Walter Benjamin and Asja Lacis, "Naples," in Walter Benjamin, *Reflections: Essays, Aphorisms, Autobiographical Writings* (New York: Schocken Books, 2007), 166.

[64] Alain Corbin, *Village Bells: Sound and Meaning in the Nineteenth-Century French Countryside* (London: Papermac, 1999), xi.

[65] Corbin, *Village Bells*, xi.

[66] Maria Rattazzi, *Portugal de relance* (Lisbon: Livraria Zeferino, 1881).

[67] Camilo Castelo Branco, *A senhora Rattazzi* (Porto/Braga: Livraria internacional de Ernesto Chardron, Editor, 1880); Urbano de Castro, *A princeza na berlinda: Rattazzi a vol d'oiseau, com a biographia de sua Alteza* (Lisbon: Typographia Portugueza, 1880); Monteiro Ramalho, *As ratices da Rattazzi: o pello nacional* (Porto: Typ. do Jornal da Manhã, 1880).

[68] Castelo Branco, *A senhora Rattazzi*, 3, 36.

poorly documented and reveals the writer's deeply ethnocentric perspective. Nevertheless, despite its satirical, misinformed, and exaggerated tone, it contains some useful firsthand information. Being a foreigner placed the author in a privileged position to notice aspects of Portuguese everyday life that seemed to her unusual. Probably the ubiquity of the sounding church bells went unnoticed by the people of Lisbon because these chimes had been part of their everyday routines for centuries—but not for Rattazzi. For her, Portugal was second only to Belgium among Catholic countries in the use of the carillon.[69] Bells were associated with a wide range of religious events, such as christenings, funerals, and other celebrations.[70] Also, because so many buildings were made of wood, there were frequent fires, and bells were used to sound the alarm.[71] Apart from the standard tolls and peals, Lisbon's bells had a widely varied repertoire. It included the national anthem, operetta arias, and urban songs.[72] The arias were drawn from Offenbach's *Orphée aux enfers* and Lecocq's *La fille de Madame Angot*, demonstrating the pervasiveness of French operetta in Lisbon. Moreover, "the voluptuous rhythm of waltzes and the spicy sauciness of the cancans were fraternally allied with the *Oremus*, with the *Alleluia*, and with the *Amen*,"[73] showing the unclear boundary between the sacred and the secular in a predominantly Catholic southern European country.

The mechanical organ (also called barrel organ or street organ) was ubiquitous in the city's streets. It relies on a pneumatic apparatus in which a set of pipes is fed with air pumped by a bellows. The tunes were stored in a cylinder to which were attached pins and staples; these activated valves that allowed the air to pass through the pipes, and the pre-programmed tune was played. The cylinder was set in motion with a hand crank and could be programmed to play different tunes. These pieces were selected by the organ grinder as he performed. Although the mechanical organs used an automated device, some of them could be played either manually or automatically. Apart from the more portable instruments, some mechanical organs were fixed and they usually appeared in fairgrounds. For example, the hoarse sound of the barrel organ was heard outside the waxwork tents in the 1905 Alcântara annual fair. There, a large Orchestrophone, a fairground mechanical organ built by Limonaire Frères, was a popular attraction.[74] Figure 5.3 shows a part of the 1905 fair where people were circulating. The fair had eateries, theaters, and

---

[69] Rattazzi, *Portugal de relance*, 28.
[70] Rattazzi, *Portugal de relance*, 28–29.
[71] Rattazzi, *Portugal de relance*, 28–29.
[72] Rattazzi, *Portugal de relance*, 28–29.
[73] Rattazzi, *Portugal de relance*, 29.
[74] *Illustração portugueza*, 8 May 1905, 429.

Figure 5.3 A feira d' Alcântara—a entrada da feira, in *Illustração Portugueza*, 8 May 1905, 418, Hemeroteca Municipal de Lisboa. The entrance to the Alcântara Fair.

other popular amusements where a part of Lisbon's population spent their time and money.

Victorian street music was perceived as a nuisance by the professional middle classes that worked from their homes in London.[75] Street musicians were frequently portrayed as an invasive disturbance of foreign origin, a stereotype caricatured by artists like John Leech in London's periodicals.[76] The Savoyard organ grinders in Victorian England were often "British performers, masquerading under exotic disguises and titles in order to increase their attraction."[77] Even so, they created a sonic annoyance that was "distinctly alien to London."[78] This means that "the foreign street musician was also an easy target during moral panics over crime and disorder."[79] The movement against street noise in the Victorian period had the professional middle classes as its main campaigners. However, the music played by street musicians "echoed middle-class tastes from the highbrow to the low," and consisted of arrangements of songs and operatic pieces, religious works, and dances.[80]

[75] Picker, *Victorian Soundscapes*, 46–52 and 65–76.
[76] Picker, *Victorian Soundscapes*, 69.
[77] Dave Russell, *Popular Music in England, 1840-1914: A Social History* (Manchester: Manchester University Press, 1997), 74.
[78] Picker, *Victorian Soundscapes*, 47.
[79] Russell, *Popular Music in England*, 74.
[80] Picker, *Victorian Soundscapes*, 63. See also Richard Middleton, "Popular Music of the Lower Classes," in Nicholas Temperley (ed.), *The Romantic Age, 1800-1914* (London: Athlone Press, 1981), 63–81.

The negative references to street musicians had a parallel in Portugal. The music periodical *Amphion* published an article in 1890 arguing that the sound of the barrel organ was a scourge that afflicted the city of Lisbon, similar to the complaints heard in England.[81] This resonates with the Victorian discourse on street music. Nevertheless, as *Amphion* was dedicated to promoting Western art music its condemnation of street music is not surprising. *O Ocidente* published a small article on itinerant musicians stating that groups of wandering musicians were frequently seen in Portuguese towns and villages.[82] These buskers were generally a singer and a guitarist or a fiddler and they played songs from successful comic operas, including their double entendre *coplas*.[83] As Pimentel wrote in *Vida de Lisboa*,

> In the complicated mechanisms of life in the capital, the street cry and the boy's songs are intimately connected with theatrical events: the music from the theater, if it pleased the audience, is soon reproduced in the street.[84]

Thus, it is possible to argue that street musicians played an important role in the spread of theatrical music across the country. They enlarged the theatrical audience both geographically and socially. The porosity of boundaries is not limited to the urban and the rural, but also has class implications. Writing in 1889, Fialho d'Almeida told of Sérgio, a former cellist of the S. Carlos orchestra. He was "reddish from the alcohol" and performed regularly in a "café of *fadistas*" in Mouraria.[85] Notwithstanding social conventions, and after years of socializing with people from the upper strata, Sérgio

> now prefers to stoop to the lower spirals of the subaltern people, where his reasonings impress, his sayings resonate, and his divine instrument saves him every night, through the virtuosity of his flair, of the grotesque shipwreck of a *camoeca* [slang for drunkenness] caught with offered grog—as a *remember* [sic, in English] of respect—by the admirers in their shirtsleeves and clogs that, to hear him play, go to the café every night.[86]

---

[81] Leitão, "A ambiência musical e sonora da cidade de Lisboa no ano de 1890," master's thesis (Universidade Nova de Lisboa, 2006), 178.

[82] *O Occidente*, 25 November 1896, 258–259.

[83] *O Occidente*, 25 November 1896, 258–259.

[84] Alberto Pimentel, *Vida de Lisboa* (Lisbon: Parceria António Maria Pereira, 1900), 52.

[85] Fialho d'Almeida, *Os gatos, publicação mensal, d'inquerito á vida portugueza* (Porto: Casa Editora Alcino Aranha & C.ª, September–October 1889), 9.

[86] Almeida, *Os gatos*, 11–12.

The café is described as a small and sordid place, frequented by drunks and prostitutes. Sérgio ignores the audience's request to play the "Chegadinho," a "street song" associated with Carnival that was collected in the *Cancioneiro de músicas populares* (see Figure 3.1). He chooses to perform the Kermess Scene from Gounod's *Faust*. Sérgio was accompanied by the resident pianist. His hand was "trembling from the grog" and "giving macabre leaps."[87] The cellist was certainly José Augusto Sérgio da Silva, who had studied in the Conservatoire and played in the orchestra of the Real Teatro de S. Carlos for thirty years.[88] However, Sérgio had mental health issues that caused him to leave the orchestra in 1884.[89] He fell into "extreme lowliness," playing daily in that café that was frequented by the "worst people who wandered through those places."[90] There, he improvised fantasies "in fados and in other popular songs, or in themes of known operas," a reminiscence of his virtuoso training.[91] Sérgio died in 1890, after "throwing himself to the wretched living that he had finally adopted." Thus, Fialho caught him in the last year of his life, transforming Sérgio in a poignant account of Lisbon's lowlife, where artistic flair was shown in marginal and ill-reputed contexts.[92] This illustrates the porosity of Lisbon's entertainment circuits, where a former musician of the most distinguished theater interacts with the people of the poor districts, complicating a direct association between class, repertoire, and space in a city that is sonically multilayered.

O primo Basílio, a novel by Queirós, contains a scene in which a black-bearded organ grinder performs Bellini's "Casta diva" on a barrel organ, attracting the people who lived nearby.[93] The barrel organ appears two more times in this novel. It breaks the silence of a Sunday evening with the sound of Bellini's *Norma* and Donizetti's *Lucia di Lammermoor*. Later, it is heard performing the finale of *La traviata*.[94] An organ grinder playing *La traviata* also appears in the horse race episode of *Os Maias*, a novel by Queirós.[95] The street organ also "added to the musical and social experience of the poor" by giving

---

[87] Almeida, *Os gatos*, 15.

[88] Ernesto Vieira, *Diccionario biographico de musicos portuguezes: historia e bibliografia da musica em Portugal*, vol.2 (Lisbon: Lambertini, 1900), 306–308.

[89] Vieira, *Diccionario*, 307.

[90] Vieira, *Diccionario*, 307.

[91] Vieira, *Diccionario*, 307.

[92] Vieira, *Diccionario*, 308.

[93] Eça de Queirós, *O primo Bazilio, episódio domestico* (Porto/Braga: Livraria Chardron, 1878), 34–36; António de Sousa Bastos, *Lisboa Velha: sessenta anos de recordações, 1850 a 1910* (Lisbon: Câmara Municipal de Lisboa, 1947), 47–58.

[94] Queirós, *O primo Bazilio*, 112 and 220.

[95] Queirós, *Os Maias: episódios da vida romântica*, vol. 1 (Porto: Livraria Chardron/Casa Editora Lugan & Genelioux Successores, 1888), 417.

people access to music they otherwise could not have heard.[96] The fleeting contact that the Lisbon poor could have with opera was probably through barrel organ arrangements. Nevertheless, it would be naive to assume that the opera selections played by the street organ gave the poor any "real share in the art music tradition of the period."[97] In *Os Maias*, the waltz from Lecocq's operetta *La fille de Madame Angot* is heard several times. It is performed by the barrel organ in the city's streets and by the wind and percussion band that was playing at the horse track.[98] This demonstrates that pieces from the music theater were circulating in other spaces and contexts. We can witness the importance of the operetta in the auditory landscapes of Lisbon's streets by connecting *Portugal de relance* with *Os Maias*. Music from *La fille de Madame Angot* was adapted and performed by church bells, by a barrel organ, and by a wind and percussion band. Thus, the same tune crossed several cultural boundaries.

The *bandas* were important in shaping the city's auditory landscape. Despite not being a mechanized ensemble, their presence was ubiquitous. Unlike mechanical instruments, they were not perceived as an epitome of modernity. However, with a significant impulse received by the amateur music movement in the last third of the 19th century many *bandas* were created. Therefore, their strong presence in the city was a recent development. The constitution of the *bandas* varied, but they usually included flutes, reed instruments, brass instruments, and percussion. Figure 5.4 shows a *banda* playing in the Aterro, an area in the western part of the city. They are playing brass instruments and marching while the crowd watches them.

There were some professional *bandas*. They were affiliated with the military or with the police, like the Banda da Guarda Municipal de Lisboa or the Banda dos Marinheiros da Armada. Others were part of voluntary societies that were sometimes connected to the trade unionist movement. The *bandas* usually performed on Sundays and bank holidays in theater halls, at balls, in outdoor gatherings, for political rallies, and in public gardens. Outdoor music was played in the Jardim da Estrela, in the Praça D. Fernando, and in the Avenida da Liberdade, and the bandstand, a new type of urban structure, was placed in some of the city's open spaces.[99] The *bandas* played a varied repertoire that included marches, waltzes, polkas, anthems, and arrangements of classical pieces like opera overtures. For example, João Rodrigues Cordeiro arranged parts of operettas like *La fille de Madame Angot* and *Barba Azul* for

---

[96] Russell, *Popular Music in England*, 76.
[97] Russell, *Popular Music in England*, 76.
[98] Queirós, *Os Maias*, vol. 2, 11, and vol. 1, 426.
[99] Leitão, A ambiência, 130–135.

Figure 5.4 Paulo Guedes, Banda de música no Aterro, Lisbon, early 20th century, Arquivo Fotográfico de Lisboa, Colecção Paulo Guedes, PT/AMLSB/PAG/000641.
A musical band in the Aterro.

wind and percussion band.[100] The impact of this movement on the city's music life cannot be overstated due to its frequent presence in public spaces and gatherings. These *banda* performances were another way to make music omnipresent and affordable.

During the peak of Offenbach's popularity in Lisbon, the church bells and all barrel organs played his music.[101] According to Queirós, even the Elevation of the Host in Lisbon's churches was made to the sound of the Général Boum's couplets, a song from of *La Grande-Duchesse de Gérolstein*.[102] This satirical statement illustrates the pervasiveness of the French operetta in Lisbon, a dominance that would end toward the end of the 19th century. The ubiquitous presence of music from the popular theater illustrates the porosity between stage, street, and domestic space. Therefore, the same repertoire was arranged to maximize its impact in different contexts. This unified and segmented the

---

[100] João Rodrigues Cordeiro, *Mosaico: extrahido da Opera Comica La Fille de Madame Angot*. Shelfmark PTBN: C.N. 523, National Library of Portugal; João Rodrigues Cordeiro, *Barba Azul: 1.º Acto (completo) da Opera Buffa*. Shelfmark PTBN: C.N. 530, National Library of Portugal.

[101] Ramalho Ortigão and Eça de Queirós, *As farpas: crónica mensal da política, das letras e dos costumes* (Lisbon: Typographia Universal, 1871), 34.

[102] Ortigão and Queirós, *As farpas*, 34.

city's spaces at the same time, where a complex relation between continuity and discontinuity and between space and sound is clearly visible. Moreover, the involuntary exposure of the people of Lisbon to the omnipresent sounds of the church bells, of the barrel organ, of the *bandas,* of the street songs, and of the cries of the peddlers was commonplace. These sounds were "always there, beyond our control, slipping under our thresholds of consciousness: a soundtrack of everyday life."[103]

Phonography in Portugal: Between the Global and the Local

Sound technologies introduced important changes in the music business at the end of the 19th century. The possibility of capturing the sound of a performance and reproducing it in different spaces and times reshaped the way people interacted with music. In this, sound was transformed into a commodity. Thus, the commodification of music was intensified with the commodification of sound itself, and different competing technologies for its reproduction were integrated in the everyday life of a city like Lisbon. Nevertheless, this was not a simple and one-dimensional process. Implementing a new commercial enterprise in a small-scale market like Portugal requires inventiveness. The interaction between the local and the global plays an important role in the Portuguese phonographic market, where both local entrepreneurs and multinational companies developed their business. The "sublime experience" of the Romantics was transformed in the Victorian era "into a quantifiable and marketable object or thing, a sonic commodity, in the form of a printed work, a performance, or, ultimately, an audio recording."[104] In the first decade of the 20th century the main European recording companies established their stores in Portugal.[105] Smaller companies relied on local agents for the distribution of their catalogue.[106] Because there were no record pressing plants in Portugal, the local market was dependent on imported goods and technicians. Thus, local traders were motivated to establish a relationship with foreign companies

---

[103] Anahid Kassabian, "Popular," in Bruce Horner and Thomas Swiss (eds.), *Key Terms in Popular Music and Culture* (Malden, MA: Blackwell, 1999), 117. About the cries of the peddlers in Lisbon, see Irkan [Fialho d'Almeida], "Os pregões," *Pontos nos ii,* 3 July 1890, 211, 214; Júlio de Castilho, *Lisboa antiga* (Lisbon: Antiga casa Bertrand, José Bastos, 1904) 184–233.

[104] John Picker, *Victorian Soundscapes,* 10.

[105] Geoffrey Jones, "The Gramophone Company," 83.

[106] Leonor Losa, "Indústria fonográfica," 633; Losa and Belchior, "The Introduction of Phonogram Market in Portugal," 7.

to be able to record and issue their phonograms. Selling phonographic goods had to combine novelty with established models.

The new type of information stored in sound recordings marks a qualitative difference between them and other goods that were sold in this period. Technological innovations played a key role in reshaping discourse networks, "the network of technologies and institutions that allow a given culture to select, store, and process relevant data," between 1800 and 1900.[107] New types of machines were developed in the last third of the 19th century. These devices took over "functions of the central nervous system, and no longer, as in times past, merely those of muscles."[108] Thus, the phonograph performed the functions of the central nervous system by recording and storing information. Therefore, phonography can be framed metaphorically as a prosthetic form of memory.[109] Associating human memory with the impression and deletion of traces on a substrate has been especially pervasive in Western culture.[110] For example, Jean-Marie Guyau's "La mémoire et le phonographe" makes a direct comparison between memory and the working of phonograph, whereby a stylus makes an inscription in the brain cells.[111] The person recollects as the needle passes over the corresponding groove, deploying the corresponding sensation.[112] This analogy was made in the early days of phonography. "La mémoire et le phonographe" was published in 1880, only a few years after Edison's first successful experiments with his phonograph. The assumption that external recording technologies can be used to supplement, expand, and enhance memory is based on the idea that they work in similar and at least compatible ways with the mechanisms of the human mind.[113] Sound recording was also associated with memory in Portugal, which illustrates the circulation of this idea. In *História do fado*, Pinto de Carvalho praises the memory of Cesária, a fado singer from Lisbon's Alcântara district, by associating it with phonography: "in her memory, like in a phonograph, she stored hundreds of verses."[114]

---

[107] Friedrich A. Kittler, *Discourse Networks, 1800/1900* (Palo Alto, CA: Stanford University Press, 1992), 369.

[108] Friedrich A. Kittler, *Gramophone, Film, Typewriter* (Palo Alto, CA: Stanford University Press, 1999), 16.

[109] Bennett Hogg, "The Cultural Imagination of the Phonographic Voice, 1877–1940," Ph.D. thesis (Newcastle University, 2008), 143–147.

[110] James Burton, "Bergson's Non-Archival Theory of Memory," *Memory Studies*, 1/3 (2008), 322.

[111] Jean-Marie Guyau, "La mémoire et le phonographe," *Revue philosophique de la France et de l'étranger*, Tome IX, janvier–juillet (1880), 317–322.

[112] Guyau, "La mémoire et le phonographe," 320.

[113] Guyau, "La mémoire et le phonographe," 320.

[114] Pinto de Carvalho, *História do fado* (Lisbon: Empreza da História de Portugal, 1903), 175.

An important point in the study of phonography is the recording of a supposedly unmediated reality. At the height of positivism, sound recording was used for scientific purposes. An intended objectivity was guaranteed by reducing human intervention.[115] The phonograph was perceived to gather quantifiable and empirical data, making it a valuable instrument for the unmediated collection of popular songs.[116]

The shaping of phonographic technologies into media facilitated their incorporation into everyday life. However, the spread of phonography was a part of a complex process through which these new devices interacted and transformed the cultures of listening.[117] "Audible techniques" predate the dissemination of sound recording, being associated especially with two professional areas: medicine and telegraphy. "Medicine and telegraphy were two fields where techniques of listening provided professional ethos and prestige" and "both the stethoscope and the telegraphic 'sounder' were technologies that crystallized already-extant techniques of listening."[118] Different sound reproducing technologies shared "a set of common operational and philosophical principles," making them "embodiments and intensifications of tendencies that were already existent elsewhere in the culture."[119] The phonograph emulates human hearing, and its diaphragm is equivalent to the eardrum. Thus, it is a tympanic technology. Fialho d'Almeida refers to the role of phonographic culture in transforming our perception of everyday life in Lisbon. He argues that "the presage of dawn seemed to make the city louder: each sound takes in the air a vivid and crystalline sonority that arrives reinforced to our ears, as if it is reverberated by the immense membrane of a phonograph."[120]

O Ocidente published an article on Thomas Edison that mentioned the phonograph in 1878.[121] It also published an account of Edison's phonograph by Francisco da Fonseca Benevides.[122] He examined how the phonograph worked in recording speech, and included an illustrated schema. This is coherent with Edison's development of the phonograph as an office tool. At its early stage, it was not designed for entertainment purposes but as an aid for memory. The article was published shortly after Edison's initial patent for the phonograph was

---

[115] Hogg, "The Cultural Imagination," 201.
[116] Hogg, "The Cultural Imagination," 201.
[117] Sterne, *The Audible Past*, 84.
[118] Sterne, *The Audible Past*, 98.
[119] Sterne, *The Audible Past*, 34.
[120] Fialho d'Almeida, *Lisboa Galante* (Porto: Livraria Civilização, 1890), 319.
[121] "O inventor Thomaz Edison," *O Occidente*, 15 September 1878, 140–141.
[122] Fonseca Benevides, "Phonographo fallante de Edison," *O Occidente*, 15 April 1878, 64.

granted.¹²³ Benevides described Edison's phonograph as a device that records and reproduces sound. However, one illustration is more specific because it pictures a man speaking into the phonograph; the caption for a similar image states that the machine was being used "for reproducing words."¹²⁴ The phonograph was used as a dictating machine, a possibility raised by Edison's focus on recording voice in his first patent and in the establishment of the Edison Speaking Phonograph Company in 1878.¹²⁵ Therefore, the article captures a moment in its development when "the phonograph appeared before a need for its function had been identified. While numerous uses were projected, none were realized."¹²⁶ In the late 1870s, the phonograph was nothing more than a "curiosity of little practical value."¹²⁷

The inconsistent development of the phonograph contributed to its slow dissemination. Its multiple applications delayed the integration of the phonograph into everyday life.¹²⁸ During its history, it "was used with varying success as an office dictating machine, a scientific instrument, a toy and a coin-slot amusement machine, but in the mid-1890s success was still around the corner."¹²⁹ For the phonograph to have widespread use, it had to undergo several alterations. This implied transforming the machine in visual, cultural, and acoustic terms.¹³⁰ The task was undertaken by manufacturers, advertisers, and consumers.¹³¹ In sum, "the phonograph could not just reproduce the sounds of musical instruments; it had to become an instrument itself."¹³² Nonetheless, some transformations that were essential to create a market for phonographs and recordings were carried out in the 1880s. They included improving Edison's phonograph and establishing the Edison Phonograph Company for its manufacture.¹³³

---

[123] Thomas A. Edison, "Improvement in Phonograph or Speaking Machines," US Patent 200,521, 19 February 1878.

[124] Benevides, "Phonographo fallante de Edison," 64.

[125] Thomas A. Edison, "Improvement in Phonograph or Speaking Machines"; Walter L. Welch and Leah Brodbeck Stensel Burt, *From Tinfoil to Stereo: The Acoustic Years of the Recording Industry, 1877–1929* (Gainesville: University Press of Florida, 1995), 19.

[126] Emily Thompson, "Machines, Music, and the Quest for Fidelity: Marketing the Edison Phonograph in America, 1877–1925," *Musical Quarterly*, 79/1 (1995), 137.

[127] Leonard DeGraaf, "Confronting the Mass Market: Thomas Edison and the Entertainment Phonograph," *Business and Economic History*, 24/1 (1995), 88.

[128] Taylor, "The Commodification of Music," 285.

[129] Pekka Gronow, "The Record Industry: Growth of a Mass Medium," *Popular Music*, 3 (1983), 54.

[130] Thompson, "Machines, Music, and the Quest for Fidelity," 140.

[131] Thompson, "Machines, Music, and the Quest for Fidelity," 140.

[132] Thompson, "Machines, Music, and the Quest for Fidelity," 140.

[133] Thomas A. Edison, "Phonograph," US Patent 386,974, 31 July 1888; Welch and Burt, *From Tinfoil to Stereo*, 25–26.

Despite the prominence given to Edison in sound recording history, other people helped to develop the phonograph during its early period. An important contribution was made by Charles Sumner Tainter while working with Alexander Bell. Tainter produced the Graphophone, a device that recorded sound onto a cylinder that was covered with a wax-like substance.[134] Recording on a more pliable surface improved sound fidelity.[135] This contrasted with Edison's phonograph, which used a tinfoil cylinder instead. Another improvement was developed by Gianni Bettini and consisted of a flexible diaphragm attached to the stylus by four radial spurs.[136] This device could be adapted to different phonograph models.[137] The rapid development of a large-scale market for recorded sound merged technological innovation and commercial strategies.[138] These efforts were directed toward marketing pre-recorded music and gave greater prominence to the phonograph as a supplier of entertainment than to its use as an office tool.[139] Over a period of thirty years, a "curiosity of little practical value" was transformed in an object that was perceived as the epitome of modernity. Edison's device was offered for sale to the public in 1896. By 1900, the phonograph was already part of modern domestic life and soon became a familiar household item.[140] Thus, the phonograph was "put to use in ways that distinctly changed the prevailing culture of music in the home."[141] It was not only perceived as a part of modern domesticity but also as a good that played an important role in defining modernity.

The Portuguese market for sound recording and reproduction was established in the last years of the 19th century. Both local entrepreneurs and international companies played a key role in this process. The activity of Francisco Santos Diniz and Joaquim Duarte Ferreira indicate that phonography was an attractive area for investment.[142] Between 1898 and 1902, Santos Diniz was granted two patents. They covered his brand Audiophone and were "intended for phonographic equipment" and an improvement on the gramophone.[143] He

---

[134] Sumner Tainter, "Apparatus for Recording and Reproducing Sounds," US Patent 341,288, 4 May 1886.

[135] Roland Gelatt, *The Fabulous Phonograph 1877–1977* (London: Cassell, 1977), 35.

[136] Gianni Bettini, "Method of Recording and reproducing Sounds," US Patent 409,003, 11 April 1889; "Apparatus for the Record and Reproduction of Sounds," US Patent 409,004, 13 August 1889.

[137] Welch and Burt, *From Tinfoil to Stereo*, 61–71.

[138] DeGraaf, "Confronting the Mass Market," 89.

[139] DeGraaf, "Confronting the Mass Market," 89.

[140] Thompson, "Machines, Music, and the Quest for Fidelity," 138.

[141] Thompson, "Machines, Music, and the Quest for Fidelity," 138.

[142] Leonor Losa, *Machinas fallantes: a música gravada em Portugal no início do século XX* (Lisbon: Tinta da China, 2013), 39–40.

[143] Losa and Belchior, "The Introduction of Phonogram Market in Portugal," 7.

sold his gramophone, *O Gigante*, in his Lisbon store.[144] Ferreira filed a patent to make and record discs and cylinders. However, the company Pinto & Meirelles, a trader in wax cylinders, complained about it and the patent was not granted.[145] This refusal made the Portuguese phonographic enterprises dependent on foreign production facilities.[146] This lasted for the next fifty years. Several labels and brands were registered in the first decade of the 20th century, which may indicate the growth of a yet incipient market for recorded sound.[147] Local agents played an important part in the Portuguese market for phonographic goods.[148] This is interesting because the country lacked record factories and recording technologies. The prominence of local traders is remarkable in dealing with a business that was devised on an international scale from the start.[149] The leading recording companies built factories, created subsidiary companies and agencies, and established a worldwide network for making and distributing phonograms.[150] Thus, the smaller dealers had either to develop a relationship with the major companies or fill the gaps left by them. This was crucial in creating a market for local popular music.

At the beginning of the 20th century, Santos Diniz also owned a store in the Praça dos Restauradores where he traded in gramophones and discs made by the Gramophone Company and by the German-based Odeon.[151] However, his company was liquidated in 1907.[152] Alberto, the son of Diniz, was a pioneer and an early enthusiast of phonography. He died in 1903 at the age of twenty-five. According to his obituary, he introduced the gramophone in Portugal and also improved it.[153] The text mentions that his mother listened to the voice of her dead son that was captured on the phonographic cylinders.[154] Thus, sound recording technologies could foster rituals of remembrance. The preservation of the voices of the dead was also a use for sound recording. It is associated with Victorian domesticity but is also present in Portugal. Archiving the voices of the dead is the subject of Barraud's painting *His Master's Voice*. The artwork that portrayed the dog Nipper listening his dead owner's voice recorded on a cylinder was bought in 1899 by the Gramophone Company and became

---

[144] Losa and Belchior, "The Introduction of Phonogram Market in Portugal," 7.
[145] Losa and Belchior, "The Introduction of Phonogram Market in Portugal," 7.
[146] Losa and Belchior, "The Introduction of Phonogram Market in Portugal," 7.
[147] Losa and Belchior, "The Introduction of Phonogram Market in Portugal," 8.
[148] Losa and Belchior, "The Introduction of Phonogram Market in Portugal,"8.
[149] Gronow, "The Record Industry," 56.
[150] Gronow, "The Record Industry," 56.
[151] *O Occidente*, 10 January 1903, 8; 19 August 1903, 176; 30 December 1904, 290.
[152] *Diário de notícias*, 10 May 1907.
[153] *O Occidente*, 20 May 1903, 111–112.
[154] *O Occidente*, 20 May 1903, 112.

the very recognizable icon of the company.[155] However, the idea of archiving sound permanently in the early period of phonography has to be placed in context. It was an intended, as well as desired, possibility and not an established reality. The potential of sound recordings to preserve sound indefinitely were a myth.[156] Although this was part of the discourse of both users and publicists from an early stage of these technologies, the technical difficulties of storing and archiving sound were significant; "the first recordings were essentially unplayable after they were removed from the machine."[157] Technical failure was only a part of the problem. Culturally, "later wax cylinder recordings and even metal or shellac disks were often treated by their makers as ephemera."[158]

The early multinational recording companies were organized in an oligopoly that relied on vertical integration. Therefore, the "control of the total production flow from raw materials to wholesale sales" was crucial in reducing competition.[159] The competing business models embraced by the recording companies were deeply associated with technological and legal constraints. Given the complex development of commercial phonography, these constraints included the holding of patents and licenses for the several steps of production. Furthermore, the variety of these processes and products had a deep impact on the recording policy of the companies. Therefore, "the success that any company was having could be mitigated by the music industry's lack of exclusive repertoire as well as its lack of technological standardization."[160]

The recording companies concentrated their attention on music that was already familiar to the public. Most pieces were not exclusive to the company or to the performer. Thus, both artists and repertoires overlapped in the catalogues of different recording companies. This is where the importance of the popular stage for the recording industry surfaces. The fact that the music was associated with a specific performer contributed to the creation and development of catalogues of the recording companies in the early 20th century. The theaters played an important role in supplying the artists and repertoires of the early phonograms. Moreover, the recording artists were predominantly actors. At this stage, "clear diction and strong stage personality were more important

---

[155] Kittler, *Gramophone, Film, Typewriter*, 69; Peter Martland, *Recording History: The British Record Industry 1888–1931* (Lanham, MD: Scarecrow Press, 2013), 55.

[156] Sterne, *The Audible Past*, 288.

[157] Sterne, *The Audible Past*, 288.

[158] Sterne, *The Audible Past*, 288.

[159] Richard A. Peterson and David G. Berger, "Cycles in Symbol Production: The Case of Popular Music," in Simon Frith and Andrew Goodwin (eds.), *On Record: Rock, Pop, and the Written Word* (London: Routledge, 1990), 119.

[160] David J. Steffen, *From Edison to Marconi: The First Thirty Years of Recorded Music* (Jefferson, NC: McFarland, 2005), 4.

than a trained singing voice."[161] This is associated with the limitations of the medium, and the recording technicians played an important role in selecting the performers. Recording famous people from the popular theater was a pervasive tendency of the early recording companies throughout the world. Portuguese stage performers like Palmira Bastos, Delfina Victor, or Jorge Roldão recorded frequently for a number of companies during the first decade of the 20th century. Relating this to the lack of technological standardization, a small pool of performers was transversally represented in the Portuguese catalogues of national and international companies. Avelino Baptista's recordings of fado were included in the 1906 catalogues of both the Companhia Franceza do Gramophone and of Phonographos Pathé, two competing ventures.[162]

The competing technologies for reproducing sound were sometimes incompatible and the leading companies worked within a framework of vertical integration. The same company could sell the same piece in cylinders and in vertical-cut flat records. A competitor could issue lateral-cut flat records with the same repertoire. This strategy favored the owners of the equipment that was manufactured by the companies themselves. Thus, the release of the same music by the same performer in different formats did not involve direct competition between companies.[163] Consequently, the relationship between sound equipment and storage media was essential in the rapid expansion of the phonographic industry. Sound equipment and recordings were marketed to the economically privileged. An advertisement for the Gramophone Company illustrates this novel form of consumption and its associated sociability:

> We are arrived at the season of gifts, of presents, of *cadeaux*, and all spirits raise the question "What should I offer?" "What can I give that is new, interesting, and lasting; that offers pleasure without being banal or becoming ordinary, and that can constantly be a graceful souvenir of my gift?" By giving a gramophone you will be cordially celebrated as the generous friend, who is well-received and always wanted because you gifted something that gives constant pleasure.[164]

The link between phonography and the affluent was reinforced by the frequent publishing of advertisements to the recording companies in periodicals

---

[161] Pekka Gronow and Bjorn Englung, "Inventing Recorded Music: The Recorded Repertoire in Scandinavia 1899–1925," *Popular Music*, 26/2 (2007), 291.

[162] Companhia Franceza do Gramophone, *Catalogo das ultimas placas feitas pela Companhia Franceza do Gramophone* (Lisbon: n.p., 1906), 2; Phonographos Pathé, *Novo catalogo e repertorio portuguez* (Porto: n.p., 1906), 17.

[163] Losa and Belchior, "The Introduction of Phonogram Market in Portugal," 9.

[164] *Illustração Portugueza*, 18 December 1905, I

that targeted these societal segments, such as the magazines *O Ocidente* or *Ilustração portuguesa*. These goods were associated with modernity, elegance, and sophistication. Nevertheless, *Ilustração Portuguesa* also advertised "the gramophone for the people or the popular gramophone."[165] This equipment was sold by the Companhia Franceza do Gramophone. However, even the cheapest machine was expensive by Portuguese standards. Therefore, phonographic products were financially inaccessible to the majority of the Portuguese population.

A technology that paralleled phonography was film. Silent movies were being shown in Lisbon at the end of the 19th century, and some pioneers recorded aspects of local everyday life. The early enthusiasts João Freire Correia and Manuel Cardoso took part in *O rapto de uma actriz*, the film that was shown in the *revista Ó da guarda*. Because these films were silent, the music had to be performed live. Matching recorded sound with the moving image was a complicated process. However, Léon Gaumont developed a process that synchronized a camera with a phonograph.[166] Correia and Cardoso made the first Portuguese film that used this technique between 1907 and 1910.[167] The film consisted of Júlia Mendes, a star of the music theater, performing the

Figure 5.5 Júlia Mendes recording a film with synchronized sound in the 1900s, in *Illustração*, 16 January 1934, 12, Hemeroteca Municipal de Lisboa. Júlia Mendes recording a film with synchronized sound in the 1900s.

---

[165] *Illustração Portugueza*, 25 September 1905, I.

[166] Léon Gaumont, "Means for Operating Synchronously Phonographs and Kinematographs," US Patent 752, 394, 16 February 1904.

[167] *Illustração*, 6 January 1934, 12.

song "Grisette" (probably from Lehár's *The Merry Widow*), a piece she had recorded for the Gramophone Company. The session took place in a courtyard in Lisbon's Rua da Palma and is reproduced in Figure 5.5. The singer is seen against what seems to be a theatrical set while two pairs of men operate the phonograph and the kinematograph, respectively, under the supervision of a fifth. This illustrates the role the stars of the popular theater played in the early cinema and phonography in Portugal. The film promoters relied on the prestige of the stars to attract audiences, and the performers reinforced their fame by extending their presence to a show where they were disembodied and did not compete with their original activity at this stage.

The Establishment of Pathé in Portugal

The multinational recording companies were established in Portugal in the first decade of the 20th century. They included the French-based Compagnie Générale de Phonographes, Cinématographes et Appareils de Précision, owned by the brothers Charles and Émile Pathé. Pathé was created in 1900 through the merger of two companies: the Compagnie Générale de Cinématographes, Phonographes et Pellicules and the Manufacture Française d'Appareils de Précision. The first company was owned by the Pathé brothers and traded in phonography and film. The Manufacture Française was founded by René Bünzli and Pierre Victour Continsouza and concentrated on film. Pathé became the dominant company in the French phonographic market.[168] Its establishment in Portugal reflects the pervasiveness of Parisian models as epitomes of modernity and cosmopolitanism. The sources related to Pathé in Portugal are scarce. The exact date of its establishment is unknown, but it was operating locally as early as 1906. It had a store in Porto and an office in Lisbon, and these facilities traded in a variety of goods. The stores sold phonographs, gramophones, blank cylinders, cylinders with pre-recorded music, and parts and accessories for these machines.[169] Moreover, Pathé ran a wax cylinder recording room in its Porto premises, where a part of its local catalogue may have been recorded.[170]

The business models of the early recording companies relied on patented technology. Thus, the control of patents and licenses influenced the actions of the companies in their targeted markets. Furthermore, it affected the machines and the storage media that could be traded by a company. The most important

---

[168] Gelatt, *The Fabulous Phonograph 1877–1977*, 177.
[169] Phonographos Pathé, *Novo catalogo e repertorio portuguez* (Porto: n.p., 1906).
[170] Phonographos Pathé, *Novo catalogo e repertorio portuguez*.

media for storing sound were the phonograph cylinder and the gramophone disc. Making and replicating these competing media was achieved through different processes,—which are frequently evoked when analyzing the shortcomings of the mass production of cylinders.[171] Multiple master copies of the early cylinders were made by repeating the performance of a given piece on one or several phonographs.[172] Then, the cylinder was duplicated onto a blank cylinder. This was made with the help of a pantograph. In spite of a considerable loss of quality, this process allowed twenty-five to one hundred good copies to be made. Of course, it was an insufficient number to supply an expanding mass market.[173] The development of molding in the first years of the 20th century allowed the master record to be more easily replicated.[174] With this technique, the recorded wax cylinder was plated to create a mold. Molding became the standard procedure for duplicating cylinders, allowing a much larger number of good copies to be obtained.[175] Creating a master recording on a flat disc was far more complicated than making a master cylinder, and could not be made at home. However, discs offered the possibility of mass production from a very early stage. Their replication was easier and better suited for industrial production. The piece was recorded onto a master metallic disc that could be covered with a workable substance, like wax. Then, an acid wash converted the semi-permanent grooves made by the recording stylus into permanent imprints.[176] A sequence of positive and negative copies of the master disc was then made through electroplating. This produced a stamper, which is a metal disc that was a negative copy of the master. The stamper was fitted into a press and was used to replicate the disc in a pliable substrate, like shellac.[177] This allowed for both the preservation of the master disc and for the production of a large number of quality copies.

Pathé started to trade with machines similar to the "Eagle" model of Columbia Graphophone and its cylinders, and expanded its catalogue to gramophones and discs around 1905–1906.[178] Therefore, the 1906 Portuguese

[171] Burt and Welch, *From Tinfoil to Stereo*, 111–126.

[172] Burt and Welch, *From Tinfoil to Stereo*, 82; William Howland Kenney, *Recorded Music in American Life: The Phonograph and Popular Memory, 1890–1945* (Oxford: Oxford University Press, 2003), 42.

[173] David Morton, *Sound Recording: The Life Story of a Technology* (Santa Barbara, CA: Greenwood Press, 2004), 27–28.

[174] Kenney, *Recorded Music in American Life*, 42.

[175] Morton, *Sound Recording*, 28.

[176] Emile Berliner, "Process of Producing Records of Sound", US Patent 382,790, 15 May 1888; "Sound-record and Method To Make Same," US Patent 548,623, 29 October 1895.

[177] Matthias Worgull, *Hot Embossing: Theory and Technology of Microreplication* (Oxford: William Andrew, 2009), 3–8; Steffen, *From Edison to Marconi*, 48–51.

[178] Amitabha Ghosh, "Pre-commercial Era of Sound Recording in India," *Indian Journal of History of Science*, 34/1 (1999), 54.

catalogue may be Pathé's first publication to include local cylinders and discs. Pathé-Frères was operating under Edison licenses and used Edison-related devices for all its European recordings.[179] They used large-diameter cylinders to produce the master records, which were transcribed onto smaller-diameter cylinders.[180] These were sold in three different sizes. Recording masters on cylinders persisted after the company's venture into discs. To make flat records, the sound of the master cylinder was transferred to a disc by using a pantograph.[181] This was similar to duplicating cylinders, and was very direct since Pathé's cylinders and discs were vertically cut. Thus, their grooves were of constant width and variable depth. Because the company was working under Edison's licenses, this avoided juridical complications of patent infractions. Consequently, the discs made by Pathé were very different from those of their competition. They were vertically cut, center-start, and revolved between 90 and 100 rpm, contrasting with the discs made by the Gramophone Company, which were laterally cut, outside-start, and revolved at approximately 70 rpm.[182]

The form of cylinders and discs was associated with their success. Until the development and mass marketing of hard plastic cylinders their frailty was a significant deterrent to their use.[183] This situation prevailed until 1906–1907, when the Indestructible Phonographic Record Company started its trade. Moreover, frailty posed difficulties for the preservation of cylinders. The number of surviving cylinders in Portugal is very small. Storage is also an important consideration when comparing cylinders and discs. Since cylinders could not be effectively stacked the manufacturers had to develop storage cabinets specifically for them. The 1906 Portuguese Pathé catalogue advertised a cabinet that could store up to sixty-four large cylinders, presenting its "spinning library" as an attractive piece of living-room furniture.[184] This was part of the process through which the phonograph became a household item. Phonographic goods were developed in ways that blended in with the surrounding furniture. Discs were sturdier and could be stacked and stored in bulk, something that placed them as collectables.[185] Thus, "records are possessed like photographs; the nineteenth century had good reasons for coming up with phonograph record albums alongside photographic and postage-stamp albums, all of them herbaria of artificial life."[186]

[179] Burt and Welch, *From Tinfoil to Stereo*, 79.
[180] Burt and Welch, *From Tinfoil to Stereo*, 79.
[181] Ghosh, "Pre-commercial Era of Sound Recording in India," 54.
[182] Burt and Welch, *From Tinfoil to Stereo*, 142; Phonographos Pathé, *Catalogo*, 3.
[183] Sterne, *The Audible Past*, 299–301.
[184] Phonographos Pathé, *Catalogo*, 11.
[185] Thompson, "Machines, Music, and the Quest for Fidelity," 142.
[186] Theodor W. Adorno, "The Form of the Phonograph Record," *October*, 55 (1990), 58.

Nevertheless, an analysis based on technology falls short in explaining the dominance of the flat disc over the phonographic cylinder. A recurrent argument was that the phonograph had multiple uses, as it could record and reproduce sound. This enhanced its introduction in the mass market when compared with the gramophone's sole functionality of reproducing pre-fixed sounds. However, "the manufacturers of cylinder talking machines considered their machines' capability to record anywhere a great sales advantage over the new disc talking machines; the disc machines could not provide such capability."[187] The possibility of homemade phonograph recordings promoted an "active engagement from Victorians, who could readily make their own amateur records at home rather than purchase them."[188] This feature created a major cultural change in the early 20th century as the gramophone became the main supplier of recorded sound in a household. Victorian domesticity favored specific ways of informal archiving, which included family albums or home sound recordings, and the parlor was the place where the "formal presentation and the maintenance of family identity" occupied center stage.[189] It had no room to accommodate mass entertainment, since it was intended to be an unviolated space in a profane world, a retreat from ever-encroaching modernity.[190] The living room replaced the parlor in the early 20th century.[191] This reflected a transformation in domestic living space. The earlier parlor was a space "largely populated with hand-crafted goods and family-specific cultural productions."[192] It was transformed into a room that was "considerably more informal in decor and arrangement" that "admitted more and more mass produced goods."[193] Moreover, "the middle-class consumer culture that would provide the cultural, economic, and affective basis for building collections of recordings and extensive listening to prerecorded music was only just emerging as these machines [gramophones] became available."[194]

The first pages of Pathé's Portuguese catalogue advertise the company and its store, recording room, and workshop, also presenting its phonographs, gramophones, cylinders, cylinder storage cabinets, and accessories such as horns or diaphragms.[195] Most of the catalogue is dedicated to the repertoire. It

---

[187] Burt and Welch, *From Tinfoil to Stereo*, 81.
[188] Picker, *Victorian Soundscapes*, 112.
[189] Sterne, *The Audible Past*, 204.
[190] Holly Kruse, "Early Audio Technology and Domestic Space," *Stanford Humanities Review* 3 (1993), 6.
[191] Sterne, *The Audible Past*, 204.
[192] Sterne, *The Audible Past*, 204.
[193] Sterne, *The Audible Past*, 204.
[194] Sterne, *The Audible Past*, 204.
[195] Phonographos Pathé, *Catalogo*, 1–12.

is arranged by performer, which shows the dominance of content over media. The prominence of performers had been crucial for the recording industry since its early stages. Most artist sections include a photograph and a handwritten note by the performer. If it was a group, the leader would write the note. These notes praise the fidelity of the Pathé machines. The actress/singer Palmira Bastos even compared the recordings made by a Pathé phonograph to a "photograph of the voice."[196] This draws an interesting parallel between phonography and phonography. This comparison can be analyzed from different perspectives. It features in a text that advertises a company on the basis that the fidelity of the sound recording is on the same level as the fidelity of the photograph. Moreover, it links two technologies that were perceived as guarantors of objectivity or as neutral conveyors of reality. Therefore, the idea that the phonograph captured the "real" and inscribed it into the cylinder was important in its advertising. This discourse on fidelity can be found throughout the early history of phonography and reveals a "kind of faith in reproducibility."[197] Listeners were encouraged to discern the different "sonic signatures" of the apparatus as their familiarity with sound reproduction devices grew.[198] The impossibility of achieving a gold standard for these recordings established a framework in which "the best available or the preferable became a stand-in for the true."[199] One point that emanates from this discussion is reproducibility itself. Moreover, it poses the relationship between the "original" and the "copy" differently. The correspondence between live music and recorded music worked mostly in the imagination of the listeners.[200] Thus, a correspondence between them had to be made since "the sound event is created for the explicit purpose of its reproduction."[201] Therefore, "copy and original are products of the process of reproducibility."[202] In this sense, the narrative that draws a direct path from original to copy through a process of technological mediation must be reframed, because the creation of a contrast between original and copy itself is only admissible due to the very possibility of sound reproduction. "We can no longer argue that copies are debased versions of a more authentic original that exists either outside or prior to the process of reproduction."[203]

The music recorded by Pathé was varied and mirrored the work of the recording artists in the local entertainment market. Recordings were sold in

---

[196] Phonographos Pathé, *Catalogo*, 14.
[197] Sterne, *The Audible Past*, 274.
[198] Sterne, *The Audible Past*, 275.
[199] Sterne, *The Audible Past*, 275.
[200] Sterne, *The Audible Past*, 284.
[201] Sterne, *The Audible Past*, 241, 284.
[202] Sterne, *The Audible Past*, 241.
[203] Sterne, *The Audible Past*, 241.

three distinct formats: as discs and as two sizes of cylinders. Palmira Bastos, a star of the popular music theater, recorded songs from plays. She had already performed a large part of her repertoire (if not all) on Portuguese and Brazilian stages before recording the songs.[204] The recordings include pieces from Offenbach's *La Périchole* and *Barba-azul*, Audran's *La poupée*, Clérice's *O moleiro d'Alcalá*, and Cyriaco de Cardoso's *O solar dos Barrigas*, as well as songs from the *revista Tim tim por tim tim*.[205] This reinforces the practice of recording companies to hire famous performers to perform pieces that were already part of their repertoire and were associated with them by the audiences. Avelino Baptista recorded fados and "popular songs" as well as a piece from the operetta *Os sinos de Corneville*.[206] He was a distinguished performer of fado associated with Coimbra. However, an autonomous Coimbra tradition was not yet in place. Eduardo Barreiros recorded operetta, fados and "popular songs," while the *cançoneta* was the genre more recorded by Duarte Silva.[207] Fados and "popular songs" occupied a dominant place in the recordings of Isabel Costa or Cristina Tapa.[208] Apart from solo songs, Pathé recorded some duets and choruses from operettas and *revistas*.[209] In addition, its catalogue included monologues performed by the actor and playwright Pedro Bandeira.[210] The variety of the theatrical offering is partly reflected in the Pathé catalogue, illustrating the role played by the operetta and the *revista* in the marketing of cultural goods. Some pieces were not associated with the theater. For example, the famous singer and guitarist Reinaldo Varela recorded fados with Portuguese guitar accompaniment and also recorded a few guitar solos.[211] The actress Rafaela Fons recorded a number of Spanish and Latin American songs.[212] The catalogue also included instrumental pieces for solo piano, for Portuguese guitar and Spanish guitar, and for mandolin and piano.[213] *Bandas* were also represented in the catalogues of the recording companies. The Band of the Municipal Guard of Porto and the Band of the Real Oficina de S. José recorded anthems, marches, rhapsodies, and dances.[214] The Oficina was a religious institution devoted to the care and education of young men whose

---

[204] Eudinyr Fraga, "Teatro brasileiro no fim do século XIX," *Luso-Brazilian Review*, 35/2 (1998), 14–15.

[205] Phonographos Pathé, *Catalogo*, 15.

[206] Fraga, "Teatro brasileiro no fim do século XIX," 17.

[207] Phonographos Pathé, *Catalogo*, 23–24, 29.

[208] Phonographos Pathé, *Catalogo*, 21, 35.

[209] Phonographos Pathé, *Catalogo*, 21, 47.

[210] Phonographos Pathé, *Catalogo*, 49.

[211] Phonographos Pathé, *Catalogo*, 47, 54.

[212] Phonographos Pathé, *Catalogo*, 53–54.

[213] Phonographos Pathé, *Catalogo*, 61.

[214] Phonographos Pathé, *Catalogo*, 51, 57–58.

family could not support them. The attention given to the *bandas* is associated with the fact that wind and percussion instruments were easier to record than string instruments.[215] This contributed to the proliferation of this type of recording. Nevertheless, Pathé and other companies recorded solo string instruments. However, recording *bandas* was both a reflection and a promotion of this type of ensemble in Portugal and elsewhere, a growing tendency in this period.[216] Although most of the repertoire had been previously issued in other forms, phonography introduced a novel form of relation between the listener and the music, a connection that fostered a specific form of privacy and of property. Moreover, the commodification of sound presupposes private property, and is associated with an acoustic space that relied on privacy and individuality.[217]

The Companhia Franceza do Gramophone

The Gramophone Company was established in Britain and traded exclusively in gramophones and discs. It contrasted with Pathé, which sold both phonographs and gramophones, and their associated products. The gramophone was developed by Emile Berliner as a hand-operated device.[218] It was later improved with a spring motor patented by Eldridge Johnson.[219] This facilitated its introduction into the mass market that was being created. As a result of this, "in the first years of the century, the Gramophone Company had a virtual monopoly on the record market in Europe, thanks to its initial control of Berliner's sound recording patents."[220] Their record pressing plant was built in Hannover in 1898, and was run by Emile Berliner's brother, Joseph. This reduced their dependence on American imports.[221] From that year on, the company assembled gramophones, manufactured disc records, and marketed the finished products.[222] It was clearly organized on a model of vertical integration. The early recording of gramophone discs faced an important obstacle.

---

[215] Steffen, *From Edison To Marconi*, 106.

[216] See the recording sheet of the march "Le drapeau de la liberté" by the Musique de la Garde Republicaine, Paris, January 1904. Serial number 2454, extant both in the EMI Archive and in the British Library.

[217] Sterne, *The Audible Past*, 138.

[218] Emile Berliner, "Gramophone," US Patent 564,586, 28 July 1896. (This letter states that the English patent for the gramophone was granted on 8 November 1887).

[219] Eldridge E. Johnson, "Spring-motor," US Patent 689,884, 31 December 1901.

[220] Gronow and Englung, "Inventing Recorded Music," 285.

[221] Geoffrey Jones, "The Gramophone Company," 80.

[222] Peter Martland, *Recording History*, 53.

A Bell-Tainter patent covered the use of wax as a recording substance.[223] To avoid legal issues, Gramophone's early master discs were first etched in zinc.[224] However, when the Bell-Tainter patent expired in 1900, the company began to use wax to record their masters, improving the sound quality of the product.[225]

The creation of the Gramophone Company was a complex operation that stretched from 1897 to 1900 and involved American and British agents.[226] The Gramophone Company secured the control of the British and European patents held by Emile Berliner and by Eldridge Johnson for the gramophone and its related goods.[227] It also secured a dominant multinational role by creating subsidiary companies and marketing branches in Germany, Italy, France, Russia, Austria-Hungary, and Australia. In addition, it created a network of local agents, who were partly responsible for selecting artists and repertoires to be recorded for a branch.[228] Portugal was part of the area covered by the Compagnie Française du Gramophone (French Gramophone Company) as a result of the division of the European market into several regions. By 1898, the Gramophone Company had opened a salesroom in Paris. Alfred Clark, an American former associate of Edison, developed a partnership with them in the subsequent year. Clark established a selling agency in Paris, known as the Compagnie Française du Gramophone, and, as a manager and partial owner, he became responsible for recording music from the places supervised by his company.[229] The earliest recordings in Portugal for the Gramophone Company were made in Porto between late October and early November 1900.[230] They were part of a European venture led by William Sinkler Darby, an American engineer trained by Emile Berliner.[231] In this journey, Darby made seventy

---

[223] Sumner Tainter, "Recording and Reproducing Sounds," US Patent 341,287, 4 May 1886.

[224] Emile Berliner, "Sound-record and Method of Making Same," US Patent 548,623, 29 October 1895.

[225] Welch and Burt, *From Tinfoil to Stereo*, 109; Ogilvie Mitchell, *The Talking Machine Industry* (London: Sir Isaac Pitman, [1922]), 38; Morton, *Sound Recording*, 38.

[226] Martland, *Recording History*, 46–61.

[227] Martland, *Recording History*, 25, 54.

[228] Martland, "A Business History of the Gramophone Company Ltd: 1897–1918," Ph.D. thesis (Cambridge University, 1992), 95, 110; Gronow and Englung, "Inventing Recorded Music," 285.

[229] Jones, "The Gramophone Company," 83.

[230] Susana Belchior, "Sinkler Darby's 1900 Expedition for the Gramophone Company in Portugal," in Pekka Gronow and Christiane Hofer (eds.), *Contributions to the History of the Record Industry: Beiträge zur Geschichte der Schallplattenindustrie*, vol. 5 (Vienna: Gesellschaft für Historische Tonträger, 2010), 15.

[231] Paul Vernon, *A History of the Portuguese Fado* (Aldershot: Ashgate, 2000), 59; Gronow and Englung, "Inventing Recorded Music," 282; Martland, *Recording History*, 53.

pressings of Portuguese artists, reflecting the company's international strategy of recording local performers whose repertoire was being popularized through other media.[232] Despite pressing the records of Sinkler Darby's 1900 recording sessions, the Companhia Franceza do Gramophone needed three years to become established in Portugal.[233] Nevertheless, its Porto recordings were included in a catalogue featuring French, Italian, Spanish, and Portuguese records issued around 1900.[234] Starting toward the end of 1903, this company relied on a number of local agents to sell their goods, like Santos Diniz and Carlos Calderon (in Lisbon) and Artur Barbedo (in Porto). Given the prominence of local agents and the role the popular stage played in the company's output, it is possible that Calderon might have been involved in the development of the company's Portuguese catalogue before establishing his record business. He was already an integrated professional in the theater, and became involved with the Sociedade Phonographica Portugueza, a local venture that traded in phonographic goods.[235] With Arthur Barbedo he registered the brand Ideal in 1906.[236] Ideal was a partnership with the German firm Beka Records that became part of the Carl Lindström group in 1910. The Portuguese firm kept its relationship with Beka, and Calderon became the Portuguese representative of Odeon.[237] Knowledge of the technical process enabled the recording engineers to identify the voices that were better suited for recording purposes making them the most important individuals in the process of selecting the artists to be recorded.[238] Thus, the ability to project the voice was valued over other aspects. Apart from relying on local agents, the Companhia Franceza do Gramophone established a store that traded exclusively in its goods. It was located in the center of Lisbon but it did not last long. The company also developed a lasting and aggressive advertising campaign in local periodicals. They promoted their Lisbon facilities, the company's agents, the artists, the music, and the machines in a series of graphically appealing page-long advertisements.[239] However, this shop closed in 1906 and the company's catalogue

---

[232] Belchior, "Sinkler Darby's 1900 Expedition," 17.

[233] Losa, "Indústria fonográfica," 633; Losa and Belchior, "The Introduction of Phonogram Market in Portugal," 7.

[234] Grammophon, *Verzeichnis französischer, italienischer, spanischer, portugiesischer Platten* (Berlin: J. S. Preuss, [1900]).

[235] Losa, *Machinas fallantes*, 69–74.

[236] Losa, *Machinas fallantes*, 57.

[237] Losa, *Machinas fallantes*, 72.

[238] Peter Martland, *Since Records Began: Emi, the First 100 Years* (London: Batsford, 1997), 25–27; Martland, *Recording History*, 12.

[239] Losa and Belchior, "The Introduction of Phonogram Market in Portugal," 7. See *Illustração portugueza*, 19 December 1904, II.

of January 1910 stated that Francesco Stella had become the local agent. His store was located in Rua da Assunção, in Lisbon's commercial district.[240]

At the time, phonographic products were marketed to the well-to-do, and the advertising strategy of the Companhia Franceza do Gramophone associated the ownership of the gramophone and its records as signs of social prestige. Thus, in the late 19th and early 20th centuries, owning phonographic products bestowed prestige and implied modernity. Apart from the "popular gramophone" mentioned above, a number of advertisements linked phonography with social status and distinction. Most of the repertoire advertised belonged to the company's international catalogue, consisting of records from Gramophone's more prestigious labels, like Monarch or Concert.[241] An interesting case that contrasts with the overall tendency to record repertoires that were already known to the audience is included in one of these advertisements.[242] Ruggiero Leoncavallo's "Mattinata" was composed for a Caruso Concert Red Label recording in which the composer played the piano. Its royalties belonged to the Italian subsidiary of the Gramophone Company, prefiguring the dominant model for the recording industry of the later part of the century. Moreover, the sheet music published in Germany by Roehr includes the catalogue number for both Italian and German Gramophone recordings of the song.[243] Sound recording and sheet music were not perceived as competing but as complementary goods whose symbiotic relationship could boost the sales of each.

The Companhia Franceza do Gramophone published an advertisement in *Ilustração Portuguesa* stating that the best Christmas gift would be a gramophone, a "chic and elegant present."[244] It also mentions the "luxury gramophones" that were available in the company's Lisbon outlet. These advertisements presented the gramophone as an icon of sophistication, revealing Gramophone's advertisement strategy. The company promoted gramophones and discs as high-quality goods, while their strategy was to produce cheap records for a volume market.[245] This efficient marketing strategy stressed the symbolic value of phonographic goods, indicating that people were paying for prestige and modern sophistication. The British record dealerships that traded in the Gramophone Company's goods were prestigious piano dealers that

---

[240] Companhia Franceza do Gramophone, *Catalogo geral dos discos* (Lisbon: Companhia Franceza do Gramophone, 1910).

[241] *Illustração portugueza*, 3 July 1905, III.

[242] *Illustração portugueza*, 3 July 1905, III.

[243] Ruggiero Leoncavallo, *Mattinata* (Berlin: Roehr A.G., [1904]).

[244] *Illustração portugueza*, 18 December 1905, I.

[245] Martland, *Recording History*, 162.

occupied premises in the areas in which potential costumers circulated.[246] This strategic placement of phonographic products was a way of capitalizing on the respectability of the retailers. Pianos embodied social status in the first part of the 19th century and gramophones were their 20th century counterpart. Moreover, the dealers argued that trading on recorded sound helped to promote the sales of their sheet music.[247] This developed differently in Portugal. Most music stores did not sell phonographic goods. Nevertheless, they were situated in the same areas as the gramophone stores. This shows that "consumption is always spatial: it is based on the spatial-aesthetic arrangement, associations, and display of commodities in social space."[248]

However, there is a lack of reliable information pertaining to Gramophone's local recordings between Darby's recording expedition and the *Supplemento ao catalogo de discos portuguezes* (Supplement to the Catalogue of Portuguese Records) published in November 1905. Nevertheless, Alfred Clark informed the mother company in 1904 that "of the discs sold in Portugal about two-fifths are Italian, two-fifths Spanish, and one-fifth Portuguese."[249] This might be a generalization, but it confirms the existence of local recordings from an early stage. Moreover, an advertisement published in *Ilustração portuguesa* supports Clark's statement.[250] It included information on "freshly arrived records"—like sheet music publishers, recording companies promoted their goods focusing on novelty.[251] Most consisted of imported music from the company's international catalogue but there were also a few local recordings. The repertoire includes Italian opera arias performed by famous singers like Enrico Caruso, Mattia Battistini, or Luisa Bresonier. They belonged to the high-end segment of the company's offering, the Monarch Red Label or the Concert Red Label. The advertisement also included records by French, Italian, Spanish, and Portuguese military bands that were released on the company's Concert Black label. The band of the Guarda Municipal de Lisboa (Municipal Guard of Lisbon) recorded waltzes, gavottes, and mazurkas by Portuguese composers. They also recorded Portuguese anthems and marches, such as the "Hino da Carta," the "Hino da Restauração," and "A Portuguesa," as well as the Brazilian national anthem. Its repertoire was

---

[246] Martland, *Recording History*, 173.

[247] Martland, *Recording History*, 173.

[248] Alexander Styhre and Tobias Engberg, "Spaces of Consumption: From Margin to Centre," *ephemera*, 3/2 (2003), 121.

[249] Correspondence between Alfred Clark, Compagnie Française du Gramophone, and the Gramophone & Typewriter's offices in London, 5 May 1904. I would like to thank Susana Belchior for this reference.

[250] *Illustração portugueza*, 3 July 1905, III.

[251] *Illustração portugueza*, 3 July 1905, III.

Figure 5.6 Advertisement of the popular gramophone, in *Illustração Portugueza*, 25 September 1905, Front cover verso, Hemeroteca Municipal de Lisboa. Advertisement of the popular gramophone.

varied and included the popular stage. The *banda* also recorded numbers from the operetta *A capital federal* and the *revista Nicles!* .[252] One advertisement for the "popular gramophone" illustrates the early stage of market segmentation. The advertisement, reproduced in Figure 5.6 concentrates exclusively on the "popular gramophone." It compares its price with other gramophone models. Moreover, the repertoire was local and totally coincident with the *Supplemento ao catalogo de discos portuguezes*.[253] This reveals a complex strategy undertaken by the Companhia. They attempted to maximize the impact of the advertising campaigns by addressing the taste markers of different social strata. The most expensive models were associated with their high-end labels and the local popular repertoire was advertised with cheaper machines. Needless to say, the Portuguese market was dominated by the local genres.

[252] Companhia Franceza do Gramophone, *Catalogo das ultimas placas feitas pela Companhia Franceza do Gramophone* (Lisbon: n.p., 1906).
[253] *Illustração portugueza*, 13 November 1905, III.

At the beginning of the 20th century, advertisements that emphasized the most prestigious recordings of the company's international catalogue coexisted with publications promoting cheaper machines and local repertoire. As discussed above, the local repertoires consisted predominantly of well-known songs: fado, *cançoneta, canção popular* (popular song). The catalogues also included arrangements of pieces from *revistas* and operettas for instrumental ensembles, instrumental pieces recorded by wind bands (such as marches and anthems), and comical ("eccentric") monologue or dialogue sketches.[254] These correspond almost directly to the segments presented by Gronow and Englund in their work ("Singing actors, Singing comedians, Choirs and vocal ensembles, Spoken word, Wind bands, Solo instruments, Miscellaneous, Revue artists, comedians, declamation").[255] This illustrates that the selection of the artists and repertoires by the early recording companies obeyed the same rules in several countries.

In the early stage, the discs of the Companhia Franceza do Gramophone's were organized by labels and by dimension. In the Portuguese catalogues from 1905 to 1907, the repertoire was divided into 12-inch Monarch records, 10-inch Concert records, and 7-inch "small plate" records.[256] Nevertheless, there is a section in the 1907 catalogue devoted to the Zonophone label.[257] This indicates that a new perspective in market segmentation was arising. As mentioned above, the colors of the labels, especially the Monarch Red and the Concert Black, were included in the company's advertisements from an early stage. This information was included in the 1908 Portuguese catalogue. The company offered 12-inch Monarch records (with red, pink, green, and buff labels), 10-inch Concert records (only specifying its red and pink labels for the "artistic recordings"), and 10-inch Zonophone records.[258] It no longer included 7-inch discs. The separation by label was reflected in the pricing of the records. The Monarch labels were the most expensive of the catalogue, followed by the Concert labels. Zonophone records were the cheapest, a fact that relates to the history of the company. Initially, the International Zonophone Company was owned by Frank Seaman and manufactured and traded the

---

[254] Losa and Belchior, "The Introduction of Phonogram Market in Portugal," 9–10.

[255] Losa and Belchior, "The Introduction of Phonogram Market in Portugal," 9–11; Gronow and Englung, "Inventing Recorded Music," 288–293.

[256] Companhia Franceza do Gramophone, *Supplemento ao catalogo de discos portuguezes* (Lisbon: n.p., 1905); Companhia Franceza do Gramophone, *Catalogo das ultimas placas feitas pela Companhia Franceza do Gramophone* (Lisbon: n.p., 1906); *Compagnie Française du Gramophone, Repertoire portuguais: Disques "Gramophone" & disques "Zonophone" double-face* (n.p.: n.p., 1907).

[257] Compagnie Française du Gramophone, *Repertoire portuguais*.

[258] Companhia Franceza do Gramophone, *Novo catalogo de discos portuguezes* (Lisbon: n.p., 1908).

same goods as the Gramophone Company.[259] However, in the summer of 1903 it was bought by Gramophone and became its budget label.[260] This shows a dual strategy that relied on marketing the most prestigious discs and machines to a high-end market while developing a popular catalogue to cater to a growing mass market.[261] Therefore, the early phonographic industry reflected and amplified the segmentation between art and entertainment as part of a strategy for maximizing profit.

The mass production of double-sided discs transformed the recording industry. The German-based Odeon presented its first double-sided records in a 1904 Leipzig fair.[262] This format rapidly became the industry's standard. Until then, recordings were made either on a cylinder or in a single-sided disc. Thus, each recording corresponded to a single work. Thereafter, the same record was able to contain two pieces. This development was frequently used in the advertisements of the companies, which emphasized novelty.[263] The new technique changed the ratio use value/exchange value in a favorable way for the consumer. Although the Portuguese advertisements that promoted double-sided records by the Companhia Franceza do Gramophone date from 1905, the first local catalogue to include them was published in 1907. This indicates that the first double-sided records were foreign. Nevertheless, the 1907 catalogue included both single-sided and double-sided records. The double-sided records belonged to the Zonophone label. This reflects the role played by the Zonophone in Gramophone's catalogue management as a producer of cheap records and machines for a larger market, contrasting with the high-end goods represented by more prestigious labels of the group.

The most complete source for studying the Companhia Franceza do Gramophone's Portuguese venture is the 1908 Portuguese catalogue. It is a comprehensive publication and includes records from earlier catalogues. The year 1908 was a fruitful one for recording. A "truly typical and original repertoire" that included Portuguese regional songs and fados accompanied by Portuguese guitar was selected.[264] New singers apart from the "ones who are used to sing in every talking machine" were hired and taken to Paris to record the new selections.[265] This indicates that the pool of recording artists

---

[259] Welch and Burt, *From Tinfoil to Stereo*, 100–101.
[260] Gronow and Englung, "Inventing Recorded Music," 285.
[261] Martland, *Recording History*, 164.
[262] Worgull, *Hot Embossing*, 4–5.
[263] *Illustração portugueza*, 18 December 1905, I.
[264] Companhia Franceza do Gramophone, *Novo catalogo de discos portuguezes* (Lisbon: n.p., 1908), 1.
[265] Companhia Franceza do Gramophone, *Novo catalogo*, 1.

was growing as well as the repertoire. The catalogue is divided into local and foreign records. Foreign records were subdivided into new recordings and re-issues, with the latter mixing criteria like performers, media types, and labels. Moreover, its Portuguese section appears to be segmented inconsistently by genre, label, or artist. It begins with a section that contains songs and *cançonetas* that had been written specifically for the gramophone by people like Baptista Diniz.[266] The catalogue includes solo popular songs with choruses and duets, as well as a "repertoire of fados." They were presented as the "truly typical fado, solely accompanied by the Portuguese guitar."[267] This shows that the notion of authenticity was already associated with this genre from a very early stage. A large number of early fados were recorded with piano accompaniment, which may indicate that their sheet music was used for the recording session.[268] This demonstrates the spread of musical goods in the Portuguese leisure market, whereby a product of sound recording was based in another commodity. Moreover, the technological limitations of the acoustic recordings may have influenced the choice of the piano over the Portuguese guitar. The piano was easier to record because of its greater ability to project sound.[269]

The catalogue includes discs that, on one side, contained solo pieces for the Portuguese guitar (fados or waltzes) and sung fados on the other.[270] Portuguese regional songs were selected in their "absolutely typical fashion" from places like Minho, Alentejo, and Coimbra.[271] A large number of these integrated the *Cancioneiro de músicas populares*, by Neves and Campos. Thus, the *Cancioneiro* provided the sheet music for their recording. Opera numbers were recorded with a large orchestra by Portuguese artists. These include the "Desgarrada" of Alfredo Keil's *Serrana*, and Puccini's "Mi chiamano Mimì" (from *La bohème*) and "Vissi d'arte" (from *Tosca*).[272] In the catalogues of Pathé and Companhia Franceza do Gramophone it is clearly stated when a selection had orchestral accompaniment. This serves to clearly distinguish them from the more frequent records that were accompanied by the piano. However, recording an orchestra acoustically raised important issues. Musical works were significantly transformed for recording.

[266] Companhia Franceza do Gramophone, *Novo catalogo*, 2–5.
[267] Companhia Franceza do Gramophone, *Novo catalogo*, 5–6.
[268] Rui Vieira Nery, *Para uma história do Fado* (Lisbon: Público/Corda Seca, 2004), 138–140; Leonor Losa, "'Nós humanizámos a indústria': reconfiguração de produção fonográfica e musical em Portugal na década de 60," master's thesis (Universidade Nova de Lisboa, 2009), 36–37.
[269] Leonor Losa, personal communication, 4 July 2010.
[270] Companhia Franceza do Gramophone, *Novo catalogo*, 6–7.
[271] Companhia Franceza do Gramophone, *Novo catalogo*, 7–10.
[272] Companhia Franceza do Gramophone, *Novo catalogo*, 7–10.

Instruments that did not record well, like cello and double bass, were substituted by tubas and trombones.[273] Therefore, recording an orchestra often involved a transformation of instrumentation and of the composer's intent. Orchestral pieces had to be adapted to produce a better recording. This complicates Adorno's statement that phonography only stored and recorded music "that was already in existence before the phonograph record and is not significantly altered by it."[274] Music had to be substantially altered so it could meet the audience's expectations.

The 1908 catalogue includes instrumental recordings of dances, anthems, and rhapsodies performed by the band of the Guarda Municipal de Lisboa.[275] It also comprises spoken pieces (the "eccentric and monologue" category). The companies started to re-issue single-sided records as double-sided discs when these became widely available. Therefore, a large part of the music recorded on the double-sided records had already been issued as single-sided discs.[276] This reveals a strategy that aimed to maximize the profit generated by the company's repertoire. A strand focused on new recordings while the other concentrated on re-issues. The recordings of famous performers like Avelino Baptista, Duarte Silva, Manassés de Lacerda, Reinaldo Varela, César Nunes, Almeida Cruz, Eduardo Barreiros, Jaime Silva, and Júlia Mendes were re-issued in this process. This indicates that some songs and performers were part of the local entertainment market for a significant period. The Portuguese catalogue also advertised imported records, including bands and orchestras, Baroque to Romantic chamber and orchestral music, and virtuosos like Kubelik and Sarasate.[277] However, the foreign music is dominated by operatic selections performed by famous singers and recorded in single-sided discs. The price for these pieces was higher than for the double-sided records, and proportional to the number of soloists involved.[278] This shows that these recordings were directed to a high-end market. They had money to attend the Real Teatro de S. Carlos and to buy expensive records as a form of social distinction. Therefore, the association of opera with forms of entertainment that, to a certain extent, reflected a type of cultural capital (its "high-art" segment) played a key role

---

[273] Suisman, "'Sound, Knowledge, and the 'Immanence of Human Failure,'" 23.

[274] Theodor W. Adorno, "The Form of the Phonograph Record," *October*, 55 (1990), 57.

[275] Companhia Franceza do Gramophone, *Novo catalogo*, 11–13.

[276] Compagnie Française du Gramophone, *Repertoire portuguai* and Companhia Franceza do Gramophone, *Novo catalogo*.

[277] Companhia Franceza do Gramophone, *Novo catalogo*, 19–28.

[278] Companhia Franceza do Gramophone, *Novo catalogo*, 28–32.

in Gramophone's marketing strategy. Nevertheless, this seems to have had a limited impact in Portugal.

This strategy was based on the conspicuous and systematic differentiation of records through their distinct packaging and pricing. This began when Gramophone's Fred Gaisberg toured Russia and recorded singers of the Imperial Opera, and a local dealer suggested he sold the discs with conspicuous red labels.[279] This can be interpreted as a strategy to enhance the symbolic meaning of these goods, a shared strategy of the Gramophone Company and the Victor Talking Machine Company.[280] In October 1901 Victor was formed in Camden, New Jersey, by Eldridge Johnson to sell gramophones and records. Given their proximity with Berliner, they developed a strong commercial relationship with the Gramophone Company, and formalized their relationship in an agreement signed in June 1907, dividing the world market between them.[281] This illustrates the strong transatlantic relations between these institutions, which was central to their positioning in the worldwide market.

The printing of a separate catalogue for Red Label records in America and their distinctive label color supported the claim made by the Gramophone Company and by Victor and their dealers that these goods were qualitatively distinct from their competition.[282] Consequently, the object reflected and embodied a strategy of market differentiation that relied on the symbolic capital of these recordings. Each single-sided disc contained a "single and singular music performance," and aimed to create a surrogate aura in the age of the mechanical reproduction of the work of art, "a kind of counter-narrative to consumer society itself—an illusion of uniqueness based on mass-produced intimacy."[283] This clearly echoes Adorno's notion of pseudo-individuation. Nevertheless, it is repositioned from popular music to art music because recorded opera became a commodity that occupied a dominant position among the companies.[284] Thus, a division between art music and popular music is blurred through commodification.

---

[279] David Suisman, *Selling Sounds: The Commercial Revolution in American Music* (Cambridge, MA: Harvard University Press, 2009), 105.

[280] David Suisman, *Selling Sounds* 111.

[281] Frank Hoffman, *Encyclopedia of Recorded Sound* (London: Routledge, 2004), 901.

[282] Suisman, *Selling Sounds*, 111.

[283] Suisman, *Selling Sounds*, 111.

[284] Theodor W. Adorno, "On Popular Music," in Richard Leppert (ed.), *Essays on Music: Theodor W. Adorno* (Berkeley: University of California Press, 2002), 437–470.

Local Entrepreneurs in the Portuguese Phonographic Market

José Castelo Branco created the Sociedade Fabricante de Discos—Disco Simplex C. B. in the beginning of the 20th century. Simplex was a local company that created an important local record catalogue.[285] The store was in the Rua das Portas de Santo Antão (then Rua de Santo Antão, parallel to the Avenida da Liberdade), and originally imported Dutch bicycles. Bicycles were then introduced in several countries as a fashionable and modern product.[286] This framework is similar to the worldwide spread of phonographic goods. Simplex began to advertise records and talking machines in 1905, indicating that their business had changed.[287] Castelo Branco conducted an advertising campaign to promote his venture that included giving away 125 talking machines in November 1909.[288] Simplex sold records from its catalogue and from the German-based Odeon.[289] Figure 5.7 shows the store at the beginning of the 20th century. The small shop traded in talking machines, and on "double-face discs containing the best novelties." It also sold records by Simplex and by Odeon.

By the 20th century the geographic spectrum of the international recording companies in Portugal had widened. Up to this point, these were based either in France (like Pathé) or in Britain (like the Gramophone Company). However, smaller German labels played a very important role in the local record business.[290] This is because of "the lack of investment on the part of international companies and the poor system of agencing and distribution of phonograms" in Portugal.[291]

The *Boletim da propriedade industrial* published Simplex's registration for a record brand in August 1906.[292] According to the surviving discs and their 1908 catalogue, Simplex's output mirrors the local offering of the other recording companies. It concentrates on theatrical and regional songs.[293] These were

---

[285] Losa and Belchior, "The Introduction of Phonogram Market in Portugal," 7–11.

[286] G. B. Norcliffe, *The Ride to Modernity: The Bicycle in Canada, 1869–1900* (Toronto: University of Toronto Press, 2001).

[287] *Illustração portugueza*, 12 November 1906 and 20 April 1908.

[288] *Illustração portugueza*, 25 October 1909.

[289] Municipal Archive of Lisbon, shelfmark PT/AMLSB/AF/JBN/000985.

[290] Losa and Belchior, "The Introduction of Phonogram Market in Portugal," 10.

[291] Losa and Belchior, "The Introduction of Phonogram Market in Portugal," 10.

[292] Losa and Belchior, "The Introduction of Phonogram Market in Portugal," 8. See Ministério das Obras Públicas, Comercio e Industria. Repartição da Industria, *Boletim da propriedade industrial*, August 1906, 316.

[293] Losa and Belchior, "The Introduction of Phonogram Market in Portugal," 10; Discos Simplex e Odeon, *Catalogo para 1908* (Lisbon: Discos Simplex, 1908).

Figure 5.7 Joshua Benoliel, Casa Odeon, gramophones and discs, Lisbon, early 20th century, Arquivo Fotográfico de Lisboa, Colecção Joshua Benoliel, PT/AMLSB/JBN/ 000985. Casa Odeon, a store that traded in gramophones and discs in Lisbon.

performed by Duarte Silva, Eduardo Barreiros, Isabel Costa, Júlia Mendes, Emília d'Oliveira, or Reinaldo Varela. It illustrates the reliance of the recording industry on a small number of artists whose recording contracts did not contemplate exclusivity. Moreover, Simplex sold arrangements for *banda* of anthems, marches, dances, and theatrical songs performed by both local and German ensembles. Their catalogue also included Spanish songs, operatic selections, tangos, French operetta and a few solo instrumental recordings.[294] The 1908 catalogue is arranged by size and repertoire and its records are all double-faced. Its organization is similar to the 1908 Gramophone catalogue. The Portuguese agents were dependent on imported goods and technicians, which motivated a strong relationship between local traders and foreign companies. Therefore, the absence of recording equipment and engineers in Portugal barred local record publishers from producing their own catalogue.[295] To compensate, a beneficial relationship between foreign companies and small Portuguese record publishers had to be established. This gave a more prominent role to the local dealers and fostered a stronger interaction between

---

[294] Discos Simplex e Odeon, *Catalogo para 1908* (Lisbon: Discos Simplex, 1908).
[295] Losa and Belchior, "The Introduction of Phonogram Market in Portugal," 10.

them and the foreign recording companies. This proximity is illustrated in the reliance of Castelo Branco on German companies to record and release the repertoire for Simplex. Therefore, a "mixed series" of recordings was released, and companies like Beka, Odeon, or Homophon used certain prefixes to identify Portuguese recordings in their catalogues.[296] Conversely, the references of some Portuguese recordings conformed to the series of the multinational companies. Thus, Portuguese recordings became available by both local labels and by international companies.[297]

A 1905 group of Simplex and Homophon records illustrates this tendency. They were recorded by Hermann Eisner, then manager/owner and technical director of the company, in a single expedition that took place in May 1905.[298] The Simplex and the Homophon phonograms recorded in 1905 started with a spoken announcement saying "Disco Simplex."[299] This indicates that the recordings were meant to be released by Simplex. Moreover, the discs released by both companies were probably pressed in the same plant.[300] Thus, Simplex records followed a different business model than the multinational companies like Pathé or the Gramophone Company. Simplex created a partnership with foreign companies to record and press their discs. This relationship between local and multinational companies is characteristic of peripheral markets, like Portugal. Nevertheless, small companies of other countries used the same strategy. Therefore, the activity of a small number of local entrepreneurs that worked closely with German-based companies was fundamental for the growth of a recording market.[301] People like Castelo Branco adopted a strategy in which commercial interests were shared and negotiated between local and foreign companies. This was possible because of the close relationship between them, and that contrasts with the "more distant and imposing" position adopted by the larger companies.[302]

---

[296] Losa and Belchior, "The Introduction of Phonogram Market in Portugal," 8.
[297] Losa and Belchior, "The Introduction of Phonogram Market in Portugal," 8.
[298] Losa and Belchior, "The Introduction of Phonogram Market in Portugal," 8–10.
[299] Losa and Belchior, "The Introduction of Phonogram Market in Portugal," 9.
[300] Losa and Belchior, "The Introduction of Phonogram Market in Portugal," 9.
[301] Losa and Belchior, "The Introduction of Phonogram Market in Portugal," 10.
[302] Losa and Belchior, "The Introduction of Phonogram Market in Portugal," 10.

Conclusion

"Burning in a fever of greatness, Lisbon had felt the need for other streets, other styles, other interiors: something that was consistent with the ideals, the habits, and the workings of its modern life."[1] This remark by Fialho d'Almeida captures the fundamental changes that merged urban planning, everyday life, and modernity in Lisbon. This chapter brings together topics that permeate the entire book but were addressed separately. Therefore, it traces lines of thought that, despite their ubiquitous presence, were only allowed to emerge at certain points. However, given the fragmentary nature of the book, these concluding remarks do not intend to force the materials into a coherent narrative. They aim to highlight the most important ideas without losing track of the contradictory and ever changing qualities of nationalism and modernity.

I would like to start by examining the polarity between art and entertainment. This process is associated with the expansion of the market for cultural goods in which commercial entertainment venues provided the ideal setting.[2] Popular theaters, fairs, and circuses illustrate the rise of a leisure culture that relied on large audiences and marks clearly the widening gap between art and entertainment.[3] So-called Western art—or "serious"—music feeds on the idea of social distinction. Art was meant for the cultured few and entertainment for the ignorant masses. Categorizing and naming was part of this process. In the Portuguese dictionary written by Cândido de Figueiredo "art" is defined as a set of conventions and as a synonym for skill or artifice.[4] It does not contain any reference to an autonomous field of cultural production. However,

---

[1] Fialho d'Almeida, *Lisboa galante* (Porto: Livraria Civilisação, 1890), 16.

[2] On this issue see Derek B. Scott, "The Rift between Art and Entertainment," in *Scott, Sounds of the Metropolis: The 19th-Century Popular Music Revolution in London, New York, Paris and Vienna* (Oxford, Oxford University Press, 2008), 85–115.

[3] Scott, "The Rift between Art and Entertainment," 88.

[4] Cândido de Figueiredo, *Nôvo diccionário da língua portuguêsa*, vol. 1 (Lisbon: Livraria Tavares Cardoso & Irmão, 1899), 135.

two series of the music periodical *Arte Musical* (Musical Art) had already been published before the dictionary. *Arte Musical*, whose series were published in 1873–1875 and in 1890–1891, focused on art music. However, the Portuguese ethnologists of the time studied the local "popular arts." This indicates the polysemic character of "art" in Portugal, as well as its varied meaning in different contexts.

The rift between art and entertainment was not uniform. In some countries the split was made between Austro-German art music and Italian opera. The opposition between instrumental music and Italian opera was also circulating in Portugal. Public concerts were held and orchestras were formed.[5] However, they had a limited impact on a market dominated by the popular theater. The dominance of the Real Teatro de S. Carlos and the late introduction of French and German art music in Lisbon place the rift between art and entertainment in another context. Some people believed that Offenbach's operettas acted as surrogates for the German operas until these were performed in Lisbon.[6] Thus, a genre that originated with the mass market and was not seen as art was thought to be an improvement on the dominance of Italian opera. Nevertheless, the line that separates art from entertainment varies according to time and place. The dominance of the *revista* for a sustained period of time transformed the discourse concerning opera and operetta; if art was eternal, the *revista* was transient. The same play was reworked over and over again to to reflect changing current events. People bought a ticket to a *revista* so they could laugh at current matters and to see the half-naked chorus girls; others rented a box to hear the *prime donne* at the opera.

However, if art was a polar opposite to popular entertainment, tracing the boundaries of the latter is a complex process. This separation is difficult to map in Lisbon, where a small pool of musicians and actors catered to a growing audience for both, with the same person working in different venues and contexts. Prolific composers of operetta and *revista* for Lisbon's stages worked in the Real Conservatório de Lisboa or in the Real Teatro de S. Carlos, institutions that were linked to art music. Their activity changed according to the different institutions they worked for. Members of the orchestra of the Real Teatro de S. Carlos who never wrote operas were frequently employed as composers for theaters that staged operettas and *revistas*. Prominent musicians worked in different roles in a variety of cultural spaces, their roles shifting according to the place they were currently employed. Augusto Machado taught

---

[5] Maria José Artiaga, "Continuity and Change in Three Decades of Portuguese Musical Life 1870—1900" (Ph.D. thesis, Royal Holloway, University of London, 2007).

[6] Ramalho Ortigão and Eça de Queirós, *As farpas: crónica mensal da política, das letras e dos costumes*, vol. 7 (Lisbon: Typographia Universal, 1876), 71–72.

in the Conservatoire and directed the Real Teatro de São Carlos, where he had his opera *Laurianne* performed—an example of his activity in local art music. However, he also wrote several operettas that were staged in popular theaters. Hence, the same person composed for different places and audiences. In other cases, performers in the orchestra of the São Carlos were also musical directors of theatrical companies and composed a large number of *revistas* and operettas. Some even conducted *bandas*.

Another dichotomy that permeates this book concerns the ideas of tradition and modernity. These are deeply connected and should be analyzed as a dialectical relationship. The rapid transformation of human modes of experience associated with "modern" life suggests a complex interaction of technological innovations, economic development, and political processes, all of which reshaped the everyday life of the Portuguese. "Modernity" points to a notion of space and of historical time that marked a distinction between "modern" and "pre-modern" worlds. Therefore, the idea of tradition became predominantly associated with a static vision of a pre-modern world. It contrasted with the fast pace and the constant change of modern society. However, seeing tradition as a residual trace of the pre-modern world in modern societies proves to be problematic. It relies on an evolutionist conception of culture that does not account for the interpenetration between the modern and the traditional. The separation between them in Lisbon is amorphous and elusive since elements of both worlds coexisted. The new forms of separating public and private spaces that are embodied in modern boulevard culture spilled over into the older parts of the old city. Moreover, popular traditions were used politically to attest to the antiquity of the Portuguese nation, necessary to preserve the country's historical past. These traditions were presented as timeless, achronological, or subject to a conception of historical time other than the modern. Thus, the same country displays traces of different historical times existing concurrently and develops a particular relationship with them.

Derrida's notion of the constitutive outside emerges when one studies the intertwining and embedding of tradition and modernity. "The constitutive outside is a relational process by which the outside—or 'other'—of any category is actively at work on both sides of the constructed boundary, and is thus always leaving its trace within the category."[7] Consequently, a binary opposition between tradition and modernity, a prevalent idea in Western modernity, is problematic because these categories are ontologically relational. Therefore, tradition is the space in relation to which modernity is encoded,

---

[7] Wolfgang Nater and John Paul Jones, "Identity, Space, and Other Uncertainties," in Georges Benko and Ulf Strohmayer (eds.), *Space and Social Theory: Interpreting Modernity and Post-Modernity* (London: Blackwell, 1997), 146.

performed, and commodified. It "marks the alterity of the inside, fashions its borders, assigns its social significance, and supervises its relations with other boundaries."[8] Conversely, "the constructed inside [in this case, modernity], which is both agent and victim of this territorializing process, extends beyond itself to become another's outside within."[9] Therefore, interpreting tradition as a residual trace of a pre-modern past becomes extremely difficult because these categories are not static. However, their boundaries have to be shown as strict in order to maintain (and not to contain) the category.[10] Thus, despite a binary opposition between tradition and modernity that is frequently evoked in the efforts of the Portuguese Regeneração, the boundaries between them are blurred.

Hobsbawm situates the "invented" forms of tradition within modernity and associates them with the modern nation-state.[11] Invented traditions "are responses to novel situations which take the form of reference to old situations, or which establish their own past by quasi-obligatory repetition."[12] Moreover, they are a "set of practices, normally governed by overtly or tacitly accepted rules and of a ritual or symbolic nature, which seek to inculcate certain values and norms of behavior by repetition, which automatically implies continuity with the past."[13] Thus, invented traditions played an important role in producing national and patriotic symbols. They promoted an unbroken continuity between the past and the present. This attempt to ground nation-states in a remote past and the use of their alleged antiquity as a form of validation of a contingent reality is associated with a modern conception of historical time. Invented traditions can be framed in the "attempt to structure at least some parts of social life" within the ever-changing modern world, an argument that resonates with the ahistorical and static view of popular culture forwarded by several Portuguese ethnologists.[14] However, Hobsbawm presents a reductive view of tradition. He defines it as a space that relies on purported notions of invariance and fixedness, excluding conventions or routines that have no "significant ritual or symbolic function as such."[15] Hobsbawm also draws a distinction between tradition and custom, presenting the latter as a relatively

---

[8] Nater and Jones, "Identity, Space, and Other Uncertainties," 146.

[9] Nater and Jones, "Identity, Space, and Other Uncertainties," 146.

[10] Nater and Jones, "Identity, Space, and Other Uncertainties," 146.

[11] Eric J. Hobsbawm and Terence Ranger (eds.), *The Invention of Tradition* (Cambridge: Cambridge University Press, 1992).

[12] Eric J. Hobsbawm, "Introduction," in Eric J. Hobsbawm and Terence Ranger (eds.), *The Invention of Tradition*, 2.

[13] Hobsbawm, "Introduction," 1.

[14] Hobsbawm, "Introduction," 2.

[15] Hobsbawm, "Introduction," 2–3.

flexible concept that is prevalent in traditional societies (that, in this context, may be understood as pre-industrial).[16] This line of reasoning raises important questions. First, Hobsbawm's view of tradition relies on a functionalist perspective on ritual and symbols which tends to reduce (or even exclude) the ritual and symbolic aspects of everyday life. This is incompatible with my work on Bourdieu's notion of *habitus* used in this book. Second, the distinction between tradition and custom is highly problematic when one is dealing with a culturally heterogeneous country, which is the normative arrangement for most nation-states. For example, Portugal was a predominantly agrarian country with a few industrialized areas. Therefore, different types of social organization coexisted within the same territory. If Portuguese ethnology predominantly studied popular culture in rural communities, the folklorists acted as mediators not only between the rural and the urban, but also between customs and tradition. Consequently, folklorists played an important role in creating a stabilized tradition. They crystallized elements associated with dynamic traditional practices and articulated them in a more static idea of tradition.

A topic that permeates the discussion concerning tradition and modernity is the urban/rural divide. The perspective in which the rural is the central stage for an authentic tradition dominated the work of several writers, some of whom aimed to link coeval popular culture to the nation's glorious past. Therefore, the idealized production of the rural aimed to bind space and time together in one historical category. Creating the essence of the urban and the rural relied on their demarcation as self-contained entities. This was used to ground and validate political action. However, interpreting the rural world as the site where an "authentic" popular culture needs to be rescued from urbanization tends to disregard the symbiotic relations and the porosity of boundaries between these spaces. For example, the rise in internal migration from the country to the city contributed to the transformation of cultural practices in both places. Furthermore, toward the end of the 19th century, the significant emigration of both men and women from predominantly rural areas to countries such as Brazil reshaped Portuguese everyday life and is well documented in the coeval sources. Elements associated with the rural world and, therefore, with modes of life that were seen as traditional were ubiquitous in the urban landscape. This is due to a symbiotic relation between the city and the country that surfaced with urbanization. The city had to rely on the countryside for the supply of basic products. Thus, the peddlers, who were mostly inbound from the rural outskirts of Lisbon known as the *região saloia*, were a constant presence in the city's life. They traded in markets, such as the Praça da Figueira,

---

[16] Hobsbawm, "Introduction," 2.

in their fair stalls, or in the city's streets with their carts and baskets. Their cries were part of the auditory landscape of the city. Another element that reinforces the porosity between the urban and the rural is the use of regional songs, dances, and characters in the urban entertainment market. This staging of the rural was part of the process in which the vernacular was aestheticized. Conversely, the spread of urban theatrical songs in the countryside evidences the fluidity of boundaries between the country and the city, and complicates the essentialist perspective promoted by the ethnologists.

The dialectic relation between the local and the global is correlated with the distinctions of tradition/modernity and urban/rural. The growing commodification of music created a transnational market in a period when most trade was conducted with or within national economies, in which the colonial world was included.[17] Although the global commerce worked predominantly at an international level, cultural goods relied in transnational processes. This shows a tendency toward deterritorialization that would be transferred to other kinds of products throughout the 20th century. Giddens points to the "disembedding" mechanisms in modernity.'[18] They "prize social relations free from the hold of specific locales, recombining them across wide time-space distances."[19] Moreover, in contemporary societies "the reorganisation of time and space, plus the disembedding mechanisms, radicalise and globalise pre-established institutional traits of modernity; and they act to transform the content and nature of day-to-day social life."[20] Despite focusing on late modernity, this insight proves very useful to the understanding of the transnational entertainment market.

Therefore, the "national" is not a space that is clearly demarcated. It is a logic inherent in this process that takes place between the local and the global. Therefore, it becomes possible to articulate both levels through the nation-state to create and maintain a nation that is symbolically efficient during a period of intense social change in local and global levels. Moreover, the constant negotiation of tensions and boundaries between the local and the global, tradition and modernity and, to some extent, urban and rural is a constant feature of the modern nation-state. The notion of cosmopolitanism surfaces in discussing modernity and transnationalism. Understandings of cosmopolitanism in the 19th century indicate "reflective distance from one's original cultural affiliation, a broad understanding of other cultures and customs, and

---

[17] Eric J. Hobsbawm, *The Age of Empire: 1875–1914* (London: Abacus, 2004), 41–42.

[18] Anthony Giddens, *Modernity and Self-Identity: Self and Society in the Late Modern Age* (Stanford, CA: Stanford University Press, 1991), 2.

[19] Giddens, *Modernity and Self-Identity*, 2.

[20] Giddens, *Modernity and Self-Identity*, 2.

a belief in universal humanity."[21] Moreover, a "cultivated detachment from restrictive forms of identity" underpins the notion of cosmopolitanism.[22] Thus, cosmopolitanism is a disembedding mechanism of modernity, associated with the break between cultural practices and specific places. The new Portuguese railways made European traveling easier. They shortened the time required to import foreign goods. This facilitated the circulation in Portugal of "modern" products that were mostly associated with the sophistication of Parisian life. Railway transportation accelerated the process through which goods that were traded transnationally were incorporated into everyday life. Musical instruments, sheet music, gramophones, and records made their way to Lisbon's entertainment market rapidly. This is important because Portugal had to import many cultural goods since the local production facilities were scarce.

An exclusive association between cosmopolitanism and the economically privileged can be misleading. More affluent people were able to travel, and could afford pianos, player pianos, gramophones, phonographs and their associated products. They were part of a transnational flow of people that can be framed in a context of cosmopolitanism. Nevertheless, the spread of products associated with the transnational entertainment market in Portugal adds a new layer of complexity to this issue. The performance of Offenbach's Parisian operettas in theaters directed at the popular segments of Lisbon's society is a symptom of this process. However, the operettas had to be translated and adapted to the local context so they could be understood by the audience. The production and recording of "modern" and "vernacular" musical styles, such as the Brazilian *maxixe* or the Portuguese fado, by Portuguese artists and their incorporation in the catalogues of multinational phonographic companies intensified this relationship between the local and the global. These events contributed to the rapid spread in Portugal of cosmopolitanism throughout several social strata. Thus, leisure and cosmopolitanism were not exclusive to the well-to-do. The internationalist strands associated with trade unionism epitomize this process. Popular modernity integrates in its fabric the local and the global, and vernacular forms of cosmopolitanism relied, precisely, on the disembedding mechanisms that were developed with modernity.

The association between technological innovation, objectivity, and modernity pervades this book. Technologies that reduced human intervention in capturing and registering information were developed in this period.

---

[21] Amanda Anderson, *The Powers of Distance: Cosmopolitanism and the Cultivation of Detachment* (Princeton, NJ: Princeton University Press, 2001), 63.

[22] Amanda Anderson, "Cosmopolitanism, Universalism, and the Divided Legacies of Modernity," in Pheng Cheah and Bruce Robbins (eds.), *Cosmopolitics: Thinking and Feeling beyond the Nation* (Minneapolis: University of Minnesota Press, 1998), 266.

Photography, phonography, and film are related to a new form of objectivity that relied on mechanical apparatuses to guarantee its neutrality. Moreover,

> aperspectival objectivity was the ethos of the interchangeable and therefore featureless observer—unmarked by nationality, by sensory dullness or acuity, by training or tradition; by quirky apparatus, by colourful writing style, or by any other idiosyncracy [sic] that might interfere with the communication, comparison and accumulation of results.[23]

This paradigm was predominantly used in the natural sciences and can be traced back to late 18th-century philosophy.[24] It relies on the Kantian notion of disinterestedness.[25] Objectivity was valued in the transnational network of scientists that was established during the 19th-century because it embodied the ideal of communicability, a tendency that is related to the notion of cosmopolitanism addressed above.[26]

However, the application of the "modern technologies of the Real" was not exclusively scientific.[27] Their spread in the global market of cultural goods was an important development. This illustrates a type of objectivist thought that underpins an essential part of Western culture. It has its most significant symptoms in the development of a positivist science as well as of aesthetic movements such as naturalism and realism. However, although the technologies mentioned above were seen as mechanical conveyors of reality, their usage is more complex. Consequently, making a univocal reading of this cultural tendency is highly problematic. If naturalist and realist ideas permeated the market for cultural goods, the ubiquitous presence of allegory is also quite significant. For instance, the *revista* was based on a structure that relied heavily on allegory and personification. It dominated Lisbon's theaters, and coexisted with realist and naturalist plays. Photographs of scenes from the *revista* were published in several periodicals as well as on postcards. This indicates the importance of realistic modes of representation that relied on mechanical and chemical processes even when depicting the allegoric content of the plays. Another symptom of this process can be found in the work of

---

[23] Lorraine Daston, "Objectivity and the Escape from Perspective," *Social Studies of Science*, 22/4 (1992), 609.

[24] Daston."Objectivity and the Escape from Perspective," 606–607.

[25] Daston."Objectivity and the Escape from Perspective," 606–607.

[26] Daston."Objectivity and the Escape from Perspective," 608–612.

[27] Amanda Weidman, "Guru and Gramophone: Fantasies of Fidelity and Modern Technologies of the Real," *Public Culture*, 15/3 (2003), 453–476.

Portuguese ethnologists, who used a philological approach based on positivist paradigms to study popular myths and stories. Despite the coexistence of several codes, there is a predominantly objectivist mode of representation in various spheres and commodities. These rely sometimes on technologies then perceived and promoted as the epitome of modernity. Postcards were a new product in the 1870s, and sound recordings entered the market and people's homes in the 1900s.

An important characteristic of some of these technologies was their ability to capture reality through mechanical and chemical processes. As argued before, it is possible to draw from Barthes to frame the developing technologies of photography, phonography, and film. They were purveyors of analogue data that introduced new modes of representation into the market for cultural goods. Thus, the rise of iconographic and phonographic cultures has to be framed as part of a larger process. The process relied on the incorporation of visual and auditory analogue depictions of reality in a market that, in the middle of the 19th-century, was predominantly concentrated on goods that relied on a code for their interpretation.[28] Moreover, the representations that were made possible with the "modern technologies of the Real" reshaped human experience under the sign of modernity.

The entertainment market played a key role in building, spreading, and naturalizing the modern nation in Portugal between 1867 and 1910. This period was one of intense social change across Europe. This book has addressed a heterogeneous set of elements such as class, gender, ethnicity, technology, tradition, modernity, domesticity, and production of space. Moreover, it studies how the link between music and the modern nation was forged in the popular theater. In nation-building, the transnational market for cultural goods is bound to an analysis that has to account for the permeable and complex interaction between several scales of cultural production. These comprise the local, the global, the regional, and the national.

The construction of identity and alterity is fundamental to create a symbolically efficient nation-state. Moreover, it requires a particular approach in the study of a country like Portugal. On the one hand, Portugal was a peripheral European country that depended heavily on foreign capital for its modernization. Also, the country developed a significant interchange with its former colony Brazil and maintained colonies on several continents. The colonial and post-colonial worlds were a constant presence in the definition of Portugal as a nation, a feature that was brought to the foreground at several points in

---

[28] Roland Barthes, "The Photographic Message," in Roland Barthes, *Image-Music-Text* (New York: Hill and Wang, 1978), 17.

the country's history. This was clear during the crisis following the British Ultimatum, and grew in significance in the country's international positioning throughout most of the 20th-century. Therefore, incorporating colonial ideology into the fabric of a European nation relied on the construction and naturalization of an asymmetrical bond between the metropolis and the colonies. Moreover, the spectral presence of a purportedly golden age, the heyday of the Portuguese Empire, was an important part of the construction of the continental nation-state that intersected time and space, history and geography. This stance did not change with the Portuguese Republic. The alternative idea of a nation that did not rely on the monarchy was developed toward the end of the 19th century. It was staged in the popular theaters, and set to music by several composers. Moreover, leisure was used to facilitate its spread in a growing market. People circulated in the city and heard the same pieces over and over again in different formats. Thus, music helped to set the scene for the modern nation, a nation that was constantly negotiated in Portugal. Thus, when the Republic was instated, there were changes made, but the *revista* maintained its dominance in the theatrical circuits. This happened because the genre could easily accommodate the constantly shifting social and political scene in its portrayals. Moreover, plays kept on circulating in Portugal and Brazil, revealing the transnational connections in the Portuguese-speaking entertainment markets.

What was the role music played in the creation, dissemination, and internalization of the modern nation? In some direct instances, the performance of patriotic marches, such as "A Portuguesa," fueled patriotic feelings in difficult moments of Portuguese history. These pieces were also performed in the theaters and at home, a result of the commodification of music. People could play "A Portuguesa" on the piano or listen to it on a record whenever they wanted. Thus, the use of commodified music was intensified in this period. This indicates another important trait that placed music as an effective conveyor of nationalist or patriotic ideologies, its ability to cross boundaries of physical and social space. Therefore, music was an important activity where the "composite image" of modern Portugal was promoted and internalized through pleasure. Pleasure loosened social conventions and was used as an escape from the daily routines imposed by modern life for the theatergoing audience of Lisbon. Therefore, pleasure acted as a facilitator for the modern nation to become naturalized and internalized. Consequently, promoting patriotism and modernity in the entertainment market commodified the nation and made its consumption pleasurable for the audience. The commodification of Portugal paralleled but also relied on the commodification of music. This indicates that an articulated entertainment system was in place. A theatrical show generated a set of commodities that extended the scope of that universe to the city's streets as well as to domestic spaces, and incorporated the repertoire of the music theater in different contexts of everyday life. Moreover, it intersected social strata, space, and time.

However, promoting the nation through entertainment was not exclusively confined to the direct use of nationalist propaganda, such as patriotic marches. It was a logic that permeated the market for cultural goods. For example, positive press reviews received by several operas and operettas by Portuguese composers were a form of promoting an attachment of the readers to a nationalist agenda. The use of music in the *revista* is symptomatic of the promotion of a nationalist logic that underpinned a significant segment of the country's cultural goods. Its structure in closed numbers allowed for a selection of varied symbols associated with the nation-state and with the transnational entertainment market. These were presented and internalized by the audience, who were also able to reproduce these repertoires domestically. The music included in the *revista* ranged from transnational musical styles (such as the waltz) to aetheticizations of the urban and rural Portuguese vernacular (such as the fado or the *chula*). Thus, music that was perceived as epitomizing modern cosmopolitan sophistication and local repertoires were played side by side. Therefore, the Portuguese entertainment market and the rise of several types of musical theater are inextricably bound to the complex process through which Portugal was established, presented, developed, and commodified as a modern nation-state.

GLOSSARY

banda: a marching band, a wind and percussion ensemble.

chula: a type of regional dance form the north of Portugal.

compère or *commère*: an always-on-stage character who bonds to the loose sketches of the *revista*.

copla: generic name for the sung part of a sketch in a musical revue, often published in booklets that include the lyrics of all songs of the play, the *coplas*.

corridinho: a type of regional dance from the south of Portugal.

fadista: fado singer or player, a popular character frequently associated with Lisbon's outcasts.

fado: a genre of urban popular song and dance developed in Lisbon in the 19th century. "Fado" is sometimes used as a generic synonym for popular song.

mágica: a theatrical genre that relies on supernatural plots.

Maxixe: an Afro-Brazilian salon dance that was in fashion in the late 1800s and the early 1900s.

moda: a generic term for popular songs and dances, especially used in Alentejo (south of Portugal).

quadro: a sketch of a musical revue.

revista: a musical revue, a popular play divided in sketches that comments on current events, and includes music and dance.

varina: a female migrant from the Ovar region (center of Portugal) dressed in regional costumes who sold fish in Lisbon.

zarzuela: the Spanish equivalent of the operetta. It includes singing, dancing and spoken dialogue, frequently incorporating regional subjects and musical genres.

REFERENCES

Primary Sources

PERIODICALS

Almanach de A Lucta
Ámanhã
O archeólogo português
A arte musical
A capital: diário republicano da noite
O Elvense
A mascara: arte, vida, theatro
A Revolução de Setembro
A semana de Lisboa
L'assiette au beurre
A voz do operário
O berro
Branco e negro: semanário ilustrado
Contemporânea
Diário de notícias
Diário illustrado
O Grande Elias
Illustração
Illustração Portugueza
O micróbio
O Occidente
O paiz
Pontos nos ii
Revista Lusitana
Serões: revista mensal ilustrada
Le temps

Books and Articles

Abreu, Jorge de, "Da Monarchia á República (Narrativas da revolução de 4 e 5 de Outubro de 1910)," *A capital: diário republicano da noite*, 21 November 1910, 4.

Almeida, Fialho d', *Actores e autores* (Lisbon: Livraria Clássica Editora, 1925).

Almeida, Fialho d', *Os gatos, publicação mensal, d'inquerito á vida portugueza* (Porto: Casa Editora Alcino Aranha & C.ª, September–October 1889).
Almeida, Fialho d', *Lisboa Galante* (Porto: Livraria Civilisação, 1890).
Almeida, Fialho d', *Pasquinadas (jornal d'um vagabundo)* (Porto: Livraria Chardron, Lello & Irmão, 1904).
Almeida, Fialho d', *Saibam quantos...* (Lisbon, Livraria Clássica Editora, 1912).
Almeida, Fialho d', *Vida Irónica* (Lisbon, Livraria Clássica Editora, 1914 [1892]).
American Annual Cyclopaedia and Register of Important Events (New York: D. Appleton, 1888).
Andrada, Miguel Leitão de, *Miscellanea* (Lisbon: Imprensa Nacional, 1867).
Andrada, Miguel Leitão de, *Miscellanea do sitio de N. Sª. da Luz do Pedrogão Grande* (Lisbon: Matheus Pinheiro, 1629).
Anjos, João Maria dos, *Novo methodo de guitarra* (Lisbon: Livraria de António Maria Pereira, 1889).
Arriegas, Artur, *A canção da minha terra: fados* (Lisbon: Impressão C. do Cabra, 1907).
Arriegas, Artur, "Fadinhos," *O Casmurro*, 5 June 1905, 2.
Arriegas, Artur, "Fadinhos," *O Casmurro*, 31 July 1905, 2.
Arriegas, Artur, "Fadinhos," *O Casmurro*, 12 August 1905, 2.
Arriegas, Artur, *A trova portugueza: Fados e canções* (Lisbon: Barateira, 1922).
Arroio, António, "Introducção," in Pedro Fernandes Tomás, *Velhas canções e romances populares portugueses*, v–lii.
"O attentado de 1 de Fevereiro," *Illustração Portugueza*, 10 February 1908, 169–173.
Bastos, António de Sousa, *Carteira do artista; apontamentos para a historia do theatro portuguez e brazileiro* (Lisbon: Antiga casa Bertrand, José Bastos, 1899).
Bastos, António de Sousa, *Diccionario do theatro portuguez* (Lisbon: Imp. Libânio da Silva, 1908).
Bastos, António de Sousa, *Lisboa Velha: sessenta anos de recordações, 1850 a 1910* (Lisbon: Câmara Municipal de Lisboa, 1947).
Bastos, Teixeira, *A crise: estudo sobre a situação política, financeira, económica e moral da nação* (Porto: Livraria Internacional de Ernesto Chardron, 1894).
Baudelaire, Charles, "Le Peintre de la vie moderne," in *Œuvres complètes de Charles Baudelaire*, vol. 3 (Paris: Calmann Lévy, 1885), 51–114.
Benevides, Francisco da Fonseca, "Phonographo fallante de Edison," *O Occidente*, 15 April 1878, 64.
Benevides, Francisco da Fonseca, *O Real Theatro de S. Carlos de Lisboa desde a sua fundação em 1793 até à actualidade: estudo histórico* (Lisbon: Typ. Castro Irmão, 1883).
Benevides, Francisco da Fonseca, *O Real Theatro de S. Carlos de Lisboa: memorias 1883–1902* (Lisbon: Typographia & Lithographia de Ricardo de Sousa Salles, 1902).
Borba, Tomás, "Dansas e cantos populares da nossa terra," *Illustração Portugueza*, 23 December 1907, 833–838.
Botelho, Abel, *Amanhã!* (Porto: Livraria Chardron, 1902).
Braga, Teófilo, *Cancioneiro e romanceiro geral portuguez* (Porto: Typographia Lusitana, 1867).
Braga, Teófilo, "As melodias portuguesas," in Neves and Campos, *Cancioneiro*, vol. 1, v–vii.
Branco, Camilo Castelo, *A senhora Rattazzi* (Porto/Braga: Livraria internacional de Ernesto Chardron, Editor, 1880).
Brazão, Eduardo, *Memórias de Eduardo Brazão que seu filho compilou e Henrique Lopes de Mendonça prefacía* (Lisbon: Empresa da Revista de Teatro, 1925).
Capelo, Hermenegildo, and Roberto Ivens, *De Benguella ás terras de Iácca; descripção de uma viagem na Africa central e occidental*, 2 vols. (Lisbon: Imp. Nacional, 1881).
Capelo, Hermenegildo, and Roberto Ivens, *From Benguella to the Territory of Yacca: Description of a Journey into Central and West Africa*, 2 vols. (London: Sampson Low, Marston, Searle, & Rivington, 1882).
Carvalho, Maria Amália Vaz de, *Mulheres e creanças: notas sobre educação* (Porto: Joaquim Antunes Leitão e Irmão, 1880).

Carvalho, Pinto de, *História do fado* (Lisbon: Empreza da História de Portugal, 1903).
Carvalho, Pinto de "O triste fado," *Illustração portugueza*,11 February 1907, 169–172.
Castilho, Júlio de, *Lisboa antiga* (Lisbon: Antiga casa Bertrand, José Bastos, 1904).
Castro, Urbano de, *A princeza na berlinda: Rattazzi a vol d'oiseau, com a biographia de sua Alteza* (Lisbon: Typographia Portugueza, 1880).
Chagas, João, "O fado (palavras d'um revoltado)," *O berro*, 12 April 1896, 3.
Chagas, João, *1908: subsidios criticos para a historia da dictadura* (Lisbon: João Chagas, 1908).
Chagas, Pinheiro, *As colonias portuguezas no seculo XIX* (Lisbon: António Maria Pereira, 1890).
Charpentier, Mademoiselle, *Méthode de piano* (Paris: Firmin-Didot, 1875).
Coelho, José Simões, "O povo e o teatro," *Ámanhã*, 1 August 1909, 1–4.
"A crise do theatro," *A Paródia*, 6 February 1901, 2.
Dias, Carlos Malheiro, *Cartas de Lisboa: terceira série (1905–1906)* (Lisbon: Livraria Clássica Editora, 1907).
Dolge, Alfred, *Pianos and Their Makers* (Covina, CA: Covina Publishing, 1911).
Félix, Pedro, "João Black," in Salwa Castelo-Branco (ed.), *Enciclopédia da música em Portugal no século XX*, vol. 1, 144.
Ferreira, Isidoro Sabino, *Memorias do Actor Izidoro* (Lisbon: Imprensa de J.G. de Sousa Neves, 1876).
Figueiredo, Cândido de, *Novo diccionario da língua portuguesa*, 2 vols. (Lisbon: Livraria Tavares Cardoso & Irmão, 1899).
Fuschini, Augusto, *O presente e o futuro de Portugal* (Lisbon: Companhia Typographica, 1899).
Galtier, Joseph, "Visite au Portugal: Déclarations de S. M. D. Carlos Ier,"' *Le temps*, 14 November 1907, 1.
Ganivet, Angél, *Idearium español* (Granada: n.p., 1897).
Harrington, Carlos, *Improvisos (Fados)* (Lisbon: Typographia Costa Braga, 1892).
Harrington, Carlos, *Versos de Carlos Harrington, para guitarra, orchestra ou piano* (Lisbon: Impr. Lucas, 1907).
Herculano, Alexandre, *História de Portugal*, vol. 1 (Lisbon: Casa da Viúva Bertrand e Filhos, 1853 [1846]).
Irkan [Fialho d'Almeida], "Gloria aos vencidos!," *Pontos nos ii*, 5 February 1891, 42–3.
Irkan [Fialho d'Almeida], "Os pregões," *Pontos nos ii*, 3 July 1890, 211, 214.
Jean-Guyau, Marie, "La mémoire et le phonographe," *Revue philosophique de la France et de l'étranger*, Tome IX, janvier-juillet (1880), 317–322.
Jonson, G. C. Ashton, "Mechanical piano-players," *Journal of the Royal Musical Association*, 42/1 (1915), 15–32.
Laranjeira, Manuel, *O pessimismo nacional* (Lisbon: Padrões Culturais Editora, 2008 [1907-8]).
Lima, Magalhães, *La Fédération Ibérique* (Paris: Imprimerie Gautherin & Cie,1892).
Lobato, Gervásio, *Lisboa em camisa* (Lisbon: Empreza Litteraria de Lisboa, 1882).
Longworth, Dames, and M. and E. Seemann, "Folklore of the Azores," *Folklore*, 14/2 (1903), 125–146.
Machado, Júlio César, "Jacobetty," *Diário de Notícias*, 6 June 1889, 1.
Machado, Júlio César, *Os theatros de Lisboa* (Lisbon: Mattos Moreia & C.ª, 1875).
Madureira, Joaquim, *Impressões de theatro* (Lisbon: Ferreira & Oliveira, L.da, Editores, 1905).
Martins, Oliveira, *O Brazil e as colonias portuguezas* (Lisbon: Livraria de António Maria Pereira, 1888).
Martins, Oliveira, *História de Portugal*, vol. 2 (Lisbon: Bertrand, 1887).
Martins, Oliveira, *Portugal contemporâneo*, 2 vols. (Lisbon: António Maria Pereira, 1895).
Martins, Oliveira, *As raças humanas e a civilisação primitiva*, 2 vols. (Lisbon: Bertrand, 1881).
Massano, Augusto, et al., *O Elvense: Numero brinde aos senhores assignantes em 1894* (Elvas: Typographia d'O Elvense, 1894)
Melo, Adelino das Neves e, *Musicas e canções populares colligidas da tradição* (Lisbon: Imprensa Nacional, 1872).
Mesquita, Alfredo, "Chronica occidental," *O Occidente*, 10 February 1908, 26.

Mesquita, Alfredo, "Do omnibus ao automóvel," *Illustração portugueza*, 24 September 1908, 233-238.
Miguéis, José Rodrigues, *A escola da paraíso* (Lisbon: Estúdios Cor, 1960).
Mitchell, Ogilvie, *The Talking Machine Industry* (London: Sir Isaac Pitman, [1922]).
M.O., "O Phonola," *O Occidente*, 28 February 1905, 46
Moore, Isabel, "Portuguese Folk-songs," *Journal of American Folklore*, 15/58 (1902), 165-169.
"A morte de um grande actor comico: Alfredo de Carvalho," *Illustração portugueza*, 18 April 1910, 508-509.
Murguía, Manuel, *Historia de Galicia*, vol. 1 (Lugo: Imprenta de Soto Freire, Editor, 1865).
Neves, César das, and Gualdino de Campos, *Cancioneiro de músicas populares*, 3 vols. (Porto: Tip. Ocidental—Empresa editora César, Campos & Cª, 1893, 1895, 1898).
Neves, Hermano, *Como triumphou a Republica* (Lisbon: Empreza Liberdade, 1910).
Nogueira, António Francisco, *A raça negra sob o ponto de vista da civilisação da Africa; usos e costumes de alguns povos gentilicos do interior de Mossamedes e as colonias portuguezas* (Lisbon: Typographia Nova Minerva, 1880).
Noronha, Eduardo, "Visconde S. Luiz Braga," *O grande Elias*, 21 January 1904, 1-2.
Ortigão, Ramalho, and Eça de Queirós, *As farpas: crónica mensal da política, das letras e dos costumes* (Lisbon: Typographia Universal, 1871).
Ortigão, Ramalho, and Eça de Queirós, *As farpas: crónica mensal da política, das letras e dos costumes* (Lisbon: Typographia Universal, 1872)
Ortigão, Ramalho, and Eça de Queirós, *As farpas: crónica mensal da política, das letras e dos costumes*, vol. 7 (Lisbon: Typographia Universal, 1876).
Ortigão, Ramalho, and Eça de Queirós, *As farpas: crónica mensal da política, das letras e dos costumes*, vol. 2 (Lisbon: Typographia Universal, 1878).
Ortigão, Ramalho, *As farpas*, vol.1 (Lisbon: Livraria Clássica Editora, 1948).
Osório, Paulo, "Wagner em S. Carlos," *Illustração portugueza*, 1 March 1909, 281-288; 8 March 1909, 289-295; 15 March 1909, 329-333; 22 March 1909. 353-358.
Palmeirim, Luiz Augusto, *Os excentricos do meu tempo* (Lisbon: Imprensa Nacional, 1891).
Pato, Bulhão, *Memorias: homens politicos*, vol. 2 (Lisbon: Typographia da Academia Real das Sciencias, 1894).
Pedroso, Consiglieri, *Portuguese Folk-Tales* (London: Folk-Lore Society, 1882).
Peixoto, Rocha, "A arqueologia e a etnografia nos bilhetes postais," *Etnográfica*, 4/1 (2000), 185-188.
Peixoto, Rocha "O cruel e triste fado," *Etnográfica*, 1/2 (1997 [1897]), 331-336.
Pimentel, Alberto, *As alegres canções do norte* (Lisbon: Livraria Viúva Tavares Cardoso, 1905).
Pimentel, Alberto, "A guitarra," in Pimentel, *Fotografias de Lisboa* (Lisbon: Frenesi, 2005 [1874]), 73-78.
Pimentel, Alberto, *Notas sôbre o Amor de Perdição* (Lisbon: Guimarães & C.ª, 1915).
Pimentel, Alberto, *A triste canção do sul: subsídios para a história do Fado* (Lisbon: Livraria Central, 1904).
Pimentel, Alberto, *Vida de Lisboa* (Lisbon: Parceria António Maria Pereira, 1900).
Pinto, Serpa, *Como eu atravessei Africa: Do Atlantico ao mar Indico*, 2 vols. (London: Sampson Low, Marston, Searle, and Rivington, 1881).
"Por encostas e ladeiras," *Illustração portugueza*, 8 February 1909, 165-168.
Portugal, Direcção Geral de Estatística, *Relatorio sobre o censo da populaçao* (Lisbon: Imprensa Nacional, 1896).
Queirós, Eça de, *Os Maias: episódios da vida romântica*, 2 vols. (Porto: Livraria Chardron/Casa Editora Lugan & Genelioux Successores, 1888).
Queirós, Eça de, *O primo Bazilio: episódio doméstico* (Porto/Braga: Livraria Chardron, 1878).
Queirós, Eça de, *A relíquia* (Porto: Typ. de A. J. da Silva Teixeira, 1887).
Quental, Antero de, *Conferencias democraticas: Causas da decadencia dos povos peninsulares nos ultimos tres seculos* (Porto: Typographia Commercial, 1871).

Ramalho, Monteiro, *As ratices da Rattazzi: o pello nacional* (Porto: Typ. do Jornal da Manhã, 1880).
Ramos, Manuel, "Cancioneiro de Músicas Populares," in Neves and Campos, *Cancioneiro*, vol. 3, v–viii.
Rattazzi, Maria, *Portugal de relance* (Lisbon: Livraria Zeferino, 1881).
Reis, Jaime Batalha, "Introdução," in *Eça de Queirós, Prosas bárbaras* (Porto: Lello & Irmão, 1912), 5–53.
"A revista Agulha em Palheiro no Theatro Apollo," *Illustração portugueza*, 10 April 1911, 456.
"As revistas do anno actualmente em scena nos theatros de Lisboa," *Illustração Portugueza*, 24 January 1910, 105.
Reys, Luís da Câmara, "A miséria em Lisboa," *Serões: revista mensal ilustrada*, November 1908, 334–342.
Ribas, João António, *Album de musicas nacionaes portuguezas: constando de cantigas e tocatas usadas nos differentes districtos e comarcas das províncias da Beira, Traz-os-montes e Minho* (Porto: C. A. Villa Nova, 1860).
Rimanso, João [João Chagas], "Epistola ao sr. conselheiro João Franco—salvo o devido respeito," in *A paródia*, 4 May 1907, 2.
Rosa, Augusto, *Memórias e estudos* (Lisbon: Livraria Ferreira, 1917).
Rosa, Augusto, *Recordações da scena e de fóra da scena* (Lisbon: Livraria Ferreira, 1915).
Sampaio, Albino Forjaz de, *Chronicas immoraes* (Lisbon: Livraria Cálssica Editora, 1908).
Santos, Machado, *A Revolução Portuguesa: relatorio de Machado Santos* (Lisbon: Papelaria e Typographia Liberty, 1911).
Sarmento, Martins, *Os Lusitanos: questões de etnologia* (Porto: Typ. de Antonio José da Silva Teixeira, 1880).
Sarmento Martins, "Para o pantheon lusitano," *Revista Lusitana*, 1 (1888/1889), 227–290.
"A 'Serrana': opera portugueza de Alfredo Keil," *O paiz*, 2 September 1910, 1–2.
Simão, Veiga, *A nova geração; estudo sobre as tendencias actuaes de litteratura portugueza* (Coimbra: F. França Amado, 1911).
Simmel, Georg, "The Metropolis and Mental Life," in Gary Bridge and Sophie Watson (eds.), *The Blackwell City Reader* (Cambridge: Blackwell, 2002 [1903]), 11–19.
Sousa, Avelino de, *O fado e os seus censores: artigos colligidos da Voz do Operario: Crítica aos detractores da canção nacional* (Lisbon: Avelino de Sousa, 1912).
Sousa, Teixeira de, *Para a história da Revolução*, vol. 1 (Coimbra: Moura Marques & Paraísos, 1912).
Steffanina, Celestino, *Subsidios para a historia da Revolução de 5 de Outubro de 1910* (Lisbon: Typographia do Commercio, 1913).
Teles, Basílio, *Do ultimatum ao 31 de Janeiro: esboço de Historia politica*. (Porto, B. Telles, 1905).
Tomás, Pedro Fernandes, *Canções populares da Beira: acompanhada de 52 melodias recolhidas para piano* (Figueira da Foz: Lusitana, 1896).
Tomás, Pedro Fernandes, *Velhas canções e romances populares portugueses* (Coimbra: França Amado, editor, 1913).
Unamuno, Miguel de, *Por tierras de Portugal y de España* (Madrid: V. Prieto, 1911).
Unamuno Miguel de, "Sobre el marasmo actual de España," in Miguel de Unamuno, *En torno al casticismo: cinco ensayos* (Madrid: Residencia de Estudiantes, 1916), 187–219.
Unamuno, Miguel de, "La tradición eterna," in Miguel de Unamuno, *En torno al casticismo: cinco ensayos* (Madrid: Residencia de Estudiantes, 1916), 15–54.
Vasco, Neno, *Da Porta da Europa: factos e ideias, 1911–1912* (Lisbon: Biblioteca Libertas, 1913).
Vasconcelos, Leite de, "Canções do berço: segundo a tradição popular portuguesa," *Revista Lusitana* 10/1–2 (1907), 1–86.
Vasconcelos, Leite de, *História do Museu Etnológico Português* (Lisbon: Imprensa Nacional, 1915).
Vasconcelos Leite de, "Museu ethnographico português," *Revista Lusitana*, 3 (1895), 193–250.

Vasconcelos, Leite de, "Observações sobre as cantigas populares," *Revista Lusitana*, 1 (1889), 143-157.
Vasconcelos, Leite de, *Religiões da Lusitania: na parte que principalmente se refere a Portugal*, 3 vols. (Lisbon: Imprensa Nacional, 1897, 1905, 1913).
Veiga, Estácio da, *Antiguidades monumentaes do Algarve: tempos prehistoricos*, 4 vols. (Lisbon: Imprensa Nacional, 1886, 1887, 1889, 1891).
Verde, Cesário, *O livro de Cesário Verde* (Lisbon: Typographia Elzeveriana, 1887).
Vieira, Ernesto, *Diccionario biographico de musicos portuguezes: historia e bibliografia da musica em Portugal*, 2 vols. (Lisbon: Lambertini, 1900).
Vieira, Ernesto, *Diccionario musical* (Lisbon: Lambertini, 1899).
Vieira, Ernesto, *A musica em Portugal: resumo historico* (Lisbon: Clássica Editora, 1911).
Vieira, Ernesto, "Orquestra," in Ernesto Vieira, *Diccionario musical* (Lisbon: Lambertini, 1899), 392-393.
Viterbo, Sousa, "Cancioneiro de músicas populares," in Neves and Campos, *Cancioneiro*, vol. 2, v-vii.
Wagner, Richard, *My Life* (London: Constable & Robinson, 1996).
Wolzogen, Hans von, *Thematischer leitfaden durch die musik zu Rich. Wagner's festspiel Der ring des Nibelungen* (Leipzig: E. Schloemp, 1876).

Patents and Brands

Ball, H. P., "Perforated device for music-rolls," US Patent 778.835, 18 February 1902.
Berliner, Emile, "Gramophone," US Patent 564,586, 28 July 1896.
Berliner, Emile, "Process of producing records of sound," US Patent 382,790, 15 May 1888.
Berliner, Emile, "Sound-record and method to make same," US Patent 548,623, 29 October 1895.
Bettini, Gianni, "Apparatus for the record and reproduction of sounds," US Patent 409,004, 13 August 1889.
Bettini, Gianni, "Method of recording and reproducing sounds," US Patent 409,003, 11 April 1889.
Brocherioux, Emilien Jean Baptiste, Paul Joseph Tochon, Alfred Fortier, Leon Victor Marotte, "Composition for sound-records," US Patent 842,070, 22 January 1907.
Edison, Thomas A., "Improvement in phonograph or speaking machines," US Patent 200,521, 19 February 1878.
Edison, Thomas A., "Phonograph," US Patent 386,974, 31 July 1888.
Gaumont, Léon, "Means for operating synchronously phonographs and kinematographs," US Patent 752, 394, 16 February 1904.
Johnson, Eldridge E., "Spring-motor," USPatent 689,884, 31 December 1901.
Portugal. Ministério das Obras Públicas Comércio e Industria, *Boletim da propriedade industrial*, 2ª série—18º anno (Lisbon: Imprensa Nacional, 1903), 6 July 1901.
Tainter, Sumner, "Apparatus for recording and reproducing sounds," US Patent 341, 288, 4 May 1886.
Tainter, Sumner, "Recording and reproducing sounds," US Patent 341,287, 4 May 1886.

Printed Librettos, Coplas, and Cançonetas

Abranches, Aristides, *Amar sem conhecer: zarzuela em 3 actos* (Lisbon: Livraria Popular de Francisco Franco, n.d.).
Abranches, Aristides, *Fausto, o petiz: opereta phantastica em 3 actos e 4 quadros* (Lisbon: Livraria Popular de Francisco Franco, n.d.).
Abranches, Aristides, *As três rocas de cristal* (Lisbon: Carvalho, [1874]).
Aquino, Luís d', Barbosa Júnior, and Filipe Duarte, *Coplas da revista Ó da guarda: em 3 actos e 12 quadros* (Lisbon: A Liberal, 1907).

References

Araújo Luís de, *Intrigas no bairro: paródia às óperas cómicas* (Lisbon: Livr. Económica de Domingos Fernandes, 1864).

Azevedo, Arthur de, *A capital federal: opereta de costumes populares brazileiros* (Lisbon: Livraria Popular de Francisco Franco, n.d.).

Barranco, Mariano, *Marron glacé: juguete en un acto y en prosa* (Madrid: Impr. de C. Rodríguez, 1883).

Bastos, António de Sousa, *Coplas, tangos, fados e córos de: "Tim Tim Por Tim Tim: revista do ano de 1888" de Sousa Bastos: Edição de luxo, ornada com o retrato da actriz Pepa*.(Lisbon: Typographia de Alfredo da Costa Braga, 1889).

Bastos, António de Sousa, *Em pratos limpos: revista do anno de 1896* (Lisbon: Costa Sanches, 1897).

Bastos, António de Sousa, *A nove: revista em 3 actos e 15 quadros* (Lisbon: Impr. Lucas, 1909).

Bastos, António de Sousa, *Sal e pimenta: revista phantastica em 3 actos e 11 quadros* (Lisbon: Livraria Popular de Francisco Franco, n.d.).

Bastos, António de Sousa, *Sinos de Corneville: opereta original em 1 acto* (Lisbon: Liv. Economica, 1879).

Bastos, António de Sousa, *Talvez te escreva!...: revista em 3 actos e 12 quadros* (Lisbon: n.p., n.d.).

Bastos, António de Sousa, *Tim tim por tim tim de 1898: coplas, fados, córos e tangos* (Lisbon, Libanio & Cunha, 1898).

Bastos, António de Sousa, *Tim tim por tim tim: revista do anno de 1888* (Lisbon: Typographia de Alfredo da Costa Braga, 1889).

Bastos, António de Sousa, *Tim tim por tim tim: revista phantástica e de costumes em 1 prólogo, 3 actos e 12 quadros* (Lisbon: Livraria Popular de Francisco Franco, n.d.).

Câmara, D. João da, and Gervásio Lobato, *O solar dos Barrigas* (Lisbon: Livraria Popular de Francisco Franco, n.d.).

Castro, Urbano de, and Gervásio Lobato, *Mam'zelle Nitouche: vaudeville em 4 actos* (Lisbon: Liv. Economica, n.d.).

Chaves, Pedro Carlos d'Alcantara, *Revista do anno de 1859: scena com pretenções a comica e adubada com alguma musica original* (Lisbon: Viuva Marques & Silva, [1860]).

Correia, Machado, and Acácio Antunes, *O anno em três dias: revista phantastica* (Lisbon: Instituto Geral das artes graphicas, 1904).

Dantas, Júlio, *A Severa: drama em quatro actos* (Lisbon: M. Gomes, 1901).

Diniz, Baptista, and Esteves Graça, *Coplas de O anno em hora e meia* (Lisbon: Imprensa Lucas, 1905).

Fernandes, Eduardo, *O poeta Bocage: opereta em 3 actos* (Lisbon: Impr. Lucas, 1902).

Ferreira, Andrade, *Os melhoramentos materiais: revista de 1859. Comédia satírica e fantasmagórica em 3 actos e 4 quadros por um curioso observador* (Lisbon, Typ. de Joaquim Germano de Sousa Neves, 1860).

Garcia, Camanho, and Ayres Pereira da Costa, *P'rá frente: revista em 3 actos e 12 quadros* (Lisbon: Impr. Lucas, 1907).

Garrido, Eduardo, *Boccacio: opera comica em tres actos, accommodada á scena portugueza* (Lisbon: Imprensa Nacional, 1884).

Garrido, Eduardo, *As georgianas: ópera burlesca em três actos* (Lisbon: Typographia Universal de Thomaz Quintino Antunes, 1868).

Garrido, Eduardo, *A Grã-duqueza de Gérolstein: ópera burlesca em três actos e quatro quadros* (Lisbon: P. Plantier, 1869).

Garrido, Eduardo, *A Grã-duqueza de Gérolstein: ópera burlesca em três actos e quatro quadros* (Lisbon: Typographia Universal de Thomaz Quintino Antunes, 1868).

Garrido, Eduardo, *A Grã-duqueza de Gérolstein: ópera burlesca em três actos e quatro quadros* (Lisbon: Typographia Universal de Thomaz Quintino Antunes, 1869) [second edition].

Garrido, Eduardo, *O moleiro d'Alcalá: opera comica em 3 actos e 4 quadros* (Lisbon: Livraria Popular de Francisco Franco, n.d.).

Jacobetty, Francisco, *Coplas das vistorias... do Diabo* (Lisbon: Eduardo Roza, 1884),

Junqueiro, Guerra, and Guilherme d'Azevedo, *Viagem à roda da Parvónia: relatorio em 4 actos e 6 quadros* (Lisbon: Off. Typ. da Empreza Litteraria de Lisboa, 1879).
Lima, Câmara, *Em nome do padre... :revista de costumes e acontecimentos* (Lisbon: Typographia de Palhares e Cª, 1908).
Lobato, Gervásio, and D. João da Câmara, *O burro do senhor alcaide* (Lisbon: Livraria Popular de Francisco Franco, 1904).
Meneses, António de Sousa de, *O tutti-li-mundi: revista do ano de 1880* (Lisbon: Imp. Cruz, 1881).
Mesquita, Alfredo, and Dias Costa, *Na ponta da unha!: revista em 3 actos e 12 quadros* (Lisbon: Livraria Popular de Francisco Franco, n.d.).
Oliveira, Joaquim Augusto de, *A gata borralheira: mágica em 3 actos e 16 quadros* (Lisbon: Livraria Popular de Francisco Franco, n.d.).
Oliveira, Joaquim Augusto d, *Revista de 1858: em dois actos e dez quadros* (Lisboa: Escriptorio do Teatro Moderno, 1859).
Paiva, Acácio de, and Ernesto Rodrigues, *A.B.C.: Revista em 3 actos e 12 quadros* (Lisbon: Impr. Lucas, 1908).
Palha, Francisco, *Barba azul: ópera burlesca em 3 actos e 4 quadros* (Lisbon: Typographia Franco Portugueza, 1868).
Rodrigues, Ernesto, Félix Bermudes, and Marçal Vaz, *Agulha em palheiro: revista de costumes portugueses em 3 actos e 10 quadros* (Lisbon: Imprensa de Manuel Lucas Torres, 1911).
Roussado, Manuel, *Fossilismo e progresso: revista* (Lisbon: Typographia Rua da Condessa nº3, 1856).
Schwalbach, Eduardo, *Agulhas e alfinetes: revista do anno de 1898 em 3 actos e 12 quadros* (Lisbon: Livraria Popular de Francisco Franco, n.d.).
Schwalbach, Eduardo, *O barril do lixo: revista de costumes e acontecimentos* (Lisbon: Livraria Popular de Francisco Franco, n.d.).
Schwalbach, Eduardo, *Formigas e formigueiros: revista de costumes e acontecimentos em 3 actos e 9 quadros* (Lisbon: Livraria Popular de Francisco Franco, n.d.).
Schwalbach, Eduardo, *O reino da bolha: revista de costumes e acontecimentos em 3 actos e 12 quadros* (Lisbon: Livraria Popular de Francisco Franco, n.d.).
Schwalbach, Eduardo, *Retalhos de Lisboa: revista de costumes e acontecimentos* (Lisbon: Livraria Popular de Francisco Franco, n.d.).

Printed Music

Almeida, Joaquim d', *Fausto de Gounod* (Lisbon: Lence & Viúva Canongia, [1873]).
Alvarenga, Francisco, *O fado do Zé Povinho: cantado pelo actor Marcelino Franco no Tutti himundi, revista do anno de 1880* (Lisbon: Lence &Viuva Canongia—Lith. R. das Flores, 1881).
Arroyo, João, *Liebe und Verderben: Lyrisches Drama in 3 Akten nach der Portugiesischen Novelle C. C. Branco's* (Mainz: Schott, 1909).
Bramão, Carlos Augusto Pereira, *O marido mata a mulher? Polka da comedia do mesmo titulo para piano* (Lisbon: Lence & Viúva Canongia, 1872).
Cardoso, Ciriaco de, Gervásio Lobato, and D. João da Câmara, *O burro do Sr. Alcaide: ópera cómica: canções populares* (Lisbon: Lith. R. das Flores, n.d.).
Cardoso, Ciríaco, Gervásio Lobato, and D. João da Câmara, "Carta" (n.p.: n.p., n.d., MNT: 36970).
Cardoso, Ciríaco, Gervásio Lobato, and D. João da Câmara, "Coplas dos foguetes" (n.p.: n.p., n.d., MNT: 36971).
Cardoso, Ciríaco, Gervásio Lobato, and D. João da Câmara, "Coro das velhas" (n.p.: n.p., n.d., MNT: 36973).
Cardoso, Ciríaco de, Gervásio Lobato, and D. João da Câmara, *O solar dos barrigas: Duetto dos P.P.* (n.p.: n.p., n.d.).
Cardoso, Ciríaco, Gervásio Lobato, and D. João da Câmara, "Valsa" (n.p.: n.p., n.d., shelfmark MNT: 36969).

Carvalho, Francisco, and Bernardo Lisboa, *O mugunzá: lundu bahiano* (Rio de Janeiro: Edições Buschmann & Guimarães).
Carvalho, Rio de, and Alfredo de Moraes Pinto, *Meios de transporte: cançoneta original* (Lisbon: Liv. Económica de F. Napoleão de Victoria, 1887).
Carvalho, Rio de, Júlio Rocha, and Baptista Machado, *Fado alfacinha: para piano* (Lisbon: Lith. R. das Flores, n.d.).
Carvalho, Rio de, Júlio Rocha, and Baptista Machado, *O Tournure é cousa boa: para piano* (Lisbon: Lith. R. das Flores, n.d).
Correia, Machado, Acácio Antunes, and Filipe Duarte, *O anno em três dias: Coplas da lavadeira/Coplas do Kodack* (Lisbon, Salão Neuparth, n.d.).
Duarte, Filipe, Acácio Antunes, and Machado Correia, *O anno em 3 dias: coplas da lavadeira* (Lisbon: Neuparth & Carneiro, 1904).
Duarte, Filipe, *Fado do colete encarnado* (Lisbon: Neuparth & Carneiro, n.d.).
Fado liró (Lisbon: Neuparth & Carneiro, n.d.), shelfmark PTBN: C.N. 1669 A. National Library of Portugal.
Fado Roldão: cantado na peça José João no Theatro do Principe Real (Lisbon: Livraria Popular de Francisco Franco, n.d.).
Fausto: musica di Carlo Gounod (Lisbon: Sassetti, [1859]), shelfmark M.P. 1302//1 V., Biblioteca Nacional de Portugal.
Fereal, César, Henrique Lopes de Mendonça, and Alfredo Keil, *Serrana: drama lyrico em três actos* (n.p.: n.p., 1899).
Frondoni, Ângelo, *A rosa de sete folhas* (Lisbon: Lence & Viuva Canongia, 1870).
Gazul, Freitas, *Retalhos de Lisboa: revista do anno de 1895: O amanhã fado cantado pelo actor Queiroz* (Lisbon: Lith. R. das Flores, n.d.).
Gazul, Freitas, *Sal e pimenta: revista de Sousa Bastos* (Lisbon: Lith. R. das Flores, 1894).
Les grands succès de l'opéra: collection choisie de morceaux célèbres des opéras anciens et modernes: couplets des lettres dans La Grande Duchesse de Gerolstein pour piano (Porto: C A Villa Nova, n.d.).
Jacobetty, Francisco, and Rio de Carvalho, *O microbio: revista de 1884 de F. Jacobety: músicas das coplas mais applaudidas: tal qual a família ... pegue-lhe ... pegue-lhe* (Lisbon: Lith. R. das Flores, n.d.).
Jacobetty, Francisco, and Rio de Carvalho, *O microbio: revista de 1884 de F. Jacobety: músicas das coplas mais applaudidas: tenho um cavaquinho ... tra la la ... : redução para piano forte* (Lisbon: Lith. R. das Flores, n.d.).
Keil, Alfredo, and Henrique Lopes de Mendonça, *A Portugueza: marcha* (Lisbon: Neuparth & C.ª, n.d.), shelfmark PTBN: C.I.C. 78 A. National Library of Portugal.
Keil, Alfredo, *Donna Bianca: drame lyrique en quatro parties et un prologue* (Paris: G. Hartmann, [1888–1890]).
Keil, Alfredo, *Irene: leggenda mistica (dramma lirico) in quattro parti* (Lipsia: Stamperia Musical di C. G. Roder, [1893–1896]).
Leoncavallo, Ruggiero, *Mattinata* (Berlin: Roehr A.G., [1904]).
Macedo, F. S. L., *Morceau sur l'opéra La Grande Duchêsse de Gérolstein de J. Offenbach* (Coimbra: Litografia de Macedo e Filho, n.d.).
Machado, Augusto, and Henrique Lopes de Mendonça, *Tição negro: farça lyrica em 3 actos sobre motivos de Gil Vicente* (Lisbon: Neuparth & Carneiro, n.d.), shelfmark PTBN: A.M. 348 A, Biblioteca Nacional de Portugal.
Machado, Augusto, and Henrique Lopes de Mendonça, *Tição negro: farça lyrica em três actos sobre motivos de Gil Vicente* (Lisbon: Neuparth & Carneiro, [1902–1910]) [Alvorada, Ensalada]. Shelfmark PTBN: A.M. 383 A., National Library of Portugal.
Machado, Augusto and Henrique Lopes de Mendonça, *Tição negro: farça lyrica em três actos sobre motivos de Gil Vicente* (Lisbon: Neuparth & Carneiro, [1902–1910]) [Coplas, Dueto]. Shelfmark PTBN: A.M. 287 A., Biblioteca Nacional de Portugal.
Machado, Augusto and Henrique Lopes de Mendonça, *Tição negro: farça lyrica em três actos sobre motivos de Gil Vicente* (Lisbon: Typ. Annuario Commercial, 1907).

Musard, Philippe, *A costureira* (Lisbon: J. I. Canongia [1853]).
Musard, Philippe, *La couturière: valse sur des motifs d'Offenbach* (Lisbon: Sassetti, [1855–60]).
Oliveira, Joaquim Augusto de, Salvador Marques, and Filipe Duarte, *Canção de Belphogor (Fado)* (Lisbon: Salão Neuparth, n.d.).
Rente, Francisco Alves, *Quadrilha sobre os principais motivos da revista do anno Etc e tal* (Porto: Costa Mesquita, n.d.).
Ribeiro, Guilherme, *Suzanna: opera comica num acto: fantasia brilhante* (Lisbon: Augusto Neuparth, [1883]).
Schwalbach, Eduardo, and Filipe Duarte, *Agulhas e alfinetes: Duetto das vaidosas* (Lisbon: Neuparth & Comp., n.d.).
Strauss, Johann, *Boccacio: quadrilha para piano: Opera comique de F. Suppé* (Porto: Costa Mesquita, [1882]).
Strauss, Johann, *Orphée aux enfers: quadrille-cancan sur l'opera de J. Offenbach: pour piano* (Lisbon: Sassetti, n.d.).

Catalogues

Compagnie Française du Gramophone, *Repertoire portuguais: Disques "Gramophone" & disques "Zonophone" double-face* (n.p.: n.p., 1907).
Companhia Franceza do Gramophone, *Catalogo das ultimas placas feitas pela Companhia Franceza do Gramophone* (Lisbon: n.p., 1906).
Companhia Franceza do Gramophone, *Catalogo geral dos discos* (Lisbon: Companhia Franceza do Gramophone, 1910).
Companhia Franceza do Gramophone, *Novo catalogo de discos portuguezes* (Lisbon: n.p., 1908).
Companhia Franceza do Gramophone, *Supplemento ao catalogo de discos portuguezes* (Lisbon: n.p., 1905).
Discos Simplex e Odeon, *Catalogo para 1908* (Lisbon: Discos Simplex, 1908).
Grammophon, *Verzeichnis französischer, italienischer, spanischer, portugiesischer Platten* (Berlin: J. S. Preuss, [1900]).
Grandes Armazéns do Chiado, *Catálogo de Novidades: Inverno de 1910* (Lisbon: A Editora, 1910).
Phonographos Pathé, *Novo catalogo e repertorio portuguez* (Porto: n.p., 1906).
The Aeolian Company, *Bulletin of New Music for the Pianola Pianola-Piano, Orchestrelle and Aeolian Grand* (New York: Aeolian Company, 1911).

Iconography and Cartography

ABC [poster], Lisbon, Teatro Avenida (1908), PT-ADPRT-COL-CDAC-017-034-01699, Porto District Archive.
O anno em três dias [postcards]. Shelfmarks MNT: 32135, MNT: 32179, MNT: 32271, and MNT: 32388, National Theater Museum (Lisbon).
Beijos de burro [program], Lisbon (Teatro Chalet do Rato), [1903]. Shelfmark MNT: 17092, National Theater Museum (Lisbon).
Benoliel, Joshua, *Casa Odéon, gramofones e discos*, PT/AMLSB/AF/JBN/000985, Municipal Archive of Lisbon.
Coimbra, o gaiteiro, costume dos arrabaldes [postcard], Coimbra, Pap. Borges, [1904]. Record number Fel_028588-AL-RE, ETH-Bibliothek Zürich, Bildarchiv, Feller Collection.
Coimbra, Uma serenata d'estudantes [postcard], Coimbra, Pap. Borges, [1904]. Record number Fel_028589-AL-RE, ETH-Bibliothek Zürich, Bildarchiv, Feller Collection.
Colyseu dos Recreios, and Empreza Santos, *Opera lyrica A Serrana: argumento* [program] (Lisbon: Typ. Almeida, Machado & C.ª, 1901). Shelfmark PTBN: M.9 A., National Library of Portugal.
Delgado, Nery, and Carlos Ribeiro, *Carta geológica de Portugal* (Lisbon: Direcção Geral dos Trabalhos Geodésicos, 1876). Shelfmark PTBN: C. Par. 70, National Library of Portugal.

Fernandes, J., *Vénus: Americanas* [postcard], Lisbon, Pap. Typ de Paulo Guedes e Saraiva, [1906]. Shelfmark PTBN: P.I. 5755 P., National Library of Portugal.
A grande avenida [poster], Lisbon, Teatro do Rato (1887), PT-ADPRT-COL-CDAC-017-034-01706, Porto District Archive.
Pinheiro, Columbano Bordalo, *Trecho difícil*, 1885. Inventory number CMAG: 928, Casa-Museu Dr. Anastácio Gonçalves (Lisbon).
Pontos nos ii [poster], Lisbon, Chalet da Rua dos Condes (1886), PT-ADPRT-COL-CDAC-017-034-01677, Porto District Archive.
Raios X [program], Lisbon, (Teatro da Trindade), [1904/1905]. Shelfmark MNT: 112557, National Theater Museum (Lisbon).
O solar dos barrigas [program], Lisbon (Teatro da Rua dos Condes), 1892. Shelfmark MNT: 29871, National Theater Museum (Lisbon).
Tição negro [postcard], Lisbon: Union Postale Universelle, [1902]. Shelfmark PTBN: A.M./C.3//6, National Library of Portugal.
O tutti-li-mundi [poster], Lisbon, Teatro da Rua dos Condes (1881), PT-ADPRT-COL-CDAC-017-034-01728, Porto District Archive.
Tição negro [poster], Lisbon, Teatro Avenida, [1902]. Shelfmark MNT: 18062, National Theater Museum (Lisbon).
Tim tim por tim tim [poster], Lisbon, Teatro da Avenida (1889), PT/ADPRT/COL/CDAC/005/002/01708, Porto District Archive.
Venus [postcards], [1906]. Shelfmarks PTBN: P.I. 63 P., PTBN: P.I. 64 P., PTBN: P.I. 65 P., PTBN: P.I. 66 P., National Library of Portugal.

Manuscript Sources

Bastos, António de Sousa, and Júlio Soares, Revista do anno de 1879, 1880. Lisbon, National Library of Portugal, Shelfmark PTBN: M.M. 1071.
Cordeiro, João Rodrigues, *Barba Azul: 1.º Acto (completo) da Opera Buffa*. Shelfmark PTBN: C.N. 530, National Library of Portugal.
Cordeiro, João Rodrigues, *Mosaico: extrahido da Opera Comica La Fille de Madame Angot*. Shelfmark PTBN: C.N. 523, National Library of Portugal.
Correspondence between Alfred Clark, Compagnie Française du Gramophone, and the Gramophone & Typewriter's offices in London, 5 May 1904.
Duarte, Filipe, O fado [uncatalogued manuscript in the National Library of Portugal].
Duarte, Filipe, Favas contadas: Revista de costumes e acontecimentos em 3 actos [uncatalogued manuscript in the National Library of Portugal].
Duarte, Filipe, Nicles: Revista do anno 1900 [uncatalogued manuscript in the National Library of Portugal].
Duarte, Filipe, A Severa [instrumental score, ff. 32v.–33r, and vocal score, uncataloged manuscripts in the National Library of Portugal].
Duarte, Filipe, A Severa [vocal score, uncatalogued manuscript in the National Library of Portugal].
Garrido, Eduardo, *Os sinos de Corneville: opera-comica em 3 actos e 4 quadros*. Shelfmark PTBN: COD. 12136, National Library of Portugal.
Keil, Alfredo, and Henrique Lopes de Mendonça, A Portugueza—Marcha. Shelfmark PTBN: M.M 345//3, National Library of Portugal.
Machado, Augusto, and Henrique Lopes de Mendonça, *Tição Negro*: orchestra, 1902. Shelfmark PTBN: A.M. 171, National Library of Portugal.
Machado, Augusto, and Henrique Lopes de Mendonça, Tição negro: libreto, 1902. Shelfmark PTBN: A.M./C.5//96,, National Library of Portugal.
Machado, Augusto, Maria da Fonte: Comédia em três actos, 1878. Shelfmark PTBN: A.M. 318, National Library of Portugal.
Meillac, Henri, Ludovic Halévy, and Jacques Offenbach, A Perichole: opera burlesca em 3 actos e 4 quadros. Shelfmark PTBN: COD. 11735.

Paróquia de Socorro: Livro de Registos de óbito 1833–1852, PT/ADLSB/PRQ/PLSB53/003/O10, 143v.
Recording sheet of the march "Le drapeau de la liberté" by the Musique de la Garde Republicaine, Paris, January 1904. Serial number 2454, extant both in the EMI Archive and in the British Library.

Secondary Sources

Adorno Theodor W., "The Curves of the Needle," *October*, 55 (1990), 49–55.
Adorno, Theodor W., "The Form of the Phonograph Record," *October*, 55 (1990), 56–61.
Adorno, Theodor W., "On Popular Music," in Richard Leppert (ed.), *Essays on Music: Theodor W. Adorno* (Berkeley: University of California Press, 2002), 437–470.
Alexandre, Valentim, "Questão nacional e questão colonial em Oliveira Martins," *Análise Social*, 31/135 (1996), 183–201.
Almeida, Miguel Vale de, "Anthropology and Ethnography of the Portuguese-Speaking Empire," in Prem Poddar, Rajeev S. Patke and Lars Jensen (eds.), *A Historical Companion to Postcolonial Literature: Continental Europe and Its Empires* (Edinburgh: Edinburgh University Press, 2008), 435–39.
Alves, Daniel Ribeiro, "A República atrás do balcão: os lojistas de Lisboa na fase final da Monarquia (1870–1910)," Ph.D thesis (Universidade Nova de Lisboa, 2010).
Anderson, Amanda, "Cosmopolitanism, Universalism, and the Divided Legacies of Modernity," in Pheng Cheah and Bruce Robbins (eds.), *Cosmopolitics: Thinking and Feeling beyond the Nation* (Minneapolis: University of Minnesota Press, 1998), 265–289.
Anderson, Amanda, *The Powers of Distance: Cosmopolitanism and the Cultivation of Detachment* (Princeton, NJ: Princeton University Press, 2001).
Anderson, Benedict, *Imagined Communities: Reflections on the Origin and Spread of Nationalism* (London: Verso, 1991).
Andrade, Adriano da Guerra, *Dicionário de pseudónimos e iniciais de escritores portugueses* (Lisbon: Biblioteca Nacional de Portugal, 1999).
Araújo, Maria João Rodrigues de, "The reception of Wagner in Portugal (1880–1930),: Ph.D. thesis (University of Oxford, 2004).
Artiaga, Maria José, "Continuity and Change in Three Decades of Portuguese Musical Life 1870—1900," Ph.D. thesis (Royal Holloway, University of London, 2007).
Askew, Kelly, *Performing the Nation: Swahili Music and Cultural Politics in Tanzania* (Chicago: University of Chicago Press, 2002).
Attali, Jacques, *Noise: The Political Economy of Music* (Minneapolis: University of Minnesota Press, 1985).
Balibar, Étienne, "The Nation Form," in Étienne Balibar and Immanuel Wallerstein, *Race, Nation, Class: Ambiguous Identities* (London: Verso, 1991), 86–106.
Barata, José de Oliveira, *História do teatro português* (Lisbon: Universidade Aberta, 1991).
Barnett, Kyle S., "Furniture Music: The Phonograph as Furniture, 1900–1930," *Journal of Popular Music Studies*, 18/3 (1996), 301–324.
Barthes, Roland, *Camera Lucida* (London: Vintage Books, 2000).
Barthes, Roland, "The Photographic Message" in Barthes, *Image-Music-Text* (New York: Hill and Wang, 1978), 15–31.
Barthes, Roland, "Rhetoric of the Image," in Barthes, *Image-Music-Text* (New York: Hill and Wang, 1978), 32–51.
Bastos, Glória, and Ana Isabel de Vasconcelos, *O teatro em Lisboa no tempo da Primeira República* (Lisbon: Museu Nacional do Teatro, 2004).
Becker, Howard S., *Art Worlds* (Berkeley: University of California Press, 2008).
Belchior, Susana, "Sinkler Darby's 1900 Expedition for the Gramophone Company in Portugal," in Pekka Gronow and Christiane Hofer (eds.), *Contributions to the History of the Record*

Industry: Beiträge zur Geschichte der Schallplattenindustrie, vol. 5 (Vienna: Gesellschaft für Historische Tonträger, 2010), 15–24.

Benchimol, Jaime, *Pereira Passos: um Haussmann tropical* (Rio de Janeiro: Secretaria Municipal de Cultura, Turismo e Esportes, 1992).

Benjamin, Walter, and Asja Lacis, "Naples," in Walter Benjamin, *Reflections: Essays, Aphorisms, Autobiographical Writings* (New York: Schocken Books, 2007), 163–173.

Benjamin, Walter, *The Arcades Project* (Cambridge, MA: Harvard University Press, 1999).

Benjamin, Walter, "Little History of Photography," in Walter Benjamin, *Selected Writings*, vol. 2, *1927–1934* (Cambridge, MA, Harvard University Press, 1999), 507–530.

Benjamin, Walter, "Paris—Capital of the Nineteenth Century," *New Left Review*, 1/48 (1968), 77–88.

Benjamin, Walter, *The Work of Art in the Age of Mechanical Reproduction* (London: Penguin Books, 2008).

Benjamin, Walter, *The Writer of Modern life: Essays on Charles Baudelaire* (Cambridge, MA: Harvard University Press, 2006).

Benson, Richard, *The Printed Picture* (New York: Museum of Modern Art, 2008).

Berman, Marshall, *All That Is Solid Melts into Air: The Experience of Modernity* (London: Verso, 1983).

Bhabha, Homi K., "Dissemination: Time, Narrative and the Margins of the Modern Nation," in Bhabha, *The Location of Culture* (London: Routledge, 1994), 139–170.

Bispo, A. A.,"Luso-brasileirismo, ítalo-brasileiros e mecanismos performativos: representações teatrais e revistas: Nicolino Milano," *Revista Brasil-Europa* 107/3 (2007), http://www.revista.brasil-europa.eu/107/Nicolino-Milano.htm, accessed 12 November 2009.

Blake, Jody, *Le Tumulte Noir: Modernist Art and Popular Entertainment in Jazz-Age Paris, 1900–1930* (University Park: Pennsylvania State University Press, 1999).

Bohlman, Philip, "Traditional Music and Cultural Identity: Persistent Paradigm in the History of Ethnomusicology," *Yearbook for Traditional Music*, 20 (1988), 26–42.

Born, Georgina, and David Hesmondhalgh, "Introduction," in Born and Hesmondhalgh (eds.), *Western Music and Its Others: Difference, Representation, and Appropriation in Music* (Berkeley: University of California Press, 2000), 1–58.

Born, Georgina, "Music and the Materialization of Identities," *Journal of Material Culture*, 16/4 (2011), 376–88.

Bottero, Wendy, "Relationality and Social Interaction," *British Journal of Sociology*, 60/2 (2009), 399–420.

Bourdieu, Pierre, and Loïc Wacquant, *An Invitation to Reflexive Sociology* (Oxford: Polity Press, 1992).

Bourdieu, Pierre, *La distinction. Critique social du jugement* (Paris: Éditions de Minuit, 1979).

Bourdieu, Pierre, "The Forms of Capital," in Mark Granovetter and Richard Swedberg (eds.), *The Sociology of Economic Life* (Boulder, CO: Westview Press, 2001), 46–58.

Bourdieu, Pierre, "La parenté comme représentation et comme volonté," in Pierre Bourdieu, *Esquisse d'une théorie de la pratique, précédé de Trois études d'ethnologie kabyle* (Paris: Éditions du Seuil, 2000), 83–215.

Bourdieu, Pierre, *Outline of a Theory of Practice* (Cambridge: Cambridge University Press, 1977).

Bourdieu, Pierre, "Social Space and Symbolic Power," *Sociological Theory*, 7/1 (1989), 14–25.

Bourdieu, Pierre, "The Social Space and the Genesis of Groups," *Theory and Society*, 14/6 (1985), 723–744.

Boym, Svetlana, *The Future of Nostalgia* (New York: Basic Books, 2001).

Branco, Jorge Freitas, and Salwa Castelo-Branco (eds.), *Vozes do povo: a folclorização em Portugal* (Oeiras: Celta Editora, 2003).

Branco, Jorge Freitas, "A fluidez dos limites: Discurso etnográfico e movimento folclórico em Portugal," *Etnográfica*, 3/1 (1999), 23–48.

Branco, Luiz de Freitas, *Comemoração do centenário da "Casa Sassetti"* (Lisbon: Sassetti & C.ª, 1948).
Brown, Julie, "Bartók, the Gypsies, and Hybridity in Music," in Born and Hesmondhalgh (eds.), *Western Music and Its Others* (Berkeley: University of California Press, 2000), 119–142.
Buck-Morss, Susan, *The Dialectics of Seeing: Walter Benjamin and the Arcades Project* (Cambridge, MA: MIT Press, 1991).
Burton, James, "Bergson's Non-Archival Theory of Memory," *Memory Studies*, 1/3 (2008), 321–339.
Cabral, João de Pina, "A antropologia em Portugal hoje," in Pina Cabral, *Os contextos da antropologia* (Lisbon: Difel, 1991), 11–41.
Câmara Municipal da Póvoa de Lanhoso (ed.), *História da coragem feita com o coração—Actas do congresso "Maria da Fonte—150 anos—1846/1996"* (Póvoa do Lanhoso: Câmara Municipal da Póvoa de Lanhoso, 1996).
Carvalho, Mário Vieira de, *Eça de Queirós e Offenbach* (Lisbon: Edições Colibri, 1999).
Cascudo, Teresa, "A década da invenção de Portugal na música erudita (1890–1899)," *Revista portuguesa de musicologia*, 10 (2000), 196–208.
Castelo-Branco, Salwa, and Manuela Toscano, "'In Search of a LOST World': An Overview of Documentation and Research on the Traditional Music of Portugal," *Yearbook for Traditional Music*, 20 (1988), 158–192.
Castelo-Branco, Salwa, "Etnomusicologia," in Salwa Castelo-Branco (ed.), *Enciclopédia da música em Portugal no século XX*, vol. 2 (Lisbon: Círculo de Leitores, 2010), 419–432.
Catroga, Fernando, *O republicanismo em Portugal* (Lisbon: Editorial Notícias, 2000).
Catroga, Fernando, "Ritualizações da História," in Luís Reis Torgal, José Amado Mendes, and Fernando Catroga, *História da História em Portugal*, vol. 2 (Lisbon: Temas & Debates, 1998), 221–362.
Charney, Leo, and Vanessa Schwartz, "Introduction," in Charney and Schwartz (eds.), *Cinema and the Invention of Modern Life* (Berkeley: University of California Press, 1995), 1–14.
Charnow, Sally, "Commercial Culture and Modernist Theatre in Fin-de-siècle Paris: André Antoine and the Théâtre Libre," *Radical History Review*, 77 (2000), 60–90.
Chartier, Roger, and J. A. González, "Laborers and Voyagers: From the Text to the Reader," *Diacritics*, 22/2 (1992), 49–61.
Chiesa, Lorenzo, "Lacan with Artaud: fouis-sens, jouis-sens, jouis-sans," in Slavoj Žižek (ed.), *Lacan: The Silent Partners* (London: Verso, 2006), 336–364.
Clifford, James, *Routes: Travel and Translation in the Late Twentieth Century* (Cambridge, MA: Harvard University Press, 1997).
Comaroff, John, and Jean Comaroff, "Images of Empire, Contests of Conscience," in Comaroff and Comaroff, *Ethnography and the Historical Imagination* (Boulder, CO: Westview Press, 1992), 181–214.
Corbin, Alain, *Village Bells: Sound and Meaning in the Nineteenth-Century French Countryside* (London: Papermac, 1999).
Cruz, Gabriela, "L'Africaine's Savage Pleasures: Operatic Listening and the Portuguese Historical Imagination," *Revista portuguesa de musicologia*, 10 (2000), 151–180.
Cymbron, Luísa, "Entre a tradição italiana, a reforma garrettiana e as motivações políticas— os compositores de ópera na Lisboa de meados do século XIX," in Luísa Cymbron, *Olhares sobre a música em Portugal no século XIX* (Lisbon: Edições Colibri/CESEM, 2012), 1–38.
Cymbron, Luísa, "Francisco de Sá Noronha e L'Arco di Sant'anna: para o estudo da ópera em Portugal (1860–70)," master's thesis (Universidade Nova de Lisboa, 1990).
Cymbron, Luísa, "Machado, Augusto," Grove Music Online, ed. L. Macy, http://www.oxfordmusiconline.com, accessed 5 November 2009.
Cymbron, Luísa, "A ópera em Portugal 1834–1854: o sistema produtivo e o repertório nos teatros de S. Carlos e de S. João," Ph.D. thesis (Universidade Nova de Lisboa, 1998).

Cymbron, Luísa, "As orquestras dos teatros de ópera em Lisboa e no Porto durante o século XIX," in Luísa Cymbron, *Olhares sobre a música em Portugal no século XIX* (Lisbon: Edições Colibri/CESEM, 2012), 77–114.

Cymbron, Luísa, "O teatro de Scribe em Lisboa após a vitória liberal (1834–1853)," in Luísa Cymbron, *Olhares sobre a música em Portugal no século XIX* (Lisbon: Edições Colibri/CESEM, 2012), 171–208.

Cymbron, Luísa (ed.), *Verdi em Portugal 1843–2001* (Lisbon: Biblioteca Nacional de Portugal, 2001) [exhibition catalogue].

Dalhaus, Carl, *Nineteenth-Century Music* (Berkeley: University of California Press, 1991).

Darnet, Brenda, *Cyberpl@y: Communicating Online* (Oxford: Berg, 2001).

Daston, Lorraine, and Peter Galison, "The Image of Objectivity," *Representations*, 0/40 (1992), 81–128.

Daston, Lorraine, "Objectivity and the Escape from Perspective," *Social Studies of Science*, 22/4 (1992), 597–618.

de Certeau, Michel, *The Practice of Everyday Life*, vol. 1 (Berkeley: University of California Press, 1988).

DeGraaf, Leonard, "Confronting the Mass Market: Thomas Edison and the Entertainment Phonograph," *Business and Economic History*, 24/1 (1995), 88–96.

DeNora, Tia, *After Adorno: Rethinking Music Sociology* (Cambridge: Cambridge University Press, 2003).

Dias, Jorge, "Bosquejo histórico da etnografia portuguesa," *Revista Portuguesa de Filologia*, 2 (1952), 1–64.

Dias, Nélia, "The Visibility of Difference: Nineteenth-Century French Anthropological Collections," in Sharon Macdonald (ed.), *The Politics of Display: Museums, Science, Culture* (London: Routledge, 1998), 36–52.

Duttlinger, Carolin, "Imaginary Encounters: Walter Benjamin and the Aura of Photography," *Poetics Today*, 29/1 (2008), 79–101.

Eagleton, Terry, *Walter Benjamin or Towards a Revolutionary Criticism* (London: Verso, 2009).

Elliker, Calvin, "Toward a Definition of Sheet Music," *Notes, Second Series*, 55/4 (1999), 835–859.

Elliott, Richard, *Fado and the Place of Longing: Loss, Memory and the City* (Aldershot: Ashgate 2010).

Fernandes, Abílio, *Lisboa e a electricidade* (Lisbon: EDP, 1992).

Ferreira, Hélder, and António Azevedo, *Armazéns do Chiado: 100 anos* (Mafra: Elo, 2001).

Foucault, Michel, *Histoire de la sexualité: La volonté de savoir*, vol.1 (Paris: Gallimard, 1976).

Fraga. Eudinyr, "Teatro brasileiro no fim do século XIX," *Luso-Brazilian Review*, 35/2 (1998), 3–17.

França, José-Augusto, *O Romantismo em Portugal: estudo de factos socioculturais* (Lisbon: Livros Horizonte, 1974).

Francmanis, John, "National Music to National Redeemer: The Consolidation of a "Folk-Song" Construct in Edwardian England," *Popular Music*, 21/1 (2002), 1–25.

Freire, Vanda, "Óperas e mágicas em teatros e salões do Rio de Janeiro e de Lisboa," in *Anais do XV Encontro Anual da ANPPOM* (Rio de Janeiro: UFRJ, 2005), 232–241.

Frith, Simon, *Performing Rites: On the Value of Popular Music* (Cambridge, MA: Harvard University Press, 1998).

Frith, Simon, *Popular Music: Critical Concepts in Media and Cultural Studies*, vol. 2 (London: Routledge, 2004).

Gammon, Vic, "Folk Song Collecting in Sussex and Surrey, 1843–1914," *History Workshop Journal*, 10/1 (1980), 61–89.

Gellner, Ernest, *Nations and Nationalisms* (Oxford: Blackwell, 2006).

Ghosh, Amitabha, "Pre-Commercial Era of Sound Recording in India," *Indian Journal of History of Science*, 34/1 (1999), 47–58.

Giddens, Anthony, *A Contemporary Critique of Historical Materialism: The Nation State and Violence* (Cambridge: Polity Press, 1985).
Giddens, Anthony, *Modernity and Self-Identity: Self and Society in the Late Modern Age* (Stanford, CA: Stanford University Press, 1991).
Gitelman, Lisa, "Media, Materiality, and the Measure of the Digital; or, the Case of Sheet Music and the Problem of Piano Rolls," in Lauren Rabinovitz and Abraham Geil (eds.), *Memory Bytes: History, Technology, and Digital Culture* (Durham, NC: Duke University Press, 2004), 199–217.
Gluck, Mary, *Popular Bohemia: Modernism and Urban Culture in Nineteenth-Century Paris* (Cambridge, MA: Harvard University Press, 2005).
Gomart, Emilie, and Antoine Hennion, "A Sociology of Attachment: Music Amateurs, Drug Users," *Sociological Review*, 46/S (1998), 220–247.
Gonçalves, Isabel, "A introdução e a recepção da ópera cómica nos teatros públicos de Lisboa entre 1841 e 1851," *Revista portuguesa de musicologia*, 13 (2003), 93–111.
Gonçalves, Isabel, "A música teatral na Lisboa de oitocentos: uma abordagem através da obra de Joaquim Casimiro Júnior (1808–1862)," Ph.D thesis (Universidade Nova de Lisboa, 2012).
Goonewardena, Kanishka, et al., "On the Production of Henri Lefebvre," in Kanishka Goonewardena et al. (eds.), *Space, Difference, Everyday Life: Reading Henri Lefebvre* (London/New York: Routledge, 2008), 1–24.
Gordon, Rae Beth, "From Charcot to Charlot: Unconscious Imitation and Spectatorship in French Cabaret and Early Cinema," *Critical Inquiry*, 27/3 (Spring 2001), 515–549.
Goulemot, Jean-Marie, and Eric Walter, "Les centenaires de Voltaire et de Rousseau: Les deux lampions des lumières," in Nora, *Les lieux de mémoire*, vol. 1, 381–420.
Gronow, Pekka, and Bjorn Englung, "Inventing Recorded Music: The Recorded Repertoire in Scandinavia 1899–1925," *Popular Music*, 26/2 (2007), 281–304.
Gronow, Pekka, "The Record Industry: Growth of a Mass Medium," *Popular Music*, 3 (1983), 53–75.
Gunn, Simon, "Translating Bourdieu: Cultural Capital and the English Middle Class in Historical Perspective," *British Journal of Sociology*, 56/1 (2005), 49–64.
Hall, Patrik, "Nationalism and Historicity," *Nations and Nationalism*, 3/1 (1997), 3–23.
Hall, Stuart, "Encoding/decoding," in Centre for Contemporary Cultural Studies (ed.), *Culture, Media, Language: Working Papers in Cultural Studies, 1972–79* (London: Hutchinson, 1980), 128–138.
Hanák, Péter, *The Garden and the Workshop: Essays on the Cultural History of Vienna and Budapest* (Princeton, NJ: Princeton University Press, 1999).
Harney, Lucy D., "Zarzuela and the Pastoral," *MLN*, 123/2 (2008), 252–273.
Harvey, David, *Paris, Capital of Modernity* (London: Routledge, 2005).
Henkin, David M., *The Postal Age: The Emergence of Modern Communications in Nineteenth-Century America* (Chicago: University of Chicago Press, 2007).
"History of the pianola—piano players," Pianola Institute (2008), http://www.pianola.org/history/history_pianoplayers.cfm, accessed 2 August 2010.
Hitchcock, H. Wiley, and Pauline Norton, "Cakewalk," *Grove Music Online*, ed. L. Macy, http://www.oxfordmusiconline.com, accessed 5 December 2009.
Hobsbawm, Eric J., *The Age of Empire: 1875–1914* (London: Abacus, 2004).
Hobsbawm, Eric J., "Introduction," in Eric J. Hobsbawm and Terence Ranger (eds.), *The Invention of Tradition* (Cambridge: Cambridge University Press, 1992), 1–14.
Hobsbawm, Eric J., *Nations and Nationalism since 1780: Programme, Myth, Reality* (Cambridge: Canto, 1992).
Hoffman, Frank, *Encyclopedia of Recorded Sound* (London: Routledge, 2004).
Hogg, Bennett, "The Cultural Imagination of the Phonographic Voice, 1877–1940," Ph.D. thesis (Newcastle University, 2008).

Holland, Frank W., and Arthur W. J. G. Ord-Hume, "Reproducing Piano: 1. History and Technical Development," *Grove Music Online*, ed. L. Macy, http://www.oxfordmusiconline.com, accessed 10 August 2010.

Huebner, Steven, "Gounod, Charles-François," *Grove Music Online*, ed. L. Macy, http://www.oxfordmusiconline.com, accessed 10 July 2010.

Johnson, James, *Listening in Paris: A Cultural History* (Berkeley: University of California Press, 1996).

Jones, Geoffrey, "The Gramophone Company: An Anglo-American Multinational, 1898–1931," *Business History Review*, 59/1 (1985), 76–100.

Kassabian, Anahid, "Popular," in Bruce Horner and Thomas Swiss (eds.), *Key Terms in Popular Music and Culture* (Malden, MA: Blackwell, 1999), 113–123.

Kenney, William Howland, *Recorded Music in American Life: The Phonograph and Popular Memory, 1890–1945* (Oxford: Oxford University Press, 2003).

Kirshner, Lewis A., "Rethinking Desire: The *objet petit a* in Lacanian Theory," *Journal of the American Psychoanalytical Association*, 53/1 (2005), 83–102.

Kittler, Friedrich A., *Discourse Networks, 1800/1900* (Palo Alto, CA: Stanford University Press, 1992).

Kittler, Friedrich A., *Gramophone, Film, Typewriter* (Palo Alto, CA: Stanford University Press, 1999).

Koetsier, Teun, "On the Prehistory of Programmable Machines: Musical Automata, Looms, Calculators," *Mechanism and Machine Theory*, 36 (2001), 589–603.

Kohl, Philip L., "Nationalism and Archaeology: On the Constructions of Nations and the Reconstructions of the Remote Past," *Annual Review of Anthropology*, 27 (1998), 223–246.

Koza, Julia Eklund, "Music and the Feminine Sphere: Images of Women as Musicians in 'Godey's Lady's Book,' 1830–1877, " *Musical Quarterly*, 75/2 (1991), 103–129.

Kracauer, Siegfried, *Jacques Offenbach and the Paris of His Time* (New York: Zone Books, 2002).

Kruse, Holly, "Early Audio Technology and Domestic Space," *Stanford Humanities Review* 3 (1993), 1–14.

Lacan, Jacques, *Écrits: A Selection* (London: Routledge, 2001).

Lacan, Jacques, *The Ethics of Psychoanalysis, 1959–1960* (New York: Routledge Chapman & Hall, 1992).

Laclau, Ernesto, "Ideology and Post-Marxism," *Journal of Political Ideologies*, 11/2 (2006), 103–104.

Laclau, Ernesto, *On Populist Reason*, (London: Verso, 2007).

Lains, Pedro, "The Power of Peripheral Governments: Coping with the 1891 Financial Crisis in Portugal," *Historical Research*, 81/213 (2008), 485–506.

Lamb, Andrew, "Operetta," *Grove Music Online*, ed. L. Macy, http://www.oxfordmusiconline.com, accessed 6 November 2012.

Lamb, Andrew, et al., "Revue," *Grove Music Online*, ed. L. Macy, http://www.oxfordmusiconline.com, accessed 5 December 2009.

Leal, João, *Antropologia em Portugal: mestres, percursos e transições* (Lisbon: Livros Horizonte, 2006).

Leal, João, *Etnografias portuguesas (1870–1970): cultura popular e identidade nacional* (Lisbon: Publicações D. Quixote, 2000).

Leal, João, "The Hidden Empire: Peasants, Nation Building, and the Empire in Portuguese Anthropology," in Roseman and Parkhurst (eds.), *Recasting Culture and Space in Iberian Contexts*, 35–53.

Lefebvre, Henri, *Introduction to Modernity: Twelve Preludes* (London: Verso, 1995).

Leitão, Rui, A ambiência musical e sonora da cidade de Lisboa no ano de 1890, master's thesis (Universidade Nova de Lisboa, 2006).

Leppert, Richard, "The Female at Music: Praxis, Representation and the Problematic of Identity," in Leppert, *Music and Image: Domesticity, Ideology and Socio-cultural*

Formation in Eighteenth-Century England (Cambridge: Cambridge University Press, 1988), 147–175.

Leppert, Richard, "Sexual Identity, Death, and the Family Piano," in *19th-Century Music*, 16/2 (1992), 105–128.

Lin, Nan, "Building a Network Theory of Social Capital," *Connections*, 22/1 (1999), 28–51.

Löfgren, Orvar, "Scenes from a Troubled Marriage: Swedish Ethnology and Material Culture Studies," *Journal of Material Culture*, 2 (1997), 95–113.

Lopes, Maria Virgílio Cambraia, *O teatro n'A Paródia de Rafael Bordalo Pinheiro* (Lisbon: Imprensa Nacional-Casa da Moeda, 2005).

Lopes, Rui Cabral, "Filipe Duarte," in Salwa Castelo-Branco (ed.), *Enciclopédia da música em Portugal no século XX*, vol. 2, 385.

Losa, Leonor, and João Silva, "Edição de música. 1. Geral" in Salwa Castelo-Branco (ed.), *Enciclopédia da música em Portugal no século XX*, vol. 2 (Lisbon: Círculo de Leitores, 2010), 391–392.

Losa, Leonor, and Susana Belchior, "The Introduction of Phonogram Market in Portugal: Lindström Labels and Local Traders (1879–1925)," in Pekka Gronow and Christiane Hofer (eds.), *The Lindström Project: Contributions to the History of the Record Industry: Beiträge zur Geschichte der Schallplattenindustrie*, vol. 2 (Vienna: Gesellschaft für Historische Tonträger, 2010), 7–11.

Losa, Leonor, "Indústria fonográfica," in Salwa Castelo-Branco (ed.), *Enciclopédia da música em Portugal no século XX*, vol. 2 (Lisbon: Círculo de Leitores, 2010), 632–643.

Losa, Leonor, "Joaquim Tomás del Negro," in Salwa Castelo-Branco (ed.), *Enciclopédia da música em Portugal no século XX*, vol. 3, 904.

Losa, Leonor, *Machinas fallantes: a música gravada em Portugal no início do século XX* (Lisbon: Tinta da China, 2013).

Losa, Leonor, "'Nós humanizámos a indústria': reconfiguração de produção fonográfica e musical em Portugal na década de 60," master's thesis (Universidade Nova de Lisboa, 2009).

Macdonald, Sharon, "Preface," in Sharon Macdonald (ed.), *The Politics of Display: Museums, Science, Culture* (London: Routledge, 1998), ix–xiii.

Manuel, Peter, *Popular Musics of the Non-Western World: An Introductory Survey* (Oxford: Oxford University Press, 1990).

Marinho, Maria José, "Jaime Batalha Reis e Celeste Cinatti: diálogo sobre um retrato incompleto," *Análise social*, 42/182 (2007), 281–284.

Martin, James, "The Political Logic of Discourse: A Neo-Gramscian View," *History of European Ideas*, 28/1–2 (2002), 21–31.

Martins, Mónica, Lina Santos, and Catarina Latino, "Hino Nacional," in Salwa Castelo-Branco (ed.), *Enciclopédia da música em Portugal no século XX*, vol. 2 (Lisbon: Círculo de Leitores, 2010), 617–618.

Martland, Peter, "A Business History of the Gramophone Company Ltd: 1897–1918," Ph.D. thesis (Cambridge University, 1992).

Martland, Peter, *Recording History: The British Record Industry 1888–1931* (Lanham, MD: Scarecrow Press, 2013).

Martland, Peter, *Since Records Began: Emi, the First 100 Years* (London: Batsford, 1997).

Mascarenhas, João Mário (ed.), *Grandella, o grande homem* (Lisbon: Câmara Municipal de Lisboa, 1994).

Medeiros, António, "Imperialist Ideology and Representations of the Portuguese Provinces during the Early Estado Novo," in Sharon R. Roseman and Shawn S. Parkhurst (eds.), *Recasting Culture and Space in Iberian Contexts* (NY: SUNY Press, 2008), 81–99.

Mencarelli, Fernando Antonio, "A cena aberta: a interpretação de 'O Bilontra' no teatro de revista de Arthur Azevedo," master's thesis (Unicamp, 1996).

Mencarelli, Fernando Antonio, "A voz e a partitura: teatro musical, indústria e diversidade cultural no Rio de Janeiro (1868–1908)," Ph.D. thesis (Unicamp, 2003).

Mendonça, Manuela (ed.), *História da Companhia Carris de Ferro de Lisboa em Portugal*, 2 vols. (Lisbon: Companhia Carris de Ferro de Lisboa, S.A./Academia Portuguesa de História, 2006).
Middleton, Richard, "Afterword," in Ian Biddle and Vanessa Knights (eds.), *Music, National Identity and the Politics of Location* (Aldershot: Ashgate, 2007), 191–203.
Middleton Richard, "Musical Belongings: Western Music and Its Low-Other," in Born and Hesmondhalgh (eds.), *Western Music and Its Others*, 59–85.
Middleton, Richard, "Popular Music of the Lower Classes," in Nicholas Temperley (ed.), *The Romantic Age, 1800–1914* (London: Athlone Press, 1981), 63–81.
Middleton, Richard, "Popular Music: I. Popular Music in the West, 1. Definitions," *Grove Music Online*, ed. L. Macy, http://www.oxfordmusiconline.com, accessed 5 June 2014.
Middleton, Richard, *Studying Popular Music* (Milton Keynes: Open University Press, 1990).
Middleton, Richard, *Voicing the Popular: On the Subjects of Popular Music* (London: Routledge, 2006).
Mónica, Maria Filomena, *Eça de Queiroz* (Melton: Tamesis, 2005).
Mónica, Maria Filomena, "Os fiéis inimigos: Eça de Queirós e Pinheiro Chagas," *Análise social*, 36/160 (2001), 711–733.
Mónica, Maria Filomena (ed.), *A formação da classe operária portuguesa: antologia da imprensa operária, 1850–1934* (Lisbon: Fundação Calouste Gulbenkian, 1982).
Moreau, Mário, *Coliseu dos Recreios: um século de história* (Lisbon: Quetzal Editores, 1994).
Moreau, Mário, *O Teatro de S. Carlos: dois séculos de história*, 2 vols. (Lisbon: Hugin Editores, 1999).
Morton, David, *Sound Recording: The Life Story of a Technology* (Santa Barbara, CA: Greenwood Press, 2004).
Nater, Wolfgang, and John Paul Jones III, "Identity, Space, and Other Uncertainties," in Georges Benko and Ulf Strohmayer (eds.), *Space and Social Theory: Interpreting Modernity and Post-Modernity* (London: Blackwell, 1997), 141–161.
Negus, Keith, *Popular Music in Theory: An Introduction* (Middletown, CT: Wesleyan University Press, 1996).
Nery, Rui Vieira, and Paulo Ferreira de Castro, *História da música* (Lisbon: Imprensa Nacional-Casa da Moeda, 1991).
Nery, Rui Vieira, *Para uma história do Fado* (Lisbon: Público/Corda Seca, 2004).
Neves, Larissa de Oliveira, "As comédias de Artur Azevedo—em busca da história," Ph.D. thesis (Unicamp, 2006).
Nora, Pierre (ed.), *Les lieux de memoire*, vol. 1 (Paris: Gallimard, 1984).
Norcliffe, G. B., *The Ride to Modernity: The Bicycle in Canada, 1869–1900* (Toronto: University of Toronto Press, 2001).
Oberdeck, Kathryn J., "Contested Cultures of American Refinement: Theatrical Manager Sylvester Poli, His Audiences, and the Vaudeville Industry, 1890–1920," *Radical History Review* (1996), 40–91.
Ord-Hume, Arthur W. J. G., "Mechanical Instrument," *Grove Music Online*, ed. L. Macy, http://www.oxfordmusiconline.com, accessed 21 July 2010.
Ord-Hume, Arthur W. J. G., "Mechanical Instruments: Introduction," in John Shepherd, et al., *Continuum Encyclopedia of Popular Music of the World*, vol. 2 (Performance and Production) (London: Continuum, 2003), 323–329.
Ord-Hume, Arthur W. J. G., "Player Piano," *Grove Music Online*, ed. L. Macy, http://www.oxfordmusiconline.com, accessed 21 July 2010.
Osborne, Peter, "Modernity Is a Qualitative, Not a Chronological, Category," *New Left Review*, I/192 (1992).
Outeirinho, Maria de Fátima, "A mulher: educação e leituras francesas na crónica de Ramalho Ortigão," *Intercâmbio* (1992), 148–161.
Paddison, Max, "The Critique Criticised: Adorno and Popular Music." *Popular Music*, 2 (1982), 201–218.

Parsons, Deborah L., *Streetwalking the Metropolis: Women, the City, and Modernity* (Oxford: Oxford University Press, 2000).
Pellow, Deborah, "The Architecture of Female Seclusion in West Africa," in Denise Lawrence-Zúñiga and Setha M. Low (eds.), *The Anthropology of Space and Place: Locating Culture* (Cambridge: Blackwell, 2003), 160–184.
Pereira, Maria da Conceição Meireles, "O brasileiro no teatro musicado português—duas operetas paradigmáticas," *População e sociedade*, 14–15/2 (2007), 163–179.
Pereira, Nuno Teotónio, "Pátios e vilas de Lisboa, 1870–1930: a promoção privada do alojamento operário," *Análise social*, 29/127 (1994), 509–524.
Pestana, Maria do Rosário, "César das Neves," in Salwa Castelo-Branco (ed.), *Enciclopédia da música em Portugal no século XX*, vol. 3, 909–910.
Peterson, Richard A., and David G. Berger, "Cycles in Symbol Production: The Case of Popular Music," in Simon Frith and Andrew Goodwin, *On Record: Rock, Pop, and the Written Word* (London: Routledge, 1990), 117–133.
Picker, John M., "The Soundproof Study: Victorian Professionals, Work Space, and Urban Noise," *Victorian Studies*, 42/3 (2000), 427–453.
Picker, John M., *Victorian Soundscapes* (Oxford: Oxford University Press, 2003).
Pickering, Michael, *History, Experience and Cultural Studies* (London: Macmillan, 1997).
Prado, Décio de Almeida, *História concisa do teatro brasileiro: 1570–1908* (São Paulo: Edusp, 1999).
Raimundo, Luís, "Para uma leitura dramatúrgica e estilística de Serrana de Alfredo Keil," *Revista portuguesa de musicologia* 10 (2000), 227–274.
Ramos, António Alberto, "A memória de João Black e o fado como canção de protesto," *Sítios e Memórias*, 2 (1997), 63–68.
Ramos, Rui, "A ciência do povo e as origens do estado cultural," in Branco and Castelo-Branco (eds.), *Vozes do povo*, 25–35.
Ramos, Rui, *D. Carlos (1863–1908)* (Lisbon: Círculo de Leitores, 2006).
Ramos, Rui, *João Franco e o fracasso do reformismo liberal (1884–1908)* (Lisbon: Imprensa das Ciências Sociais, 2001).
Ramos, Rui, *A segunda fundação*, vol. 6, in José Mattoso (ed.), *História de Portugal* (Lisbon: Círculo de Leitores, 1994).
Rebello, Luiz Francisco, *História do teatro de revista em Portugal*, 2 vols. (Lisbon: Publicações D. Quixote, 1984).
Rebello, Luiz Francisco, "Opereta," in Salwa Castelo-Branco (ed.), *Enciclopédia da música em Portugal no século XX*, vol. 3 (Lisbon: Círculo de Leitores, 2010), 935–938.
Rebello, Luiz Francisco, "Teatro de revista," in Salwa Castelo-Branco (ed.), *Enciclopédia da música em Portugal no século XX*, vol. 4, 1248–1253.
Rebello, Luiz Francisco, *O teatro naturalista e neo-romântico (1870–1910)* (Lisbon: Instituto de Cultura Portuguesa, 1978).
Rebello, Luiz Francisco, *O teatro romântico (1838–1869)* (Lisbon: Instituto de Cultura e Língua Portuguesa, 1980).
"The reproducing piano—Hupfeld DEA," Pianola Institute (2008), http://www.pianola.org/reproducing/reproducing_welte.cfm, accessed 2 August 2010.
"The reproducing piano—Welte-Mignon," Pianola Institute (2008), http://www.pianola.org/reproducing/reproducing_welte.cfm, accessed 2 August 2010.
Ribas, Tomaz, *O Teatro da Trindade: 125 anos de vida* (Porto: Lello & Irmão, 1993).
Risebero, Bill, *Modern Architecture and Design: An Alternative History* (Cambridge, MA: MIT Press, 1982).
Robertson, Jennifer, *Takarazuka: Sexual Politics and Popular Culture in Modern Japan* (Berkeley: University of California Press, 1998).
Robertson, Jennifer, "Theatrical Resistance, Theaters of Restraint: The Takarazuka Revue and the 'State Theater' Movement in Japan," *Anthropological Quarterly*, 64/4 (1991), 165–177.

Robinson, Jennifer, *Ordinary Cities: Between Modernity and Development* (London: Routledge, 2006).
Rodrigues, Isabel Maria, "As avenidas de Ressano Garcia," in *Boletim Lisboa Urbanismo*, 13 (Sept./Oct. 2000), 20–23; 14 (Nov./Dec. 2000), 30–34.
Roell, Craig H., *The Piano in America, 1890–1940* (Chapel Hill: University of North Carolina Press, 1989).
Rosa, Joaquim Carmelo, "'Essa pobre filha bastarda das artes': a Escola de Música do Conservatório Real de Lisboa nos anos de 1842–1862," master's thesis (Universidade Nova de Lisboa, 1999).
Rothenbuhler, Eric W., and John Durham Peters, "Defining Phonography: An Experiment in Theory," *Musical Quarterly*, 81/2 (1997), 242–264.
Ruiz, Carmen del Moral, *El género chico: Ocio y teatro en Madrid (1880–1910)* (Madrid: Alianza Editorial, 2005).
Ruiz, Roberto, *O teatro de revista no Brasil: do início à I Guerra Mundial* (Rio de Janeiro: Ministério da Cultura, Instituto Nacional de Artes Cênicas, 1988).
Russell, Dave, *Popular Music in England, 1840–1914: A Social History* (Manchester: Manchester University Press, 1997).
Said, Edward W., "Invention, Memory, and Place," *Critical Inquiry* 26/2 (2000), 175–192.
Said, Edward, "Opponents, Audiences, Constituencies, and Community," *Critical Inquiry*, 9/1 (September 1982), 1–26.
Samson, Jim, *Virtuosity and the Musical Work* (Cambridge: Cambridge University Press, 2004).
Sandroni, Carlos, *Feitiço decente: transformações do samba no Rio de Janeiro, 1917–1933* (Rio de Janeiro: Jorge Zahar Editor/UFRJ, 2008).
Santos, Fernando Piteira, "A fundação de 'A voz do operário'—do 'abstencionismo político' à participação no 'congresso possibilista' de 1889," *Análise social*, 17/67–69 (1981), 681–693.
Santos, Gonçalo Duro dos, *A escola de antropologia de Coimbra, 1885–1950* (Lisbon: Imprensa das Ciências Sociais, 2005).
Santos, Maria de Lourdes Lima dos, *Intelectuais portugueses na primeira metade de Oitocentos* (Lisbon: Editorial Presença, 1988).
Santos, Maria de Lourdes Lima dos, "Para a análise das ideologias da burguesia," *Análise social*, 14/53 (1978), 39–80.
Santos, Victor, *Leal da Câmara—um caso de caricatura: a sátira na atitude política portuguesa* (Sintra: Câmara Municipal de Sintra, 1982).
Santos, Vítor Pavão dos, *A revista à portuguesa* (Lisbon: O Jornal, 1978).
Sardo, Susana, "Música popular e diferenças regionais," in Mário Ferreira Lages and Artur Teodoro de Matos (eds.), *Portugal: Percursos de Interculturalidade*, vol. 1 (Lisbon: ACIDI, 2008), 407–476.
Schmiedgen, Peter, "Interiority, Exteriority and Spatial Politics in Benjamin's Cityscapes," in Andrew Benjamin and Charles Rice (eds.), *Walter Benjamin and the Architecture of Modernity* (Prahran: re.press, 2009), 147–158.
Schor, Naomi, "Collecting Paris," in John Elsnera and Roger Cardinal (eds.), *The Cultures of Collecting* (Cambridge, MA: Harvard University Press, 1994), 252–274.
Schwartz, Vanessa R., *Spectacular Realities: Early Mass Culture in Fin-de-Siècle Paris* (Berkeley: University of California Press, 1998).
Scott, Derek B., "The Sexual Politics of Victorian Musical Aesthetics," *Journal of the Royal Musical Association*, 119/1 (1994), 91–114.
Scott, Derek B., *The Singing Bourgeois: Songs of the Victorian Drawing Room and Parlour* (Aldershot: Ashgate, 2001).
Scott, Derek B., *Sounds of the Metropolis: The 19th-Century Popular Music Revolution in London, New York, Paris and Vienna* (Oxford: Oxford University Press, 2008).
Seta, Fabrizio della, "L'imagine di Meyerbeer nella critica italiana dell'Ottocento e l'idea di 'dramma musicale,'" in Maria Teresa Muraro, *L'opera tra Venezia e Parigi* (Florence: Olschki, 1988), 147–176.

Shuker, Roy, *Understanding Popular Music* (New York: Routledge, 1994).
Silva, Augusto Santos, "O Porto em busca da Renascença (1880–1911)," *Penélope: revista de história e ciências sociais*, 17 (1997), 51–69.
Silva, Hugo, "Júlia Mendes," in Salwa Castelo-Branco (ed.), *Enciclopédia da música em Portugal no século XX*, vol. 3, 769.
Silva, João, "O diário 'A Revolução de Setembro' (1840–1857): Música, poder e construção social de realidade em Portugal nos meados do século XIX," master's thesis (Universidade Nova de Lisboa, 2007).
Silva, Joaquim Palminha, "Armazéns Grandella: como nasceram e o que foram," *História*, 112 (1988), 4–27.
Silva, Manuel Deniz, "Música e cinema: 1 Do início do cinema à introdução do 'sonoro' (18961930)," in Salwa Castelo-Branco (ed.), *Enciclopédia da música em Portugal no século XX*, vol. 3, 841–843.
Silva, Raquel Henriques da (ed.), *Lisboa de Frederico Ressano Garcia, 1874–1909* (Lisbon: Câmara Municipal de Lisboa/Fundação Calouste Gulbenkian, 1989).
Singer, Ben, "Modernity, Hyperstimulus, and the Rise of Popular Sensationalism," in Charney and Schwartz (eds.), *Cinema and the Invention of Modern Life*, 72–99.
Smith, Anthony D., *The Ethnic Origins of Nations* (Oxford: Blackwell, 1987).
Smith, Woodruff, *Consumption and the Making of Respectability, 1600–1800* (London: Routledge, 2002).
Sobral, José Manuel, "O Norte, o Sul, a raça, a nação—representações da identidade nacional portuguesa (séculos XIX–XX)", *Análise social*, 39/171 (2004), 255–284.
Sobral, José Manuel, "Race and Space in the Interpretation of Portugal: The North-South Division and Representations of Portuguese National Identity in the Nineteenth and Twentieth Centuries," in Sharon R. Roseman and Shawn S. Parkhurst (eds.), *Recasting Culture and Space in Iberian Contexts* (New York: SUNY Press, 2008), 205–224.
Sorensen, Janet, "Alternative Antiquarianisms of Scotland and the North," *Modern Language Quarterly*, 70/4 (2009), 416–441.
Souza, Silvia Cristina Martins de, "Um Offenbach tropical: Francisco Correa Vasques e o teatro musicado no Rio de Janeiro da segunda metade do século XIX," *História e Perspectivas*, 34/January–June (2006), 225–259.
Stallybrass, Peter, and Allon White, *The Poetics and Politics of Transgression* (Ithaca, NY: Cornell University Press, 1986).
Stavrakakis, Yannis, and Nikos Chrysoloras, "'(I Can't Get No) Enjoyment: Lacanian Theory and the Analysis of Nationalism," *Psychoanalysis, Culture & Society*, 11/2 (2006), 144–163.
Steffen, David J., *From Edison to Marconi: The First Thirty Years of Recorded Music* (Jefferson, NC: McFarland, 2005).
Steinmetz, George, "Bourdieu's Disavowal of Lacan: Psychoanalytic Theory and the Concepts of 'Habitus' and 'Symbolic Capital,'" *Constellations*, 13/4 (2006), 445–464.
Sterne, Jonathan, *The Audible Past: Cultural Origins of Sound Reproduction* (Durham, NC: Duke University Press, 2003).
Stocking, George W.Jr. (ed.), *Objects and Others: Essays on Museums and Material Culture* (Madison: University of Wisconsin Press, 1985).
Storey, John, "Inventing Opera as Art in Nineteenth-Century Manchester," *International Journal of Cultural Studies*, 9/4 (2006), 435–456.
Straw, Will, "Systems of Articulation, Logics of Change: Communities and Scenes in Popular Music," *Cultural Studies*, 5/3 (1991), 368–388.
Styhre, Alexander, and Tobias Engberg, "Spaces of Consumption: From Margin to Centre," *ephemera*, 3/2 (2003), 115–125.
Suisman, David, *Selling Sounds: The Commercial Revolution in American Music* (Cambridge, MA: Harvard University Press, 2009).
Suisman, David, "Sound, Knowledge, and the 'Immanence of Human Failure,'" *Social Text*, 102, 28/1 (2010), 13–34.

Taylor, Timothy D., "The Commodification of Music at the Dawn of the Era of 'Mechanical Music,'" *Ethnomusicology*, 51/2 (2007), 281-305.
Teixeira, Nuno Severiano, "Politica externa e politica interna no Portugal de 1890," *Análise social*, 23/4 (1987), 687-719.
Tengarrinha, José, *Imprensa e opinião pública em Portugal* (Coimbra: Edições Minerva, 2006).
Thebèrge, Paul, *Any Sound You Can Imagine: Making Music/Consuming Technology* (Hanover, NH: Wesleyan University Press, 1997).
Thompson, Emily, "Machines, Music, and the Quest for Fidelity: Marketing the Edison Phonograph in America, 1877-1925," *Musical Quarterly*, 79/1 (1995), 131-171.
Tick, Judith, "Passed Away Is the Piano Girl: Changes in American Musical Life, 1870-1900," in Jane Bowers and Judith Tick, *Women Making Music: The Western Art Tradition, 1150-1950* (Urbana: University of Illinois Press, 1986), 325-348.
Tilly, Charles, "The State of Nationalism," *Critical Review: A Journal of Politics and Society*, 10/2 (1996), 299-306.
Titon, Jeff Todd, "Knowing Fieldwork," in Gregory Barz and Timothy J. Cooley, *Shadows in the Field: New Perspectives for Fieldwork in Ethnomusicology* (Oxford: Oxford University Press, 2008), 87-100.
Tone, Andrea, *The Business of Benevolence: Industrial Paternalism in Progressive America* (Ithaca, NY: Cornell University Press, 1997).
Traubner, Richard, *Operetta: A Theatrical History* (London: Routledge, 2003).
Turner, Victor, "Are There Universals of Performance in Myth, Ritual, and Drama?," in Richard Schechner and Willa Apel, *By Means of Performance* (Cambridge: Cambridge University Press, 1997), 8-18.
Turner, Victor, "Frame, Flow and Reflection: Ritual and Drama as Public Liminality," *Japanese Journal of Religious Studies*, 6/4 (1979), 465-499.
Turner, Victor, *From Ritual to Theater: The Human Seriousness of Play* (New York: PAJ Publications, 1982).
Turner, Victor, *The Ritual Process: Structure and Anti-Structure* (Hawthorne, NY: Aldine de Gruyter, 1997).
Turner, Victor, "Symbolic Studies," *Annual Review of Anthropology*, 4 (1975), 145-161.
Valente, Vasco Pulido, *O poder e o povo: A Revolução de 1910* (Lisbon: Alhetheia, 2010).
Vaule, Rosamond B., *As We Were: American Photographic Postcards, 1905-1930* (Boston, MA: David R. Godine, 2004).
Vernon, Paul, *A History of the Portuguese Fado* (Aldershot: Ashgate, 2000).
Vickery, Amanda, "Golden Age to Separate Spheres? A Review of the Categories and Chronology of English Women's History," *Historical Journal*, 36 (1993), 383-414.
Vieira, António Lopes, *Os transportes públicos de Lisboa entre 1830 e 1910* (Lisbon: Imprensa Nacional-Casa da Moeda, 1982).
Villaverde, Manuel, "Rua das Portas de Santo Antão e a singular modernidade lisboeta (1890-1925): arquitectura e práticas urbanas," *Revista de História da Arte*, 2 (2006), 142-176.
Walkowitz, Judith R., *City of Dreadful Delight: Narratives of Sexual Danger in Late-Victorian London* (Chicago: University of Chicago Press, 1992).
Ward, Peter, *A History of Domestic Space: Privacy and the Canadian Home* (Vancouver: University of British Columbia Press, 1999).
Weidman, Amanda, "Guru and Gramophone: Fantasies of Fidelity and Modern Technologies of the Real," *Public Culture*, 15/3 (2003), 453-476.
Welch, Walter L., and Leah Brodbeck Stensel Burt, *From Tinfoil to Stereo: The Acoustic Years of the Recording Industry, 1877-1929* (Gainesville: University Press of Florida, 1995).
Williams, Raymond, *The Country and the City* (New York: Oxford University Press, 1975).
Williams, Raymond, "Culture Is Ordinary," in Raymond Williams, *Resources of Hope* (London: Verso, 1989), 3-18.
Williams, Raymond, *Keywords* (London: Fontana Press, 1988).

Wittmann, Michael, "Meyerbeer and Mercadante? The Reception of Meyerbeer in Italy," *Cambridge Opera Journal*, 5/2 (1993), 115–132.
Wolff, Janet, "The Invisible Flâneuse. Women and the Literature of Modernity," *Theory, Culture & Society*, 2/3 (1985), 37–46.
Worgull, Matthias, *Hot Embossing: Theory and Technology of Microreplication* (Oxford: William Andrew, 2009).
Yon, Jean-Claude, *Jacques Offenbach* (Paris: Gallimard, 2000).
Young, Clinton David, "Zarzuela: or Lyric Theater as Consumer Nationalism in Spain, 1874-1930," Ph.D. thesis (University of California San Diego, 2006).
Žižek, Slavoj, *Enjoy Your Symptom!* (London: Routledge, 2008).
Žižek, Slavoj, *For They Know Not What They Do* (London: Verso, 2008).
Žižek, Slavoj, *The Sublime Object of Ideology* (London: Verso, 2008).

INDEX

Abranches, Aristides, 91
Albergaria, Sá de, 102
alegres canções do norte, As, 166, 177–180
Almeida, Fialho d', 22, 67, 104, 119, 121, 122, 190, 195–196, 250, 256, 283
Almeida, Joaquim de, 221
Alpoim, José Maria de, 36, 37
Amanhã (magazine), 18
Amphion (periodical), 250
Anderson, Benedict, 16, 94
Antoine, André, 114
António Maria, O (periodical), 120, 126
Araújo, Luís de, 99
Arriegas, Artur, 129, 173, 175–176
  canção da minha terra: fados, A, 173
Arrieta, Emilio, 79
Arroio, João, 86, 159
Arroio, António, 163
Arte Musical, 284
Avenida da Liberdade, 51, 53–54, 56–57, 66, 69, 70, 71, 72, 75, 124, 145, 224, 252
Azevedo, Arthur, 102
Azevedo, Guilherme de (Gil Vaz), 121

banda (wind band), 5, 32–33, 154, 218, 252–254, 268–269, 281
  Guarda Municipal de Lisboa (*banda*), 126, 252, 273–274, 278
Baptista, Avelino, 261, 268, 278
Baptista Diniz, Eduardo, 225, 277
Barbieri, Francisco, 79, 92
Barbosa du Bocage, Manuel Maria, 99
Barreiros, Eduardo, 268, 278, 281
Barthes, Roland, 216, 244–245, 291
Bastos, João, 109
Bastos, Teixeira, 4, 35, 38
Bastos, Palmira, 119, 120, 213, 261, 267–268
Batalha Reis, Jaime, 81–82
Baudelaire, Charles, 9, 64, 65

Becker, Howard, 95–96, 111–112
Benfey, Theodor, 42
Benjamin, Manuel, 120
Benjamin, Walter, 10, 58–61, 63–65, 150, 208, 247
Benoliel, Joshua, 111, 143–144, 208
Berliner, Emile, 269–270
berro, O (periodical), 168
Bhabha, Homi, 15
Black, João, See Salustiano Monteiro, João
Borba, Tomás, 162
Bordalo Pinheiro, Manuel Gustavo, 125, 201, 229
Bordalo Pinheiro, Rafael, 90, 106, 118, 132, 171, 229
Botelho, Abel, 17, 32, 61, 199, 201
  Amanhã! (novel), 17, 19, 32, 199, 201
Bourdieu, Pierre, 2, 73, 157, 184, 189–192, 200, 287
  habitus, 70, 130, 165, 190–192, 200, 287
Braamcamp, Anselmo José, 31
Braga, Teófilo, 13, 41–42, 157–158, 163, 166
branco e negro, O (magazine), 86
Brasil-Portugal (magazine), 98, 115
Brazão, Eduardo, 100, 120
British Ultimatum (1890),
  and African colonial borders, 3, 32, 44–45
  and anti-British sentiment, 27, 34
  and popular culture, 43, 169, 229–230
  and Portuguese nationalism, 3–4, 31–32, 34, 45, 103, 132, 230, 291–292
  and republicanism, 34–35, 132
  and freedom of press, 122
Brun, André, 100, 111–114, 127, 132, 143–144
Buíça, Manuel, 4, 227

Caballero, Manuel, 79
cabo da caçarola, O (play), 141
cabralistas, See de Costa Cabral, António Bernardo

Calderon, Carlos, 127, 140–141, 271
Câmara, D. João da, 103, 105, 107, 112, 140, 173
Camões, Luís de, 98
Campos, Gualdino de, 155–160, 227
canção de Portugal: o Fado and *O faduncho, A* (periodical), 173
Cancioneiro de músicas populares, 22–23, 139–140, 155–160, 163, 167–168, 227, 251, 277
cançoneta (musical genre), 224–225, 228–229, 268
Cândido de Figueiredo, António, 168, 182, 283
Canongia Júnior, Joaquim Ignacio, 219–220
Capelo, Hermenegildo, 44
Cardoso, Cyríaco de, 103, 105, 107–109, 112, 127, 159, 183–184, 268
Cardoso, Manuel, 262–263
Carvalho, Alfredo de, 129
Carvalho, Pinto de, 164–168, 173, 255
  História do fado, 164, 166, 173, 255
Casella, Cesare, 198–199
Casimiro Júnior, Joaquim, 117–118
Casino Lisbonense, 4, 42
Casmurro, O (periodical), 175
Castelo Branco, Camilo, 85, 86, 247
  Como ela o amava, 85
  Amor de perdição, 86
Castelo Branco, José, 280, 282
Castro, Urbano de, 91
Certeau, Michel de, 63–64
Chagas, João, 3, 36–37, 168–169
Chartier, Roger, 16–17, 20
Coelho, Adolfo, 13, 41–42, 163
Coelho, José Simões, 18–19
Coelho, Latino, 116
Coliseu dos Recreios, 71, 73, 86
Companhia Franceza do Gramophone, 163, 225, 236, 261–262, 269–277
Consiglieri Pedroso, Zófimo, 41–43, 163
Contemporânea (magazine), 83
corja: semanario de caricaturas, A (periodical), 173
Correa Vasques, Francisco, 93–94
Costa, Alfredo, 227
Costa, Isabel, 268, 271
Costa Cabral, António Bernardo da, 29–30, 36, 97, 99

Daddi, João Guilherme, 68
Dantas, Júlio, 99–100
Delgado, Nery, 46
Domingos Bomtempo, João, 68
D. Carlos I, 34, 36, 37, 82, 173, 227
D. João VI, 27
D. Luís, 44, 82
D. Luís Felipe, 227
D. Manuel II, 227

D. Maria II, 29, 187
D. Miguel I, 27, 29, 67
D. Pedro I of Brazil, 26–27, 28–29
D. Sebastião, 157
Doux, Émile, 67–68
Duarte, Filipe, 22, 99–100, 109, 115, 126, 127, 143–144, 146
Duarte Ferreira, Joaquim, 258–259
Dumas, Alexandre, 67, 198–199
  The Count of Monte Cristo, 198–199

Edison, Thomas, 256–258, 265
ephemera, cultural, 22, 36, 78, 98, 104, 115, 122–124, 206, 209, 212, 260

fado,
  and class, 2, 101, 109, 132, 141, 151–152, 164–176
  and nationalism, 18, 109, 139–143, 159, 168–170, 277, 289
  fadistas, 66, 118, 136, 140–141, 165, 174, 250, 255
  fado menor, 101, 110
  and popular culture, 24, 100, 109–110, 139–143, 154, 162, 175–176, 268, 275
Faria, Bento, 109
Farrobo, The Count of, 27–28
Faust, 221–222, 251
Fernandes, Eduardo, 99, 120, 227
Fernandes Tomás, Pedro, 157, 161, 163
  Canções populares da Beira, 157, 161
Filgueiras, Luiz, 94, 115, 126, 127
flâneur, 63–65, 129
Fontes Pereira de Melo, António Maria, 30, 31
Franco, João, 36–37, 38, 122–123
Freire Correia, João, 262–263
Frondoni, Ângelo, 93
Fuschini, Augusto, 26, 77

Galhardo, Luiz, 115, 127
Garcia, Frederico Ressano, 53–54
Garrido, Eduardo, 89, 91, 107, 204
Garrett, Almeida, 68, 84, 85, 87
Gatzambide, Joaquín, 79, 92
Gazul, Freitas, 84, 102, 126
Geração de 70 (1870 Generation), 42, 81
Ghislanzoni, Antonio, 84
Gobineau, Arthur de, 45
  Essai sur l'inégalité des races humaines, 45
Gramophone Company, 201, 236, 259–261, 263, 265, 269–270, 272, 276, 279, 282
Grandella, Francisco, 58, 70
  Armazéns Grandella, 58, 66
Grandes Armazéns do Chiado, 8, 58

Hall, Stuart, 2, 14
Harrington, Carlos, 171–173

Index

Harvey, David, 63–64
Haussmann, Georges-Eugène, 9, 54, 59, 63, 89
Herculano, Alexandre, 12, 40, 84
Hobsbawm, Eric, 12, 14, 20, 46, 286–287
Hussla, Victor, 159

Ilustração Portuguesa, 10, 82, 86, 100, 111, 145, 162, 214, 262, 272
Infante D. Henrique, 98
Ivens, Roberto, 44

Jacobetty, Francisco, 122, 123, 143
José João (play), 227
Johnson, Eldridge, 269–270, 279

Keil, Alfredo, 85–86, 97, 101, 132, 159, 223, 229–230, 277

Lacan, Jaques, 147, 149, 183–184
jouissance, 147, 149
Lacombe Casella, Felicia, 198–199
Haydée (opera), 198–199
Lacombe, Louis, 198
Lanterna mágica (newspaper), 118
Laranjeira, Manuel, 5, 37–38
Leal da Câmara, Tomás Júlio, 173–175
Leitão de Andrada, Miguel, 157
 Miscellanea do sitio de N. Sª. da Luz do Pedrogão Grande, 157
Leite de Vasconcelos, José, 13, 41–43, 46, 48–49, 157, 161–163
 Revista Lusitana, 43
Lenormant, François, 42
Liberal Revolution (1820), 23, 26, 67
Lisboa em 1850, 116
Lisboa, Bernardo, 130–131
Livraria Popular de Francisco Franco, 205, 219, 227
Lobato, Gervásio, 91, 103, 105, 107, 112, 200
 Lisboa em camisa, 200
Lopes de Mendonça, António Pedro, 87, 199
Lopes de Mendonça, Henrique, 85, 97, 132, 229
low-other, 96, 99, 109, 130, 136, 151–152, 164, (see also revista)
lundu (Afro-Brazilian dance), 102, 130–131
 lundu-canção, 130

Machado, Augusto, 84–85, 95, 97, 99, 212, 223, 284–285
Machado, Bernardino, 47–48
Machado, Júlio César, 78–79
mágica (Portuguese genre), 107–108, 115, 121, 143
maxixe (Afro-Brazilian dance), 102, 120, 130–131, 137, 289
Maria da Fonte (revolt), 29, 69
Marques, Salvador, 70, 143

Marques Pinto, Augusto, 83
marselheza: supplemento de caricaturas, A (periodical), 173–175
Matos, Júlio de, 41
Mendes, Júlia, 100, 278, 281
Mercadente, Saverio, 80–81
Middleton, Richard, 146, 181
Milano, Nicolino, 102, 141–143
Miró, António Luís, 68
modernity,
 and leisure/entertainment, 5–7, 9–11, 18, 28, 30, 48, 60–61, 72, 75–76, 149, 289
 and technology, 19, 25, 30, 188, 236–237, 240, 246, 258, 289–291
 and tradition, 74, 129, 143, 146–147, 152, 160–161, 285–288
 and transience, 8–9, 147, 164
 and urban space, 2, 7, 9–10, 11–12, 23–25, 28, 49–51, 53–63, 72, 75, 129, 146–147, 288
Monteiro de Almeida, Eugénio, 99
Morais Pinto, Alfredo de, 228
Moreira, Cruz, 120
Moreira de Sá, Bernardo Valentim, 83
Moura Barreto, Nuno de (Duke of Loulé), 30
Murguía, Manuel, 177, 181
Musard, Philippe, 222
Museu Arqueológico do Algarve, 48
música ligeira (light music), 183–185

nationalism,
 and culture, 2, 14, 41, 158–159, 288–289, 293
 and ethnicity, 13, 46–47, 158, 163, 176–178
 and folklore, 40–41, 151–153, 155, 158–160, 163–164
 Herderian nationalism, 15, 43, 153, 165
 and history, 12–15, 158, 164–165
 and music theatre, 5–6, 18–19, 75–76, 84–88, 94–97, 101–103, 109, 116–117, 127, 139, 146–147, 150, 177–178
 nation-building, 11–15, 18–19, 40, 43, 76, 80, 94–95, 150, 151–152, 176, 181–182
 national symbols, 12, 14, 16–17, 150, 153, 228
 and 'the people', 1–2, 15, 17, 41–42, 158, 163–164
 and republicanism, 2, 4, 127, 163
 Romantic nationalism, 28, 40–41, 43, 84, 153–154
Negro, Tomás del, 18, 95, 126, 140–141
Neuparth, Eduardo, 218–219, 223, 230
 Neuparth & Carneiro, 235, 237, 239
Neves, César das, 155–160, 163, 227
Nogueira, António Francisco, 181
 raça negra sob o ponto de vista da civilização da África, A, 181

Ocidente, O, 44, 81, 103, 213, 237, 239, 250, 256, 262
Odeon, 236, 259, 271, 276, 280,
Offenbach, Jacques, 79, 81, 89–94, 99, 143, 147, 204, 222, 248, 253, 268, 284, 289
Oliveira, Emília d', 281
Oliveira, Joaquim Augusto de, 107, 117, 143
operetta, (generic traits) 6–7, 10, 22, 24, 69–70, 71, 74, 75, 79, 87, 88–94, 95, 97–104, 204–206, 284
operettas
  Barba-azul, 204, 222, 252–253, 268
  burro do Sr. Alcaide, O, 103–105, 106, 108, 204, 222
  Capital federal, 102, 274
  Cócó, Reineta & Facada, 105, 105n.162
  fado, O, 109–111
  fille de Madame Angot, La, 252–253
  georgianas, As, 204, 222
  Grã-duquesa de Gérolstein, A, 204, 222, 253
  Maria da Fonte, 97, 99
  Périchole, A, 91–92, 268
  Rosa Engeitada, 126, 140, 152
  Severa, A, 99–101, 109, 126, 140, 152
  sinos de Corneville, Os, 204–205, 268
  solar dos Barrigas, O, 105–106, 207, 223, 228, 268
  Suzanna, 101–102, 223
  Tição negro, 210, 214, 222, 227
  Tribofe, O, 102 See *Capital federal*
  valete de copas, O, 105, 107
Oliveira Martins, Joaquim Pedro, 27–29, 45, 68, 170, 181
Orquestra da Real Câmara (Royal Chamber Orchestra), 189

Palha, Francisco, 71, 89, 91–93, 116
Palmerim, Luís Augusto, 87
Partido Histórico, 30, See also Partido Progressista
Partido Regenerador, 30, 36
Partido Progressista (Progressive Party), 30, 31, 36, 37, 122
paródia, A, 36–37, 126
Passeio Público, 51–53
Pato, Bulhão, 66
Peixoto, Rocha, 169–170, 215–216
Pereira, Miguel Ângelo, 83–84
Pereira da Costa, Francisco, 46
Pimentel, Alberto, 13, 158, 164, 166–168, 177–181, 227, 250
  Fotografias de Lisboa, 167–168
Pinheiro Chagas, Manuel, 44–45
player piano (instrument), 234–244
  Masterspiel DEA, 243
  Phonola, 237–239, 244

Pianola, 242
Pianophon Ochestrion, 241–242
Welt-Mignon, 243
Portuguesa, A (republican national anthem), 132–133, 228–230, 233, 240, 273, 292
Portuguese First Republic (1910–1926), 32
Portuguese Republican Party, 34
Possibilist International Workers Congress (1889), 32

Queirós, Eça de, 24, 51, 53, 87–88, 90, 94, 107–108, 168, 190, 194, 199–203, 253
  Farpas, As, 90, 194
  Maias, Os, 53, 190, 195, 199, 201–203, 252
  primo Basílio, O, 51, 90, 193–195, 199–201
  relíquia, A, 168
  tragédia da Rua das Flores, A, 90
Quental, Antero de, 4–5, 173

Ramos, Manuel, 83, 159
rapto de uma actriz, O (silent film), 115–116, 262
Rates, José Carlos, 170
Rattazzi, Maria, 247–248
  Portugal de relance, 247–248, 252
Real Conservatório de Lisboa, 68, 95, 132, 160, 284
Real Coliseu de Lisboa, 71, 138
Real Teatro de São Carlos, 7, 27, 32, 52–53, 67–68, 71–74, 75–88, 90, 94–95, 115, 117, 119, 138, 190, 199, 219, 221, 230, 251, 278, 284
Recreios Whittoyne, 91, 224
Regeneração (Regeneration), 29–31, 117, 286
Regicide (1908), 3, 10, 36
Republican coup (1910), 34
revista (generic traits),
  and allegory, 24, 115–117, 132, 290
  and Brazil, 28, 102, 130–132, 150
  coplas, 22, 24, 98, 116, 203–206, 219, 224
  and dramatic structure, 6, 114–115, 128–129, 136, 139
  and the everyday, 24, 30, 66, 76, 98, 114, 122, 124–126, 132, 140, 145, 150, 176
  and gender, 51, 131, 133–136, 149
  and high/low culture, 74, 94, 112, 120–121, 136, 141, 284–285
  and metonymy, 116–118, 122, 127, 139, 150, 290
  and modernity, 6, 115–116, 135, 137, 146, 148, 150
  and multivocality of symbols, 76, 120, 136, 146–150
  and musical structure, 7, 114, 127, 130–132, 137–139, 143–144
  and nationalism, 76, 97, 116–117, 127–128, 139, 141, 145–146, 293
  and phonographic market, 7, 203, 268, 275
  and satire, 6, 30–31, 36–38, 80, 87, 90, 116–118, 121–123, 126, 133, 144–145, 148–149

revistas,
   A.B.C., 141, 143, 147, 209, 228
   Agulha em palheiros, 127–128
   Agulhas e alfinetes, 126, 134
   anno em três dias, O, 134, 136, 214, 224
   barril do lixo, O, 126, 132
   Beijos de burro, 120–121, 206–207
   Em pratos limpos, 119, 120, 129
   Etcoetera e tal, 224
   Fado e Maxixe, O, 132
   Favas contadas, 144–145
   festejo dum noivado, O, 116
   Fim de século, 119
   Formigas e formigueiros, 118, 126
   Fossilismo e progresso, 116–117
   Garotice & C.ª, 129
   gran via, La, 123–124
   melhoramentos materiais, Os, 30, 116
   micróbio, O, 123, 224
   Na ponta da unha!, 140, 143
   Nicles!, 126–127, 134, 274
   nome do padre, Em, 133
   Ó da guarda, 115, 122, 205, 262
   Parreirinha ao Limoeiro, Da, 225
   Pontos nos ii, 209, 224
   P'rá frente, 122, 140–141
   procura do badalo, 225
   Raios X, 207
   reino da bolha, O, 126
   Retalhos de Lisboa, 126, 224
   Retalhos de Lisboa e Porto, 133
   Revista de 1858, 117–118
   Revista do anno de 1879, 137, 143
   Sal e Pimenta, 119, 129, 224
   século XIV, O, 225
   Sol e sombre, 127, 135–136
   Talvez te escreva!, 119, 126
   Tam-Tam, 119, 129
   Tim tim por tim tim, 90, 119, 124–125, 129–130, 133, 205, 210, 268
   tutti-li-mundi, O, 139, 209–210, 224
   Viagem à roda da Parvónia, 121
   Vistorias do Diabo, 143
   Zás traz, 225
Rey Colaço, Alexandre, 159
Ribas, João António, 155–156
   Álbum de músicas nacionais portuguesas, 154–156
Ribeiro, Carlos, 46
Ribeiro, Hintze, 36
Rimanso, João, See Chagas, João
Rio de Carvalho, João Pedro, 91, 95, 123, 228
Rodrigues, Ernesto, 127
Rogel, José, 79, 92
Rosa, Augusto, 79, 100, 120
Ruiz, Pepa, 102, 119, 130, 133, 205

Salustiano Monteiro, João, 170–171
Sampaio, Alberto, 13, 177, 181
Sand, George, 84
   Les beaux messieurs de Bois-Doré, 84
Sá Noronha, Francisco de, 83–84, 159
Santos, Amélia, 38–39
Santos, Machado, 34–35, 38
Santos Diaz, Francisco, 258–259
Sassetti, João Baptista, 218, 222, 223
Schwalbach, Eduardo, 18, 120, 125, 132–133, 145, 160
século, O (newspaper), 17, 171
Sérgio da Silva, José Augusto, 250–251
Serões (magazine), 230
Serpa Pinto, Alexandre de, 44
setembristas, 29, 67
Silva Passos, Manuel de (Passos Manuel), 36, 68
Simplex, 280–282
Sinkler Darby, William, 270–271, 273
Smith, Anthony D., 12, 13,
Soares, Júlio, 137
Sociedade Cooperativa A Voz do Operário, 32, See *Voz do Operário*
Sousa, Avelino de, 170–171
   fado e os seus censores, O, 171
Sousa Bastos, António de, 80, 90–92, 98, 103, 118–119, 121–122, 124–126, 130, 137–138, 210
Sousa Viterbo, Francisco Marques, 158
Spanish-American War, 4, 5
Steffanina, Celestino, 38–39
Strauss II, Johann, 223–224
Strauss, Richard, 82
Suppé, Franz von, 92, 223
   Boccaccio, 92, 223
Supplemento ao catalogo de disco portuguezes, 273–274

Taborda, Francisco, 69, 117,
Tainter, Charles Sumner, 258, 270
Teatro da Alegria, 71, 138
Teatro de D. Afonso, 108
Teatro D. Amélia, 71, 72, 74, 99, 212
Teatro Apolo, 109, 113–114, 127
Teatro da Avenida, 71, 73, 80, 97, 100, 103, 111–112, 117, 122, 124, 126, 127, 141, 143, 145, 205, 210
Teatro Baquet, 108
Teatro de D. Fernando, 69, 116
Teatro do Ginásio, 30, 52, 68–69, 71, 73, 87, 89–90, 116–117, 118, 121, 205
Teatro Livre, 114–115
Teatro Moderno, 115
Teatro Nacional D. Maria II, 52, 68, 71, 74, 87–88, 199

Teatro do Príncipe Real, 69, 71, 87–88, 89–90, 109, 113–114, 115, 127, 134, 138, 140, 205, 227 See also Teatro Apolo
Teatro do Rato, 120, 123, 206–207
Teatro da Rua dos Condes, 67, 68, 69–70, 71, 87, 99, 105, 116, 118, 119, 124, 126, 132, 138–140, 143, 205, 230
Teatro do Salitre, 67, 69
Teatro de São João, 108
Teatro de São Sebastião (S. Miguel, Azores), 199
Teatro Taborda, 71
Teatro da Trindade, 3, 71, 72–73, 87–88, 89–93, 94–95, 97, 101, 102, 116, 120, 133
Teatro Variedades, 88, 116, 118
Teles, Basílio, 13, 176–177, 181
temps, Le (French newspaper), 36
triste canção do sul: subsídios para a história do fado, A, 164, 166–168
Turner, Victor, 148–149

Unamuno, Miguel de, 153–154, 177
University of Coimbra, 47–48, 216

Varela, Reinaldo, 268, 278, 281
Vasco, Neno, 39–40
Vasco da Gama, 98

Vasconcelos, Joaquim de, 83
Vaz, Marçal, 127
Vaz de Carvalho, Maria Amália, 188–189, 192–194
Veiga, Estácio da, 48
Velhas canções e romances populares portugueses, 162–163
Vénus (play), 212–213
Verde, Cesário, 63
  sentimento de um occidental, O, 63, 65–66
Viana, Francisco, 170
Viana da Mota, José, 159
Vicente, Gil, 97, 210
Victor, Delfina, 94, 261
Vieira, Ernesto, 166
voz do operário, A (periodical), 32, 171

Wagner, Richard, 80, 81–83, 94, 115
Williams, Raymond, 2, 8,

zarzuela, 24, 69, 71, 76, 79–80, 87, 88–94, 96–97, 99–100, 103–104, 114, 124, 138, 150
  zarzuela grande, 92, 96
  genero chico, 96, 99–100, 105, 150
Zé Povinho (portuguese national character), 118, 132, 139, 147, 22